Reframing Ethics Through Dialectics

Also available from Bloomsbury

Advances in Experimental Philosophy of Free Will and Responsibility,
edited by Thomas Nadelhoffer and Andrew Monroe
The Ethics of Generating Posthumans, edited by Calum MacKellar
and Trevor Stammers
The Futility of Philosophical Ethics, by James Kirwan
The History and Ethics of Authenticity, by Kyle Shuttleworth

Reframing Ethics Through Dialectics

A New Understanding of the Moral Good

Michael Steinmann

BLOOMSBURY ACADEMIC
LONDON • NEW YORK • OXFORD • NEW DELHI • SYDNEY

BLOOMSBURY ACADEMIC
Bloomsbury Publishing Plc
50 Bedford Square, London, WC1B 3DP, UK
1385 Broadway, New York, NY 10018, USA
29 Earlsfort Terrace, Dublin 2, Ireland

BLOOMSBURY, BLOOMSBURY ACADEMIC and the Diana logo are
trademarks of Bloomsbury Publishing Plc

First published in Great Britain 2023
This paperback edition published 2024

Copyright © Michael Steinmann, 2023

Michael Steinmann has asserted his right under the Copyright, Designs
and Patents Act, 1988, to be identified as Author of this work.

For legal purposes the Acknowledgments on p. vi constitute
an extension of this copyright page.

Cover image: Overlapping pieces of multi-coloured construction paper
on illuminated white backdrop (© Mint Images / Getty Images)

All rights reserved. No part of this publication may be reproduced or transmitted in any
form or by any means, electronic or mechanical, including photocopying, recording, or
any information storage or retrieval system, without prior permission in writing from the
publishers.

Bloomsbury Publishing Plc does not have any control over, or responsibility for, any third-
party websites referred to or in this book. All internet addresses given in this book were
correct at the time of going to press. The author and publisher regret any inconvenience
caused if addresses have changed or sites have ceased to exist, but can accept no
responsibility for any such changes.

A catalogue record for this book is available from the British Library.

A catalog record for this book is available from the Library of Congress.

ISBN: HB: 978-1-3502-8688-7
PB: 978-1-3502-8692-4
ePDF: 978-1-3502-8689-4
eBook: 978-1-3502-8690-0

Typeset by Integra Software Services Pvt. Ltd.

To find out more about our authors and books visit www.bloomsbury.com
and sign up for our newsletters.

Contents

Acknowledgments	vi
Introduction	1

Part One Foundations

1	The Right Beginning	13
2	Morality as an Exception	21
3	A Different Type of Notion	31
4	Expressing the Good	45
5	The Reality of the Good	85

Part Two Failures

6	Five Ways of Failing the Good	105
7	What Moral Theories Try to Achieve	111
8	The Dialectics of Generality	121
9	The Dialectics of Reason	143
10	The Dialectics of Inherent Goodness	161

Part Three Foolishness

11	Moral Nonetheless	187

Notes	222
Bibliography	259
Index	268

Acknowledgments

I would like to thank my friends and colleagues at Stevens Institute of Technology who have discussed the project with me over the years and given me much helpful advice, especially Garry Dobbins, John Horgan, Jennifer McBryan, James McClellan III, and Gregory Morgan. I would also like to thank Matthias Bormuth, University of Oldenburg, and Ulrich von Bülow, Deutsches Literaturarchiv Marbach, for our many spirited conversations. Furthermore, I want to thank Yunus Tuncel, New York University, for the many opportunities to work together and exchange ideas. In addition, I would like to thank the members of the panel on ethics at the World Congress for Philosophy in 2018 for their interest in my work. Thanks go to the many students I had the honor to engage with over the course of the years, not only at Stevens Institute of Technology but also in previous years at the University of Tübingen and the University of Freiburg. Discussing moral theories with young, bright, and critical persons has been invaluable in showing me the limitations of these theories. I also want to thank the team at Bloomsbury which made the production of this book a pleasure and the anonymous reviewer who helped me clarify many points. Finally, I want to thank Steffen Friede for his constant encouragement and support.

Introduction

Wherever one looks in the vast field of moral philosophy, one cannot but notice the failure of the theories and positions that are being presented. Upon closer examination, contradictions emerge in each theory, which make it so that one cannot even imagine an end to the debates and controversies in the field. There are of course many good reasons to defend this position or that, and most moral philosophers are serious people, in both their personal commitments and their analytic stringency. Much effort and good will are applied by them to articulate, examine, and justify moral positions. Remarkable results have come from this too, theoretical accounts that dive deeply into the intricacies of moral life and come up with well-reasoned and inherently plausible arguments to defend one position or another. I myself did not have the impression that I was doing anything spurious when earlier in my life I traced the legacy of the ancient idea of the good life in modern ethics or defended a deontological position.[1] And yet, all positions and theories fail insofar as the contradictions that emerge result in none of the positions being ultimately tenable (at least I cannot think of one that would be tenable upon close examination). One particular theory can always be replaced by another, which is then held for equally valid reasons than the previous one until it is being replaced by yet another theory, and so on. One could perhaps live with the fact that a final theory has not been found yet in moral philosophy, but I am not sure that one can live with the fact that it is not even clear whether such a theory is possible or not. For moral reasons alone, should there not be agreement among those working in the field?[2]

This book, like many others perhaps, is testament to a great disillusion. Working in moral philosophy as a scholar and teacher, I grew more and more wary and suspicious over time. At some point, I decided that I did not want to examine particular theories anymore, or compare one theory to another, but find out what causes the failure of all theories.[3] I started looking for the systematic conditions that affect them and make it so that they are caught, willingly or not, in a web of contradictions and mutual oppositions. This led to the present book in which I try to show how dialectical structures can emerge in *all* moral theories and positions. I am therefore not wedded to any one theory in particular (or so I hope, as one should leave it to the scrutiny of others to find out where one's tacit assumptions and prejudices lie).

Some might think that it is naïve to expect a final consensus in moral philosophy, others might think that the endlessness of controversies is precisely what keeps this philosophy alive and interesting. (Truth to be told, the controversies keep at least the moral philosophers alive insofar as they are academics.) Yet others might say that it is by no means a new thing to lament the status of the discipline. Moral philosophy was a questionable affair from its very beginning, which one can see, among others, in Socrates' struggle with the sophists who simply did not buy his commitment to justice. In modernity, there exist a plethora of attacks on morality, following the holy trinity of suspicion—Nietzsche, Marx, and Freud. Skeptics are free to choose the type of criticism that they prefer.

However, many of these attacks come from outside of morality, rejecting it as a whole or rejecting at least its main assumptions. The attacks can of course bring many interesting insights, but I for one am not ready to distance myself from the phenomenon in such a way. The contradictions that I will show are inherent; they are morality's own product, so to speak, and do not imply that moral positions are, say, disingenuous, fictitious, or merely strategic.

Given that I want to take morality seriously and support its ambition, it is perhaps not useless to state what my criticism of moral theories does *not* imply, or what it does *not* target. First, I do not suppose that the main problem with theories in morality would be that they are precisely that, too theoretical. It is often said that commitments to morality are spontaneous and unarticulated, and that theoretical reflection destroys the naturalness and inner strength of the goodness in people's hearts. Such a desire to rely on some innate impulse of goodness always appeared as wishful thinking to me. One can say, of course, that the academization of morals, with its ever-increasing specialization, presents a problem of its own. It would no doubt be preposterous to suggest that no one could be moral if they could not clearly explain the difference, say, between utilitarianism and virtue ethics. Still, the fact that a great deal of reflection is spent on moral life indicates to me that humans do like to question what they feel and cannot simply stop exploring their own nature.

I am also not bothered with the widespread abuse of moral thought. Such abuse exists in many facets. For example, one can only deplore the arbitrary manner in which positions are often defended and presented as preferable compared to others, as well as the focus on mere technicalities in the articulation of arguments as if the main purpose of moral philosophy were, like in a courtroom, to get away with certain claims. It is also hard to overlook the hypocrisy and misappropriation of ethics in professions and industries where, instead of doing one's job as decently as one can, one merely talks about how decent one is. There is pseudo-morality, a lot of it, like there is pseudo-science, and there is moralism, the use of moral qualifications for the sole purpose of blaming others and elevating oneself over them. Contrary to all of this, I want to present and criticize theories and positions that I consider as genuine, serious ones, because only for such positions contradictions matter at all.

In tracing the systematic conditions that affect moral theories, I use dialectics as my analytical tool. The failure of moral theories can be explained through the dialectical structures that emerge both within each theory and in the relation between them. Dialectics has gone mostly out of favor nowadays, but it seems to me that without it is impossible to provide a holistic account of what moral theories are able and unable to achieve. I believe that a real contribution can be made to the current field of studies by re-animating (and of course re-formulating) this methodical approach. The paradigm for a dialectical reconstruction of moral positions can be found in Hegel's philosophy but I do not follow his approach to the letter or adopt his own systematic intentions. As a tool, dialectics allows one to look at theories in a more inter-connected way but it should not be used as a Procrustean bed. I do not believe that the theoretical options in morality can be fully exhausted and represented in some sort of system.[4]

One advantage of the dialectical perspective is that it makes no assumptions about the intentions that drive moral theories or about the existence of logical inconsistencies. As already said, theories do not fail because they are faulty in some way but because of their structure *as theories*. They fail, in other words, precisely because they establish a way to act morally. Each theory and position entails what I call a moral determination. The term "determination" refers both to the specific content of actions and intentions *and* to the fact that this content provides a reason to act. Agents can only be moral if they are moral in specific ways. They have to decide, among others, about the extent and universality of the principles that they adopt, about the method that guides their thinking in finding the appropriate determination (whether it is reasoning, intuition, feeling, or something else), and about the ability of human practice to absorb and realize moral qualities, that is, about the question whether actions are valued inherently or only because of their consequences. The various determinations that follow from these decisions define the theories in contrast to each other.

I will argue that all determinations prove to be either inherently contradictory or insufficient to reach their intended goal, moral action. In its most schematic form, I assume that moral determinations are either not determined enough and can then be suspected to be empty and ineffective, or end up being too determined. In case of the latter, they either turn into their own opposite or become discriminatory and antagonistic toward other positions which it would also be moral to have. The failure to be appropriately determined engenders the dynamic in the field of moral philosophy insofar as theories, whether consciously or not, respond to, and try to fix, other theories' deficiencies.

It might seem as if the dialectical approach to morality would force me to adopt a skeptical or relativistic stance toward moral objectivity. This is not the case, but it takes some effort to show why it is so. In thinking about the failure of moral theories, I realized that a detour was needed. It became a quite substantial detour, eventually, and almost a book of its own. The detour led to the first part of this monograph, which traces the outlines of a theory of the good. Combining the perspective on failure with a strong and non-relativistic, non-skeptical account of the moral good may seem like a contradiction on my end. Does one not exclude the other? I do not think they do. If I want to show why moral theories fail, I have to show that there is indeed something to fail. If there is no such thing as a moral action because there is no quality or content that defines particular actions as such, then there can also be no failure. One could then disregard the whole talk about morality and devote one's attention to psychology, politics, and similar things. As said before, I take the ambition of moral theories quite seriously.

Switching gears between the focus on failure and the focus on what is being failed does not always come easy. What was explained so far is treated in *Part Two: Failures*, but now is the time to address the things said in *Part One: Foundations*. *Part One* starts from a simple question which, like most simple questions in philosophy, is surprisingly difficult to answer. What is morality, and what makes this phenomenon distinct from other normative domains? Ordinary discourses are full of normative statements: practical challenges require constant focus and attention from the agent ("You have to keep the windows closed because so many mosquitos are coming in"); interactions with others are guided by conventions and expected patterns of behavior ("You really should have left a bigger tip"); and the social world is structured by regulations and laws that tell the agent what to do ("You cannot make a left turn here"). Does morality possess a normative quality of its own, a quality that would be both specific and distinct, or can it be reduced eventually to practical considerations, conventions, and the law? Some might suspect that after all, morality is not even needed in human life given that laws, conventions, and practical know-how all guide our actions quite successfully.

I believe that morality is indeed a distinct phenomenon. As such, it is based on two main elements that exist in correlation. On the one hand, morality requires the individual's act of self-determination (more on the other part later). Conventions, laws, and practical constraints are always already there: we have to follow them anyway and can fall back on them if there is doubt about practical matters. In order to act morally, it takes a special impulse and decision. Historically speaking, morality needs the environment of advanced societies which allow for individuals to question their behavior and adopt a new, personal determination. The existence of morality is, as it were, a sign for the decadence of societies which have become unable to provide sufficient justification for their customary practices or their politics and laws. Critics like Nietzsche have always sensed that the flower of morality grows in the swamps of cultural decay, real or perceived.

The focus on self-determination means that there is something irreducibly subjective in morality. The moral philosophy of the last centuries has often been afraid of subjectivity. At least since the period of Enlightenment, its goal has been to identify the objective factors that drive moral life: the infallible mechanism of sentiments, the law-like content of rational decisions, the empirically validated amount of well-being that is achieved, and so on. Analytic philosophy has only exacerbated this trend toward a scientific foundation of morality, with its fascination for the semantic analysis of rules, norms, and principles. One could get the impression that moral philosophy is really just that, a debate about the right meaning of words.

I am of course a little polemical here. There always has been a focus on subjective factors, for example, on the factor of motivation. Once we have found the right rules, how do we make agents adopt them? Hume, among others, was right in saying that if one starts from mere rules, no agent is ever moved to act. Instead, one has to start from their feelings. But in saying this, Hume assumed that there is a natural, regularly occurring impulse in agents, rooted in their habitual sympathy toward others. I do not believe that agents always act morally from such a disposition, or any similar one, but that more often than not they have to decide, intuitively or not, that they *want* to do so, perhaps even beyond the immediate range of their sympathetic connection to others. It is inevitable to go back to a decidedly individual impulse, even if this impulse sits uncomfortably with moral theories because it cannot be explained or deduced from any prior disposition or reason.

The subjective impulse to be moral is also necessary to establish the meaning of moral principles and rules. It is surprising that this fact has been given so little attention. Many take it for granted, it seems, that such a thing as morality exists and that the norms which are invoked are genuinely moral. To take an example: if there happens to be a viral pandemic, officials can issue the rule to wear a face mask in order to prevent the spread of viruses through people's breath. "Wear a mask" can then be understood in a variety of ways. It is first of all a practical consideration that tells people to prevent viruses from floating in the air. Wearing a mask can also become a new convention which then entails a certain pressure to conform and perhaps even social sanctions. Wearing a mask could also be required by law. Finally, an agent can decide to wear a mask even if the legal regulations are not strict, the conventions not fully uniform, and the practical considerations fraught with a certain percentage of doubt. They can decide that they want to contribute to as much public safety as possible, follow the law, or show a considerate attitude toward other people's health. In that case, what is left out by practical considerations, conventions, and the law is filled in by morality. We could go through similar examples, looking at the various rules and principles that are used. In each case we could show that their meaning is far from obvious and that it is only the agent's intention that turns them into a moral determination.

As said before, the subjective element, self-determination, is only one of the two main elements of morality. The other element lies in the content that agents adopt in their determination. What type of content is this? Given that self-determination is based on a radically individual impulse to act, the content could be anything. Any moral principle will do. However, if the impulse is indeed undetermined, so that the individual could technically decide for anything, then one needs a criterion that decides and completes the determination to act in one way rather than another. If one asks an individual: "Why do you act like that?" the answer can of course be: "Because my maxim has universal validity for all rational beings" or "Because I believe that I can increase the well-being of a great number of people." But the other person can continue to ask: "Why universal validity?" "Why well-being and not, say, equality?" In that case, the individual's final answer has to be something like this: "Because it is the moral thing to do." I will argue that "the moral thing" is synonymous to the good and that the final answer that is needed in order to complete a moral determination is given by the moral good. In the full phenomenon of morality, individual self-determination is correlated to the good, I believe. The other half of my endeavor in *Part One* is devoted to explaining and justifying this idea of the good. Terminologically, I refer to it as the absolute good.

It might seem anachronistic to talk about an absolute good but I believe that it is possible to conceive of it without falling back into an obsolete form of metaphysics. I will assume that the absolute good is the one basic notion of morality. That is, I will assume that the good is not one notion among many in moral philosophy. The distinction between the good and the right, or the good and the just, is often taken to imply that the good, the right, and the just are all equally fundamental notions. I believe instead that all notions in morality can be analyzed in a way that leads back to the good as the most basic and fundamental idea. Why is justice important if not because it is good, and why should I do what is right if not because that is good, too? One can of course ask: why should the good be the most fundamental notion in morality and not any other? To this question, I have no real answer. The good has been the fundamental notion in classical ancient ethics and I do not see any reason to choose another. As a philosopher, one always thinks, writes, and talks in a given natural language which is at the same time the language of a particular historical constellation. There could be another basic notion in morality, indeed, but it seems to me that in order to find it, one would have to follow a very different tradition altogether.

The good is termed absolute in my approach because it incorporates all possible aspects of goodness: character traits like virtue, beneficial outcomes of actions, the legitimate freedom of persons, etc. The good is also the source of moral obligations, the only possible one, I believe, if ones takes morality as an autonomous discipline. I understand the idea of the good in a wider meaning than some of the current Neo-Aristotelian approaches do, which are based on a more concrete and more naturalistic idea of the good, for example, the good as human well-being. For me, the good is first and foremost a formal notion which is rooted in the practice of giving and asking for reasons. The good is the reason for which something is desired or done, which means that it cannot be identified with any particular state, experience, or activity. We desire well-being because it is good, but we also desire equality because it is good, and so on. No particular thing can fill in the meaning of "good." I do have to explain, of course, what I think it is that we refer to by referring to something as good. My answer will be that the good is the uncoerced consistency of purposes. What this means will, hopefully, become clear in the course of *Part One*. In any case, even if I indicate a descriptive content in the idea of good, as I believe one can, this content is formal and cannot be identified with any empirical state of affairs.

There are many reasons for which the idea of an absolute good may be hard to accept in the current landscape of philosophy. I only want to point out two tendencies here. One is the tendency toward pluralism which can manifest itself as a tendency toward inclusiveness, democracy, individualism, and non-foundationalism, among others. My claim that there is one, unitary notion of the good, and not rather many forms and instances of the good, or simply many goods, may seem either futile, a desire for an ultimately unreachable foundation, or downright oppressive with respect to the diversity of moral life. I think that I have an answer to such objections, which the following remarks will give.

The other tendency can be subsumed under the title of non-cognitivism. There are again many variations. Humeanism, emotivism, care ethics, and the like, all share a negative view on the possibility of a conceptual analysis. If there is an absolute good, in the sense that all moral notions can be traced back to the notion of the good, then moral determinations have to involve a conceptual content. There are some modern defenders of concepts, like Scanlon, but overall it seems safe to say that conceptual contents do not enjoy a central role in current philosophy. It seems that modernity, in its eagerness to overcome metaphysics, has thrown the baby out with the bath water and forgotten that even if metaphysical insights may no longer be valid the conceptual language on which they were based can still be important for us. Concepts occupy a particular place. Compared to the rules of formal logic and semantics, they have a concrete meaning. Concepts allow for material inferences in the sense that one conceptual content can be related to, or expressed through, other conceptual contents. These inferences are not reducible to formal logic. Compared to empirical beliefs, concepts refer to ideal or intellectual objects, like the good which designates a quality that cannot be identified in any physical way. As already said, modern philosophy often follows the model of science, advertently or not, and then has a hard time acknowledging truths that are neither purely formal nor purely empirical. I believe that this scientific orientation makes it difficult to deal with the specific status of moral ideas. We have to hold on to concepts, it seems, if only to be able to hold on to these ideas.

The analysis in *Part One* is based on a reconstruction of the Platonic notion of the good. I believe that Plato's philosophy offers an account of the good not only as the highest notion of morality but also as an inclusive notion that comprises all other moral notions in a totality of conceptual relations. However, just as I am not interested in an exegesis of Hegel's dialectic, I am also not interested in a detailed interpretation of Plato's philosophy. The conceptual framework of the absolute good is plausible beyond the confines of his own metaphysical assumptions, I believe.

Readers might ask themselves what all these reflections amount to. Are there any practical outcomes of my analysis of the good? There are some. To begin with, the analysis can change attitudes and expectations toward the purpose and power of moral theories. Theories, insofar as they are action-guiding, are meant to be sufficient to make actions moral, both subjectively and objectively: they establish ways for the agent to be adequately and fully determined in their desire to act morally and they identify the content that determinations need to have in order to be considered moral. But despite their best efforts, theories contribute to the endless polemics and controversies that mark the field of morality. Not only history, it seems, but also moral philosophy is all-too often written by winners: authors happily point out the deficiencies in other theories and declare themselves superior in a comparison whose rules they have defined themselves. The notion of the absolute good has therefore a critical and corrective function. It throws all theories off balance and urges their proponents to recognize the limitations that all positions inevitably possess.

At the same time, the perspective of the absolute good allows us to see that the stakes are actually higher than one might think in relying on particular moral theories. If it were not possible to conceive of such a good, then all partial realizations of the good and all moral theories would be adequate and sufficient for what they want to achieve. One would then have to say that any theory that establishes at least some moral good is fine. But many moral theories, despite their attempt at being sufficient, actually achieve too little because they have stopped somewhere on the way toward a more inclusive moral conception.

It might seem that from a practical point of view my approach leads to some kind of benevolent pluralism. This is most definitely not the case, because for a pluralistic understanding of morality there can also be no failure. For it, all approaches to being good are more or less equally valid. I hold instead that none are valid, if only they are examined closely enough. Also, if one cannot decide for a particular moral position and act on it, despite its contradictions, then one has not really tried to be moral at all. I do not think that anything is gained, morally speaking, from a pluralist position.

Alternatively, one could suspect that if I am not a pluralist then I am eventually a moral nihilist because my conclusion could be that if all positions fail it does not matter which one is taken. But then again, no one would really make any attempt at being moral. From my perspective, there is no way around the paradox that one has to be moral despite its failure. Beckett's famous dictum, it seems, applies to morality, too: "Try again. Fail again. Fail better." This means that although there is a practical application of my analysis, insofar as a different attitude toward the nature and validity of moral theories can emerge, one should not expect a new morality in the sense of a practical solution. What follows from the recognition of the paradoxes in morality has to be left open.

At this point, it is necessary to switch gears one more time and introduce the last part of the book, *Part Three: Foolishness*. Some theories and positions are more aware of morality's dialectic than others. I call them rescue attempts because they start from the awareness of the hopelessly contradictory nature of moral positions and yet try to salvage a commitment to the good in the various ways that seem possible for them. Rescue attempts stand in contrast to what can be called classical, or strong, theories, which believe in the ability of defining and realizing an absolute good. Kant's, Hume's, and Mill's theories, for example, are classical in this regard. The dialectic of moral determinations arises only inadvertently in them.

In referring to non-classical positions as foolish, I think of Paul who called the Apostles fools ("fools for Christ," to be precise).[5] Committing to morality despite its contradictions makes one a sacred fool of sorts, not an idiot.[6] The three positions that I will describe follow the basic dialectical structure of moral determinations. Idealism, firstly, starts from the awareness that moral determinations may be empty and ineffective but turns that into a promise. Determinations that seem ineffective now only have not been realized and exhausted yet and can so be used to anticipate a more adequate moral future. Responsibility, secondly, starts from the fact that determinations may be too determined and turns that into a special commitment, addressing significant moral issues forcefully and running head-on into the contradictions that this creates. It is then always at risk of becoming immoral for moral reasons. Forgiveness, thirdly, reacts to the antagonistic nature of moral qualifications and tries to escape the logic of blame, punishment, and retribution. In doing so, it transcends the moral point of view altogether toward an absolute good that, once achieved, would not need moral categorizations anymore. Forgiveness, too, can be suspected to become immoral because it gives up the seriousness of moral ideas by pretending that one should not care about the wrongdoing that occurs.

None of the three attitudes has played a significant role in classical theories. They do not allow to be based on general principles or on a reliable method of reasoning (with the exception of idealism, as *Part Three* will show). I believe, however, that moral philosophy needs to expand and give such theories a more central space. On the other hand, I also do not want to suggest non-classical positions as the only viable alternative, if only for the reason that it is impossible to prescribe a non-generalizable position.

The fact that this book ends with forgiveness gives me a fitting motive to end this introduction, too. Authors often ask for forgiveness from their readers, but with my endeavor, this plea is far from rhetorical. I have to ask for indulgence with my attempt at approaching many wide-ranging topics. Each reader might have their preference in the trajectory from foundations to failures and to the foolishness of morality's rescue attempts, and perhaps not everyone will appreciate the trajectory as whole. But it seems to me that one cannot really grasp the paradoxes and contradictions in moral thought without showing both what it is trying to achieve and where it falls short.

Part One

Foundations

1

The Right Beginning

Varieties of Normativity

One has to begin at the beginning, but what *is* the right beginning for an inquiry into the nature of morality? One can of course begin at any point in this field rich of approaches and traditions, but is there a point at which one can see what morality is without already presupposing it? That is, a point at which one can see the phenomenon emerging in its distinctiveness from a background of other phenomena? Approaches to moral philosophy have often the tendency to begin at any point they see fit in order to make far-reaching claims, which then are claims from *within* the field of morality but not from its beginning. Again, there is nothing necessarily wrong with this. Insofar as morality deals with things that are highly significant for the personal and interpersonal life of human beings, any investigation into the field can lead to valuable insights, at least for some. Serious and truthful insights can be made without defining the field to which they refer in proper sense, which is true for other fields as well. One does not have to be able to give a definition of beauty in order to make meaningful statements about art. Hence, not everyone would agree that there even is a problem of the right beginning. It seems all the more plausible that there is none as the very idea of a beginning, of an origin, ultimately seems to imply a foundation, a sort of "foundationalism," which for some bears insurmountable difficulties.

Without resorting to any pompous philosophical terminology, and without deciding anything about the possibility of a foundation, one can ask two simple questions: what is the phenomenon we refer to when we talk about "morality"? Does it exist as a separate thing? And if there is indeed such a phenomenon, under which conditions are we supposed to talk about it? If one person, for example, makes the claim that particular actions violate the dignity of human beings, and another one says that they are also economically harmful, then the first person can be said to have raised a specifically moral concern independent from any economic benefit or harm. In situations like this, morality is inevitably invoked as a specific condition, criterion, dimension, aspect, etc., of human life and the discourses pertaining to it. The very fact that we can make such distinctions means that we cannot avoid the question of *what it is* we talk about. The second question can be understood in an equally simple way. Before engaging in a more technical analysis of concepts, methods, procedures of justification, and the like, we can say that not all phenomena are talked about in the same way. Some things can be approached by way of neutral, analytic thinking while others require personal experience and commitment. We make such distinctions almost naturally in relation to the various aspects of human life. Moral philosophy, therefore, cannot rely on being always already located within a particular field of discourse where certain forms of arguments are valid without the need of distinguishing them from those used in other fields.

It is important to note that at this stage of our inquiry the distinctiveness of morality cannot be shown by separating moral judgments from statements on natural or physical facts. This distinction can only be made at a later point, once a more elaborated notion of the moral good will have been reached. In order to get started, we can presuppose that moral judgments simply *are* distinct from judgments about natural facts, not only in their linguistic form (semantically or pragmatically) but also in their conceptual content. All we need to say here is that moral judgments seem to have a meaning of their own, which prima facie cannot be reduced to physical descriptions. Not even a hard physicalist can deny this assumption, it seems. The real challenge we are facing lies somewhere else. It stems from that fact that we have to distinguish moral judgments from other judgments that bear a normative content. Normativity is by no means specific to morality. The same can be said for prescriptive language. We can distinguish at least three dimensions of human practice in which normative judgments, whether expressed in prescriptive sentences or not, are made without possessing a specifically moral meaning.[1]

First, practical considerations. The statement "I have to eat something" is normative and not the description of a physical fact. Although it refers to a physical condition—the need of a human body for food—this condition is mentioned in light of the practical decisions that agents have to take. The physical condition is relevant for a human being who is concerned with their bodily well-being. Such a concern comprises its own normativity, a set of practical considerations, rules, provisions, advices, etc., without possessing a specifically moral content.

Second, social conventions. The statement "You should call and thank her for the gift she sent us" is also normative without a specifically moral content. It refers to the conventions that rule human interactions and determine what an individual ought to do in a given situation—conventions like showing gratitude, noticing the presence of others in a room, asking for their well-being, responding to their physical or emotional distress, etc. In all these cases, a particular form of behavior is expected and can be fulfilled without having the explicit intention of being benevolent or considerate toward others. The distinction between conventions and morality is of course not always easy to draw, and every convention can be interpreted in a morally relevant way. For example, not showing one's gratitude can be interpreted as a negligent or even aggressive act. The important point, however, is that conventions *can* be separated from morality. In many cases, all they require from an individual is to be sociable or polite. Conventions reduce the friction and uncertainty in human interactions. If one "gets along with others" a basic requirement for interaction is fulfilled, and very often no further questions have to be asked.

Third, the law. Very similar to conventions, the important point about a legal system is that it can function without moral considerations. Established laws make it superfluous and at times even counter-productive to ask whether a particular action is morally reprehensible or not. If an action is prohibited by law, it can be prosecuted and sanctioned according to given procedures and scales. The notion of harm, for example, designates the impact of an action on others which needs to be avoided or minimized, because by definition no one wants to make the experience of harm. Once the legislator has determined what counts as harm, the legal system can regulate all questions pertaining to it, without any further moral justification.

What, then, is moral normativity? Before we can begin answering this question, some methodological remarks need to be made. The first one concerns the problem that our approach might seem question-begging. It may seem we are saying that morality is distinct from other forms of normativity because the other forms are not moral. However, morality may after all not be fundamentally different from practical considerations, conventions, and the law. What we call "moral" could be a variation or combination of any of these three, so that our attempt at finding the beginning of morality as a distinct phenomenon would not only be based on circular logic but also in vain. On the other hand, the distinction between moral and non-moral forms of normativity can be found in common assumptions that seem hard to deny. If we take again the statement "You have to eat something" and assume that it is directed at someone who refuses to eat, then we can say that besides any practical considerations regarding the inevitable need for food it can also carry a moral meaning. The speaker can intend to say that the agent they address has an obligation to care for themself and that being healthy is a goal which is worth being pursued for its own sake. At the very least, one cannot exclude that the statement has more than a merely practical meaning. What there is "more" in it would then correspond to what we usually call "moral." It would not be comprised in the otherwise trivial remark that every human being has to eat. It seems, therefore, that we have valid reasons to start from a working hypothesis according to which morality would be a normative dimension of its own. But this is not the only remark we have to make before we can start in proper sense.

Beyond Formalism and Empiricism

The three forms of normativity mentioned so far—practical, conventional, legal—are independent of their respective linguistic form, we believe. Whether judgments are expressed in prescriptive language or not has no bearing on their normative content, which is first and foremost conceptual. Practical considerations and social conventions are often expressed as a matter of fact ("One has to eat every six hours," "One does not walk away without saying 'Thank you'"), and laws can simply describe the actions they prohibit or require, and the penalties they stipulate. Assertive statements of this kind say only indirectly what a person should do, ought to do, has an obligation to do, etc. The claim we are making here might not be acceptable for those with strong empiricist inclinations.[2] By introducing the idea of a conceptual content we explicitly disregard the linguistic forms in which judgments are made, which is an original sin for all empiricists. For us, normativity does not require an unambiguous linguistic expression. We also assume that the conceptual content bears essential differences which allow us to distinguish between practical, conventional, legal, and, eventually, moral norms. These distinctions are also not visible in the linguistic forms that are used. An isolated statement, even if it is prescriptive, does not show whether it is meant in a practical, conventional, or legal sense. If one says, for example, "You have to stop at the stop sign," one can express a practical consideration ("Not to stop is dangerous"), a convention ("Everyone around here does it"), or a legal rule ("It is required by law"). One needs to know the context in which the statement is made in order to understand its specific normative content, or one has to ask for additional statements and explanations.[3]

For moral philosophy, it would therefore be wrong to limit the analysis of principles and rules to what is expressed in a particular linguistic form. In addition, no rule and principle should be deemed moral just because it has some normative content. Before one can accept a rule, or the expression of a rule, as a specifically moral claim, one has to determine that it does in fact carry a moral sense. Upon a closer look, many principles are more ambiguous than it seems. The Golden Rule, for example—"Do unto others as you would have them do unto you"—is commonly understood as one of the most fundamental expressions of the moral intuitions we hold toward others. Nonetheless, in certain contexts it could well be understood as expressing nothing more than a convention. In its least demanding sense, the Golden Rule requires no more than a sort of mutual distance between everyone's interests and needs. It is possible, or at least not excluded definitely, to read it in a merely negative way as a rule that tells us to be polite and tolerant, and not to interfere with the business of others.[4] This is of course not the way in which the Golden Rule is traditionally understood. It may even seem absurd to say that the rule is *not* a moral principle. But it is only possible to see more than a rule of convention in it if it is in fact given a specifically moral interpretation. The moral sense does not lie in the formula itself as if we just needed to look at it in order to see what it means.

A similar point can be made with respect to the principle "Do not harm." As mentioned before, avoiding harm can also be the goal of legal rules. One can define harm as whatever individuals refuse to suffer from others. In this purely formal sense, harm can be regulated without any further moral justification. The fact that individuals have interests and needs is as obvious as the fact that their interests and needs have to be balanced against those of others. To add a moral dimension to this mutual balance is not necessary at all. Neither is it necessary to justify in moral terms the regulations that are put in place. For the sake of theoretical economy, one should give a moral justification only for rules that cannot be justified otherwise. This means, again, that the principle "Do not harm" acquires moral sense only if one adds such sense to it. One can ask, for example, what we owe to each other over and beyond the mutual distance that we keep (what kind of protection, care, respect, etc.).

An example from medical ethics can help us illustrate the distinction between the moral and non-moral meaning of principles and rules. Medical ethics has made a point of distinguishing the general principle of "non-maleficence" (avoiding harm) from the limited principle of "beneficence" (doing good). The latter can be considered supererogatory because it is often hard to determine how the well-being of others can be increased and whether one should try to increase it at all, whereas it is almost always evident how one can avoid causing harm to them. But despite this difference, the two principles can be taken to mean the same.[5] If "non-maleficence" means nothing more than "Act according to your best professional knowledge and experience," then it only refers to the standards that all medical practitioners are expected to follow. In this case, it is normative, although merely as a *convention* and *practical consideration*, and remains clearly distinct from beneficence. On the contrary, if the principle is understood to mean something along the lines of "Reduce human suffering wherever you can," then it acquires a specifically moral sense. In this case, its ultimate purpose is "beneficence," an active promotion of the well-being of patients through the reduction of suffering. This shows, again, that the moral dimension of given rules cannot be made evident by resorting to mere formulas but only by finding the genuinely moral content that gives meaning to them.

We have to introduce a further differentiation. On the one hand, moral philosophy has to avoid the *empiricist* temptation of resorting exclusively to prescriptive linguistic expressions. On the other hand, it has to avoid the *formalist* temptation of resorting to abstract principles such as the Golden Rule or the do-no-harm rule. Empiricism and formalism, in the sense we take them here, are closely linked to each other insofar as both suggest that moral normativity is directly expressed in isolated statements and formulas. While we have shown how we want to understand the term "empiricism," we have to say more about the problem of formalism in the approach to moral principles and rules.

Nowadays, morality is often characterized by resorting to certain general notions that serve as criterion on which moral judgments are based. According to this approach, one has to distinguish, among others, between forms of morality based on duty, utility, virtue, or care. Morality then comes in the guise of certain "theories," as deontology, utilitarianism, virtue ethics, or ethics of care, which have to be understood as different ways of organizing and justifying moral judgments. All these approaches are eventually formalistic. Taken in an isolated, abstract manner, the notions cannot represent the structure and content of concrete moral determinations. Duty requires, for Kant, a strong concept of reason whereas for others it refers to the rules and obligations that are given in a context of social interaction. The idea of "prima facie duties" designates such an empirical conception of duty, very different from the one that is expressed in the categorical imperative.[6] The notion of duty has a different meaning in both cases. Similar things can be said for virtue: without the support of an axiological anthropology, like the one found in ancient ethics, the assumption of virtuous habits and actions remains essentially arbitrary. Utilitarianism, in turn, can cover anything from a quantitative calculation of the outcomes of actions (in the formal sense of consequentialism) to a general interest in the well-being of others (Mill's idea of happiness). Finally, with respect to care, one has to consider the particular inter-personal relations that allow it to exist, because no one can have an attitude of care toward everyone else. The principle is by definition non-universal. This means that no moral term, concept, and principle, and consequently no moral theory, has meaning outside of a particular understanding of human practice and the specific, theoretical and non-theoretical conditions embedded in it. Moral terms and theories are contextual, in the twofold sense that they emerge out of a given context of human practice and in turn create a context of their own, a particular framework through which human practice is understood.⁷ If we want to capture this contextual nature in one word, we can say that moral terms, as well as moral theories, are *historical*. This does not mean that moral theories should be analyzed in reference to their historical backgrounds or by tracing normative claims back to conditions of social or economic hierarchies. Doing so does not explain morality at all. "Historical" rather means that each theory exists as a specific framework. Moral theories, and the terms they use, contribute to the unfolding of moral philosophy as a series of different and often disconnected forms of discourse. Moral philosophy does not exist independent from this unfolding in a timeless or neutral form.⁸

The historical character also explains why moral philosophy as a whole is struck by such an astonishing cacophony. With every new approach, its scope is shifted to another point, which means that new approaches rarely solve the problems of older approaches but rather discover or even create new ones. The difference between deontology and utilitarianism, for example, is by no means limited to the fact that for the former certain actions, such as lying, are strictly immoral, while for the latter the very same action can be justifiable because of the outcome it creates. Stating the difference in such a simplistic way would presume that both theories are located on an even level and can be directly compared. But from one theory to the other, what is different is more than the evaluation of specific actions. The idea of theory itself, of its notions, basic arguments, and procedures of justification, is more or less incomparable, and the whole purpose of moral thinking, the way it is supposed to impact and guide human practice, by no means remains the same. Likewise, it would be wrong to assume that particular theories can be used to criticize others: although different theories are contrary in many points, they are almost never logically opposed. Were they opposed in such a way, they would either eliminate or complement each other and end up forming an overall unity, which is obviously not the case. Moral philosophy has to deal with an open, unlimited, and at times even innovative variety of approaches.

We should not exaggerate this variety, of course. To begin with, moral theories can hardly be called theories if one defines "theory" as a closed and self-sufficient set of inferential assumptions. The complexity of human practice could never be translated into such a pure theoretical form. Moral theories overlap because the experiences on which they are based overlap as well. All we can say here is that moral frameworks are specific, which allows for both their similarity and difference, their overlap and distinction.

With all that has been said so far, our quest for the right beginning in moral philosophy seems to have taken a fatal blow. If all approaches to morality are historical, then how can there be a right beginning at all? At which point in the sequence of the contexts of moral thought can we, so to speak, jump in and say that it truly begins? Is there any context that is privileged over the others? What comes first chronologically does not have to come first conceptually, so we cannot expect any help from the actual history of moral thought. If we want to designate a beginning, we simply have to choose. This means that our choice inevitably will be a circular one: whether we want it or not, we have to choose our point of departure in light of the goal we want to reach, because otherwise we would have no reason to choose it at all. Does this mean that we have to give up the question we started from? The answer is no. Insofar as the idea of the beginning of morality can only be approached in a circular way, circularity does not represent a logical flaw but a necessary condition, which then has to be accepted and dealt with as such. All we have to presuppose is that the idea of a beginning is valid at all. And as we have seen, it is valid because it is possible to ask for the demarcation between moral and non-moral normativity. At one point or another, morality begins as a specific phenomenon and other normative considerations end.

Our task is the following then. We have to find a criterion that allows us to determine the beginning of morality in a way that reduces the arbitrariness lying in every circular approach. This criterion has been found. Every definition of morality has to show in which sense it is distinguishable from practical, conventional, and legal normativity. Although the nature of morality cannot be deduced from such a distinction, once it has been found it will be evident as being distinct. Thus, if our idea of the beginning of morality can be used to explain both its distinctiveness and its specific place within the totality of normative practices, we have good reason to assume that we have identified it in a non-arbitrary way. It seems valid to assume that an approach which would *not* be able to account for the distinctiveness of morality would be more prone to arbitrariness than ours.

2

Morality as an Exception

Conventions and Obedience

As said before, every comprehensive effort in moral philosophy, every moral "theory" emerges and develops historically. In order to identify the point at which morality distinguishes itself from other forms of normativity, we have to follow one particular way in which this distinction appears. We find this way in Nietzsche's work. We could of course have chosen other philosophers, such as Plato or Kant, and any choice we make can only be justified in a circular way. All we can do is hope that the choice of Nietzsche's approach will prove valid through the coherence of our inquiry as a whole.

In *Daybreak*, Nietzsche introduces his idea of a "morality of custom."[1] According to this idea, morality, as it is understood in Western thought, originated from the customs that were followed and maintained throughout the course of human civilization, long before the advent of philosophy. Customs already comprised their own morality, their own set of intentions and attitudes that the members of a given community had to adopt. For Nietzsche, customs cannot be reduced to mere patterns of behavior but entail a subjective dimension in which the required behavior is intended explicitly and given an additional, personal valorization. Whatever the behavior, individuals had to be brought to accept willingly what they were socially required to do. Otherwise the customs could not function over an extended period of time.

Following Nietzsche's analysis, we encounter a certain polyvalence of the term "morality." In the wide and formal meaning of the term, "morality" refers to all subjective attitudes bearing normative content. Not only conventions but also laws and practical considerations have a "morality" of their own, an attitude through which the individual cherishes and adopts what is deemed inevitable or obligatory. The aim of our inquiry concerns a narrower understanding of the term: "morality" in the specifically moral sense of the word. We should, however, not suppress this polyvalence of the term "morality" all-too hastily as it indicates once more the problem we have to solve. Nietzsche's claim that there are forms of morality which do not correspond to the specifically moral understanding of the term only emphasizes that we have to be aware of grasping the distinctiveness of the phenomenon. As said before, it is impossible to use the terms employed in moral philosophy in an abstract way, isolated from the context in which they appear. Not even the term "morality" has a non-historical meaning. In German, Nietzsche distinguishes the "morality of customs" from "morality" in the more philosophical sense, by referring to the former as "*Sittlichkeit der Sitten.*" However, the distinction between "*Sittlichkeit*" and "*Moral*" is not strict and both terms can be used synonymously.[2] In English, "morality" can also mean both, subjective attitudes related to values and norms (which then can also be attached to conventions, laws, and practical considerations) and the principles and rules that are organized under the title of a moral philosophy.

One more remark on terminology: as far as the distinction between morality and ethics is concerned, we will only use the former term. Although in ordinary and academic language, "ethics" and "morality" can often be used synonymously, the meaning of the terms varies according to the context in which they are used. Where we could use "ethics" as term for the philosophical reflection on, or the system of, moral attitudes, we will use "moral philosophy" instead. For some, "ethics" refers to the ingrained habits of our life, which are tied to particular social contexts and behaviors, while "morality" holds universal validity.[3] We leave open whether this is the case. Also, in the current use, "ethics" often seems to refer only to rules and the respective rule-based behavior, for example, in the idea of "professional ethics" or the "codes of ethics" that businesses and organizations stipulate for their members. Morality, instead, seems to refer to rules, rule-based behavior, *and* the inner, personal attitude of agents. If this is so, then agents are able to act ethically without having a specifically moral attitude. Although we cannot assume that all uses of the terms can be classified this way, the inner attitudes of agents are crucial for our approach, which means that "morality," for us, is a better, more inclusive term.

In its pre-modern sense, the morality of custom consists mainly in the obedience toward the forms of traditional behavior. Customs are practices that determine life over the course of various generations. They are the old, ingrained ways of living that are always already in place when a new generation comes along. Customs are represented as a higher authority which has to be obeyed for the simple reason that it is higher than any individual's viewpoint. Whether customs are useful or not remains irrelevant in this regard. For Nietzsche, the main motivation for obeying the imperatives of convention is fear. The individual is held to fulfill the required customs as perfectly as possible, sometimes even by making considerable personal efforts.[4] Again, it is helpful to emphasize that for him customs are not merely patterns of behavior. All practices have to be accompanied and sustained by subjective attitudes or intentions. This point is important because it shows how customary practices pervade the very core of individual life. By requiring the individual to embrace them willingly, and sometimes even lovingly, they serve the purpose of minimizing the variability that inevitably comes with every new member of a group. Customs not only have the tendency to become comprehensive, insofar as they cover and determine all aspects that are vital for the conduct of life; "all education and care of health, marriage, cure of sickness, agriculture, war, speech and silence, traffic with one another and with the gods."[5] More important, customs lay a claim on individuals to sacrifice themselves; not necessarily in a literal, physical sense but such to make sure that the ultimate goal of individual life is no other than the continuation of the customary practice. Whenever morality is limited to the morality of customs, there can be no such thing as a strictly individual interest in leading a good life. Individuals have to desire subjectively what the customary practices require them collectively to do. Desiring something different would mean to isolate oneself from the community; it would mean to be morally reprehensible. Individuals can be blamed even in the case in which they want to fulfill the customary norms on their own account and in a particular, individual way. The norms are followed not so much because of *what* they require agents to do but because it is taken to be mandatory *that* they are fulfilled. As said before, the morality of customs is essentially obedience, arising out of and accompanied by coercion.[6] Customs not only do not need a rational justification or an individual's consent, they preclude and sometimes even condemn the assumption that they could depend on an individual's will.

One could of course doubt that traditional societies, or all societies in which customary practices are sustained, really have such a decidedly oppressive and irrational character as Nietzsche attributes to them. It seems easy to find examples of societies which could be used to modify or even contradict his analysis. However, the point of the analysis does not lie, at least not primarily, in its empirical truth but rather in the conceptual structure that it reveals. No customary practice would have binding force if individuals could decide whether they want to follow it or not. From the individuals' point of view, customs have to appear as unquestionable, as an object of admiration or fear, even if not everyone might personally be fearful or feel oppressed.

This brings us to the question of morality in its specifically moral form. For Nietzsche, this form emerges as an "exception" to conventional morality.[7] At a certain point, a morality of self-command and self-moderation begins to be formed, which does not depend on the obligations that the morality of custom entails. The individual begins to choose rules of behavior that are to their "very own advantage" and amount to their "personal key to happiness."[8] Although the new morality does not have to contradict the customs in their normative content, on the other hand, it does no longer obey the authority of communal life. The specifically moral form of morality is based on an individual's self-determination beyond or aside of the community to which they belong. The new morality appears as evil, or better: it *is* evil insofar as it denies the validity of conventions and of all that is deemed appropriate and good from a conventional point of view. If we modern people do not think that our understanding of morality was originally evil, Nietzsche states, this is so because we are simply not used to wonder about its beginnings, where the new morality had to detach itself from previous forms.[9] Historically, he attributes the beginning of morality to Socratic and Christian roots. For both, the main goal was an individual's personal fulfillment.

To be clear: the idea that morality in its specifically moral form was driven by evilness when it first emerged does not concern its intended content. It only concerns the individual impulse to adopt and realize a certain moral idea. Evilness, in other words, is defined from the viewpoint of conventions for which any strictly individual behavior is impermissible. Nietzsche's point is that morality, whatever its purpose and content, emerged as an essentially individual determination. The morality of custom was the primary form of morality and required a strong anti-social stance to be overcome. The individual not only had to start acting in different ways, they also had to develop a new inner attitude and resolve. For this reason, there had to be an element of destructiveness or even craziness in the way the new morality emerged and asserted its existence.[10]

The Threefold Structure of Self-Determination

We have to explain in more detail what we mean by saying that the specifically moral form of morality is essentially individual. As pointed out before, this form of morality does not necessarily contradict the normative content of customs. The deviation from conventional practice results, first and foremost, from a purely individual impulse to act. In conventional practice, the impulse for individual behavior is based on the behavior of the group to which the individual belongs, while in practical considerations the impulse is triggered by the impact of the outside physical or social world. In the specifically moral form of morality the individual posits themself, in Nietzsche's words, as an "exception"; neither group behavior nor practical conditions nor the law have the decisive influence on the actions they perform. Whatever reason the individual adopts, they see themself as the independent author, or the origin, of their decision. "I might do so as you say, but not because you want me to, or because I have to, but because *I* think it's right."[11] The term "impulse" that we use here is deliberately vague and not meant to define in any way the nature of individual agency. All it says is that the immediate cause of an individual's action is ascribed to them alone, that they act "on their own account." We could have used the term "motivation" instead, but motivations can also be understood as externally influenced.[12]

Furthermore, the specifically moral form of morality has to be adopted in a way that incorporates the normative content into the practical conduct and the habitual attitudes of individual life. In Nietzsche's words, the normative content has to appear as the individual's "most personal advantage," as the way the individual henceforth wants to live. While the first element, the individual impulse, captures the *origin* of the new morality, the second element states that it has to appear as a new *reality* of individual life. The specifically moral form of morality deviates from the morality of custom not only as an impulse to act individually but also as a new set of habits and practices (new at least insofar as they are now sustained by the individual and not by the collective, even if the content can remain more or less the same). The ways in which this can occur are manifold and may differ to a great degree, especially if one takes Nietzsche's own examples of Socratic and Christian morality into account. But in any case, without leading to a new reality of individual life the idea of an exceptional individual impulse would remain void. The impulse has to be transferred into a more or less constant form of practice.

Finally, the new morality has to comprise a purpose or an end. It is not only incorporated into practices or attitudes but also constitutes an overarching goal for the individual's life, a genuine "key to happiness." This way, the specifically moral form of morality achieves a teleological dimension. There are again many ways in which such a dimension can be realized; happiness is only one of them and can also be defined in various ways. The important point is that morality, for Nietzsche, could not exist without an inherent teleology. The assumption of an overarching goal complements the previous two elements: for each individual impulse to act, as well as for each newly adopted conduct, the question can be raised what they are good for and why they should be adopted at all. Given that an individual form of morality needs sufficient reason to deviate from the morality of custom, it is necessary for the individual to be able to state the final purpose of their decision. The decision would remain somewhat dangling in the air, that is, it would appear unmotivated if there were no final "because" that would guide the individual's point of view. The individual needs to have sufficient reason to posit themselves as an exception and to adopt their own conduct of life. "This is how I want to act and live from now on." This argument is by no means based on the assumption of a fixed and given teleological structure of human life, nor does it need a moral anthropology of sorts.

The last point can also be explained from another perspective. Self-determination cannot happen as an isolated act, or even a series of isolated acts, because this would leave the very meaning of the act unclear. It may then well result from random impulses. Self-determination needs the articulation and assertion of preferences which determine how the individual wants to act in all cases, future and hypothetical, that such preferences concern. An individual determines themself by determining, and subsequently maintaining, their preferences. The concept of preferences would deserve more attention, but we cannot engage in a deeper discussion here.[13]

To sum up, we can say that the specifically moral form of morality is essentially individual insofar as it emerges through an individual impulse to act, as an individual attitude and life conduct, and for the sake of the individual's fulfillment. All three moments are comprised in, and necessary for, the idea of individual self-determination, which is the term we will mostly use in the following. In objective terms, the structure of self-determination entails the origin, the reality, and the end of individual self-determination; in subjective terms it entails the impulse, the life conduct, and the personal goal related to it.

We should add that this structure is by no means limited to the premises of Nietzsche's thought. For example, Korsgaard identifies a similar structure in her reading of Plato's *Republic*. It is worthwhile to explain her interpretation in more detail, also because it deviates from ours in one important point. For Korsgaard, Plato's "principle of justice" is a "constitutive principle ... of action."[14] Through actions, individuals both acquire and express what she calls their "practical identity."[15] Action, for her, is "self-constitution."[16] The identity that gets constituted this way needs to be a "unified" one, because without unity individuals are not really in control of their agency, or better: they do not possess agency in proper sense. Perhaps they only react to stimuli and are "at the mercy of accident,"[17] or they let themselves be determined by others.[18] Justice is therefore no external standard but allows the individual to follow a universally valid determination in each case and develop a lasting commitment to act in specific ways.[19] Justice, in other words, makes action possible in the full sense of action as expression and realization of the agent's identity. Eventually, "only good action really is action."[20]

From our perspective, Korsgaard's conception seems to follow an ontologizing tendency. Her understanding of justice is more Aristotelian than Platonic, it seems, insofar as she seems to assume that normative principles become effective as traits of an agent's character which in turn is nothing other than their pattern of behavior. All is present and held together in the enactment of the agent's normative identity. We do not require such a unification. For us, there are actions and there is the normative outlook beyond them, for example, the agent's preferences. Both belong together, but the preferences extend as a projection into the future and so retain a precarious, hypothetical quality. Instead of understanding "constitution" as a making of oneself, we take it in a weaker sense, as a mere arrangement of an agent's practices and views. For us, self-determination can remain an open-ended task, whereas Korsgaard describes it as resulting in "a single identity, … a coherent life."[21]

We can now answer the question raised in the previous chapter. There, we asked for the criterion that defines morality in its distinctiveness compared to practical considerations, conventions, and laws. The answer, or at least the first part of the answer, can be now: a normative content is understood in a specifically moral sense if it belongs to a specifically individual act of self-determination. Moral normativity can be found where an individual has the explicit intention of wanting to be good, in the sense of wanting to be good by their own impulse, by incorporating a specific goodness into their attitudes and conduct, and by understanding such goodness as an inherent part of the personal fulfillment they are striving for. The formula "wanting to be good" is of course ambiguous and can be understood in a variety of ways, but in the present context it can help us delineate the distinctive character of morality. It can be distinguished from the fact of "having to be good." Practical constraints, conventions, and laws all entail reasons which are external to an individual's self-determination insofar as their binding force can be attributed to physical conditions, the rules of group behavior, and a given legal system. For morality instead, the decisive cause to perform good actions stems from a strictly individual resolve.

As said in the previous chapter, rules and norms, such as the rule not to harm others, are not genuine to morality. We can now say that in order to count as a specifically moral determination, the individual must be willing not to harm others without needing to be forced to adopt such a decision; they must act accordingly in a more or less consistent and continuous way (because they would contradict the morality of their own impulse if they failed to do so); and they must see the avoidance of the harm of others as a desirable goal of their life.

If we wanted to explain our understanding of morality by using more traditional terms, we could say that no rule or normative content is specifically moral unless its adoption results from autonomy, becomes relevant for an individual as the habit to perform virtuous behavior, and is seen as the final good of life. These terms—autonomy, virtue, and the final good—are only meant to illustrate the outcome of our analysis. It is not necessary here to resort to a more elaborated moral theory. On the other hand, the terms are helpful to delineate the distinctiveness of morality compared to other forms of normativity. Traditional theories are less inclined to exclude the subjective dimension of morality than modern ones. Modern theories often focus heavily on the objective content of moral ideas by discussing the meaning, justification, and application of principles and rules. But in order to engage in such a discussion, the theories have to presuppose that the rules are in fact moral, which is not self-evident. Morality is part of a living human practice and cannot be limited to an abstract system of principles and norms; principles and norms have meaning only if they can be incorporated into an individual's conduct and are pertinent to their self-determination.

Morality is also no tool for social regulation, as some want to have it, because even if it were moral agents would first have to ask why such tools are binding for them, which in turn would call for their self-determination. All social regulations and standards are governed by outside authority, if only the authority of collective behavior, but moral determinations are by definition, or at least ideally, independent from such influences.[22]

To illustrate this point once more: the difference between the command "Do not lie!", uttered by a police interrogator, and the command "Do not lie!", spoken in a moral sense, is precisely the fact that the latter is no purely external obligation. From a moral point of view, it should be the agent's own intention to tell the truth. The reference to self-determination gives what can be called the second why. If one asks "Why should I do x?", the first answer is "Because x is good," whereas self-determination is the answer to the question "But why should I do what is good?" This question can only be answered by saying something like "Because you should want to do so." Even a phrase as neutral as "You ought to do x" entails that we willingly accept a certain obligation, that we should want, that is, embrace and actively follow it. Metaphorically speaking, the obligation does not only concern our actions, the things that we do, but also our hearts. Some might ask whether this does not mean that no moral obligations can be binding and we fall into some sort of subjectivism according to which agents can choose which duty to follow. Our answer is that the anxious attempt at securing bindingness by ruling out the subjective acceptance of the agent has it backwards: if standards and rules were disconnected from agents, there would be no reason to adopt them anyway and morality's demands would have no chance ever to succeed.[23]

A Correlational Approach

Nietzsche's analysis, which we were mostly following so far, cannot lead us to a full account of morality. It only gives us half of it. Morality cannot be understood by focusing solely on the subjective dimension we have described so far. The individual adoption of rules is a necessary condition for an action to be moral but it is not in itself sufficient. What we have left out is the content of the individual's determination, which is needed to complete and define the act as moral.[24] Even if moral principles do not have to stand in opposition to practical, conventional, and legal ones, they eventually have to acquire their own, specific content. This means that we have to look for another historical context in order to describe the missing piece. Such context is not difficult to find: as we have seen, one of Nietzsche's historical models is Socrates. Socrates', or better Plato's approach to morality will allow us to move beyond Nietzsche and identify the content of moral self-determination.

For Plato, and for us following him, this content is given in the notion of the good. The following chapters will show why we think that the good can eventually be understood as absolute good, as the fundamental notion on which all morality is based. With respect to our initial question of the beginning of morality, we will then be able to give the second part of the answer: morality emerges as distinct phenomenon in the correlation between individual self-determination and the good. Analyzing morality in its complete form requires, we believe, a correlational approach.

The correlational approach pursues a twofold purpose: on the one hand, it restores the irreducibly subjective dimension of morality; on the other hand, it shows that the content of all different moral notions can be traced back to one, both fundamental and comprehensive notion. Our inquiry makes morality both more subjective and more objective at the same time. Emphasizing the correlation may seem to imply that there can be no self-determination without the good and vice versa. This is obviously not the case: not all forms of self-determination are moral, and it is possible to realize the good, or something good, without intending it in any way. Like in Kant's famous distinction between legality and morality one can follow the letter of the moral law without embracing its spirit. What we will describe instead is the full phenomenon of morality which we need to grasp first before we can explain any deficiency.

If we wanted to give this description a normative spin, we could say that self-determination represents the seriousness in all efforts at realizing the good. The good can be achieved in various ways, sometimes even unwillingly or by chance, but as responsible agents we are bound to create it as complete as it can be. The good calls, so to speak, for the appropriate self-determination on our side.[25] On the other hand, self-determination could become self-centeredness if it would not result in a practical conduct that is not also objectively good. In morality, all good is based on individual impulse but at the same time no good must be based on individual impulse alone.

To conclude, we can illustrate the need for a correlational approach by looking briefly at another conception that also considers self-determination as essential for morality. Assessor Wilhelm, or person "B" in Søren Kierkegaard's *Either-Or*, holds that what he calls the "ethical" must not be confused with ethics as a philosophical discipline or a set of rules. It rather indicates a way of being, a way in which a person lives and acts.[26] In more specific terms, being ethical means choosing between good and evil. This does not mean that being ethical would be identical to being good: being ethical means first and foremost recognizing that there is a choice between good and evil and that the individual has to make that choice.[27] The individual has to choose "absolutely"[28] and cannot remain indifferent; they have to choose, not something, but eventually "to will."[29] The choice has to be carried out with great "earnestness"[30] and a "quiet dignity" takes hold of the person once it is performed.[31]

For Kierkegaard, the moral good cannot be thought outside of the act of choice: "The good is because I will it, and otherwise it is not at all."[32] This can of course not mean that the individual would create the good in any way,[33] or that the author would subscribe to some sort of decisionism for which whatever is chosen is therefore also good. The point is rather that the good does not really exist unless it is chosen and incorporated into a person's actions and attitudes. Neither can the good exist unless it is explicitly preferred to evil: "When I choose the good, I choose *eo ipso* the choice between good and evil."[34] Evil, in turn, is not simply a diminishing, or an absence, of the good, but emerges as alternative together with the good and also has to be directly chosen. From these few remarks, we can retrieve another, powerful argument for the subjective dimension of morality. For Kierkegaard too, moral principles achieve their proper, specifically moral meaning only if adopted in an act of self-determination.

In *Either-Or*, the relation of the good to individual choice entails that all moral principles have to be internalized. Duty can be no external standard. The ethical person takes it on "like a garment, it is for him the expression of his innermost essence."[35] However, this does not imply that there is no distinction between the choice, or self-determination, and its content. The distinction remains visible because the choice is always only a particular act, or the act of a particular agent, whereas the good, for Kierkegaard, is general. In certain cases, the two coincide. He refers, for example, to the "secret" of conscience in which "the individual himself is the general."[36] But such a full internalization of moral principles is precisely that, a "secret" and a unique, ultimately inexplicable act. It can never be reached in a final,stable, and habitual form. Integrating the generality of the moral good into one's life is a task and an "eternal responsibility" for the individual.[37] The risk of moral failure always exists.[38]

The general, eventually, *does* remain external.[39] The individual might find temporary "rest" in it,[40] but as an individual, their highest purpose in life does not lie in the ethical but in faith. Kierkegaard is less interested in the dialectic of the particular and the general than in the transcending of the sphere of general principles, and the ethical, altogether. We cannot follow this line of thought.[41] What counts for us is that on the level of morality, despite the goal of internalizing and absorbing general principles, Kierkegaard too has to assume that there is a correlation between self-determination and the good in which both retain their proper nature. We see therefore again that it is necessary to devote attention to the notion of the good itself.

3

A Different Type of Notion

Some Remarks on Semantics and the Systematic Status of the Good

Before we can proceed, it seems wise to trace the outlines of our conception of the good, especially in the form of the absolute good. The notion of the good is deceptively simple, which is why should not assume that everyone agrees on what it entails.

For us, the absolute good is the good without restriction or qualification, which means that there is one and only one, unitary or unified, good. It is impossible for something to be good in a way that is ultimately not included in the absolute good. The notion of the absolute good is comprehensive and inclusive, referring to the most perfect good that can be assumed in the sphere of human practice. It must not be confused, however, with divine perfection, or with the person of God as incorporation of an absolute good. The absolute good, as we see it, is the entailment of the good that we have reason to intend and realize in our acts of self-determination. It is exclusively the human good.

For some, it might seem that the assumption of an absolute notion leads us back to a metaphysical conception that has no right to exist in modern philosophy. But as the following will show, the notion of the absolute good can be developed by unfolding no more than the normative assumptions that we make in our actions. No metaphysical insight is needed for it, except for one which has already been mentioned: in order to refer to an absolute good, one has to concede that a conceptual analysis is meaningful and that the meaning of moral ideas is not limited to formulaic rules and linguistic utterances. The term "metaphysical" can of course be understood in a number of ways. Strictly speaking, it is possible to call our approach metaphysical, too, insofar as the use of concepts implies a non-reductionist and non-physicalist stance. Such an understanding of the term would be mostly negative. What we definitely want to exclude is a positive understanding in the sense of speculative metaphysics. For Plato, the idea of the good provided the foundational structure of all reality, and for scholastic philosophy, goodness was an attribute of the supreme being and subsequently of all created entities. We do not think of the good in such a way, as a general ontological characteristic of things, and we do not use it to seek for a speculative vision of the world. Again, the good is real in actions simply because of the normative assumptions that agents make.

In the following, we will argue that the good is both the simplest and most comprehensive notion in morality. All other notions, and all other principles, rules, obligations, etc., can be questioned as to whether they contribute to what is good, or whether their intended content is good at all. For example, what is right, in the sense of what is required from agents, ethically speaking, can only be so if it is also eventually good. Otherwise, it could not be accepted as right. The same holds for all other, more specific notions, for duties, virtues, justice, increased happiness, and the like. Although the good has often been taken in a narrower sense, for example, as the goal of personal aspirations toward a good life, we do not think that such limitations are tenable. It seems artificial to say that what we call "good" is so only for us whereas what is good in an objective sense requires another term.[1]

One might ask how the understanding of the good as absolute relates to the status of moral self-determination as an *exception*. Moral self-determination is dependent on an individual's particular and unique decision to be good. Does this not imply that the content of this decision is particular and unique, too? The answer is no. Morality only entails that our actions are determined in a way that does not arbitrarily limit the quality and extent of the good. We can of course make a distinction between the absolute good in the sense of the one, encompassing good that has no limitations whatsoever—the truly absolute good—and the good that can be intended and realized in a particular case. The good of all human practice is different from my good, your good, etc. But the distinction is not practically relevant. Insofar as an individual agent can only act in a particular case, the absolute good is all that can be good *for them*. The absolute good, in turn, includes what is good *here and now*. Particular instantiations of the good are all direct manifestations of the one absolute good, or better: it is neither possible nor necessary to seek for an absolute good beyond the good that can be conceived as absolute in a given case. It would be meaningless to look, in any particular action, for an absolute beyond the absolute that is intended or realized. Otherwise, one would have to say that acts of self-determination create their own particular good, which would be absurd: it would then not be clear whether their content could even be called "good," because what is good for one person does not have to be good for another. Conversely, if the content of the acts of moral self-determinations can be more than merely subjectively good, then it also has to be absolutely good and has to be considered a part of the absolute good proper.

If we had to situate our approach in the debate between realist and anti-realist approaches to morality, we would fall decidedly on the side of moral realism. But although we think that the good exists as a descriptive quality of decisions, attitudes, and actions, we do not believe that it exists in any kind of analogy to physical facts. In Korsgaard's words, we assume a "procedural," not a "substantive," moral realism. Procedural realists think "that there are answers to moral questions," while substantive realists go further in assuming that these questions can be answered by relating to "a certain part of the world" in the sense of a natural fact.[2] In the following, we will not put much emphasis on the label of realism. We believe that this label presents a number of challenges that we do best to avoid.[3] On the other hand, we clearly want to avert the thrust of anti-realist arguments. Anti-realists have to say, in one way or another, that the good is *only* a construct, tied to particular socio-cultural practices and interests. It seems to us that no such restriction is possible. Obviously, the good *is* always the human good insofar as only the world of actions is relevant here. In this sense, it would not be impossible to say that the good is a construct of human practice. But nothing is gained for our analysis by calling the good a construct, because even a construct can become an inherent quality of action. Anti-realist approaches to the good do eventually not represent a true alternative to realist approaches, given that whatever is valid for human practice has some sort of reality in it. Anti-realists can only avoid this conclusion by making the good a purely subjective matter, which we reject.

Admittedly, there are some serious, anti-realist objections to our approach that we will have to consider as we go along. Most objections lead to what will be called fragmentarian conceptions of the good according to which there can only be aspects of goodness, but no absolute good. We will try to show in which sense all these arguments are either defective or self-refuting.[4] With the notion of the absolute good we will also employ the idealizing potential of moral claims, that is, morality's promise to allow for a glimpse at a better world. Insofar as the absolute good is conceived as inclusive as it can be, it is also forward-looking and cannot be used to settle for what is only the lesser evil in each case. However, this does not mean that the good is a mere ideal or the expression of some sort of utopia because this would make it valid only for a future over which we have no control. The necessary counterpart of any utopian outlook to the future is a nihilistic attitude toward the present. The absolute good has to be conceived as being absolute *here and now*; its realization cannot be postponed to a future point. This means, again, that any restriction of the validity of the absolute good—and saying that something is but an ideal or a utopia *is* a restriction—does not seem legitimate to us. Morally speaking, the better world we can think of is the world we would have reason, and should feel obliged, to produce here and now, as impossible as this seems most of the times.

We should note that ours is no foundational approach. The absolute good is no ultimate ground from which other principles can be deduced. It is rather the totality of the elements that are comprised in whatever particular good we choose. If ever, the absolute good is not a principle *a quo* but a principle *ad quem*, that is, a principle toward which our analysis proceeds. The absolute good follows from the idea of particular goods, or from goods insofar as they reveal themselves as particular, not the other way around. We can say that the absolute good is the completion of the idea of good, not that it provides its very foundation. Self-determination, on the other hand, provides no foundation either. Although the moral good has to be pursued in and for an individual's determination, it does not follow that it can be deduced from it. The existence of a *moral* form of self-determination presupposes the good as its correlational content.

Readers should also not expect our correlational approach to be a new theory of morality. Morality is nowadays often presented in "theories," which for the most part are sets of criteria that allow one to decide which actions are good, permissible, praiseworthy, etc., and which ones not. But we do not want to identify new criteria as an alternative to existing ones. The first part of this inquiry rather takes a step back: it seems to us that one first has to be clear about the nature and meaning of morality before any practical applications can be found. Nothing in our approach to moral problems is therefore new or supposed to represent some sort of innovation to the field. We attempt a mere *restitutio ad integrum* of morality, an unreduced picture, fuller than what is often given of it.

Another possible objection runs as follows. What individuals think to be moral has to be deemed so unless proven otherwise. Compared, for example, to the field of medicine in which wrong assumptions can potentially be fatal, human practice can deal with a great deal of confused moral ideas. Sometimes even confused ideas can do the job and lead to desirable results. Moral life should not be governed by pedantism but be treated with a healthy dose of pragmatism, trusting that agents usually follow good intentions and that grave aberrations are eventually dealt with by the police. According to such a pragmatic approach, it would not only be impossible to define the constitutive elements of morality, it would also be completely unnecessary. And it could potentially even be harmful, given that human practice is *sui generis* and best not bothered by an overly analytic approach. It is difficult to counter such objections. Compared to a radically pragmatic understanding of morality, our approach is decidedly rationalist, insisting on the possibility that a fundamental conceptual structure can be identified in the phenomenon. We are only able to argue for this approach based on the inherent plausibility that it will, hopefully, achieve.

Despite the assumption of an absolute good, we do not require univocity of the term "good," in the sense that any mention of the term refers to the good as absolute. Different ways of being good have to be addressed differently. The important point is that all different ways can eventually be shown as mere aspects and parts of one unified good. In addition, we assume that among the different ways of being good the moral good occupies a special place. It is eventually no mere subspecies of the good. In morality, we believe that agents strive for the full realization of the good. Why should they deviate from conventions or the law if not for a higher, more complete form of the good? The moral good, then, is by definition a specific qualification of the good, but insofar as it designates both the ultimate and most comprehensive meaning of the good, it stands for, and incorporates, the absolute good. From an intensional point of view, one can use the terms "good" and "moral good" as distinct, but extensionally, one has to assume that they are one and the same. This identity of the absolute and moral good also entails a particular relation between moral normativity and the normativity of practical considerations, conventions, and the law. Although all forms of normativity have their own criteria according to which they can be defined and used independent from each other, the moral good captures what is truly and ultimately good in practical considerations, conventions, and the law. All normativity, in other words, either comes from or leads to moral normativity. We will explain in the following why we think this is so.[5]

In debates on the topic, there is no agreement on the relation between the terms "good" and "morally good." According to Ross, the moral good is a "special sense," a "limitation" of the word good, "which is originally expressive of indefinite commendation."[6] This statement is true with respect to the use of ordinary language in which words acquire meaning in the context they are used, and in which every use is in a sense "special" and "limited." The term good in the sense of a moral qualification is always just one among many possibilities of use. On the level of conceptual analysis, however, we cannot assume that all uses are equivalent. Taken as a concept, the moral good can integrate and complete all reasons for which something can be qualified as good, even if no ordinary language speaker has to be aware of this meaning. While Ross thinks of the good too broadly, Moore seems to limit the uses of the term artificially to the moral good when he claims to investigate "what is meant by calling them [various things—M.S.] good, a matter which is reserved for Ethics only."[7] This position does not seem convincing either, given that even in ethics, or moral philosophy, we have to assume the existence of different forms of normativity.[8]

Some philosophers deny that in relation to the good the absolute is a meaningful notion. Kraut, for example, argues that whatever is good is good for someone, whereas "the property of absolute goodness ... has [no] useful role to play in moral philosophy or in everyday practical thinking."[9] If something could be absolutely good, it could be so without being good for someone.[10] This would not only exclude the "variability" that comes with "relative goodness," because the absolutely good would be the same in relation to each individual agent.[11] The absolutely good would also "depersonalize ... our relationships" insofar as agents would then be considered as "mere instruments to be used for the creation of value."[12] For Kraut, goodness is not like beauty, which is a quality incorporated in objects, not in the relation to them.[13] This criticism of the absolute good seems unconvincing. The absolute goodness that Kraut rejects is a straw-man which represents only a reduced version of the notion.

Kraut traces the notion back to the *Principia Ethica* without acknowledging that the understanding of absoluteness is actually richer in Moore's text. Admittedly, Moore's own approach is somewhat ambiguous and lends itself to misunderstandings. There are at least three aspects of the absolute good that can be distinguished in his work. First, the absolute good is "the *best* state of things *conceivable*, the Summum Bonum."[14] As such, it is encompassing, or a "whole."[15] Second, the absolute good is the good in itself.[16] Saying of something that it is "absolutely good"[17] is another way of saying that it has "intrinsic value."[18] Third, the absolute good is the intrinsic good insofar as it can be considered "existing absolutely by itself."[19] Moore uses what he calls a "method of isolation"[20] in order to look past egoistic or instrumental interests and see "what things are worth having *purely for their own sakes*."[21] It seems that Kraut combines the second meaning of the absolute good with the isolating view of the third meaning, which is really only a method and should not be considered a property of the good. This leaves the first meaning out, which is well able to integrate the fact that whatever is good is also relative, or good for someone. Moore cites friendship, or "personal affection,"[22] among the things that are absolutely good, and it is hard to see how "affection" could turn into the cold, impersonal property that Kraut imagines absolute goodness to be. In our approach, we assume that while the absolute good has intrinsic value, because there is no higher good beyond it, it is at the same time inclusive and good for those participating in it.[23] This point will be addressed extensively in the following analysis.

Can the Good Be One? The Distinction between Formal and Classificatory Notions

Before we can explain the elements that constitute the absolute good, another important question needs to be addressed. We can explain it first in reference to Plato. The Platonic notion of the good is notoriously difficult to understand. One of the main problems lies precisely in the assumption of the good as unified phenomenon, or as one. For Plato, there is one idea of the good that provides the foundation for all particular instantiations of the good, such as the particular virtues. This idea is hard to define, as is stated in some mysterious passages in the *Republic*.[24] In addition, the idea of good is for Plato a metaphysical principle that provides the foundation for all forms of being. Our investigation cannot proceed to such a level: it cannot engage in a discussion of the idea of good as the highest *mathema* of all, nor can it trace the ontological function of the idea, which would force us to go far beyond the realm of human practice. Doing so would not only require too much space; it would also not be necessary for the understanding of the good in matters of morality. Our approach can stay limited to a lower level, so to speak, on which we lay out the various elements of the good without searching for the ultimate principle of their unity. The difficulties arising on the practical level alone are no doubt enough to fuel an inquiry of its own.

But there are other reasons which make the assumption of the oneness of the good difficult to explain. According to some well-known arguments, it is doubtful whether the good can even be considered as one. In the *Nicomachean Ethics*, Aristotle claims that the term "good" is used like the term "being," that is, in many senses, which makes it impossible for it to have one, unified meaning.[25] Different things are good in different ways, depending to the category that is used; if we ask *what* is good, we can say that god or the intellect is good; if we ask *how* something is good, we can say it is so through the virtues that it has; if we ask *in which relation* something is good, we can say it is so because of its usefulness, and so on. In each case, the attribute "good" refers to something different which is good in its own, particular way; it can designate, among others, a substance, a quality, a quantity, a relation, a determination of time, or a determination of place. Of course, in each of these cases the same term is used, which means that at least on the linguistic level there exists a unifying element. But according to Aristotle, the meaning of the term is the same only *kat' analogian*. By no means are we allowed to take categories that are only related as identical and turn them into one unified, general notion.

Following Aristotle's line of thought, one has to ask whether the good is really the most fundamental notion and content of all morality. An individual can strive for justice, prudence, and other moral qualities, all of which can be called "good." Do they all possess the same kind of "good" and are they called "good" for the same reason? It seems that, if ever, they possess goodness in different ways. For example, it seems hard to see how the goodness of moderation and self-restraint can be the same as the goodness of a just and fair distribution of wealth. The inner variety of human practice does not seem to allow for a unified notion. If this argument is true, then we either have to give up the idea of the good as one, because we have to admit that it does not correspond to anything in human practice, or reduce it to the status of an abstract idea, a generalization that would serve a purpose in analyzing moral phenomena but would have no practical significance whatsoever because it is too general to reach down to the level of practical decision-making.[26]

Even more difficult, if not paradoxical, does it seem to claim the oneness of the good with respect to the other forms of normativity. Whoever wants to install a good faucet in their bathroom seems to look for something very different compared to a person who is looking for a good birthday gift, while both are looking for something different compared to someone striving to reach a good divorce settlement. The good in practical considerations, conventions, and the law makes it seem difficult to find even an analogous meaning of the good; or, again, if the meaning is analogous then only in the way of a highly generalized notion which again would have no practical significance.[27]

We can counter these objections by introducing a distinction that concerns the very nature of the notion of the good. Not all notions are of the same kind and used in the same way. We will distinguish here between formal and classificatory notions. The latter refer to particular things, or groups of things, such as numbers, elephants, and pieces of furniture. Things can be classified according to particular qualities they possess, and depending on the quality that is chosen they can be classified either as sharing a common trait or as distinct. For example, insofar as elephants are living things, or animals, they are different from pieces of furniture, but they also share with them the quality of being located in space and time. Compared to that, a formal notion applies to different things regardless of the distinctive qualities they have. One can say, for example, that all things, insofar as they are *something*, are also countable, so that one can apply the notion of countability to them without presupposing that they share any such quality. Elephants, pieces of furniture, and numbers are all countable but do not form a common class of things; we cannot find countability as a common trait in them, that is, as a trait that would allow us to describe them in any specific way.[28] While classificatory notions presuppose that the quality used for the classification can be identified in the respective things, in one way or another, formal notions do not presuppose that at all. They represent a conceptual scheme that remains distinct from the things to which it is applied and serves a purpose only in allowing us to describe and interpret them. Countability, to take our example, is important only *for us*, insofar as it makes things intelligible from a certain point of view.

As far as the good is concerned, it is a formal notion. This became indirectly clear in the objections cited above which all take the good as a classificatory notion. They all assume that the good is an intrinsic quality of actions or intentions. Based on that, in presupposing that the good is one they also have to presuppose that all things classified as good share a common trait. But then they encounter precisely the problem that the trait cannot be identical because different things are good in different ways. Taken as a classificatory notion, the good is pluralistic and contextual and refers to as many ways of being good as there are things which can be good, including the possibility of different degrees of goodness. Helping a friend move to a new apartment fosters the important good of friendship; yet, it is not only a different but also a lesser good compared to helping refugees find shelter and food. The ways in which actions can be classified as good are infinite. If we take the good in such a pluralistic way, it is hard to see why we need a common notion at all. We can use other words to replace "good," such as "laudable," "permissible," and "virtuous," which sometimes fit the things they classify even better than the empty notion of the good. A classificatory notion is very often a rather dispensable tool if one looks at the amount of individual traits it is supposed to gather into one. For this reason alone, the good cannot be classificatory but has to be formal.

The following analysis will show in more detail what it means for the good to be a formal notion. Here, a few remarks have to suffice. We can use the example of the different forms of normativity mentioned above. Installing a good faucet in one's bathroom, finding a good birthday gift, and reaching a good divorce settlement are all actions that are good in different ways. However, all of them are striving toward something purposeful, representing the desire to arrange one's life in a meaningful and beneficial way. (The relation between "good" and "purposeful" that we indicate here will become clear in the following.)[29] Even a faucet is ultimately more than an ordinary tool insofar as it is part of the things that surround us and support the many needs and interests that we have, like the need and interest of having water readily available for us. The same can be said for a divorce settlement that seeks to take advantage of the other partner. Even if its purpose would be a rather narrow and egoistic one, it would still be a settlement according to the rules of law, so that it would be purposeful as a legal solution to a given problem. One could say that it is good at least insofar as a legal clarification of the case was reached. These examples show that the common notion of the good can be applied to very different cases—cases that have nothing in common insofar as both the practical situations and the underlying intentions are very diverse. In all three cases, the good is only a concept that *we* use in order to understand the meaning of the decisions that are made. And yet, we do see something common in all cases, something that could not be seen without the formal notion. The details of the cases would make us blind, so to speak, if we could not read them in light of the one, overarching notion of the good. The examples also show that formal notions are untouched by the problem that arises in the classificatory approach, that is, by the problem how the general notion goes along with the multitude of things it is supposed to cover. We do not have to decide for either one: not for the multitude of things which would force us to give up the general notion nor for the general notion which would in turn require us to overlook the range of variety that things possess. In formal notions, the multitude is left alone; no attempt is made to identify similar traits or force diverse characteristics into common groups. Instead, the concept hovers over the realm of individual things, allowing for a unified interpretation of highly varied traits. All actions can be seen as good *precisely because* no action has to be good in the same way than any other.

Historically, the most famous expression for this status of the good can be found in Plato, in the enigmatic remark according to which the good is not the same but "beyond being," letting being come to the fore.[30] Whatever this statement means, it clearly mentions that the good is not a trait or quality on the level of particular things but a quality that overarches and concerns all things, regardless of what or how they are. Formal notions were also important in the medieval discussions of transcendentals. The transcendentals were deemed to be the first and most common notions—first because they cannot be deduced from others, and most common because they apply to all parts of reality and things. The notions that were given such a status were being, unity, truth, and good, or *ens, unum, verum*, and *bonum*.[31] The transcendentals played an important role in metaphysics—they encompass all nature insofar as it is created by God and also define His attributes—but are based first and foremost on a logical distinction. In more recent times, formal notions have played a role in phenomenological theories.[32]

In current moral philosophy, the distinction between formal and classificatory notions is rarely mentioned. One exception is Korsgaard who distinguishes, in a way analogous to ours, between formal and substantive notions. For her, this distinction denotes two separate types of moral theory: "A substantive conception of morality identifies morality in terms of its content, while a formal conception of morality identifies it with a method of reasoning about practical issues."[33] She rightfully states that the distinction "has frequently been ignored in philosophy, and I believe that this has been a source of confusion."[34] Korsgaard's main example of a substantive conception is utilitarianism because it prescribes not a method but a specific moral content, utility, whereas Kant's approach is formal in being based solely on the "*logic* of practical reason."[35] Only an approach like Kant's can entail unconditional principles, because for it no content is valid unless it stands the test of deliberation required by the categorical imperative.[36] The maximization of utility that is prescribed by utilitarian theories is dogmatic: it does not follow from the agent's own interest in happiness but is imposed on them as a particular rule, which can therefore not be universally binding.[37]

While Korsgaard's distinction parallels ours, she seems to take it too far. From our perspective, it seems best to keep the logic of notions distinct from the classification of moral theories. One could conceive of a version of utilitarianism that would be based on a formal understanding of utility. Utilitarian calculations could also be seen as a mere method. Conversely, even Kant has to assume some substantive contents in his theory, for example, the idea of humans as ends in themselves. One could also imagine different conceptions of justice, some of which would be formal whereas others would be substantive. It also does not seem tenable to tie the distinction between the two types of notions to distinctions in conditionality. Whether Kant is able to determine the unconditional bindingness of moral principles can well be debated but has no bearing on the status of the notions that he uses. As we will show later, all moral theories incur dialectical tensions: what may appear as mere logic of reasoning can eventually appear to be dogmatic. Finally, Korsgaard's idea of formality as a method of deliberation seems to put too much emphasis on the psychological dimension of moral thought. Formal notions can be defined by their meaning and do not require a specific thought process to be distinguishable from substantive contents. The thought process illustrates their meaning but does not constitute it.

Other current theories rely on a classificatory or, in Korsgaard's terms, substantive understanding of the good. Kraut's emphasis on the relative nature of the good as good-for leads him to a "theory of well-being."[38] The theory holds that "what is good for S is the flourishing of S, or what leads to it."[39] Flourishing, in turn, is interpreted along the lines of what he calls "developmentalism"[40]:

> Above all, it is plants, animals, and human beings that flourish when conditions are favorable. They do so by developing properly and fully, that is, by growing, maturing, making full use of the potentialities, capacities, and faculties that (under favorable conditions) they naturally have at a nearly stage of their existence.[41]

Developmentalism has normative force insofar as it gives "a convincing and attractive picture of human life as it should be lived when all goes well."[42] Based on these ideas, Kraut is able to articulate a comprehensive theory of the good, which is not so much systematic than summative and rich in detail. He too thinks that the good is the fundamental notion of morality,[43] which then explains and justifies more specific concepts and rules.[44]

The question is whether his theory of well-being is eventually a theory *of the good*. As mentioned before, Kraut is convinced that it is unnecessary to think about goodness as a distinct property: "Goodness is not an abstruse or abstract subject ... The best way of thinking about good—that is, thinking of it as a matter of flourishing—lies ready to hand in commonsense, practical thought."[45] The good exists as the particular good of plants, animals, and humans insofar as they all flourish and develop in specific ways. There are as many forms of the good as there are effective ways of living well. Now one can certainly call all these ways of flourishing forms of the good, but is that even necessary? Kraut's developmentalism would allow for other concepts and still be a viable theory, if it even needs unifying concepts at all given his emphatic reference to "common sense." Be this as may, it amounts to a "category mistake" if a theory does not distinguish adequately between the good life of humans and goodness as a property of its own. Both are related but have to be addressed separately.[46]

Theories that interpret the good as well-being also have difficulty to distinguish between the moral and non-moral good. We can show this in relation to Kinghorn's approach which shares many similarities with Kraut's. Kinghorn also interprets the good as flourishing but does not follow Kraut's Aristotelian perspective.[47] He rather follows Hume in developing "a thoroughly subjective approach to welfare, where one's flourishing ultimately depends solely on one's mental states."[48] Mental states are the only things that are intrinsically good.[49] The resulting theory of the good can be defined as an "ethical hedonism."[50] For such an approach, the distinction between the moral and non-moral good is not "of any importance."[51] Two reasons are mentioned for this. First, morality is a "fuzzy-edged concept, not allowing for a sharp distinction between the moral and the nonmoral."[52] The distinction is in many cases just a matter of degree.[53] Second, a theory of the good does not need a "sharp distinction" anyway. Moral and non-moral properties are both defined as forms of goodness, and moral properties can be singled out as being no more than "really important aspects of people's ... flourishing."[54] Morality concerns the things that affect well-being most, but this implies for Kinghorn that it still only has meaning insofar as it is rooted in experiences of pleasure or pain.

This deflationary approach to the moral good seems to rest on the same category mistake than the one mentioned before. Kinghorn can only account for varying instances of goodness and has no place for the property of good, taken as such, which means that he also has no place for any categorical differences in the good. We do not believe that the distinction between moral and non-moral properties is in any way "fuzzy-edged," as he assumes. There is a clear conceptual difference, it seems, between, say, an obligation and a desirable goal. Kinghorn would probably object that both obligations and goals are rooted in mental experiences and have to be associated with degrees of pleasure, but this would only show that in his approach conceptual distinctions are made irrelevant from the start. We can then ask, again, why he even needs to label his approach a theory *of the good* and does not simply call it an account of human flourishing.[55]

Attributive and Predicative Uses of "Good"

There are other discussions in moral philosophy which also seem to contradict our claim that "good" is a formal notion. According to a widely accepted distinction, adjectives can be either "predicative" or "attributive," whereby "good" is taken to belong to the side of attributive terms.[56] "In the phrase 'a red book' 'red' is a predicative adjective, ... for 'is a red book' logically splits up into 'is a book' and 'is red.'" In the attributive sense, the adjective cannot be logically separated from its noun: "'X is a forged banknote' does not split up into 'x is a banknote' and 'x is forged', nor 'x is the putative father of y' into 'x is the father of y' and 'x is putative.'"[57] Being red does not depend inherently on the object that is red, whereas being forged depends on things of which it makes sense to say that they are forged. A putative father, in turn, might not be a father at all, while a book is still a book even if its cover has a different color. Another example can be found in the distinction between a big flea and a small elephant: the flea is big *for a flea*, in the attributive sense of the term, because otherwise it follows that the flea is bigger than the elephant.[58] The distinction between predicative and attributive adjectives is "logical" insofar as it does not have to be visible in the grammatical use of the terms. This is especially important for the use of "good," which can "stand ... by itself as a predicate, and is thus grammatically predicative." But even in such cases, "some substantive has to be understood, as there is no such thing as being just good or bad, there is only being a good or bad so-and-so."[59] One cannot say "This house is good" without saying in which sense it is understood as "good." "Good" is therefore, in this account, an attributive adjective. If this were true, however, then "good" would also be a classificatory notion, in the way we have described this type of notion here: the meaning of classificatory notions depends on individual objects and their traits, while formal notions are detached and can be applied to all objects indistinctively. Formal notions seem to be aligned with the predicative use of adjectives.

We do not have to accept this conclusion. To show why this is the case, we first have to note that the distinctions formal/classificatory and predicative/attributive are not congruent. A formal notion like "good" can be used both in a predicative and attributive sense, we believe.[60] As we will see in the following chapter, the attributive use of the good is possible through the use of other formal notions that further express its meaning. We only have to be careful not to adopt certain conclusions that some want to draw from the attributive use of "good," namely the pluralism of the good. We assume that while "good" can be used in an attributive sense it also retains the unitary meaning that predicative terms like "red" possess. On the other hand, if "good" were to be analyzed exclusively in a predicative sense, it could not carry a descriptive meaning, which means that we would have to commit to some sort of expressivism. We want to avoid this, too.

At the first glance, it might not be clear why a predicative understanding of "good" would commit us to an expressivist interpretation. "Red" is used in a predicative sense but does have a descriptive meaning. Another example can help to explain this point. In a phrase like "Surely the destruction of the human race by nuclear weapons would be as bad as anything" the adjective "bad" can be interpreted to have a predicative sense.[61] The destruction of the whole human race is not bad *for a destruction*, it is only bad for those who are destroyed.[62] The thorough, and therefore "good," destruction of humans is evaluated through the predicative use of the adjective "bad." But as a matter of fact, even in this example the use of "bad" is eventually attributive. The destruction is not bad in and of itself but precisely *for* the human race, which means that the use of "bad" is limited and defined through the attributed properties of the destruction *of humans*. "Bad" only seems to stand alone as a detachable predicate. One could say that the phrase cited here is an abbreviation of a more complex thought that is left unexpressed. In other words, "Destruction is bad" does not function like "The house is red," because one has to ask inevitably: destruction of what and to what degree? (As a side note, what makes this analysis difficult and potentially contentious is the fact that it is not self-evident how far one is allowed to stray from the grammatical level of utterances to that of a logical or conceptual analysis. If the distance between the two levels becomes too great, one might think that the conceptual analysis is unwarranted, although we want to claim here that it is not.)

Now, if one were to insist that in the given example "bad" has to be interpreted according to the predicative use of the adjective, what meaning would it have? The only meaning it could have would be an expressivist one, stating the disapproval or negative attitude of the speaker. This meaning is often present on the level of everyday language where "good" and "bad" can be used in a purely evaluative sense. I can drink a beer on a hot day and say "This is good." Obviously, in this case any other expression of my satisfaction would do (like "aahhh"). If I am asked instead why the beer is good, I have to resort again to an attributive use, saying that it is refreshingly bitter, cold, etc. The beer that seems good to drink for me is a good beverage on that particular occasion. This means that the predicative use of "good" is either purely evaluative, as a rudimentary expression of feelings, or semantically not independent because it is based on an implicitly attributive use of the term. Nothing forces us, therefore, to adopt an overall expressivist position. We can work under the assumption that "good" ultimately always carries an attributive and descriptive meaning, even if it first seems to be used only in a predicative sense.

The predicative understanding of "good" can also have another consequence that it seems best to avoid. If the good were a self-standing predicate one could think, as Foot says, "that seeing something as good ought to be like seeing it with a halo."[63] If "good" were predicative like "red," there would have to be a special quality, a sort of "being good" that one could ascribe to individuals and that would turn them into "a good person." But then goodness would in fact be nothing more than a halo, a mysterious, supervening quality for which one would not even need to find any underlying qualities. Users of the term could of course say that "good" is no supervening quality but an inherent trait of the person. The adjective would then again be used in an attributive sense. This, however, could lead to another problematic meaning. Phrases like "These are all good people" can be the result of a hypostatization: the phrases may suggest that some forms of behavior can be turned into essential, unchanging qualities according to which some people simply are dignified and elevated over others. It is obvious that such claims can only be wrong.

The problem arises in parts because of the sortal use of "good." The predicate "good" can be meant to distinguish individuals or groups of people from those who are "bad." In itself, there is nothing problematic with this use of the term. We employ it often, for example, when we distinguish practices that are good from others that are not. But in the sortal use it is unclear whether the term is used in the predicative or attributive sense. "These are good people" can mean that a group of people can be singled out for having performed laudable acts. The group of people is then good like houses are red: goodness applies to them under certain conditions and can be taken away. The phrase can also mean, however, that these people are good *as people* so that all others who are not qualified as such would be lacking a specific quality and cannot have equal value to them. This use of the sortal function of the term has been envisioned by Nietzsche as its original one:

> It was the 'good people' themselves, that is to say, the noble, powerful, high-stationed and high-minded, who felt and established themselves and their actions as good, that is, of the first rank, in contradiction to all the low, low-minded, common and plebeian.[64]

The "noble" use of "good" that Nietzsche describes in these words is ancient. But by no means has it vanished from everyday language, unfortunately, given that it is still possible to see oneself as example of the "good" and discriminate against others who could never become as good as oneself. The use is also prevalent in all ideological attempts to prefer, say, one ethnic group over another. We see here, again, that it is important to conduct a conceptual analysis of the terms that are used because linguistic expressions, despite being intelligible and correct, have a more ambiguous meaning than it might seem.

4

Expressing the Good

First Step: The Good Is the Reason for Which Something Is Desired or Done

Under the Guise of the Good

We are now able to address the notion of the good in more detail than before. In a series of thirteen steps we will slowly unfold the various elements belonging to it. As already said, in doing so we will again be tied to a particular historical context, namely, to Plato's philosophy. We do of course assume that Plato's account of the good is valid beyond the historical context in which it appears so that conclusions can be drawn that hold *mutatis mutandis* for other approaches to the good. We will not follow Plato's writings to the letter but use them to identify the systematic characteristics of the good. Nonetheless, we are never allowed to pretend that our analysis is based on purely formal structures that could be described regardless of the context in which they appear. What we call "the good" can only be articulated in a particular, historically determined language, even if that language can be translated into other conceptual idioms.

Our starting point is the assumption that the notion of the good is rooted in the practice of giving and asking for reasons.[1] In its most formal sense, the good can be indicated as reason when the question is raised why something is desired or done. One can then say: "I want to do this *because* it is good." As reason adopted by an agent, the good can also be considered the cause of an action that is done. We will discuss this aspect later. The question "why something is desired or done" means that actions can be considered from two points of view which in the following will be distinguished as the action-centric and the agent-centric point of view. One can look at actions both as practices that occur and as the result of an agent's will, intention, or desire. "Desire" is used here as a broad, generic term that covers all volitional or emotive attitudes. The two points of view correspond to the correlational approach that we have suggested for morality as a whole.

When we say that the good is the reason for which something is desired or done, we do not mean that it is only one possible reason, chosen among others. In that case, something could be desired or done either because it is good or because it is useful, nice, convenient, etc., to do. We take "it is good to do x" as fundamental and synonymous to "having a reason to do x." The fact that it is good to do x simply *is* the reason to do x. Conversely, actions that are done for a reason can be said to be done because of the good, or because of *a* good. The distinction between "the good" and "a good" is not important for us because "the good" is the formal expression of what constitutes any particular instance of something that is considered a good. Other evaluative qualifications, such as "useful" and "nice," can also be subsumed under the good. The following analysis will show why we are able to use the notion in such a way.

Following a recent theory, one can say that agents act under the guise of the good.[2] The term "guise of the good" goes back to Thomas who held that "whatever the human being desires, they desire it under the aspect of the good. What is not desired as the perfect good, which is the ultimate end, is by necessity desired as tending toward the perfect good, because the beginning of anything is always ordered to achieve its completion."[3] Some moral philosophers doubt that such an orientation toward the good is actually a constitutive feature of practical desires and intentions. The good *can* for them function as the reason for which something is desired, intended, or done, but it seems problematic to say that acting for a reason, any reason, is at the same time acting for the sake of the good.[4] An easy way to circumvent this objection would be to say that for any practical goal a conceptual analysis can be given which contains the notion of the good, but this would only further beg the question. The theory of the guise of the good is not about the use of an analytical language but about the very structure of action.

There is in fact a certain fuzziness in the idea of the guise of the good, which is impossible to avoid. Still, we do not believe that this fuzziness forces us to give up the idea. The fuzziness can already be found in the way in which single actions are conceived. Is it the object of the action that is good or the fact that the action is performed, or just the desire and intention to perform it? The guise of the good can apply to all three. The goodness of desire, the action, and the object of the action can coincide but can also be considered separately. One can have doubts about the outcome of an action and still think that it is good to carry it out. In addition, many actions are parts of a larger practical endeavor and function as means to an end. Thomas mentions this in his formulation that actions which are not themselves the perfect good have at least a "tendency" toward it. How pronounced and dominant does this "tendency" have to be? Can it remain hypothetical or tentative? But again, the fuzziness that one encounters here does not have to be seen as an argument against the guise of the good. It is enough for us that there is in each case at least *one* aspect of an action that involves the desire for the good. The theory only needs to hold that "when an agent is motivated to act, something about the action looks good to the agent."[5] The aspect in question can be inherent to the very act or indirectly related to it as part of a larger scope. One can never rule out that an agent cares about the quality of their life as a whole in any particular action they carry out.[6] The meaning of an action can not only be found in the empirical act that is performed but requires a more inclusive focus on all potential ends that are involved.

This argument, however, does not address the most serious challenge to the idea of the guise of the good, which lies in the claim that there may be desires and intentions that have no relation whatsoever to the good. The challenge arises from the belief that if desires and intentions were related to the good, they would contain an evaluative judgment which could be used to justify the action. This does not seem to be case, for the simple reason that there can be desires which only tend toward their satisfaction, without any further interest in justification,[7] and intentions that are action-guiding without any evaluative stance that would force the agent to assess whether what they do is good.[8] What seems to drive such objections is the concern that acting may be unduly put under moral constraints and that the reality of human desires and intentions may involve a great deal of attitudes that are indifferent to the good or downright opposed to it.[9]

It seems that these objections are fighting a strawman. The guise of the good does not assume that agents make a value judgment in any explicit way or that they seek justification for each act they perform. The fuzziness in desires and intentions allows for the relation to the good to remain implicit, as a background assumption of sorts which does not have to become the main focus of the agent. We also do not have to assume that all normative considerations are moral in the strong sense of the term. We only need to say that they are normative in the minimal way in which all actions carry a normative content. The very idea of an action implies that a certain outcome is to be achieved. "I opened the window because it felt stuffy inside." As orientation toward a goal—"So that I can breathe better"—actions follow a normative outlook on how the world around us is to be arranged. Even if it is impossible to say that each desire and intention contains the proposition "What I want is good," this does not mean that such a consideration cannot enter into the agent's reflection. The objections can in fact be turned around and one can ask how it is possible to rule out definitely that the good plays any role in actions. It seems that one could only say this if desires and intentions could be cut off from any further implications and analyzed as isolated entities. I have a desire and all I want to do is satisfy it,[10] and I am acting in such-and-such way without "having a story about what justifies" my behavior.[11] But such an understanding of acting appears artificial as the mere result of an analytical operation. One can no doubt take actions apart into sole desires and intentions on the one side and justifications and moral purposes on the other. But then, are they still actions?

The analytic approach that is manifest in the objections against the guise of the good can be compared to the behavior of someone who is able to take a car engine apart but does not know how to put it back together and set it in motion. Desires and intentions are neatly isolated, but how do they drive human practices? Is a desire for desire's sake, and a mere intention, reflective of an agent's situatedness in the world? "I just want to sit still for a while": it seems hard to imagine an agent who does not pursue at least some hidden purpose in such a case. The inclination to distinguish between reasons that only motivate actions and others that justify them displays a sort of "separatist" attitude toward the reality of action.[12] That such an attitude is wrong can be shown, among others, through the phenomenon of regret. In many cases, if one regrets an action, "the failure seems internal to the desire."[13] If a desire were just that, a desire to achieve some end, then regret would have to come from an external point of view, for example, because one is scolded for having indulged too much. But regret often carries a relation to the expectations that were inherent to the desire itself, which means that the desire entails an assumption, however vague, about its fulfillment as being justifiable and good. Without this assumption, it would also seem impossible to explain why agents can deliberate about or even doubt their own desires and intentions.[14] The critics of the idea of the guise of the good seem to rescue desire and intention from the grip of moral categorizations only by attributing a simplicity to them that humans can hardly ever enjoy, or that they can enjoy only by pretending that in certain cases for some magical reason considerations of the good do not matter.

The understanding of the good as reason also leads us back to Socrates' claim according to which all actions aim at the good. The claim can be stated negatively, as assumption that no one does what is bad, or what they think is bad, which means that no one does what is bad, given that they can freely choose what to do, that there is something good they can do instead of the bad, and that they have the capacity, or the power, to go for the good.[15] The qualifying remarks that are made deserve some explanation. First, it makes no difference at this point whether the course of action that is chosen is in reality good or not. Socrates' argument holds even if the individual is wrong and chooses something that is ultimately bad. The claim only states that the individual has to have a reason for what they do, not that the beliefs supporting the reason have to be correct. Second, it seems obvious that the qualifications according to which the choice has to be voluntary and based on realistic options—realistic insofar as the individual can at least attempt to realize the good—do not add anything to the core argument. They are redundant insofar as non-voluntary actions are not based on choice and do not require the agent to have a reason at all. Sleepwalking and actions performed in a delusional state cannot be called actions at all or if so then only in an incomplete way (one can say that they have the external but not the internal qualities necessary for actions). Likewise, if there is no good that could be reached through the agent's own activity, there is also no choice involved. One can choose to walk carefully on crutches, in case one's leg is broken, but one cannot choose that the leg heals well, or that it heals at all.

Some cases are more difficult to assess than others and might raise doubt as to whether all actions aim at the good. In fantasies and hypothetical thoughts, for example, the individual can find it desirable to do something bad. Finding themself in a situation of stress, an individual may think that once the work is done they will get drunk for three days in a row. The individual wishing to do so might know that drinking is bad for their health, and that they would eventually not find it pleasant to extend their drunkenness for so long. Still, they might harbor the wish for some truly self-destructive behavior. One way to go about this case would be to say that the individual does not make any choice but only indulges in fantasies and imagination. This solution seems untenable, not only because it begs the question but also because it does not explain what it means to have a strong wish for something bad. At least in some cases it is possible to assume that an individual desires what they know is bad, even if they leave unclear whether they will act on their desire or not. A more plausible solution lies in saying that the individual imagines not an *action* but a *choice* they could make. They do not actually wish to stay drunk for three days in a row but fantasize how it would be if they could choose to do so. They simply would just like to have the choice. In this case, the agent does choose something bad but not in a realistic way: they do not delve further into the question whether the bad is doable for them at all, or whether they will still want it when the time has come and they have to assess it in the face of other options, which then might seem a better way to go.

We therefore have to specify our formula by saying that no one does what is bad if they make a realistic and effective choice.

This solution to the question how it is possible for an agent to choose something bad resolves only one of the difficulties that arise at this point. There are two other ways in which agents can miss aiming at the good. The first one is traditionally referred to as evil (the second one will be treated in the following section). Evil concerns the possibility of doing what is bad voluntarily and knowingly, that is, of doing it *because* it is bad. One might also say: of doing it as if it were the good. We cannot address such actions here. There is a certain mystery about them, insofar as the dialectic that seems to take place in evil is hard to understand and can well lead to the question whether evil actions do really exist. How can one desire the bad as if it were good, that is, how can one desire one thing and its opposite as the same thing? One may be tempted to say that even the so-called evil actions have a certain good involved, at least subjectively: aggressive actions, for example, may come from a sense of being entitled to take revenge, on society, the rich, one's personal enemies, etc. But even in such cases something evil is desired because it is evil, at least in parts, not because it is erroneously taken as something good. Again, we are not able to address this type of actions here. It also does not seem necessary to do so because even if evil exists as a strict opposite to the good, we first have to explain the reality of the latter (unless, of course, the good would typically be no more than the evil in disguise, but we believe that we can rule this possibility out).

Is There Weakness of the Will?

The second way in which agents can miss aiming at the good is traditionally discussed as lack of self-restraint, or incontinence, or in its more modern version as a weakness of the will. The question is here: how can someone act badly despite them knowing the good? The problem arises in Plato's account because reasons are assumed to be causes, which excludes the possibility of actions happening without a reason, or against a reason that would otherwise prevent them. In the phenomena that are discussed as lack of self-restraint the reason to avoid a particular action is known and yet the agent does not follow it. It may be tempting to say that such cases are an exception to, or subgroup of, actions that happen according to reason. What seems more plausible than the idea that some exceptions to the rule of reason in actions have to exist? But if there could be particular actions that occur without a reason, or against an opposing reason, then all actions could occur without a reason, or one could disregard all reasons that the agent has. It would be impossible to say where reason sets in, that is, where the actual transition from reasonless to reason-based actions would lie. We could never determine such a threshold with certainty. It seems therefore best to give up the idea that we have to allow for exceptions.

Socrates famously denied that an agent can lack self-restraint. An agent, for him, always acts on reason, that is, on the belief of pursuing something good. As we said, this belief does not have to be correct. The adopted reason can be faulty and the agent may not be able to think clearly (Socrates' word for this is *amathia*, ignorance or foolishness).[16] In this case, they do something bad but still act under some assumption that it is good. If this were not the case, if individuals could really act against their better knowledge, they would behave like slaves who do not follow their proper will. Although humans often claim that they are overcome by desire—"I really couldn't hold myself back at this point"—they cannot seriously put their own capability to reason in such a subordinate position.[17] That is, in Socrates' line of thought "I couldn't hold myself back" can never be a true statement if understood literally. In the philosophical tradition, this position has been controversial. Aristotle famously criticized Socrates for going against an obvious phenomenon, emphasizing that there can in fact be individuals lacking self-restraint without being either ignorant or foolish. However, Aristotle did not deny the fundamental claim according to which actions are caused by reasons; he only tried to explain how the apparent lack of self-restraint can occur, and in which way reasons are involved in it.[18] For the sake of our inquiry, two points can be mentioned from his nuanced analysis. We can summarize them by saying that for Aristotle, Socrates did not pay close enough attention to the complexity of reasons. It is wrong to assume, first, that a reason is a simple, indivisible thing. Reasons are based on an act of reasoning which allows for different outcomes based on the various steps that are taken. Second, it is not true that agents can have only *one* reason guiding *one* action at a time. An individual can fail to restrain themself by adopting one of the possible reasons that are involved in the case. What we call lack of self-restraint is therefore not complete foolishness, as Socrates assumed, but one possible if faulty way of acting according to reason.

Insofar as the first point is concerned, Aristotle points at the distinction between universal and particular statements. An agent might do something that goes counter to a universal proposition—in Aristotle's example, "It is good to eat dry food"—because they do not apply this proposition to the food at hand. They might misjudge the food they want to eat or simply not pay attention to its quality, that is, not "realize" (*energei*) the knowledge they possess. In this case, the agent acts against their better judgment but does not willingly or explicitly so.[19] With respect to the second point, an agent can follow a reason that is contrary to what they think is good but that does not stand in direct contradiction to it. Following again Aristotle's example, one can be convinced that it would not be good to eat too many sweet things but nonetheless follow the judgment that sweet things are a great pleasure to taste. In this case, two universal propositions are present in the agent's mind but only one of them motivates the action. If the desire for sweet things becomes strong enough, it can force the agent to adopt the proposition that fits its purpose best.[20] Here again, the agent acts against their better judgment, but not according to a judgment that directly contradicts the better one. They are not overcome by something they do not want. The proposition that they follow—"Sweets things taste good"—is only "accidentally" opposed to the proposition "Don't eat sweets," Aristotle says. It is simply *another* judgment that can be followed, so that the agent not only acts according to a reason, they also act according to a reason they more or less willingly adopt, even if they might later realize that it was not the best possible one, all things considered. This example shows that agents can have a multitude of judgments at their disposition, so that any given action can be seen in light of several, conflicting but equally motivating reasons.

Aristotle's examples cannot be subsumed under a strict definition of the lack of self-restraint, or incontinence, insofar as the agent does not really act against their will. They are incontinent only in a looser sense, insofar as one could expect a different behavior from them. Davidson, whose intent was to show incontinence as a true "paradox" of human action, remarked that many actions which are traditionally labeled as incontinent are not such in the strict sense of the term.[21] But is it clear that the phenomenon of an agent lacking self-restraint even exists in the strict, "paradoxical" sense?[22] Like in the case of evil, there are good reasons to doubt the existence of such a phenomenon. Agents can change their resolutions in the last second, or go through with an action despite having doubts, not to mention that they sometimes follow motives that remain inaccessible to themselves. In all these cases they might appear to be afflicted by a "weakness of the will," whereas their motives are in reality just more complex than one assumes. Agents can also think that from an objective, neutral point of view certain actions are bad—for example, not to work out or go for a walk—while their desire eventually leads them to quite different ones, for example, to stay home and watch a movie. Does this mean that they did not work out because they could not pull themselves together? Or does it not rather mean that the agent is not always willing to internalize objective standards, so that the course of action that is taken is subjectively preferable, and therefore "good," even in light of other, more objective points of view? Regular exercise might be the best thing to do, given one's own wish to live a healthy life, but it can go counter to other interests that are equally, or perhaps even more, important to the agent in a given situation. The agent then chooses another good, not something bad.

A similar conclusion can be reached if we take into account that the presumed weakness of the will often indicates a reprehensible moral failure. The agent is deemed incapable of following a given normative standard. Here again, it is far from clear that every agent accepts such standards in the first place. Being too weak to follow a certain norm or recommendation could be a form of protest: personal motives could stand against impersonal requirements, which means that in such cases it is not that the agent is too weak but that the standards do not make sense to them. Perhaps one could even think that the belief in weakness of the will stems less from an analysis of human agency than from particular moral judgments which are projected onto the realm of action and taken erroneously in a descriptive rather than evaluative way. At least it seems that descriptive and evaluative perspectives on the phenomenon are often mixed.[23]

Reasons as Causes

In recent times, Davidson has argued that if reasons play a role in explaining actions, then reasons can be considered as causes. What we give by mentioning the reason for an action is a causal explanation.[24] It may seem that giving such an explanation leads to a reduction of actions to physical events. However, one does not have to assume that causality only holds for events that are describable in a physical sense. If there would be no causal explanation of actions, then one would have to accept the quite unsatisfying conclusion that actions happen without a cause, distinct from all or at least most of the other kinds of events in this world. But actions have to have causes if having causes means that their occurrence can be explained, in whatever way explaining works for them. One of the assumptions that makes it difficult for some to accept a causal explanation of actions may be that if something is caused it is preceded by another event. Cause and effect would then be numerically distinct, so that the event E_1 of having a reason to act would come before the event E_2 of the action that occurs. If this were so, then the occurrence of actions would remain wholly inexplicable as one could never show how having a reason would trigger or move an event in the physical world. But the distinction of cause and effect does in fact *not* presuppose two numerically different events. "Cause" and "effect" are aspects under which one and the same event can be explained or, in Davidson's words, "rationalized."[25] The agent's intention, or the reason they adopt, makes the action occur, not, however, as another process separated from it but as part of its very process. To act means to act according to an intention or reason. One can easily show that not even in the case of physical events cause and effect need to be numerically distinct. If a ball hits a window and breaks it, what causes the breaking is the impact of the ball on the surface, which is indistinguishable from a modification of the surface that makes it burst according to certain patterns inherent in it. That is, what we call the "breaking of the window" is caused by its disposition to break in specific ways under a certain force. There is one single event that is separated into two, into E_1 ("the ball hit the window") and E_2 ("the window broke") only for the sake of explanation.[26]

Plato also assumed that reasons are causes. All particular things that are in one way or another located in space and time necessarily come from a cause (*aitia*).[27] The good, insofar as it is the reason for an action, is also the cause that explains why the action occurs. Socrates emphasizes this point in his famous criticism of material causes in the *Phaedo*: I wouldn't sit here in prison, he states, if I hadn't deemed it to be the best thing to do. All material causes that could be mentioned in order to explain why he is sitting there—he has to be physically able of sitting in prison and moving his body around—do not explain why he has decided to stay.[28] Some might ask whether eventually there needs to be another cause involved, one that would state why a certain reason is adopted. Socrates stays in prison because he thinks that it is the best thing to do, but why *does* he think it is best? It is obvious that such a question cannot be answered because it would lead to an infinite regress: if a reason had to be given for the adoption of a reason, one would always have to demand another reason. Hence, there can be no further reason that explains the adoption of a reason. The adoption of a reason is what explains an action, but the adoption itself cannot be further explained.[29] Does this mean, some might continue to object, that the adoption of reasons is an inexplicable event? And if this were so, would it not undermine the claim that actions can be explained through the reasons that cause them to occur? How can one use something that is in itself inexplicable to explain something else?

We can counter the objections mentioned here if we clarify what we mean by referring to the "adoption of a reason." It seems natural to think of a state prior to the adoption of a reason, that is, of a state in which or out of which the reason is adopted. Deliberation, reflection, or simply thinking are all words for a process out of which a certain insight, or a decision, resolve, intention, and the like, can occur. "I wasn't sure what to do, but then I thought it would be best to do x." Those who claim that there should be a reason for the adoption of a reason would certainly say that the adoption is explained only if we can explain the process of deliberation out of which it occurs. But it is wrong to expect that any such explanation can be given. First, what holds for the adoption of a reason also holds for the process of deliberation: it can well appear inexplicable, too. The mere fact that one event occurs prior to another does not give the former any explanatory force. Second, even if we could describe the process of deliberation in a somewhat well-defined way, we could never deduce the adoption of a reason from it. Nothing in the prior state can necessitate the adoption of a particular reason, for the simple fact that the agent could always have chosen another reason. Even if only one reason seems appropriate in a given case, other reasons are available and may appear only slightly less appropriate. There is at best a probabilistic chance that a specific reason is adopted in an open-ended process of deliberation. Third, "adopting a reason" is just another word for "having a reason." Having a reason is not a process in which the reason magically emerges, or is slowly articulated and grasped, but *one* mental act which consists of having one particular reason to do x. We do not have a reason unless we actually have it. At a certain point, we simply have to be aware of it. Obviously, our thinking is not always clear and at times we have to clarify and articulate what we really want. But we can only try to clarify a reason that we already have. If it turns out to be another reason than we thought, then we did not have it properly. With Scanlon, we can speak of "reasons fundamentalism" here, which he intends to mean: "no ... further explanation of reasons need or can be given: the 'grip' that a consideration that is a reason has on a person for whom it is a reason is just being reason for him or her."[30]

One of the problems—or rather pseudo-problems—that may drive the objections mentioned here is that although reasons are supposed to be discursive and based on inferences or arguments, at one point the agent who deliberates has to recur to some sort of intuition: "Then I saw what I had to do." If this were not so, we could never think of anything new, or better: none of the processes we associate with thinking could be possible if we could not at some point see or understand something we had not seen or understood before. For some, recurring to an intuition may seem to contradict the inner rationality of reason. But it is not at all impossible to conceive of a reason all at once. "I realized that the street was too wide for me to cross it with the red lights on." A belief like this involves rather elaborated reasoning, implying knowledge about the speed of cars, the duration of traffic lights, one's ability to run, and more. But the conclusion that the agent draws does not have to be spelled out in its different steps or in relation to its underlying assumptions. Although being potentially a longer argument, or a chain of inferences, they grasp it intuitively.

Obviously, all this means that there is indeed something "inexplicable" about having a reason. Instead of "inexplicable" we could say "probabilistic," but this is just another term for the same phenomenon. The probability is not quantifiable in any case. All explanations of actions are *ex post facto*: if actions actually occur, we can (hopefully) say which reasons caused them to occur. But this does not contradict the claim that actions can be explained. Actions are to be explained in a way that is specific to them, and if this includes the fact that agents do not have reasons until they actually have them, then the explanation has to take that into account. We cannot require an explanation that cannot be given for this kind of events. Otherwise, we would have to say that actions are explained only if they are explained in a fully deterministic way so that all reasons that we adopt would follow from all other reasons that we have adopted in our life. Obviously, it is not impossible to resort to such a deterministic conception, but it would be detached from the point of view that is involved in individual action which is the only one that is relevant for the scope of moral philosophy.

If we look again at Davidson's approach, we can see that he dealt with the same problem. According to his terminology, there are "primary reasons," "unconditional judgments," or "primitive actions"[31]—all terms that refer to the fact that actions, or the intentions causing them to occur, have to be described as individual events that cannot be deduced from prior events. This insight sheds light on his assumption that weakness of the will exists. According to his analysis, "the incontinent man acts, and judges, irrationally" because "he lacks … a reason for not letting his better reason for not doing *a* prevail."[32] In other words, it is "irrational" if one has a better reason but adopts another, lesser one. Even in light of Davidson's own account of action, this conclusion does not follow. If the adoption of reasons is "primitive" and has to be "unconditional" at a certain point, then it is possible for the agent to follow any reason, given only that it is a reason. Adoptions would be "irrational" only if we could say that reasons have to meet a certain standard, which is clearly not the case. It seems best to eliminate the term "irrational" altogether from the philosophy of action and assume that all reasons make behavior rational, in one way or the other. Otherwise, one introduces a normative standard of presumably rational behavior into an otherwise descriptive analysis. For cases in which the agent does not follow their best reason, or no apparent reason at all, the term "arational" seems more appropriate, as it indicates not the violation of a standard but a mere lack of thinking. "What were you thinking when you did that?" is a question we can ask, assuming that an agent has not fully used their capability for rational thought. They did not contradict themself but just were not aware of what they truly wanted.[33]

Second Step: The Good Is the One Sufficient Reason for Which Something Is Desired or Done

The notion of the good as reason, developed in the previous step, has to be specified a little more. To do so, we can say that the good is the sufficient reason for an action to be desired or done. Given that one can always choose to act otherwise than one eventually decides to do—if for practical matters this may be impossible at times, logically it can never be excluded—any reference to the good has to explain why one specific action is chosen and not another. I could be anywhere else, Socrates says in the *Phaedo*, in Megara or with the Boeotians, would I not hold it best to stay where I am, in prison.[34] There is a certain ambiguity in the idea of a sufficient reason. We have to distinguish between the sufficient reason that an agent has for doing something, and the reason that is sufficient all things considered. The former means that almost any reason can be sufficient, whereas the latter implies that only one reason is so. The fact that he could also be in Megara means that Socrates would have had sufficient reason to go there in order to escape from prison, had he wished to do so. Given the variety of options, it would be arbitrary for him to remain in prison could he not have one sufficient reason that excludes, or trumps, all other options. The good, which is the reason for his choice, can therefore not be any reason that is taken to explain why an action is done; it rather has to be the reason that explains why the action is *preferred* over others which would also have sufficient reason to occur. The good, in other words, has to have a comparative meaning; it has to determine what is better compared to other options that can also, in one way or another, be considered good. But this is not all: insofar as there always *are* other options, of which it is not logically excluded that they are better than the one which has actually been chosen, the good has to be not only comparatively but also absolutely good. It has to be best, all things considered in a given situation. The good, we can say, is the final good in a series of other desirable things, the last or highest one which decides what actually is chosen. As a reason, it is the final sufficient reason, or the one and only sufficient reason, that excludes the adoption of all other potentially sufficient reasons. ("In a given situation" means that the final good, as it is understood here, is final only within a specific context of action, not with respect to all possible contexts or human life as a whole).

It is not difficult to see how the comparative sense of the good is anchored in the practice of giving and asking for reasons. For every reason that an agent mentions it is possible to ask: "Did you only think at that moment that it was sufficient to act on, or did you assume that it was really so?" Distinguishing between the reasons that only appear to be sufficient and the ones that are in reality so is inherent to the very practice of giving reasons. One would not have to give a reason if one's choice were only a matter of momentary feelings or convictions. Among all the reasons that can be relevant in a given situation, the one that motivates the action has to outweigh all others.[35] "I could have done several things at that moment but thought it would be better to do *that*." However, with respect to the comparative sense of the good, the question can be asked again whether the action that is chosen only appears to be better or is in reality so. The comparative statement needs a criterion in order to be justifiable. Most of the things are only better than others in one particular sense, meaning that at certain times they may be better, at other times worse. For an action to be really better than all others it has to be best all things considered. One might object that it is often not possible to identify what is best. "The best thing to do" may be a guess or the result of some sort of experiment ("Let's do that and then see what happens"). But situations of uncertainty do not contradict the fact that the sufficient reason for an action is deemed to determine what is best. In fact, situations of uncertainty receive their meaning precisely from the idea that one of the choices *has* to be best, that is, that one of the choices *has* to be the right thing to do and so takes the place of the final good within the context at hand. If nothing could be best, it would not even matter whether one is uncertain.

We find various arguments in Plato that elucidate this point. All things related to justice, as well as all other things that are related to the good, are useful and beneficial through the idea of the good alone, Socrates states in the *Republic*. "If we don't know it and should have ever so much knowledge of the rest without this, you know that it's no profit to us, just as there would be none in possessing something in the absence of the good."[36] We can paraphrase this by saying that although many things are good, so that there would be sufficient reason to choose and desire them, we do in fact not choose them unless we are able to do so *because of* their being good. The one sufficient reason for choosing something is not any of the qualities it has, be they as desirable or beneficial as they can be, but the fact that we can identify them as best, all things considered. We need a point of view that allows us to look past all particular qualities and grasp what is primarily good in a given situation. Otherwise, although we might be doing good things, we would not have a goal (*skopos*) and eventually do everything randomly.[37] We can explain this also by saying that the one sufficient reason that we need in order to choose something cannot be identical to the thing we choose because if it were we could justify our choice only in a tautological way. We would then have to say, for example: "Justice should be the main concern in distributing resources because otherwise the distribution of resources would not be fair." In such cases, we would only use a slightly different term for the explanation of the very same idea. Only the good allows us to say something more, allows us to mention an additional reason for which all other particular qualities, moral or not, are chosen.

From a deeper and more existential point of view, Diotima states in her speech in the *Symposium* that humans care for nothing that belongs to them unless it is good, not even for their own limbs which they have cut away when they are bad. And not only do they want to possess the good, they want to possess it forever.[38] The reason for this desire, the strongest of all, stems from the nature of the good as reason: while the desire to achieve beauty necessarily raises the question why beauty should be desired at all, no further question needs to be asked once the good is achieved.[39] The good is the final and therefore the only truly sufficient reason. As the ultimate goal of a human life, it lies beyond all other desirable things, including beauty which represents the most desirable among all particular qualities.

This argument extends the idea of a final good within a given context to the final good of all life. One might ask what justifies this step. Why do we need *one* final good instead of the many final goods we deal with in the various parts of our life? The logic of Diotima's, or Plato's, argument can be reconstructed in the following way. The argument is rooted in the fact that human beings are inevitably choosing or desiring something. If they could stop at a particular final good that they have chosen, they could stop choosing and desiring altogether once they have reached it. Only the fact that there is one truly final good makes the desire unending and inexhaustible for them, though not necessarily because the good can never be reached but because it always remains beyond the particular goals that humans can meet. The goodness of life as a whole is not defined by its parts. Following Socrates, we can also say that the greatest good is what we want most and do not want to be deprived of.[40] While the desire for particular goods is limited and variable, the desire for the truly final good is unrestrictable and permanent. One can be deprived of it only if one is deprived of desire altogether. This means that the truly final good is the necessary correlate to all rational desires and will, or the reason that says that we have to have reasons, that is, that we have to desire and choose. In other words, it is the only sufficient reason that allows us to say why we have to look for sufficient reasons in what we do. At the same time, the final good is the necessary condition that allows individuals to say that they are following reason throughout their conduct of life. When Socrates states in the *Crito* that he follows only the reasoning (*logos*) that seems best to him, he could just as well say that he is always following reasons and finds himself concerned with identifying the sufficient reason that supports each one of his beliefs.[41] If we do not choose the best, we do not choose for a reason at all, or at least not for *our* best reason, but because of influences and conditions that force us to accept a lesser option.[42]

This all means that in order to follow the statements made in the *Symposium*, we do not have to assume a sort of teleology according to which humans would have a natural tendency to strive for the good. As said before, we avoid any metaphysical speculation and do not think that the good is rooted in any time-invariant structures of nature.[43] What humans only have to do is choose and make sure that their particular choices are done in the best possible way, but there is no final goal that simply guides them along. If this were so, humans would not have to make choices after all but simply follow that goal. In other words, all we are concerned with here is the relation between reasons, not their content. We cannot identify in advance what an absolutely good human life would look like. The place of the final good remains void.

Third Step: A Thing Is Qualified as Good insofar as It Fulfills a Purpose

Expressing the Meaning of "Good"

Taken as reason, the good can answer the question why something is desired or done. This answer is given from what can be called an agent-centric point of view. Given the contingency of any action, that is, the fact that for any action we can assume that it could also not be performed, the question can be asked why the agent decides to perform it at all. "Because it seems good to me" answers this question. But as we said earlier, one can also take another, action-centric point of view. From this point of view, an agent has reason to say that something seems good to them only if it can also be qualified as such. Without the second point of view, they could justify their decision only by referring to their subjective impression—"To me, this seems good"—but not by indicating a specific property in the action or thing. The question *why* something is desired or done therefore entails that it is possible to state *how* that particular thing or action is seen. "I have decided to do this because it is really good." Evidently, individual agents can refuse to follow this entailment by limiting their decision to an agent-centric point of view. In this case, the term "good" means nothing more than a kind of personal approval. However, in the previous steps we have seen that the good, in the way we understand it here, gives the one sufficient reason for an action that excludes the adoption of all other possible reasons. This means that it can eventually not be limited to an agent-centric point of view. Without saying how the respective action can be qualified, the reason that is given would not be fully sufficient. One could then always ask: "*You* think it is good, but *is* it really?"[44]

The use of "good" from an action-centric point of view makes it necessary to recall the distinction between formal and classificatory notions.[45] Classificatory notions refer to, or are based on, properties that can be identified in things. Tables and chairs can be classified as pieces of furniture because one can show that their features imply a particular form of use, in which case they can also be shown as distinct from tableware. "Good," instead, is a formal notion, that is, a concept or conceptual scheme which allows us to make statements about things without being instantiated by or identifiable in them. For example, by making the general statement that health is good we learn nothing particular about health, none of its characteristics nor any object on which it depends. If we want to say something more concrete, we have to resort to classificatory notions and say, for example, what it means for physical organs like our heart to work well, and how their working well contributes to our overall health. What we say by simply using "good" is something else. "Good" has meaning on the level of reasons: saying that health is good means, for example, that we have sufficient reason to prefer health over illness, or that there is a reason to prefer specific actions that contribute to health, like going for long walks.

Now, from an action-centric point of view we *do* say something about things, if only that they are good. Insofar as health is concerned, long walks are good, cigarettes are bad, and the term "good" is used to identify particular qualities in actions and things and sort them in different groups. We can say that things and actions are good with respect to health just like we can say that they are brown, big, or expensive. What we cannot say, however, is that we find the good as a characteristic quality in them, like we find hardness in the wood of a chair or strength in the palpitations of our heart. That is, although from the action-centric point of view we talk *about* things, the sortal use of the term "good" still does not mean that goodness becomes one of the inherent properties of things. We only sort things according to how the formal term can be applied to them. The formal meaning of "good" is primary and remains so.

A quick look at the role that the transcendentals played in the medieval analysis of things can help us illustrate this point. Being and good are transcendentals which both are distinct from particular things *and* apply to them in specific ways:

> Since according to the doctrine of the homonymy of being, the real natures in virtue of which things are beings will vary in accordance with kinds of things, it will follow that the real natures in virtue of which things are good will vary in just the same way. Different kinds of things will be good by virtue of instantiating different real natures, the same natures as those in virtue of which they are beings. Hence, any given thing is good by virtue of instantiating some real nature, but there is no single real nature in virtue of which all things are good. We might put this view into twentieth-century dress by saying that the property of being good is distinct from and supervenes on particular good-making characteristics and that what characteristics are good-making for a given kind of thing depends on the kind of thing.[46]

Although we are able to say which specific and material properties of things make them qualifiable as "good," goodness is not limited to these particular properties but implies a distinct, universal, and "supervening" quality.

One might ask: if we cannot identify the good in things, how are we allowed to say that they *are* good? What are the properties of actions or things to which the good refers? It seems evident that the good has to refer to something, because otherwise it would be wholly impossible to decide whether an action is legitimately qualified as good. In other words, it has to be possible to decide whether things carry the attribute good rightfully or not. If we say, for example, "The financial gains were distributed equally among all those who did the work," we cannot say that such a distribution is good unless we know *why* it is so. If we take the mere idea of an equal distribution, we have just as much reason to say that it is bad because it could be the case that some deserve more, others less. This means that something in the properties of actions or things has to allow for them being qualified as good.[47]

We find the required properties of things—their "good-making" properties, as stated in the previous citation—if we see that the good does not stand alone in its relation to particular things. If the good were the only formal concept we could use in order to make normative judgments, we could never say how it pertains to actions or things. The gap between, say, the characteristic properties of chairs and hearts, or activities such as making a promise and dividing financial gains, would remain too great: it would never be possible to exclude that the good is attributed to them in an arbitrary way, given that particular things can be good and bad in infinite ways. But the good, whenever it is attributed to things, entails other formal concepts. We have already mentioned one of them by explaining the meaning of "good" through the idea of "purposeful," in the sense that a good faucet, a good birthday present, and a good divorce settlement are all good insofar as they are good for something, or purposeful.[48] One might object that it is not immediately clear why we are allowed to assume that "good" entails "purposeful." If we take the good in and for itself, it does not contain any element that specifies its content in the way that "purposeful" does, which obviously adds a rather complex semantic dimension by stating that good things have a purpose they fulfill. But such an objection would stem from the formalist temptation to take concepts in an isolated manner by assuming that their meaning has to be evident by looking at them alone. In everyday speech, we are not affected by this temptation; words are substituted for other words, and concepts are used as entailing other concepts if their meaning becomes more specific in the context in which they are applied. The relation to particular things serves, so to speak, as a trigger that illuminates the fact that we do not only understand "good" when we use "good," but can understand it to mean something more specific, such as "purposeful." We can explain the relation between the two concepts by using the idea of expression: "purposeful" expresses, or makes explicit, the content of "good" which is only implicitly given in a context in which "good" is applied to particular things. "Purposeful" is more expressive than "good" insofar as it contains the good *and* an additional formal content. In the following, we will see more formal concepts that are expressive of the good. In a sense, all the following steps will be ways slowly to make explicit what lies implicitly in the good. In recent times, the role of expression in semantics has been emphasized by Brandom.[49] Expression, for him, means "making propositionally explicit."[50] This includes the acceptance of "material inferences" as being equally valid, that is, equally rational as inferences that follow the rules of formal logic.[51]

Formal concepts that are expressive of, or are explicating, the good serve as mediators between the good and particular things. Although they remain formal notions and cannot be instantiated by things, they are tied to the ways in which actions or things are qualified in their characteristic properties. No particular thing has a "purpose," strictly speaking, and even actions have purposes only insofar as they incorporate the intentions of agents. One will never see a purpose, so to speak, by simply staring at things; the purpose only emerges through a conceptual interpretation. On the other hand, one cannot understand "purposeful," say, with respect to faucets if one does not understand how faucets are supposed to work. The interpretative meaning of the formal concept has to be situated in a context of material characteristics. Material characteristics are the ground for the applicability, and therefore meaningfulness, of the concept; something has to be such-and-such in order to be interpreted from a conceptual stance. At the same time, formal concepts, even on the level of expressiveness, can be applied to all sorts of things, precisely because they are not fully instantiated by any of them. This allows us to answer the question raised before: the good can be attributed to particular things, and it can be decided whether it is rightfully attributed or not, because the characteristic properties of things (the ones that define them in their particular nature) can be interpreted and understood in light of expressive formal concepts. Insofar as characteristic properties and expressive formal concepts can be mutually related to each other, they allow the purely, or inexpressive, formal notion of the good to be applied to particular things.

To conclude this section, it might be helpful to remember that the status of the good with respect to particular things is also the reason why the good, and all related notions, can be considered as one. The notion of the good is not affected by the plurality of good-making properties. Some might object that the problem of pluralism re-emerges on the level of formal notions. "Good" is expressed in "purposeful," and insofar as the relation of expressiveness holds, the good is one even if expressed in another notion. But then, one can also use "purposeful" without referring explicitly to the good, which could mean that there are eventually two independent ways of being good, "purposeful" taken as such and "purposeful" as an explication of the good. It seems obvious that such an assumption would not make much sense, as one would have to explain the different meaning of "purposeful" in each case. Still, the "material inferences" which, following Brandom, hold between concepts do not possess the same logical necessity than formal ones. If one takes "purposeful" in an isolated manner, no inference leads to other notions and it can well seem that the notion is wholly independent from others. Expressiveness only sets in once one puts concepts into motion, so to speak, using them in reference to particular things and asking for an explication of their meaning. Only then can it become clear that they entertain relations to other notions, which in turn determine their own meaning. This means that if we want to show the good as one we also have to demonstrate it as absolute, that is, as comprising all other, related notions as its expressions. All following steps will be devoted to this task, step-by-step adding more specific concepts to the list that has been started here with "purposeful."

Describing Phenomena with Concepts

We can now show in more detail what it means that things have properties to which the notion "purposeful" refers. The classical place from which we can start is the idea, articulated by Plato, that things have an *ergon*. The *ergon* is the specific work a thing performs either exclusively or best, compared to others.[52] Things have essential properties which can be explained by what they do, or by the capability they have of doing something. This means that by assuming a specific purpose we do not have to believe that things respond to an external goal. The purpose is given with, and potentially fulfilled through each thing in and of itself; it corresponds to its "use."[53] We can then say that a thing is qualified as good insofar as it is adequately used, fulfills its inherent purpose, or realizes its specific work or *ergon*. Realizing a purpose applies to things as well as actions and persons: a person can be qualified as good insofar as they are knowledgeable in something, for example, master a certain craft.[54]

We can, however, not limit ourselves to Plato's conception of *ergon*, because in doing so we would be committed to thinking of purposes solely as inherent. This would exclude all other purposes that things can have and force us to adopt some sort of essentialism. We want to avoid this conclusion. What it would entail can be shown in comparison to Foot's approach, which is based on the attributive meaning of "good": "What is 'proper' or 'good' ... is determined by human life and its necessities, analogously to the way in which good or (proper) sight or locomotion or memory is determined in both animals and men."[55] Although Foot acknowledges that there are "large areas of indeterminacy,"[56] her overall idea is that normative assumptions about human life, or the designation of its "excellences and defects," are eventually determined in a "species-dependent" way: "A very great deal is in common to all human beings,"[57] and the goodness that can be attributed to particular persons "depends directly on the relation of an individual to the 'life-form' of its species."[58] This understanding of goodness does not shy away from teleological assumptions about human practice,[59] and it also involves the provocative claim that there is no conceptually significant difference between the inherent normativity of plant and animal life and the practice of humans.[60] For example, the normativity of promises can be explained in a natural way, given that "disrespect and untrustworthiness are bad human dispositions,"[61] whereas the decision of an agent who goes out despite running a high fever is "defective" given the requirements of practical rationality.[62]

For Foot, the advantages of her account lie in the many other approaches it helps to avoid. Utilitarianism with its focus on overall consequences "does not belong to the basic structure of the evaluation of human action."[63] An intrinsic evaluation has to come first before consequences can be factored in. The same holds for Humean theories insofar as they explain practical normativity according to desires that an agent wants to satisfy, which diminishes the role of all inherent normative structures. For Foot, ethics has to work the other way around, with natural goodness "setting a necessary condition."[64] Finally, the approach from natural goodness allows her to narrow the gap between moral and non-moral judgments, which gives a descriptive foundation to morality as a whole.[65] "Special praise" in the sense of moral appraisal should be reserved for cases in which it is hard to follow virtue. In all other cases, the virtuous action is the normal one, for example, when a rich person donates to charity for which no moral praise is deserved.[66] In the same vein, Foot claims that "'ought' is very close to 'should.'"[67] This rules out any moralistic, that is, rigorous and prohibitive account of morality and ties goodness to what human actions naturally pursue.[68]

There are many parallels in Foot's approach to ours. We also start from the given rationality of agency and try to avoid the influence of external moral standards. However, Foot's approach leads her to introduce other standards that seem unwarranted to us. She suggests that there are inherent purposes of rationality that humans have to follow. For example, she criticizes a burglar who gets caught because he stays in the apartment he burglarized to watch TV. According to Foot, the burglar succumbs to two "failures of practical rationality." First, because he failed to see "that there is reason not to steal" and, second, "that there is reason not to risk imprisonment for half an hour's TV."[69] As to the first failure, it evidently is in need of further justification. One could imagine at least some good reasons for a person to steal, which means that further justification has to be given if stealing is to be shown as impermissible.[70] With respect to the second failure, why can we not say that the burglar's intentions simply changed during the break-in? Perhaps he was enjoying the environment of a nice apartment, of the sort that he himself does not possess? Perhaps he secretly wanted to get caught? His actions were defective only if we assume that starting out as a burglar means that he should have followed through as a burglar, or that he had to have an almost professional idea of what a burglar does. Also, did he really "risk imprisonment" because he was caught by an overwhelming desire to watch TV? It does not seem plausible to believe that someone is so easily driven by impulses. We only could say that the burglar's actions were defective if we assumed, for example, that he better had visited a friend in whose house he could have enjoyed watching TV. But this means that we would have to construe the rationality, or failure thereof, in his actions in a rather artificial way. It seems best not to assume any given motive that would force the agent only to pursue a certain kind of action. Purposes cannot be inherent to actions in the sense that we can assume to know them in advance or infer them from some basic information. We rather have to think that purposes are determined only once a particular action is chosen, which means that they are as contingent and undetermined as all actions are in the process of their unfolding. Any essentialism in the assumption of purposes has to be avoided. Foot, instead, seems to put objective requirements first and then simply states that an agent who does not meet them "is doing what he has reason not to do."[71] She then also seems to confuse normative and explanatory notions: while all reasons explain actions, not all stipulate that the respective action *should* be done.

Furthermore, the distinction between inherent (or natural, essential, normal) purposes and external (or contingent, additional, defective) ones is by far not as clear as it might seem. For example, the pain inflicted by medical treatment serves a purpose insofar as the treatment can help to restore health. The treatment is good, first and foremost, because it is conducive to health, not in itself.[72] It obviously needs to have its own *ergon*, like the elegant cut performed by an experienced surgeon. But from the perspective of the patient who has to undergo the painful treatment, it is seen not so much in its inherent purpose—although they certainly have an interest in its being done with expertise and care—than as a necessary step toward reaching the ulterior purpose they pursue. To which of these purposes can the notion of the good refer? Obviously to all of them because in the action, inherent and external purposes are intertwined. The doctor may have a genuine interest in making the patient better or they may only perform surgeries because they pay well or they only operate because they are forced under the circumstances of a given case. (Think of a crime show scenario in which a doctor has to operate on the leader of a criminal group.) As a formal notion, "good" can apply to all these actions and does not apply in any predetermined or limited way. All possible purposes that are involved can be seen in its light.

Other examples could be cited. A table certainly has an *ergon* that determines its function but how stable does it have to be? And does a table have to be beautiful? Things can also lose their purpose or acquire other purposes than they initially possessed, like the objects ending up on a thrift store's shelf. The fact that a given thing has one inherent purpose and no other depends on the decisions that humans have made in its use. "This is the most comfortable chair in this house, I sit on it at night to read."

There is of course a point at which it needs to be decided where the good applies, and this point could then be seen to represent an "inherent purpose." All things may be good because they lead to something else, but the chain of relations has to come to an end at which a certain purpose is inherently fulfilled. Otherwise the quality "good" would not give us sufficient reason to desire or do something. It may be necessary to undergo surgery but only once a reliable surgeon is found, and the like. But in such cases, the inherent purpose is not a function of the things that are concerned but of the necessity to perform a particular action. Any action that is chosen establishes, in and through this choice, its own, inherent purpose, but it does not do so based on some given order of things.

We can further explain this point by looking again at Socrates' justification of his staying in prison in the *Phaedo*. He introduces the well-known distinction between two kinds of causes: those which are the causes of each thing, and those without which those causes cannot work. The former refers to his choice of the best, which is his decision not to escape from prison, while the latter refers to his body, his "bones and tendons," without which he would not be able to sit or carry out any decision he makes.[73] The latter, hence, refers to the necessary causes of an action, whereas the former indicates the sufficient reason for which it is performed. For Socrates, it is important that the necessary causes do not determine which action occurs, only the sufficient causes do. The necessary conditions are many, as the body has to have many parts in order to function the way it does, and could lead potentially to an infinite variety of actions. The body, in other words, is good for many things, but only the sufficient cause leads to the choice of one specific action, by choosing how the necessary causes are to be directed and employed. The sufficient cause comes with the purpose that is pursued, which in turn makes it possible to speak of one particular action that Socrates wants to perform.

To conclude, this argument also shows why we are allowed at all to describe both actions and things by using the conceptual lens of "purpose." Without engaging more deeply in the ontology of action we can say that purposes are part of what constitutes the structure of an action. The same holds for things. Although there are many ways in which things can be categorized based on their physical characteristics—modern science has taught us to proceed through many layers of description, all the way from mechanical interaction to chemical elements and the quantum level—things do not matter on the level of action unless they can be described under the category of purpose, or at least a similar category. "Purpose" states in which sense things are parts and objects of actions. On the level of our inquiry, we have to treat "purpose," and all related formal notions, as logically primitive.

The argument presented here is evidently circular, because in saying that actions cannot be described without such a notion we already assume that they are different from natural events. One might think that we need to justify the use of concepts in a more general way. But it is unclear why such a justification should be given. There seems to be nothing that prohibits us from interpreting the characteristics of things in light of formal notions. No contradiction is involved in our reference to a certain type of events as actions, not inherently and also not in relation to others, say, physicalist accounts. Conceptual and physicalist accounts are not mutually exclusive: as long as we keep our descriptions sufficiently distinct from physicalist ones and do not assume that "purpose" captures the same aspects of events than physicalist approaches do, there is no argument that could force us to renounce our claim to a conceptual point of view. A natural scientist, in turn, can say many meaningful things without having to say that their statements exclude the assumption of a purposeful structure of actions. We can call our approach tentatively a compatibilist one, without delving too much into its theoretical ramifications.

Previously, we said that the idea of purpose mediates between the good and the particular characteristics of things, but one could also ask what mediates between "purpose" and particular characteristics, given that the former is still a formal notion. The gap between concepts and things will always remain. Speaking metaphorically, concepts are only housed, or tolerated, by things insofar as things let themselves be interpreted from a conceptual stance. This makes it doubtful that it is ever possible to truly justify their use. What kind of justification is there to expect? Concepts might have a specific origin, and one could use metaphysical speculation to find out more about their source. One could, for example, speculate about the relation between logic and nature or about the creative faculties of the human mind. However, none of these speculations can tell us why there are such things as concepts in the first place. Whether concepts are divine, laws of nature, or constituted by the functions of consciousness, they have to be concepts first. Their semantics does not depend on a metaphysical story about their origin. In other words, even if concepts are "made" (constituted, constructed, etc.), they first have to be "discovered" as a particular type of things. One first needs to know how to use them before any further questions can be asked.[74]

This last point is especially important. We can say that the domain of the conceptual is both irreducible and undeniable because every attempt at denying its right to exist would have to use concepts in order to achieve its goal. If we say that concepts do not exist but only particular things do, we are already involved in a conceptual argument, at least insofar as we know what concepts are. The attempt at denying the conceptual is self-refuting. There is of course more that would need to be said in order to validate this argument. But again, nothing seems to prevent us from treating concepts on the level of our inquiry as logically primitive. The burden of proof lies with those who would like to deny us their use.

Fourth Step: Things Fulfilling a Purpose Also Have Virtues

As mentioned in the previous section, an *ergon* is for Plato the specific work that a thing performs either exclusively or best, compared to others.[75] There are two explanations for the term "best" that is used, a descriptive one and a normative one. In the descriptive sense, being best involves no comparison to other things, no competition, so to speak. It simply means that the properties of a thing are specific enough for it to be distinct from others. A table is best at what it does because otherwise one would have to use something else to fulfill the intended purpose. In the normative sense, the series of expressions continues until having a particular purpose achieves an evaluative meaning. In saying that an action or a thing is good, we can not only mean that it has a purpose, taken as a matter of fact, but also that it is desirable to have that purpose, or even that there is an obligation to be purposeful in certain ways.

The normative meaning of "purpose" can be made explicit through the use of other terms. In the context of Plato's work, one term that can do this job is "virtue." According to the *Republic*, a thing realizing its *ergon* is in possession of its genuine virtue.[76] Virtue is a sort of "health," "beauty," and "well-being" (*euhexia*) of the soul, the state in which it fulfills its essential functions.[77] This means, however, that like *ergon*, "virtue" is defined for Plato by inherent properties that are given with the characteristics of things.[78] We want to avoid this conclusion, too. In our inquiry, we can only use an extended notion of virtue, one that includes virtues based on acquired and non-essential traits. We can find such a notion in Aristotle's conception. For Aristotle, virtues reside in habits that are built over time through a sustained engagement in a certain type of action.[79] This engagement includes building an inner attitude that matches the outside actions so that agents perform them without feeling forced to do so.[80] Aristotle allows for virtues that are built in relation to contingent social matters, such as liberality and magnificence in the use of wealth.[81] Things like money can then be seen in light of a desirable moral purpose because money can lead to liberal and magnificent spending if only its owner decides to spend it this way.

A quick remark on the meaning of expressive notions in this case may be in order. On the one hand, "virtue" and the moral good are co-extensional. Actions, attitudes, and decisions that can be qualified as good also have to have virtue as one of their properties, and all virtues that someone or something possesses qualify them as good.[82] Humans and all other things are good through the presence of virtue, Socrates states.[83] In intensional terms, "good" and "virtue" are distinct. While the good does not contain descriptive elements, virtues have to be exemplified in reference to the properties of things. A person can be virtuous only if they are so in an appropriate way, given both the circumstances and their personal condition. For a soldier, courage means something different than for a moribund person. Understanding virtue can make it necessary to go all the way from formal notions to the casuistry of practical affairs. At the same time, one can always use it in a purely formal way as a synonym of "good." "Virtue" is a way to interpret actions from the perspective of the good (and from the perspective of "purpose" as well), not to classify them, which means that the notion possesses both adaptability and univocity.

Fifth Step: A Thing Is Qualified as Good insofar as It Fulfills Purposes with Uncoerced Consistency

The Harmony of the Whole as Freedom of Its Parts

In order to take the next step, we have to think of the beginning. In the second step, we saw that the good is the final sufficient reason for which something is desired or done. Agents have to choose what is best, because otherwise they would not choose by their own reason. Their choice would be forced upon them by others or by external circumstances. This condition has to be reflected in the properties of things. We need to be able to say that a thing fulfills its purpose in the best possible way, considering the given situation. In practical life it is hardly ever possible to choose the best possible thing, all things considered: most of the times we have to be satisfied with choosing what is available to us. But this means precisely that we choose what we have the strongest reason to pick: the limitations that affect all choice do not exclude that from the perspective of the formal notion of the good we have to choose what is best. In this step, we will further express what lies in the idea of an action being best, from both the agent-centric and the action-centric point of view.

Starting again from Plato, one can say that for something to be fully good it has to have all virtues that are relevant for its nature. In the *Republic*, this means that the city, if it is perfectly good, has to incorporate wisdom, courage, prudence, and justice.[84] It cannot leave any of those virtues out.[85] Socrates justifies this by saying that the perfect city has to be "one." It has to be arranged so that it is able to maintain its inner unity in every regard. Other cities fall apart into different groups; they are eventually not one but many cities taken as one. In order to reach utmost unity, each citizen has to be "one" as well, in the sense of performing only the task, the *ergon*, genuine to them. The unity of the city depends on the unity of its parts.[86] Strictly speaking, this implies that each part has to fulfill a twofold role: realizing its inherent purpose and at the same time being aware of how this purpose pertains to the unity of the whole. This twofold role becomes especially clear in the account of virtue. Wisdom, for example, as the virtue both of the ruling part of the city and the thinking part of an individual's soul, is no isolated expertise related to a particular field but concerns the city, or the conduct of life, as a whole,[87] whereas courage is not simply a specific temper, or a specific quality the guardians need to have, but allows an agent to maintain the right opinions about the law, opinions which are given through the thinking part and can be shaken by fears and desires.[88] Prudence, finally, is not located in any particular part of the city or the soul but establishes a harmony between all different parts.[89] Each virtue, hence, has a specific capability and *ergon*, but each brings it to benefit the whole to which it belongs.

From a political point of view, this conception has often been criticized as overly authoritarian. Indeed, the conception might seem to entail a forced division of labor by which each part of the city would be assigned a particular place and function from which it would not be allowed to move. The parts, it might seem, are determined, or even dominated, by the whole. But this interpretation goes counter to how Plato understands the unity of the city or soul. The virtue that concerns the city, or the soul, as a whole, or better: the virtue of the whole *as whole* is justice. As a normative idea, justice does not stipulate what the particular parts have to do but on the contrary provides "the power by which all these others came into being; and, once having come into being, it provides them with preservation."[90] The whole does not constitute or determine the particular parts but rather depends on their inherent characteristics and capabilities. It arranges all components so that they have the space they need in order to exist in their genuine way. Each part is supposed to be free, in the sense that it is able to realize its *ergon* in an uncoerced way. At the same time, being free to realize its *ergon* in an uncoerced way also means that each part's capabilities and interests are fulfilled by what it does. No part encroaches on or interferes with any other. Not only are the parts not coerced by the whole, more importantly they are not coerced by each other. In a certain sense, this means that the whole does indeed *limit* the parts. By letting them be what they are, and by establishing that each of them has to be let be what it is, it confines them to their particular capabilities. But the point is that the limit corresponds to what each part is doing anyway, that it forms no external constraint. For Plato, the whole can display an overall harmony only if the parts fit harmoniously into it. The whole is uncoerced only if its parts are uncoerced and do not create inner oppositions or strife. The just individual "becomes his own friend,"[91] which means that their soul contains no part that limits or oppresses any other. The limits that exist are such that each part has reason to accept them, whereas all external constraints would by definition be unjustified and could be rightfully refused.

Seen again from a political point of view, the *Republic* aims at a sort of natural rule. For justice to be installed, the appropriate rule has to be put in place, because even if a community is based on "friendship and consonance" (*philia kai xumphonia*)[92] an appropriate structure of governance has to be established and maintained over time. There always has to be rule, or governance, in one way or another, and the only question is how it can be guaranteed that no part subdues the others inappropriately. In the *Republic*, Plato's main concern lies with the thinking part of the soul, or the philosopher kings, who are supposed to rule because they are best suited for it. The philosophers would be "enslaved" were they prevented from exerting their leading role.[93] Following the idea of a natural rule, the roles of leadership cannot be switched because whatever is supposed to rule can only be deprived of this function if it is coerced. The leading parts containing wisdom are not free not to rule, they are in a sense confined to the purpose they fulfill. At the same time, it is in the best interest of the subordinate parts if they integrate into the whole because no part can be satisfied unless the whole city is. If one part wants to have more freedom than it deserves, then it will take away from the freedom of others and the ensuing strife will make all parts worse off. Plato uses health as a phenomenon in which rule is established in a natural way, befitting both the ruling parts and those that have to be ruled.[94] Subordination, taken in this sense, is not identical to oppression but represents the appropriate form of coordination in a composite whole. Following the comparison to health, we give admittedly a quite benevolent interpretation of the political ideas in the *Republic*. But we take the political structure only as a model, assuming that in the complexity of any individual's life a certain degree of coordination of their many interests and desires is needed so that some of them will always have to be subordinated to others.

Consistency as Source of Obligations

We can now see what this conception of unity contributes to the understanding of the good. Like a city and a soul, things that are qualified as good are necessarily complex. No single property can be the point of reference for formal notions. For example, one cannot attribute purpose to the color yellow, taken in an isolated manner. In order to fulfill a purpose, yellow has to be part of a set of properties which work together in a coordinated way. Such coordination has to be free because if any property, or part of properties, would have to be coerced in order to be in consonance with the others, it would not be good for it, even if it would help achieving a certain result. Ultimately, the goodness of the whole cannot entail that the parts suffer what is bad for them, because then the good would be constituted by the bad, which would be a contradiction.

To give another example, it is possible to say that it is good for students to study as hard as possible so that they achieve the best possible grades, even if this means that they are sleep-deprived, stressed, and robbed of the pleasures of a youthful life. However, such understanding and use of the good depends entirely on criteria that are external to the life of students, such as the performance on standardized tests, and disregards what is best according to their capabilities and needs. We have to assume that something that is qualified as good fulfills its own purposes, which means that a thing is good only if it is allowed to coordinate its purposes in an uncoerced and consistent way. The good has to refer both to the thing as a whole and to each of its parts. We can summarize this by saying that a thing is qualifiable as good if, and only if, it achieves uncoerced consistency in the realization of its purposes.

We prefer "consistency" here to the Platonic terms of consonance and harmony because it allows us to highlight the complex structure of things, whereas the latter also indicate their overall unity. The consonance of a chord (one of Plato's favorite examples)[95] can be understood both as internal arrangement and as one unified sound, but only the former says how the sound is constituted through the arrangement of its parts, and this is of interest for us here. This point is all the more important as we again want to avoid Plato's exclusive focus on inherent properties, which gives the arrangement a teleological component. Consistency does not require the completeness of a given whole in all its essential parts but can remain open-ended, as the fitting together of all purposes that happen to be relevant in a given situation and as achieving varying degrees of overall harmony.[96]

Strictly speaking, "uncoerced consistency" is redundant: if something needs to be coerced into being consistent to other parts, it is in fact *not* consistent to them.[97] But it might not always be clear that consistency has to be understood this way, which justifies the redundancy of our formula. "Uncoerced" expresses what lies in "consistency" and so helps making the meaning of the latter explicit and evident. Consistency implies the freedom of all parts, a freedom which allows them both to flourish according to their genuine interests and capabilities and to be given the space they need by all other parts. Following Plato's model, nothing should have to be *made* consistent. Everything has to contribute in an uncoerced manner to the consistency of the whole, which in turn is spread throughout each and every part equally, so that the consistency which makes the whole good is not bad for any of its parts.

The conceptual structure developed here is not limited to the sphere of ancient philosophy. We can also cite more recent approaches to morality. For example, it has been said that the obligation to achieve the uncoerced consensus of everyone concerned by a decision is grounded in the attempt at avoiding "egocentric" determinations of the good and achieving an "inclusive" discourse about the questions that are at stake.[98] We will come back later to the intersubjective meaning of consistency.

For things to fulfill their purposes in the best possible way they do not have to reach a degree of perfection which would otherwise not be genuine to them. They can only be best in what corresponds to their particular arrangement of parts. Otherwise, the good would be based on unrealistic or external demands. The "best possible way" is therefore no other than the arrangement of properties under which a thing exists at any given point. It means no more, although also no less, than the freedom of all relevant capabilities and functions. But while consistency can so be stated in a descriptive way, the notion ultimately carries a normative meaning. One can say that if a whole is to be consistent, its parts *ought* to be arranged in an uncoerced way. This aspect of the meaning of consistency has far-reaching consequences for the status of the good as the one fundamental notion of moral philosophy. If the good is indeed fundamental, then it has to provide the conceptual basis for all particular moral categories, including moral obligations. The fact that the fully sufficient good can be expressed as uncoerced consistency is no other than the source of these obligations. Realizing the good means to arrange one's actions in consistency to the actions of all others who are concerned. The good was initially defined as everything we have reason to desire and do, but we now see that the fulfilling of purposes cannot be expressive of the good unless it occurs in uncoerced consistency to other purposes. Obligations arise, so to speak, by themselves out of the explicated notion of the good through the multitude and complexity of purposes that are always and inevitably given in the practical world.

Saying that obligations "arise" from the idea of consistency has a twofold meaning. As such, the structure of uncoerced consistency provides only a formal or conceptual foundation for moral obligations. It cannot compel an agent to proceed from the consideration of their particular purposes to the consideration of all others' purposes that are concerned and to really act on the obligation to observe consistency. But this ambiguity should not surprise us. In moral philosophy, it is often left unnoticed that obligations can be seen from both an action-centric point of view ("Lying is never morally permissible") and an agent-centric point of view ("You ought not to lie"). Williams, for example, states: "Moral obligation is inescapable. ... Once I'm under the obligation, there is no escaping it, and the fact that a given agent would prefer not to be in this system or bound by its rules will not excuse him."[99] This statement provides a semantic analysis of the notion of obligation; however, such an analysis cannot say how the obligation becomes binding for the agent, despite Williams's claim. There is no contradiction in assuming that a principle or moral idea entails an obligation but does not entail it *for me*. As shown above, obligations become binding only through their relation to self-determination.[100] "This action is good, and you should want to do it." Moral obligations have to be recognized by agents so that they become the content of what they intend and want to do based on their own impulses. Otherwise, the agents may just follow conventions or legal rules. We have to recall our correlational approach and say that in the full phenomenon of morality the objective side of the consistency of purposes is also embraced from a subjective point of view.

The Distinction between Good and Right

Following Rawls, "the two main concepts of ethics are those of the right and the good."[101] We will try to show, albeit briefly, why this assumption of two fundamental notions of morality is untenable. In Rawls' conception, the notion of the good leads to a teleological theory of ethics, whereas the notion of the right belongs to a deontological approach. The good, for him, can be defined as "the satisfaction of rational desire."[102] It is both what is desired and what satisfies desire if reached. This means that the good exists in the plural as a set of "primary social goods" that individuals want to achieve.[103] Rawls states: "This variety in conceptions of the good is itself a good thing, that is, it is rational for members of a well-ordered society to want their plans to be different."[104] The most important principles that fall under the concept of right are the principles of justice. For Rawls, deontological principles have priority over teleological ones: principles falling under the concept of right are obligations that restrict the goods that individuals can purse. "In justice as fairness … persons … implicitly agree … to conform their conceptions of their good to what the principles of justice require, or at least not to press claims which directly violate them."[105]

However, even for Rawls, there is a "match," or a certain "congruence," between the two concepts, the good and the right.[106] The concepts cannot be reduced to one another or subsumed under a third; at the same time, they do not exclude one another, not only conceptually (the good does not deny the validity of the right, and vice versa), but also practically because in their actions, humans have to use both. Under an ideal scenario, individuals can freely and willingly act both according to their personal interest in the good *and* the requirements of justice.[107] They are able to see that their personal good is "consistent" with the existence of certain "constraints."[108] This is possible, among others, because the principles of justice provide a "shared point of view," or a certain objectivity, that allows for easier agreement between agents.[109] A well-ordered society both reflects and fosters their rational attitudes.

With the assumption of such a congruence, Rawls demonstrates, if only unwillingly, that the division of morality into two fundamentally different concepts cannot be maintained. The good eventually speaks the last word, contrary to his belief, because the obligations of justice are binding only insofar as they are good, both individually and collectively. If justice would not lead to a society that overall can be considered as good, then the members of society would have no reason to prefer it over other concepts, like individual freedom or the overall maximization of wealth.

Rawls introduces the distinction between the good and the right without explaining or deriving it in any way. The source he follows is Sidgwick.[110] For Sidgwick, the right is a prescriptive term whereas the good is evaluative. The right is a "dictate or imperative of reason,"[111] a "quasi-jural" notion that involves a "duty" which the agent has to follow unconditionally: "In the recognition of conduct as 'right' is involved an authoritative prescription to do it."[112] In the case of the good, "the moral ideal [is] being presented as attractive,"[113] which in a given case leaves it open whether "we ought to prefer this kind of good to all other good things."[114] There is also a difference in extension between the two terms: whereas the good is a "generic" notion that refers to many things that can be called "good," the right is a "specific" notion referring to some precisely defined duty.[115] For Sidgwick, ancient moral philosophy was based on the notion of the good, whereas modern philosophy developed the notion of the right in its distinctive meaning.

The distinction can be seen in two ways, conceptual and systematic. Conceptually, distinguishing between the good and the right expresses the important distinction between obligations, or duties, and goals. This distinction exists even if not all duties are unconditional or function as a "dictate" and "authoritative prescription," as Sidgwick says. In fact, both Sidgwick and Rawls seem to disregard the differences that exist among the principles of the right—differences, for example, between duties that do not allow for exceptions and others that do (perfect and imperfect duties in Kantian terms).[116]

From a systematic point of view, the distinction between the good and the right, again, does not hold up. Sidgwick himself concludes that eventually "the practical determination of Right Conduct depends on the determination of Ultimate Good."[117] For him, the good is primary to the right both materially and epistemologically, that is, both because it is a more comprehensive notion[118] and because it is "at once intuitively clear and certain."[119] It seems, therefore, that we have to be aware both of the plurality and the unity of moral concepts, that is, both of the distinction *and* the congruence between the good and right. The plurality allows for concepts that express specific and concrete commitments, whereas the unity is important because it shows that morality, ultimately, follows one overarching notion and does not fall apart in sets of different conceptual tools (if only for the reason that if morality were really based on two fundamental concepts, then one could ever only choose between them randomly in a given situation).

Sixth Step: The Good Is Co-extensional to Truth

In the present step and the one following, it will become clear that the two points of view that we have kept separate so far, the agent-centric and the action-centric point of view, eventually have to converge. What this means can first be shown with respect to the notion of truth. Following a well-known argument from the *Republic*, the good is co-extensional to truth. This argument can be understood in a twofold sense. First, the good is co-extensional to truth insofar as it is implied to be the truly good. While other qualities, including justice and beauty, can be desired even if they only appear to exist in someone or a thing—because it can be enough for someone to appear as just or beautiful in the eyes of others—the good is always desired as real.[120] One cannot refer to the good without referring also to its truth. Second, the agent cannot intend or realize the good without not also holding true beliefs about practical matters and their normative implications, at least insofar as they are related to the good. Otherwise the agent's beliefs could become dissociated from the intended good, or even contradict it. "Is it good what I am planning here and am I planning it right?"

This allows us to see how the two points of view converge. From the agent-centric point of view an action is chosen not only because the agent knows that it is good but also because *they know that they will know* that it is good in the way it is chosen. They know that they will identify with it as their choice, and they also know that something chosen by others, or for others, will be known as good by them. That is, they choose something as good insofar as they assume that it will allow them to realize and hold on to their preference for the good. Actions chosen as good have to *incorporate* the agent's point of view: they are not merely the result of an agent's choice, so that the choice would become irrelevant once the desired result is achieved, but have to include the awareness of why they are chosen. The good cannot be fully good if it is not also transparent as such to the agent.

From the action-centric point of view, it is required that an action that is realized because it is good can be identified as the one that was in fact chosen. Actions have to *express* the agent's point of view so that it is possible to say that the agent wanted the action in precisely the way in which it happens. If this is not the case, then actions that are good could occur randomly and not as the object of an agent's choice. Neither the agent-centric nor the action-centric point of view can exist separate from each other in the full phenomenon of moral action. An action is fully good only if it both expresses and incorporates the agent's choice: it has to be the right action, from the agent's perspective, and the agent has to be aware of and present in it. Otherwise, a different action could be performed and a different instance of the good could be achieved (whether this instance would be diminished in its goodness does not matter at this point). One could then not say that the action that is performed is truly good. From a practical point of view, it is of course always possible to choose one action over another, or simply to perform a different action, but the point is that no action should be preferred to the original one for the same reason that the original one was chosen.

The point that we make here can be given a normative spin: if the good would be realized randomly or by a lucky accident despite the agent's intention, then it would be only objectively, not subjectively, good. The agent would then not need to be moral at all because the demands of morality could be met without their contribution. Eventually, no one would ever have to listen to these demands. Conversely, if agents do have an obligation to achieve the good, then they have to be aware of it while it is realized and one has to make sure that it is the good that was supposed to be achieved. The good forces the agent to pay attention, so to speak.

Examples can help us explain this normative requirement. The agent's beliefs have to be *incorporated* into the action as a whole so that all parts, or all purposes concerned, are consistent and do not contradict each other. The attempt to achieve consistency cannot stop short at some point. If a person has the goal of overcoming their angry feelings toward another person and wants to start cooperating with them in a more productive way, they know that they have fulfilled their purpose with consistency only if they can either abandon or redirect their feelings. If the angry feelings remain latent but are otherwise unchanged, no real consistency is achieved because the agent individually still has reason not to cooperate with the other person. They either have not properly addressed their anger or act disingenuously toward the other. If the action instead does not *express* the agent's beliefs, then it could be performed in a disengaged way. The agent could be indifferent to the question whether they have actually achieved consistency and all purposes that are involved are given the consideration they deserve.

Also, if the agent's point of view is not *incorporated* in all relevant parts of an action, then it may well be that some of these parts are coerced into appearing as consistent. We can think of a self-declared vegetarian who justifies eating meat on one or more occasions by citing some presumed benefit that it brings. This person, whose resolve is not fully incorporated into their actions, tries to achieve consistency simply by justifying their inconsistency instead of addressing it as such. They fail uncoerced consistency through their false pretense. Conversely, if an action is performed that does not *express* the agent's point of view, then the agent can end up feeling coerced. We can think here of a vegetarian who agrees to eating meat under the pressure of social conformity. Even if they were to believe that there is no severe moral problem in occasionally eating meat, their action is not fully good because it is at least in part imposed on them. The agent would hold on to their vegetarian preferences if their social environment would not force them to give those up.

Many more examples could be imagined but the cases mentioned here—lack of effort, indifference, false pretense, and the submission to coercion—all clearly show a mismatch between the agent's beliefs and the good that is achieved. The agent cannot act with consistency because according to their own beliefs they cannot think of their actions as truly good.

We should add that while the examples show true belief as part and component of actions, it is also possible to see it as their purpose. For Plato, no knowledge that is forced upon the soul can remain firmly in it. Only what the soul understands in and through itself, in the sense that it confirms and re-confirms its truth, will become permanent in it.[121] Education has to come "easily" to students, so that they adopt the knowledge to be learned in the most natural way.[122] For any individual soul, being aware of the truth of things (*aletheuein*) is in itself good, that is, desirable and beneficial. The individual does not give up this knowledge voluntarily, as no one voluntarily believes in something untrue.[123] Truth is inherently good, and insofar as the good also has to be evident in its truth, we can speak of a conversion between the truth of the good and the good of truth.

Seventh Step: The Good Is Co-extensional to Beauty

The previous step showed truth and good as co-extensional. The agent both knows that their actions are good and chooses them because they are so, *and* contributes through their awareness to making them so. Their knowledge of the good is twofold; it comprises knowledge *of* the action at hand and knowledge that is incorporated *into* the action itself. However, truth and good remain ultimately distinct, just like knowing and acting have to remain separate aspects of practices. If the good is truly one, then a more perfect convergence, or better: a true coincidence of the two points of view has to exist. In ancient philosophy, this coincidence is given in the phenomenon of beauty, or the beautiful (*to kalon*). The beautiful is not only co-extensional to the good but in certain uses co-intensional.[124] Recent philosophy has no equivalent to this notion, partly because modern aesthetics has made it difficult to think of beauty in such a normative sense. We mention beauty, therefore, not because it has practical relevance for us today but because of its systematic status. (And just to say this one more time: as we make no metaphysical, or speculative, assumptions about the good, we make no such assumptions about the beautiful either and think of it, say, as the mind-independent order of the universe or nature.)[125]

The *Symposium* presents the philosophical understanding of beauty. Following the idea of an ascent toward genuine beauty, which Socrates reports having learned from Diotima, he states that beauty only appears to be a sensual and material property.[126] The phenomenon is ultimately rooted in an arrangement, or a structure, that can only be grasped by the mind and remains distinct from its particular instantiations. Beauty is knowledge and structure in one, or better: it is a structure that is constituted in and through the act of knowing it. Contemplating beauty, Diotima is referred to say, by no means leads to a "bad life." Whoever does so will produce not "copies" but true virtue in their behavior.[127] The coincidence of knowledge and structure, which is first reached in the mind, will so be extended throughout the conduct of life and provide a guiding structure for it. A similar conception can be found in the *Republic* where Socrates emphasizes beauty as congruity of soul and body.[128] Beauty, hence, is the coincidence of *all* vital aspects of human life, pervading body and soul, which are beautiful both in themselves and in the way they harmonize with one another. One could not maintain a beautiful soul if one's bodily existence were at the same time engaged in excessive desires or unlawful acts.

In light of this coincidence, the question arises how one can distinguish between the beautiful and the good. Whoever refers to beauty also refers to goodness (*kalogathia*), but this does not mean that no distinction can be made. According to the *Symposium*, the beautiful is desired in order to "beget" in it the good.[129] In the hierarchy of ends the good is final, even if one has to aim at beauty in order to achieve the ultimate goal. The *Philebus* explains this relation in more detail. The good, whenever one attempts to grasp it as such, turns into, or "escapes" into, the beautiful.[130] Beauty *is* the good, taken not in itself, but as a given, phenomenal quality.[131]

We are interested precisely in the phenomenality of the beautiful. Beauty allows us to describe the presence of the good once it is fully achieved. The good is not limited to decisions and intentions but also determines the quality of actions and the overall state of human practices. It refers to the final overall arrangement of individual and collective life. In fact, for Plato, actions, taken as such, can never be considered a final goal. Individuals act because they eventually want to *be* in certain ways.[132] Beauty is therefore a more fundamental concept than other, more process-related ones, whereby "more fundamental" means that it is more directly related to the overall result that the pursuit of the good aims to achieve.[133]

In allowing us to capture the final overall arrangement of human practice, the notion of beauty fulfills a crucial systematic role. It allows us to state in one concept, or in one word, what can be called the pervasiveness of the good. The good, taken as singular term, includes and unites all different ways in which something can be qualified as good. In the moral good, all normative perspectives and qualities, subjective and objective ones, come together, insofar as they all are expressions, or implicit elements, of the one, unified good. The explication of these elements, as well as all particular moral determinations and all practical intents, inevitably dissolves this unity. Beauty is the full phenomenon against which all moral endeavors, insofar as they focus solely on actions, on consequences, or on inner attitudes, can be seen as incomplete.

One might object that while the notion of beauty occupies an important systematic place in our inquiry, there is no need to have this place filled with that particular notion. This is certainly true. But the fact that a historical name for this place exists can hardly be undervalued as it gives our analysis a phenomenal basis. As said before, we cannot start from a neutral, non-historical point of view.

Eighth Step: The Good Entails Pleasure

The previous two steps showed the convergence of the agent-centric and the action-centric points of view. The good has to be *one*, otherwise it would not be fully sufficient. Now that we have reached this point of unity, we can again describe the elements of the good in their distinct character. Under the agent-centric point of view, the first element that will be analyzed is pleasure. Pleasure is the way in which the good, once it is fully reached, can be experienced by the agent. As already said, the good would not be absolutely good if it would subjectively be felt as bad. In one way or another, it has to be desirable, pleasing, or gratifying for the agent. Under the action-centric point of view, we will consider benefit and utility. Insofar as the good allows things to fulfill their purpose, they are useful, both for themselves and other things. Both pleasure and utility can also stand in opposition to the good but this point is not relevant here. What counts is that once the good is achieved, certain kinds of pleasure and utility are integrated into it as parts. Pleasure will be discussed in the present step, benefit and utility in the following.

Plato's account of pleasure often seems to be exclusively critical. Passages that refer to pleasure as a necessary part and consequence of the good are rare. The *Philebus* is perhaps most explicit in this regard. The good, Socrates states here, has to be sufficient (*hikanon*); it cannot lack anything a human person would rightfully need. A conduct of life that would be deprived of pleasure would not be desirable, or "wishable" (*hairetos*), neither for humans nor for animals and plants, especially if one thinks of it as extended through life as a whole.[134] Nonetheless, not all pleasures are such that they align naturally with the good. Pleasure comes in degrees, and the strongest ones are those which result from the satisfaction of needs or the relief of pain. This means that many forms of pleasure include a state that is precisely not experienced as sufficiently good.[135] For this reason, Plato distinguishes between the pleasures that remain consistent to the good and those that achieve their good through the interplay of deficiency and satisfaction. According to the *Philebus*, pleasures that belong to "the soul alone" are preferable, like intellectual and aesthetic pleasures which do not involve any previous need and desire.[136] In addition, simple and measured pleasures which follow the lead of understanding can also be aligned with the good.[137] Some pleasures are even directly beneficial, for example, pleasures related to eating and drinking insofar as they are also conducive to health. Pleasures of this kind are sought because of the good that comes with them.[138]

For a modern point of view, the insufficiency in the experience of pleasure can be seen in a quite different light. One could say, for example, that suffering, although not desirable as such, is a way toward the good, a necessary experience that an individual has to make in order to reach a deeper understanding. Not only passion, taken in the Christian sense, but also the Romantic idea of an unfulfilled longing could be mentioned here. Also, Plato does not seem to distinguish between pleasure as a feeling and as emotion. While the former can be passing and may indeed be linked to the interplay of deficiency and satisfaction, the latter is deeper and more lasting, rooted in an individual's personality. Emotions support a person's preferences and can be an essential component of their commitment to the good. For a more modern approach, one would also have to go beyond Plato's denigration of the body. But we do not have to give a complete or detailed account of pleasure here. All we need is the formal argument according to which the good would not be desirable if it did not also include a form of pleasure. The positive account of pleasure does of course not exclude the fact that some desires for gratification go against the notion of the good. Even if the general evaluation of the body has changed in modernity, we have to think of, say, greed, addiction, and aggressiveness as problematic from a moral point of view.

Ninth Step: The Good Is Co-extensional to Benefit and Utility

Benefit and utility are parts, or consequences, of the good. We use the two terms in combination, following Plato's claim that without the idea of the good justice would not be "useful" (*chresimon*) and "beneficial" (*ophelimon*).[139] The former can refer more narrowly to the practical use of things, whereas the latter designates how things pertain to an overall state of well-being. Both aspects belong together, as a thing's usefulness is relevant only insofar as it leads to well-being, and well-being, in turn, follows from the right use of things. Both notions of utility and benefit can also be seen as expression of the notion of purpose which was mentioned before.

The good cannot be harmful, Socrates states, it has to be beneficial (*ophelimon*).[140] One cannot be indifferent toward the consequences of its realization. The integrity of the good would suffer, so to speak, if it had a negative impact on agents or would not be useful in any way. Benefit and utility, hence, are co-extensional to the good: the good cannot *not* be beneficial, and what is beneficial is also good.[141] In the *Republic*, Socrates makes the distinction between things that are good in themselves, things that are good in relation to other things, and things that are good both in themselves and in relation to other things. The third kind is said to be the finest. Justice is precisely of this kind, as it is both intrinsically good and conducive to a good life as a whole. On a more practical level, reasoning and health can be said to have the same double nature.[142]

The modern understanding of the good has not always followed the idea that the notion of the good includes its positive consequences. Ross, for example, states: "The notion of the ultimately good—the notion, that is to say, of that which is good strictly for its own sake and neither for the sake of its results nor for the sake of an element in itself—is … the central and fundamental one."[143] The "ultimately good" is also called the "intrinsically good." Examples for it lie in "virtuous disposition and action," which are regarded "as having value in themselves apart from any consequence."[144] Moore holds similar ideas. According to him, "the only fundamental distinction [in ethics—M.S.] is between what is good in itself and what is good as means, the latter of which implies the former."[145] Ross's and Moore's conceptions are motivated by the attempt at keeping all utilitarian assumptions separated from the good, but compared to Plato, their attempts remain abstract. For Plato, things that are desirable only for their own sake are precisely not the objects of ethics, but of aesthetics. Beautiful things are "*kath' autha*," in and for themselves, and not "*pros ti*," in relation to something else.[146] The moral good, instead, is "intrinsically" good *and* makes individuals happy. It is desired because it changes life as a whole once it is attained, whereas beautiful objects remain perfect in themselves. Ironically, this means that Ross's and Moore's conceptions are eventually aesthetic, despite their claims at securing the moral good. We cannot engage in a discussion of utilitarianism, or consequentialism, at this point. All we can say is that such positions can be seen as expressions of a genuine interest in the good insofar as utility and benefit are essential parts of it.

Tenth Step: The Good Includes Practical Normativity

With pleasure as well as with benefit and utility we have seen that the absolute good comprises and unites particular ways of being good. It would not be truly good if it were not also good in these aspects or parts. We will now turn our approach around and show that various normative perspectives and qualities, which first seem to be good only in a particular way, eventually are also part of the absolute good. The perspectives and qualities that are relevant here are the ones mentioned at the beginning of our inquiry, where we distinguished between moral, practical, conventional, and legal normativity. The moral good is the good proper, which means that every normative content has to be expressible as a *morally* normative content. Other forms of normativity can eventually not be separate from moral normativity, we assume. This assumption will be explained in the present and the following two steps.[147]

We begin with practical normativity. In a sense, this form of normativity has already been addressed in the discussion of benefit and utility. The fact that a thing fulfills a purpose in the way of uncoerced consistency means that it is also good in practical terms, that it functions well and yields good results. Whenever we qualify something as morally good we expect it to work, as much as the given conditions allow. Otherwise, we have hardly any reason to say that it is sufficiently good. However, it is far from clear whether this relation can be turned around so that whatever works well from a practical point of view can also be said to be morally good. An example can help us to show that this is the case. If a digital service provider succeeds in giving reliable access to the internet for a large part of the population, we can say that the company's actions are both practically good, because they produce the desired results, and morally good, insofar as the ability to access information is important for citizens. We can say so even if we know that the company does not provide the service for altruistic motives but for profit. The sole fact that access to information is provided can be seen as morally good because it allows agents to fulfill more of their purposes and pursue greater consistency in their lives.

This way, practical and moral normativity are concomitant insofar as both are able to describe the very same activities. The moral dimension of an action does not need to be mentioned and can often remain implicit in one's practical endeavors. On the other hand, there can always be a point at which it needs to be thematized and expressed. One may then find that what seemed a merely practical problem possessed a moral dimension all along. We may realize, for example, that it is in no way guaranteed that there is running water and that our garbage gets removed. We then become aware that what we took as given conditions of our life did not function without a moral commitment toward, say, the workforce that is needed to perform certain activities in a reliable way.[148]

Carrying the previous example further, our digital service company may want to slow down data streams to save expenses on its end without reducing the price that customers have to pay. In this case, one could say that it does something that works well in practical terms but results in harm toward its customers, which is morally wrong. One could take this as an argument against the concomitance of the practical and moral good. But such examples do not contradict it at all. The fact that customers are worse off means precisely that things do not work well for them. What they experience is morally wrong because it is also faulty in practical terms. Even if the attempt at saving costs, taken in an isolated manner, can be seen as morally good, because it can help to sustain one's business and the livelihood of those associated with it, it is morally wrong insofar as it negatively affects others.

In assessing given situations, we need to conceive of the consistency of purposes in a detailed enough way, both in practical and moral matters. The less differentiated our view, the more we might be inclined to think of practical matters as indifferent toward the good. It is meaningless to ask, on a purely general level, whether practical effectiveness, functionality, and instrumental rationality, taken as such, can ever be considered morally good. There are undoubtedly cases, like the one we just mentioned, in which some practical goal stands in opposition to the moral good. But it is impossible for a situation to work practically well *in all regards* and at the same time be morally bad. If it is morally bad, then there has to be at least one individual, or one aspect of the situation, for which it does not work practically well, and vice versa.

We should also add that we are not concerned here with the normative dimension of things but with the normative dimension of actions. There is obviously no moral quality, say, in a screwdriver, taken in an isolated manner. This quality only comes into sight once we ask what it means to use the screwdriver well. It is morally relevant whether or not the screwdriver is used to assemble shelves in a sloppy and unstable way. From this angle, we could make our analysis even stronger and give it a normative spin. Considering the absolute good insofar as it includes practical considerations is in itself a moral obligation. It would be a moral flaw to think that practical matters and arrangements could be fully good without being also at least indirectly morally good. One would then not take them seriously enough, or not really consider the purposes of everyone concerned.

Eleventh Step: The Good Includes Conventional Normativity

Conventional normativity presents its own kind of inclusion into moral normativity. There can be no concomitance of conventional and moral normativity. Conventions consist of habits or patterns of behavior that are shared among the members of communities. Some of these patterns are ritualistic and institutional, such as marital rites, military ceremonies, or religious liturgies, while others work on the level of everyday practice, like holding doors and shaking hands. Conventional normativity implies that a form of behavior can be deemed good *because it is a convention*, and bad because it is not. Forms of behavior are desired, recommended, or required because they are the thing "one has to do" in a given social context. Three criteria have to be met to make forms of behavior conventionally good. First, conventions consist of well-established ways to act. From an agent's point of view, they are patterns that always already exist, so that the agent cannot, and must not, be creative in their regard. Second, conventions are habits that are seen as intrinsically valuable; they are followed with respect, reverence, and even fear. Third, conventions are patterns that are seen as beneficial or indispensable for the functioning of a community. These criteria can of course be combined in various ways and also exist to varying degrees. Agents might perform conventions without any positive inner attitude, sometimes even by rejecting them secretly. However, it is hard to see how they could function at all if there were not at least some members in any given community who support them personally.

The first criterion shows already why not all morally good actions are also conventionally good: not all moral actions amount to well-established patterns of behavior, and conversely not all well-established patterns of behavior can be justified by moral reasons. For example, one can say that the traditional limitation of marriage to heterosexual couples had a specific value insofar as this limitation entailed a commitment to raising children and so helped to make sure that new generations were born. Still, there seems to be no good reason to deny same-sex couples to get married as well. One simply cannot sustain the claim that the limitation of marriage to heterosexual couples is good *because* it is a long-standing convention. On the other hand, conventions can well align with, or even be supported by, moral reasons. We can see this in Socrates' attitude toward traditional Greek religion. In the *Phaedrus*, he refuses to question and rationalize mythical accounts, stating that such reflections would distract him from the task of knowing himself.[149] Socrates ridicules the "wise men" (*sophoi*) who want to be smarter than the mythological tradition because they lose sight of the values incorporated in it. He prefers to accept the tradition in all its seemingly fantastic and absurd elements rather than lose its ability to provide guidance for the conduct of life.

However, Socrates' sympathy toward traditional religion results from a very personal commitment. He is well aware that the tradition can indeed be criticized in many points. For this reason, he explicitly refrains from stating his commitment as an example that others should follow. When it comes to the impact of conventions on society as a whole, his attitude toward them is a much more critical one. Those holding conventional assumptions do not question their cognitive abilities and simply refrain from trying to reach a more reflected point of view, he states.[150]

The last point mentioned here is paramount. If conventions were criticized solely because they provide no proper guidance and can lead to bad decisions, then moral philosophy could simply leave them behind. What counts for Socrates is that they pretend to lead to decisions that are morally right. Conventions presume to do the job that morality does. Conventions can be seen as a partial and potentially inconsistent realization of the good. For this very reason, they have to be included in the latter. We can assume that it is one and the same good that is intended in both conventions and morality. Moral normativity, or the fully sufficient good, realizes what conventions only intend but fail to achieve. Conventions are a confused form of morality, not its negation, and can be criticized from within, based on their own presumption of achieving the good.

We cannot assume that the relation between conventions and the moral good is always one of peaceful integration. The criteria that conventions provide for judging practices as good are not fully convertible into moral reasons. Morality requires us eventually to adopt a post-conventional stance. Conventions are included into moral normativity either by being suspended or by becoming subordinated. The old man Kephalos famously walks away from the conversation in the *Republic* to take care of the "holy things," as he says.[151] For him, convention is a protective layer around the vulnerability of age. But his stance is acceptable only because he walks away from the task of giving reasons altogether. Like in the case of Socrates in the *Phaedrus*, conventions do not have to be given up if they limit themselves to a purely individual practice. Where they contradict it, or pretend to be more than they are, requiring general adherence from others, they can either not be preserved or need to be redefined.[152]

Twelfth Step: The Good Includes Legal Normativity

With respect to legal normativity, we encounter yet another kind of inclusion into moral normativity. To be more precise, we encounter several ways in which the inclusion works in this case, as the relation between morality and the law is complex. Only two ways shall be mentioned here. First, moral normativity can be assumed to be the foundation of the law. From a moral point of view, it is good that laws exist, rather than not, and morality provides the criterion for the justification of these laws. Under this perspective, all that is good according to legal criteria also has to be good according to moral criteria.[153] Second, the law can be separate from moral normativity because it creates procedures and institutions that function without the need for further moral justification. The legal system is independent from morality simply because it is a system. Under this perspective, if there is an inclusion into moral normativity at all, it can only mean that there is the need to modify and correct the existing practice of the law. How can this second inclusion be justified? We can only indicate some arguments that may be used. For example, it is possible to say that if the legal system is supposed to allow for decisions that have justice as their ultimate normative criterion, it has to be open to moral examination.[154] Otherwise, one would have to argue that justice in the law and justice in morality are two wholly different things, which seems absurd. Another, even simpler argument states that although the legal system, taken as such, is disconnected from everyday practice, at least to a certain degree—because it has its own internal rules—the actions that it considers are not. The moral and legal points of view cover the very same things, and they even do so in similar ways. At certain points at least the question can arise whether practices that are good from a legal point of view are also good from a moral one. Morality, eventually, cannot allow to think of the law as a fully autonomous system.[155] The two kinds of inclusion mentioned here are independent from each other. One can claim that the law has to be criticized and modified from a moral point of view without wanting to make morality the foundation of *all* law.

As far as the first inclusion is concerned, Plato gives us a maximum example for the foundation of legal through moral normativity. In the *Crito*, Socrates explains his staying in prison by stating that it would not be allowed to commit unjust acts only because one has been wronged previously. Doing unjust acts is wrong in every case.[156] If an individual were allowed to act against the law, then the force of the law would be ruined altogether.[157] The justification of this stance lies in the fact that the existing laws are the laws of his homeland. His homeland brought him up, nurtured and protected him, and so did the laws; they are nothing but the ways in which the homeland regulates all vital affairs.[158] We can paraphrase this in more modern terms by saying that for Socrates it is in any case better to have laws in force than not; not only because they guarantee the stability and protection of human life but also because they create a sense of unity and solidarity among individuals. The commonly shared law is the expression of the will of a community to preserve itself. In a more ideal scenario, the philosopher king is introduced in the *Republic* as the one who is able to guard and protect the meaning of the law.[159] The philosopher is able to look at what is truly just and beautiful and then implement it in human behavior.[160] The sphere of laws, seen in its entirety, needs a foundation, or an orientation, which it cannot provide within itself. It needs the good insofar as it is transcendent and unchanging compared to the various legal stipulations. Plato's understanding of the law is of course lacking some of the elements that would be deemed indispensable from a modern point of view, for example, the idea of a contract according to which the law is binding only because rational agents accept it as such, by their own insight and will. But the difference to modern approaches is less important than it may seem. We can rephrase his arguments by saying that the inclusion of legal into moral normativity means no more than the need of the law to be governed by reasons. A fully sufficient reason for the law cannot be given in terms of its particular legal procedures because all of them are contingent and depend on a reason to exist, and it certainly cannot result from external influences, such as social, economic, or political constellations of interest and power.

Thirteenth Step: The Good Extends to the Totality of Individuals and Things Concerned by It

The last step completes our account of the pervasiveness of the good.[161] While the previous three steps pursued a qualitative approach based on the different forms of normativity, the present step will introduce a quantitative point of view. We could also say that it will introduce the extensional side of the good: there has to be a certain number of things that are also referred to as good when "good" is ascribed to a thing. No single element of a situation can be good in isolation. As we have seen, the good belongs to the class of things that are good both in themselves and in relation to other things. The good would not be sufficient if its consequences were not also sufficiently good.[162] We now have to broaden this argument. We can say that from a moral point of view nothing can be good unless this quality can be extended to all things and persons connected to it. If one knows what is good for oneself, then one also knows what is good for the others who are part of one's realm of practice. Being good cannot be achieved by one person alone, because this would contradict the idea of an absolute good. The good would then be limited: it would be only mine, not yours, hers, theirs, etc. There are also conditions that have to be in place in order to let someone or something achieve the good. The unjust man cannot live in a community, not with humans nor with gods, Socrates states in the *Gorgias*.[163] In the *Republic*, he points out that a tyrant cannot freely walk around the city but has to be in constant fear wherever he goes.[164] No human being lives without the support by, or at least the interaction with, other human beings, which means that no human being can experience a fully sufficient good if the others who are involved cannot also achieve the good.

The same conclusion follows from the notion of uncoerced consistency. No part of the good can be free in isolation because then its freedom would induce the unfreedom of other parts, which would eventually impede the freedom that it strives to achieve for itself. Only the consistency of the whole *as whole* eliminates coercion. In the *Republic*, Socrates uses the example of a hurting finger to explain the structure of the ideal city. If one part hurts, the whole body is in pain, and analogously, if one part of the population is unhappy and dissatisfied, the city as a whole is dissatisfied.[165] No part of the community of citizens is supposed to be worse off than it is supposed to be. On the other hand, no part is supposed to be better off than it is supposed to be according to its role within the whole. Injustice can be understood precisely as a disarray of forces which refuse to stay bound and subordinated to the whole. The maximization of pleasure and benefit in isolated parts not only brings the whole into a state of imbalance, it also prevents those parts from reaching what is best for them, that is, what would be sufficiently good according to their own purposes. Eventually, the parts will not even be successful in the attempt at maximizing their own gratification, as an isolated part cannot provide the necessary conditions for its well-being all by itself.[166] This means, again, that a certain number of things have to be sufficiently good if one particular thing is supposed to be good. The good is sufficient insofar as it is inclusive and extends to all things and persons that are concerned by or connected to it.[167]

The crucial question that arises at this point is how far this extension goes, and how great the number of included things or persons has to be. In the thought experiment of the *Republic*, the context of good things has to be understood as a totality: the city is a whole that includes all relevant aspects and activities of life, not needing anything outside of itself to be sufficiently good. In the *Timaeus*, the totality is extended even further to the created *kosmos* as a whole. The world that is built has to be complete, because no unfinished thing can be beautiful, and it must include all living, animated beings, that is, all forms of life that can possibly exist.[168] For our analysis of morality it is not immediately clear how the idea of a totality of good things has to be understood. It is therefore best to state the result of this section negatively: the good must not be limited arbitrarily, in the sense that the extension to other persons and things would be possible but is prevented to occur. The extension of the good is mainly a normative idea, meant to counter the claim that a limited good can be seen as sufficient despite its possible extension to other persons and things. We will further explain this argument in the following chapter.[169]

5

The Reality of the Good

Be Consistent, Be One

The notion of the good has emerged now in the various aspects of its meaning and it has become clear, hopefully, in which sense it can be taken as *absolute*. This allows us to address the many concerns that such an idea undoubtedly will raise. We will subsume these concerns under the question of the reality of the good. The question has several layers. To get started, it is important to keep in mind that the good is no simple, abstract notion but concrete. On the one hand, the good is a formal notion that cannot be instantiated by the characteristics of particular things. It can be considered as one because it relates universally to all things. On the other hand, the good is no atomic concept: its meaning can be expressed through a series of other, more specific notions. The good does not only have unity but entails, at least implicitly, a totality of conceptual elements. Following our correlational approach, there are two series of expressions that have emerged. From the agent-centric point of view, the series goes from (1) good to (2) reason for which something is desired or done to (3) fully sufficient reason. From the action-centric view, the series of expressions goes from (1) good to (2) good as purpose to (3) virtue as normative aspect of purpose to (4) the uncoerced consistency of purposes. The good emerges as concrete through these series of expressions.

Not all moral philosophers agree about this point. G. E. Moore famously claimed that the good was "undefinable," a notion "of that simple kind, out of which definitions are composed and with which the power of further defining ceases."[1] We can certainly agree with Moore that the "good" cannot be defined if defining is understood in the traditional way as a combination of genus and specific difference. However, it is far from clear that such a type of definition is needed in order to explain the meaning of the good. The meaning can be captured quite adequately through the series of other concepts that it entails. The very idea of an inexplicable and purely simple notion also seems a contradiction in itself. How would one be able anyway to use such a thing in meaningful assertions? By understanding the good as an undefinable notion, the whole ethical system that Moore suggests seems to be based on a mysterious quality which undermines his theoretical approach. His claim of the undefinability of the good stems less from a conceptual analysis than from the naturalism of his thought, which left no room for the specific status of notions.[2] In explaining the simplicity of "good" by comparing it to "yellow" and by comparing its definition to the definition of a horse, he showed that he had considered only notions whose meaning represents physical qualities and things.[3]

In the previous chapter, we have already indicated in which sense the idea of uncoerced consistency entails obligations. The structure of the good can be expressed in a normative way and present itself as a moral imperative to agents. We now have to show in more detail what this means. Previously, we have also seen that the good implies a context of good things. One thing, or one single person, can be good only if the good that is achieved extends to all other persons and things that are concerned by or connected to it.[4] An agent cannot be fully consistent, that is, fully uncoerced in the realization of their purposes, if the others are not also consistent to them. If the individual's consistency implies an inconsistency to others, the individual is in fact no longer uncoerced and consistent to themself, because then they either will be forced to abandon the fulfillment of some of their purposes insofar as they impede, or stand in opposition to the purposes of others, or need to make the others follow their purposes, which would not only coerce them, but also add an external, inconsistent purpose to the ones that are genuine to them. No individual lives in uncoerced consistency if they have to force others to allow them to do so, because the forcing of others is not consistent to what they solely want for themself. One cannot want to be in need of forcing others. The reality of the good, hence, requires that *all* individuals act and conduct their lives in consistency to each other.[5]

Stated this way, the notion of the absolute good converges with some well-known ideas that let us imagine unity and mutual understanding among humans. The consistency of all individuals to each other would be the realization of peace on earth or the achievement of a union in which all members would be reconciled and free. But we are not concerned here with such a concrete understanding of the good. What counts instead is that *all* aspects of human practices can be conceived and arranged according to the idea of uncoerced consistency, both within one individual agent and in their relation to others. This allows us to summarize the meaning of the absolute good and condense it into a formula that captures its universal extension and applicability. Stated descriptively, the absolute good implies that individuals act in such a way that they are consistent both in what they do and believe about their own actions *and* in relation to what others do and believe about their actions. (Mentioning actions and beliefs together is important: if beliefs diverge from actions there can be no absolute good because agents are then likely to be in deficient states, such as doubt, indifference, or wishful thinking.)[6] Stated normatively, this formula amounts to one single imperative, directed at each agent: *Act in such a way that you are consistent both in what you do and believe about your actions and in relation to what all others do and believe about their actions.* The conversion of the descriptive statement into a normative claim, or an imperative, is possible because we can think of the reality of the good in a twofold way, as an existing state of affairs and as a state of affairs that each individual has reason to desire and produce.[7] We should add that consistency does not require unconditional agreement: if an agent holds wrong or inadequate beliefs, we can be consistent to them by trying to persuade them to change their opinion, and we may in the process change our own beliefs. Disagreements can amount to individual differences which do not make the overall consistency impossible.

The formula can be expanded again, for example, when it becomes necessary to explain the meaning of consistency. We can then say that the formula entails the full, uncoerced consistency of purposes taken as parts within an entirety of purposes. Strictly speaking, this expanded version is redundant because any reduction of the state of full and uncoerced consistency reduces consistency as such. At the same time, the formula can also be further condensed because it is unnecessary to say that the agent should be consistent to both themselves and others. If they are not consistent to others, then they are inconsistent toward themself, for the reasons mentioned above, and they cannot reach consistency to others without reaching inner consistency first. Consistency cannot be based on self-sacrifice and inner repression.[8] This means that the final version of the formula can be as short as this: *Act always in a consistent way.* Or, to simplify it even more: *Be consistent.* At the end, in order to understand the meaning of the absolute good for human practice, all one needs are these two words. The whole meaning of the good is folded into them, so to speak.

We have again reached a point at which our inquiry converges with well-known moral ideas. The formula that we use echoes Kant's categorical imperative, although we cannot explore the similarities and differences here. Staying within the context of Plato's philosophy, we rather find the opportunity to shorten the formula even more. The just man, Socrates states famously in the *Republic*, "sets his own house in order and rules himself, he arranges himself, becomes his own friend," so that he "becomes entirely one from many."[9] Consistency can therefore also be expressed as friendship, whereby friendship is directed both to oneself—humans are not naturally in accord with themselves—and to others. But even more fundamental is the unity, or oneness, that friendship entails. The just person, insofar as they are consistent, always remains one in their intentions and actions and does not experience a multitude of irreconcilable interests and needs. Our formula could therefore also be: *Be one*, or *Become one*, which again would mean "become one in relation both to yourself and others." This way, we have reached the ultimate condensation of the normative demands that the notion of the moral good lays upon agents.

Some might ask whether it is possible to make consistency the object of one's intentions. Is it possible to *want* consistency? It seems that one can direct practical intentions only to particular things. But this is not the case. If an individual says "I want to marry you," the content of their intention is not one particular thing, but a whole context of things. The content can be expressed even further—"I want to grow old with you," "I want to have a family with you"—until it is clear that it comprises both a variety of things and the consistency that reigns among them ("I want that everything goes well with us").[10] The more specific and concrete we conceive the contents of our intentions, the more complex they are and the more likely it is that consistency plays a role in them, even if the notion is not explicitly used. If the content includes only one thing, then it is in fact not concrete but general. If someone says "He only marries her because of the money," they look at the individual in question as a mere example of someone who is interested in money. Anyone else could also have thought that it would be nice to marry someone rich.

Consistency is also co-intended in all cases in which an agent wants to act in a morally good way. There cannot be a consistent killer, a consistent dictator, and the like. Saying, for example, that our formula would allow for a murderer to be good by acting consistently as a murderer would be nonsense, given that being a murderer is a contradiction to the purposes of others. In wanting to be good, an agent wants to avoid this kind of inconsistency.

The Spell of Fragmentarianism

We now have to consider some of the objections that can be raised against the good insofar as it is absolute. We will subsume these objections under the idea of fragmentarianism. In modern times, the practical world of humans appears as fractured. Individual consciousness relates to the external reality in a more or less skeptical way: it perceives the world as opaque, dominated either by evolutionary instincts or by social structures that escape the individual's control. No individual, it seems, can simply be moral but always represents the interests of their class, gender, or ethnic group. If someone has strong moral ideas, these ideas may appear as empty utopianism, and if someone's ideas are more realistic, then they may have cynically accepted the powers that rule the world. The modern individual is either helplessly nostalgic, lamenting the loss of life-worlds destroyed by capitalism and environmental degradation, or disengaged because nothing lives up to their standards and expectations. The convergence that we suggested previously between the agent-centric and the action-centric points of view, between willing and doing, or knowing and being, seems to have become wholly impossible. What we can achieve in the reality of practice are only fragments of the good, it seems: we may be able to piece these fragments together in our thought until some sort of consistency and unity emerges, but it only emerges in our thought. "Fragmentarianism" is one way of capturing the idea that we simply may have to accept that any attempt at realizing an absolute good is vain. And not only this: if the fragmentation of the good is inevitable, then we have to take it as a positive condition and embrace it. Would it not be presumptuous to expect human beings to reach a more perfect realization of the good than they are capable of? Is it not deeply human to accept our deficiencies, and is our skepticism about the good not a healthy thing after all? Is it not a livelier, more colorful approach to moral questions if we assume that the good appears in many pieces and to varying degrees?

To give an example for the kind of mistake that we may have committed in the previous analyses: one can say that there is no contradiction in the idea of a supreme being, or God, and that the idea can even fill the explanatory gaps we face in our attempts at understanding the universe as it is. It may be possible to explain certain phenomena better by assuming an intelligent creator than by relying on merely natural causes. Still, this does not mean that God exists and that there is no other way of explaining said phenomena. Analogously, one can say that our notion of the absolute good is fully consistent and even follows from the fact that actions are desired and performed according to reasons. Still, this does not mean that it corresponds to the reality of human practice. Our error would then have been that we have not started from this reality in all its relevant conditions. We would have isolated only one condition, the relation to reasons, and drawn conclusions from it until we arrived at a reality very different from the one that actually exists in human actions. Although we would have made no logical mistake, the result of our analysis still would not be true. It would not apply to reality because we would have strayed away into a realm where we deal only with concepts, not with actual humans and decisions. Envisioning a better world has never made the real world any better. Do we not hold on to an almost cynical *Fiat bonum, pereat mundus*, which is more concerned with the purity of notions than with their effectiveness?[11]

There are three ways in which the fragmented nature of the good can be described. These three ways follow a dialectical progression. What moves the progression is the need for the good to be determined if it is supposed to be real. Fragmentarianism denies the ability of the good to reach a proper form of determination: from its perspective, the good is characterized by either deficiency or excess, it is either not determined enough or too determined. If the good is not determined enough, then it is impossible for agents to hold its reality together. The good is then found in the fractured condition that we just described. We will refer to this condition as incompleteness of the good. If the good is too determined, then two things can follow. The good can first contradict itself and turn into its opposite. We will call this the relativism of the good. Here, the good is fragmented because there are various instances of it: my good, your good, hers, and so on. All instances are well-determined but eventually remain disparate and disconnected from each other. Relativism, despite trying to affirm a rich, diverse reality of the good, ends up denying it because no single viewpoint can be truly good, which means that eventually there is no good viewpoint whatsoever.

If the fragments of the good are too determined, then they also can appear to be discriminatory, excluding more or less aggressively other ways of being good. There is in any case a multitude of purposes that are to be made consistent in the good. Do we not often contradict ourselves or find ourselves struggling with our own impulses? And even if we fulfill our own purposes in an uncoerced way, is it not often the case that someone else, simply by fulfilling theirs, contradicts us, even denies us the right to do what we do? On the level of theory, is there not an antagonism of positions because most approaches to moral philosophy cannot be reconciled with each other? We only have to think here of the common assumption that there is an opposition between deontology and utilitarianism. One could even say that our own assumption of the absolute good is antagonistic because it excludes all other beliefs about the good. And insofar as it excludes fragmentarianism, which is after all a possible position, it just proves that fragmentarianism is true.

The three fragmentarian ways of conceiving the good that we have to consider are therefore incompleteness, relativism, and antagonism. We will try to give each way the consideration it deserves but also show why they all are self-refuting. Fragmentarianism seems a plausible position but we have to make sure that we do not succumb to its spell.

The Presumed Incompleteness of the Good

According to this position, striving for the absolute good, for full consistency, is impossible and even presumptuous because the good ever only exists in a fractured way, in bits and pieces, so to speak. The position is self-refuting. For a fragmentarian position, there is no other good achievable than an incomplete one. The achievable good, therefore, is justified as sufficient. At the same time, one cannot deny that this good is in fact incomplete. The good is even justified as sufficient *because* it is incomplete so that the agent does not need to achieve more than they can. This means that the fractured good is stated as sufficient and insufficient at the same time. One can only resolve this contradiction by admitting that the incomplete good is in fact not sufficient at all, which then means that the fragmentarian position is no longer exclusive and the idea of a fully sufficient good appears as undeniable again.

It may be possible to defend a fragmentarian position if one conceives of it in a general, high-level way, because general reflections about the limitations of human nature do not put one in a situation where one has to decide about the good that is actually desired or achieved. But it is impossible to argue for it with respect to particular actions and their consequences. An agent may be tempted to say: "The good I will achieve here is not perfect but I can't be bothered with that now." Still, they would have to admit that the good that is achieved is in fact not as complete as it should be, which raises the question why it is accepted as it is and not rather improved. The agent cannot say that they willingly strive for something which they know to be deficient or even bad. Their moral commitments cannot simply be terminated after a certain point. Physical impediments, for example, can be used as a justification to limit the good that one strives to achieve but only if the good is eventually complete within these given limitations. One must not take impediments as an excuse to strive even for less. We can find similar arguments in Plato. The greatest goods are the ones that one desires the most, Socrates states;[12] and the most beautiful appearance is the one that is loved the most.[13] Practical intentions are ultimately directed toward the greatest possible good. With respect to the conduct of life, we find him repeatedly say that his goal is not to live, but to live well.[14] The good cannot be limited to one particular aspect of life, like the pure fact of living, while all other aspects are treated with indifference.

We can relate the argument made here to the question why an individual should be moral at all. As we have seen, one can follow practical, legal, and conventional concerns without ever wanting to be good in moral sense. All three concerns allow for at least partial realizations of the good, and all cover essential aspects of human life. In many cases, their normativity is sufficient to decide about questions of conduct. Morality, seen from their perspective, may almost never be needed. This means that if the individual deviates from the given forms of normativity they need to have a reason, such as the desire to achieve a form of the good that is not satisfied on the level of the practical, legal, and conventional good. The question why be moral? can then be answered by saying that an individual can rightfully feel frustrated about the incomplete idea and justification of the good that is provided by the other forms of normativity. They may feel that these other forms are only parts of an overarching and unified account of the good. This would be enough for them to say that they have a stronger reason to desire the unified good than any of its partial versions.

The Presumed Relativism of the Good

According to the basic premise of relativism, all ways of approaching the good are equally valid and there is no way of reducing the multitude of approaches. But if this is so, then there is no reason to prefer any approach over the other. There is no reason not to change one's own position and adopt the position that others have chosen. Relativism is therefore equally self-refuting because it takes positions as sufficient and insufficient at the same time. And if positions are insufficient, then the idea of a fully sufficient good can again not be excluded.[15]

Defenders of the relativist position could try to avoid this conclusion by saying that all practical decisions are contingent and can always occur otherwise. We have to assume a relativism of perspectives because one cannot determine *a priori* which form of the good will be chosen in each different situation. But this argument would confuse the notion of the good with the act in which it is adopted and applied. Even if each practical decision is contingent as it factually occurs, the content of decisions is not, or does not have to be. We can call this confusion the realization fallacy. If the content of decisions were also always contingent, even in cases in which it is not chosen in an erroneous or deficient way, then we would have to assume that the notion of the good is attributed to things in arbitrary ways, in which case one could not even decide whether it is the notion that individuals actually want to apply. If all kinds of things can be called good, why does anything have to be called good? Nothing, however, prevents us from thinking that although all actions are performed contingently, they are also performed according to reasons which can be conceived as non-contingent.

Eventually, the relativist position can be turned on its head. If all positions are deemed equally sufficient, then they all have to be consistent to each other. No position can be excluded by any other, because this would contradict the very idea of relativism. We can then assume that there exists a position that integrates at least a certain number of approaches and turns them into one approach which would be more highly sufficient. But if this is possible, it is also possible to assume that there is one final position which would integrate all other, partial approaches. If consistency is possible at all, we have to assume that it can exist in all parts. Why stop at some point? Why should not all positions that appear as different complement each other? Relativism is in reality just another way of conceiving of the absolute good: instead of looking at it as a unity, it looks at it as a totality of specific contents. By its own premises, relativism would so be turned into its opposite.

We can again find a similar argument in Plato's work. Virtue can understand itself and vice, whereas vice can only understand vice, he states in the *Republic*.[16] Analogously, it can be said of the philosopher that they understand both knowledge and pleasure and so have the most insight into matters of human life.[17] This means that the good corresponds to a point of view which includes both the best and what is different to it. While certain things are more emphatically good than others, the fully sufficient good includes both its consequences (pleasure) and deficiencies (vice). There is only one form (*eidos*) of virtue but countless forms of vice,[18] which means that the particular and limited forms of the good are many, whereas the absolute good is one, containing and unifying all particular forms.[19]

As a last resort, the defenders of the relativist position could argue that each approach to the good is perspectivistic, in the sense that each approach is determined by strictly subjective attitudes and beliefs. We can find a refutation of such arguments in Plato as well. In the *Philebus*, Socrates states that if pleasure is assumed to be the only good, many nonsensical things (*alogia*) follow.[20] One has to deny the existence of good things outside of the feeling soul, and in the soul itself only the subjective experience of pleasure would be stated as good, which would exclude other, more object-oriented abilities, such as courage, prudence, and reason. If the meaning of the good is determined solely by one's joyful sensations, or one's subjective perspective, then one has to deny that any intrinsic property can be called good. This position is self-refuting, because the hedonist cannot deny that intrinsic properties exist: if they want to argue in favor of the goodness of pleasure, they have to assume that pleasure is intrinsically good. But then it is not possible for them to claim that only their subjective experience is the ground for calling something good; they rather have to say that what they experience as good is also objectively so. And if this is true, then things other than pleasure also have to be objectively good, for the simple reason that pleasure occurs in combination with other phenomena such as well-being and health. As we have seen, hedonism is for Plato only possible if it is part and consequence of the absolute good.[21] If the absolute good holds, hedonism holds as well, and the same is true for subjectivism as an individual reflection of the good, but the direction of the argument cannot be reversed.

The Presumed Antagonism of the Good

The third aspect of fragmentarianism, antagonism, leads to similar arguments. Antagonism is based on the idea that two, or more, positions can be held as equally sufficient despite the fact that they mutually exclude each other. But no position can be qualified as good if it directly excludes another position from achieving the good. The consistency of moral positions cannot be achieved at the price of inconsistency to others. This means that at least one position is insufficient and the idea of an antagonism is, like the previous ideas, also self-refuting. In general, the assumption of an antagonism between two moral determinations can be resolved in one of the following ways: either both determinations have to be given up because none of them is truly tenable and sufficient, or both can be reconciled and integrated into one sufficient good, thereby taking the antagonism away and reaching, like in the case of relativism, a unity of various instances of the good. To put this in simpler terms: if something is good for me, and something else good for another person, both things are good. If they contradict each other, they cannot both be good, but if they both are good, they can bear no contradiction. Either way, one cannot suppose the moral good to entail some form of antagonism.

Our answer to the challenge of moral antagonism has far-reaching consequences. Whatever contradiction one might assume in relation to the position of others cannot be definite and has to be conceived as a hurdle that ultimately can be overcome. At the end, why should we think that the others would not be able to agree to our position, and we not to theirs? Why should it be moral to assume a position to which many would not agree? This argument can also be made on the level of moral theories. A moral theory that denies other theories the ability of approaching the good cannot be tenable. Its own claim at defining the good can be denied, because if one theory contradicts another, all theories can contradict each other. A moral theory, hence, has to include all possible ways of being good. This way, the imperative of consistency can lead to both humility and benevolence: humility because the individual should assume that their stance cannot be justified if it is inconsistent to the stance of others, and benevolence because the individual should assume that their own good can be shared with, and distributed to, others. Consistency also entails the unlimited transparency of moral determinations. No position can be assumed to be so personal or so obscure that it remains forever irreconcilable to others. The same can be said about the assumption of dilemmas which will be addressed in the following section.

To conclude, another argument in favor of the antagonism of the good has to be mentioned. Current societies accept certain violent actions, for example, the killing of animals for research and the procurement of food. The killing of humans in war and the use of armed force by the police are also widely endorsed. Many oppose these practices and would like them to be abolished or at least reduced to the absolute minimum necessary. Vegans would abolish all use of animals for human benefit while pacifists would disarm the police and prevent all wars expect defensive ones. Does this not mean that modern societies are fundamentally antagonistic because there is not even an agreement on such basic things as eating habits and the protection against criminal behavior? From a moral point of view, it is not clear that there has to be an antagonism here. The arguments in favor of veganism and pacifism are strong, as it seems hard to deny that a higher good is achieved if no sentient animal and no human being need to be killed because of some presumed interest or constraint. Debates on these issues are obviously far from resolved, but we must not confuse disagreement with a fundamental moral antagonism: disagreements can never be excluded, for the simple reason that it is never clear why individuals hold a certain moral position. If they hold it for other than moral purposes, for example, because it benefits themselves, then the disagreement can persist even if the position can be shown as inconsistent.

A more fundamental antagonism could be seen in the fact that all living beings exclude others from living who could potentially have come into existence had the living not done so before. Insofar as I exist, someone else who could equally exist is prevented from being born. One could then say that each living being represses the possibility of other individual lives. But existence cannot be seen as a moral privilege, if ever it is the pre-condition for any possible privileges and obligations. Some living beings have to exist, and the commitment to the good can only start with those who do in fact exist. Non-existence can therefore not be qualified as a moral damage, and there can be no obligation toward someone who will never in any way begin to exist.[22]

Why There Are No Moral Dilemmas

The problem of moral dilemmas seems to bother quite a number of philosophers. For a dilemma to exist, one has to assume that the agent has "an obligation to do *a* and an obligation not to do *a*."[23] For example, I have to tell the truth to a patient, especially if they are terminally ill, so that they can make informed decisions about their life, and I must not tell them the truth because the effects of knowing their condition would be so devastating that it would further impact their health. One obligation contradicts the other but both stand. Or, the obligations are "equally wrong" from the perspective of the other.[24] Alternatively, even if we assume that one obligation is overriding, the other one is not destroyed.[25] The agent then still has to violate one moral obligation, either the stronger or the weaker one.

If moral dilemmas could exist, then there would be cases in which the good cannot be realized without contradiction. The question is what this would mean for moral theories. Mill claimed: "There exists no moral system under which there do not arise unequivocal cases of conflicting obligation."[26] Conflicts and dilemmas, for him, are inevitable and do not invalidate the principles on which theories are based, even if some theories fare better in dealing with conflicts than others.[27] But it is far from clear that dilemmas can be kept so neatly at the margins. If each obligation can lead to a "conflict" with other obligations, then no obligation has general meaning, not even the principle of utility. This problem does not only affect positions based on general moral ideas. A particularist may also find themselves in a situation where two sorts of actions appear as good and only one can be performed. They cannot rule out that *not* performing a certain action would not be bad for someone in a given case (that is, they cannot simply drop the other action on a whim even if the theory recommends precisely that). Any moral theory, thus, would fail *as theory* if dilemmas were to exist. Theories would have to renounce the ambition of providing a fundamental clarification of human practice and would sink to the level of a set of recommendations.

Fortunately, there is no such thing as a dilemma, at least not in the sense of a contradiction within the moral good itself. We can mention at least three reasons to support this claim. First, if we did not have general moral obligations, like telling the truth, there would not even be a moral dilemma, because a physician could then always do whatever seems best to them. The assumption of a dilemma is self-refuting because it denies the validity of the principles that are used to state the dilemma in the first place. Second, while it seems plausible that dilemmas exist if one states them in a formal, logical way, as shown above, no example that is given ever actually works. Upon closer examination, even the example used here is false. A false dilemma is one in which the answer to the question "Should the agent choose *a* or *b*?" is "neither."[28] For the patient, the point is not whether they are told the truth right to their face or are left in blissful ignorance but whether there is someone who can help and advise in such difficult a situation. The truth can be revealed step by step together with the appropriate emotional and practical support. Brutality and deception do certainly not exhaust the possibilities of human interaction. It is of course impossible to verify our claim that there is no example for a true dilemma. We can only urge the reader to approach all examples that are presented as if they were a false dilemma and then see whether they cannot in fact be analyzed in such a way.

The third point goes as follows: particular constellations in the world of practice may indeed lead to a dilemma but the dilemma can then not be attributed to a moral contradiction. It is rather just that, a practical problem. Foot mentions the example of someone who promised to be best man at A's and B's weeding but cannot do both because the two friends have scheduled their wedding for the same day. One promise inevitably has to be broken.[29] But the case seems rather unique and extremely unfortunate, to say the least (if this is your circle of best friends, could you not have coordinated with them a little bit more?). The case only shows that the world sometimes makes it impossible to fulfill a moral obligation. From that, nothing follows for the notion of the good.

What makes the question of dilemmas difficult and confusing is the fact that the term can be understood in different ways. For the sake of our analysis, we focus on the conceptual structure of a dilemma. But a dilemma is also a practical impasse that agents face: if someone feels that a certain situation presents a dilemma, then there is in fact one. The agent cannot decide what to do even if from an external point of view such a decision would well be possible. It would then be arrogant to say that the dilemma does not exist because it stems from limited or wrong beliefs. If the agent would not see a dilemma in the given case, they would be a different person. Some moral philosophers seem to talk about this kind of practical impasse when they refer to a moral dilemma. To give a complete picture, we have to mention at least some examples for such a case. Our remarks, again, have to be brief.

To begin with, there is the notorious question "Who shall die?" that can be presented in a multitude of ways. Assuming that during a pandemic not all infected patients can be given the required treatment, say, a ventilator, doctors have to triage and decide who should be left untreated. Perhaps the elderly who have not as many years to live as younger people? This criterion may be appropriate in the given case. However, it is clear that such decisions are allowed only in situations of emergency in which treatment is needed but not available for all. It has no implications for medical care in general. The criterion may also not work in all cases, for example, when there are much more old people in need of treatment than younger ones. Would then still only young people be treated? The criteria that are established in such cases are always more or less *ad hoc*. In fact, if one gives the example a more sadistic spin and thinks of a psychopath who forces an individual to choose one person from a group to be killed, it is clear that no reason for choosing anyone can exist, or that all reasons would be *ad hoc* and arbitrary. Situations of emergency may feel like a dilemma for the agent but they present in reality no moral dilemma at all. The answer to the question "What should I do?" can only be: "Whatever seems best to you," which is of course no answer at all. "Philosophy cannot be asked to solve unsolvable problems,"[30] and nothing follows for the good if a case is not decidable in moral terms.[31] Other cases of a felt dilemma may result from a certain indecision of agents. If one looks long enough at practical options, none may seem attractive enough and one becomes unable to make a decision. Sartre's famous story of the young man who does not know whether he should stay with his mother or join the resistance can be seen as an example for this.[32]

Other cases may seem to carry a greater weight. A dilemma may arise because an agent cannot let go of a particular moral commitment. For example, one may be uncertain whether medical treatment should be discontinued for a patient. One party thinks that the vital functions which make life worth living have already been lost while another party wishes to hold on and is not ready to give up hope. Hursthouse, who uses this example, is right in saying that the dilemma is solvable here because there has to be an answer, if only eventually, to the question what kind of life the patient still lives.[33] The two moral commitments can be reconciled, even if it takes care and respect and probably long deliberations to reach such a reconciliation. Resolving dilemmas too quickly and too easily may feel cynical to those who are facing traumatizing decisions. If a person had to give up a family member during a time of murderous oppression which threatened the life of all members, the person cannot be consoled by being told that at least they were able to save the others. They may carry a wound that can never be closed. It is hardly worthwhile to save conceptual consistency in the face of such a reality of human life.

Still, refusing to accept a proposed dilemma can also be important at times, because all-too often agents claim that they were facing a situation that did not leave them a choice. "We had to bomb the whole village because there were terrorists hiding in it." Showing that their dilemma is false takes away the justification for such harmful behavior. As a rule of thumb, we always have to ask: who wants a dilemma to exist? We can think of the case in which a woman murders her violent and abusive husband in his sleep, after long years of suffering from him and perhaps out of fear that the abuse might get worse and end up lethal for her. Is there a dilemma in this case? There may be one for those who think that the woman has to be punished for her deed because she should have had more respect for her husband's life. For herself, there does not have to be a dilemma because she may feel that she acted out of self-defense, pure and simple. Perhaps she feels remorse for having killed another human being but even then she would probably first blame her husband for having put her in a situation in which she had to act so drastically. If this case is a dilemma at all, she did not choose to be in it.[34] We should therefore be aware that the assumption of a dilemma is rarely innocent: all-too often we do not just register obligations that somehow exist independently but introduce them into a given case, which means that we put the agent under constraints and then blame them, if only implicitly, for having violated some form of the good. Coming back to the case of the bombing of the village, there is a dilemma only if one thinks that the lives of innocent civilians can be balanced against tactical gains. If they cannot, then it is of course no question that one should not bomb.

The Good as Paradigm, Not as Ideal

Physical versus Conceptual Things

What kind of reality is involved in the conception of the good? This question, which was always present in the previous analyses, needs to be addressed directly now. Although the ontological assumptions that we make are minimal we make at least some, and it seems necessary to explain what they are. There are two ways to think of something as real: things can be real because they are situated in time and space and they can be real as content of human thoughts and intentions. Although the number two is no physical entity and cannot be found situated in time and space, it is well-determined both in its logical properties and as part of a symbolic system. Humans can think of it clearly and distinctly. The number also determines how humans approach their surrounding world. Identifying objects as two, and not as one or three, matters for them both in intellectual and practical terms, not to mention that the ability to count is constitutive for the idea of objects itself. Numbers are part of the reality of human life, and although they have no causal power they have at least practical effects insofar as matters change once numbers are used. We can think of the absolute good in the same way: if we have a clear idea of it and can say that it is relevant for our thoughts and intentions regarding the practical world, then it is also real.

Again, the ontological assumptions that we make with this are minimal and best kept at the level of analogies to other concepts of which we also assume that they are real, like numbers. We mentioned before that we follow Scanlon who thinks of reasons as "fundamental elements of the normative domain."[35] Reasons "are not reducible" to natural properties;[36] they form a "domain" insofar as it seems unquestionable "that statements can make claims about different subjects."[37] A domain, in other words, only needs to be conceived as a specific realm of discourse without thereby making ontological commitments to identifying a certain part of the "natural world"[38] which would possess "any spatio-temporal location."[39]

The question of reality, eventually, seems more pressing on the level of practice itself. An obvious objection that can be raised at this point goes as follows: how can we say that the good is real in human practice if individual decisions, attitudes, and actions often if not always fail the good? Does human practice not give us sufficient evidence that individuals are very rarely concerned about moral questions at all and that the motives driving their actions are more likely to come from desires, instincts, and external constraints that hold their sway over them? That is, how can an idea possess reality if most individuals fail to be even aware of it? But the objection is not difficult to counter. We can think of the good as a structure of human practice even if the practical implications of this structure are failed in each individual act. To take again the example of counting: even if most individuals would prove to be incapable of using complex mathematical operations, or of using them correctly, no one would assume that the system of mathematical laws is therefore invalid and has to be given up.[40] It would be even more absurd to think that the mathematical laws have to be adapted to human errors, so that the laws of multiplication, for example, would have to be changed in order to make incorrect uses appear correct. Surprisingly, this is what defenders of a fragmentarian position in morality often do: they adapt moral ideas to the human deficiencies in order to make the latter appear as correct, instead of measuring the deficiencies against moral ideas.

To approach this problem from a different angle, one cannot say that humans fail to fly given that it is impossible for them to do so, at least without the help of machines. One cannot fail at something that one can by definition not achieve. The fact that we can say of humans that they fail moral ideas implicitly states that it would be possible for them to understand and realize these ideas in their actions. We can find similar conclusions in Kant's understanding of the morally determined will, when he says that "it is absolutely impossible by means of experience to make out with complete certainty a single case in which the maxim of an action otherwise in conformity with duty rested simply on moral grounds and on the representation of one's duty."[41] There is no contradiction for Kant in assuming that the moral law determines the reality of human practice, at least under the perspective of reason, and yet cannot ever be identified with certainty as realized in an individual's practical determinations.

Descriptive versus Normative Contents

The arguments presented here can be further refined. Numbers and the good can be understood from both a descriptive and normative point of view. The good can be both what we do and what we should or ought to do; it can be both the structure of actions and an imperative for the agent. "I don't lie to others" and "I should not lie to others" can be expressions of the same action and attitude. The same is true for numbers, which are not only elements of a given symbolic system but also provide a standard for the use and interpretation of things ("Add these up according to this method"). But even if numbers can be applied in a variety of unforeseeable ways, as such they are always already fully expressed. There is never a doubt as to whether there is a numerical reality, because the calculation that one is about to do already exists as a potential variation in the given system. Moral ideas are different in this regard. We have to distinguish between a normative idea that corresponds to an already given, fully determined reality and one that at first only exists as an imperative. In the sense of the latter, the good is not yet real but should or ought to be realized. It is hovering, so to speak, in a sort of inbetween, unfulfilled state. For moral philosophy, insofar as its principles are meant to be action-guiding, this aspect of normativity is the most important one. Moral philosophy wants to show what agents should do, now and in all future actions to come. We therefore have to ask how the reality of the good can be asserted or secured if it is only a normative, yet-to-be-realized content of practical intentions.

It is not difficult to show that the question raised here rests on a confusion. We can show this by comparing our analysis one more time to Moore's approach. He distinguishes between the notion of the good, which is undefinable for him, and the "state of things" that can be subsumed under the good: "The best ideal we can construct will be that state of things which contains the greatest number of things having positive value. … Great positive goods, it will appear, are so numerous, that any whole, which shall contain them all, must be of vast complexity."[42] Moral philosophy can envision an "ideal," which in Moore's case has to be conceived as comprehensively as possible. The question is then how one can decide what kinds of things belong to this ideal. Insofar as his approach is naturalistic, this question leads to an empirical investigation: "In order to decide correctly at what state of things we ought to aim, we must not only consider what results it is possible for us to obtain, but also which, among equally possible results, will have the greatest value."[43] For Moore, the list of elements that are included in the good cannot be given *a priori* but has to remain open. He even has to concede that it is possible that "we cannot discover what the Ideal is."[44]

For our approach, such a possibility does not exist: we know that the absolute good can be defined as the consistent and uncoerced fulfillment of the purposes of actions. The notion of the good has been expressed clearly through the various conceptual elements that it contains. One might object that we also do not know *a priori* which purposes are there to be fulfilled, and how they have to be fulfilled. But this empirical question is secondary and does not concern the notion of the good as such. As a formal notion, the good is not determined by the particular things to which it refers. This means that for us the question how the good exists can be answered in a simple way: as a notion, it is always already present to us and can be conceived as the content of an individual's practical determinations. We do not have to search for the elements that fulfill the meaning of the good, nor do we have to be afraid of not being able to discover what they are. The objection according to which the good can be at risk of having no reality because it would remain an abstract ideal results from taking it as an unfulfilled empirical reality, not as conceptual content. A normative content, even if it is not yet realized in an empirically attestable way, is always already real for the respective practical intention and for the actions that it guides.

One might say that even if this argument is true we are in no better position than Moore. By looking solely at the conceptual content, we cannot say *how* the good will be realized in individual practice, or *whether* it will be realized at all. The realization of the good is undeniably what is most important for us. But to say this again: our point is that any realization of the good, partial and confused as it may be, can be seen against the notion of the absolute good. If the good were a state of the world that we first have to identify empirically, we would indeed not be able to say what it is. Conversely, insofar as we *are* able to say what it is, we can turn the argument around and say that because the good is accessible to us as a formal notion we know which actions and which states of the world are most appropriate for it. The notion of the good does not depend on our experience of the world but on the contrary allows us to assess and measure human practice. With Murdoch, we can say that we "see the world in the light of the Good."[45] If we could not know the good in advance, however confusedly, we could never find out what is truly good. It would then even be possible that a utopian state of things has already been reached but no one was able to recognize it. In turn, whoever claims that the good is not realized yet also needs to know what it is, because otherwise they would not even know what they want to see achieved. Even Moore knows already what the notion of the good, or the ideal, entails; for him, it has to be the greatest amount of things that possess "intrinsic value."[46] Based on this idea, he actually contradicts himself by saying that these value-bearing things still have to be searched for and might perhaps never be found. One cannot use the idea of intrinsic value in any meaningful way without knowing at least tentatively to what it refers.

The question of the reality of the good is eventually not merely theoretical. It is not the case that we have a notion of the good and then need to find out whether there are actions in the world that would correspond to it. If we have the notion and understand it sufficiently well, then we also understand that *we* are the ones who are supposed to realize it. After all, it is the consistency to ourselves and others that is at stake. In the *Republic*, Socrates also shows that the validity of his idea of justice does not depend on the question whether it is realized exactly in the way it is explained. It rather serves as a model (*paradigma*) against which individual actions can be measured and compared. Agents can use it to see that their pursuit of happiness should be based on the pursuit for justice.[47] The idea of justice entails the imperative to be realized with as few modifications as possible.[48] We are anxious, therefore, to avoid any connotation to the notion of an "ideal" as one can find it in Moore's approach. The absolute good is no remote and hypothetical idea but rather the structure of things, the way in which they *are* insofar as they can potentially be arranged to be consistent to another. The notion of an ideal undermines the validity of moral claims and should never be used to justify them. Moral claims are not valid because they show us how the world could be, ideally conceived, but how it has to be here and now.

One final remark: the way in which we conceive of the absolute good avoids the problem that presents itself for other, more limited principles and the theories based on them. We do not have to assume that a transition has to be made from morally indifferent impulses to a moral content. That is, we do not have to assume that the individual has to go from a pure *is* ("I want, I like, I do," etc.) to a pure *ought*. All reasons that agents follow bear a normative content and can be related to the moral good as unity of normative contents. As no person acts alone, the question of consistency to both themselves and others is always present in the background. Logically speaking, the step from a non-moral to a moral determination does not involve a contradiction, a strict opposition, but only a contrary relation. Moral determinations are never excluded but are parts, or potential expressions, of all other, non-moral determinations. Only evil determinations present themselves as a rupture, whereas moral ones fit into the conduct of life as a whole.

How Far It Goes

The last question we have to address has been mentioned before, although it could not be treated sufficiently then. As we have seen, the absolute good has a quantitative dimension which requires each instance of the good to stand in a context of equally good things.[49] Taken in and for itself, the notion of the good implies no limitation in the way the good is realized; it is absolute insofar as it is *prima facie* unlimited. An agent cannot say that they want to act in consistency only to a particular group of people because then they would accept to be in inconsistency to others. Whoever says that they only care about the members of their nation, or about those adhering to the same faith, excludes all others from participating at the good. As already said, the question of the extension of the good is primarily normative, not empirical. We do not have to figure out who exactly is concerned, and how, but what normative perspectives should be used if anyone needs to be given further consideration.

One might ask whether the extension of the good has a temporal dimension. Is consistency extended only to the individuals that are present with oneself, that is, only to one's own generation, or are future generations included in it? It seems obvious that some future generations have to be included in it, especially the ones that will follow one's own closely, but the further into the future one goes, the less possible it seems to include individuals who do not yet exist. Again, the commitment to consistency starts with each and every individual. It starts at the present. While it is not possible to speak for generations that will exist in a very far future, because their interests and needs are wholly indeterminate for us, it is possible to speak for those future generations that will be impacted by the decisions we currently make. Most of the times, we know very well how we have to arrange the world in order to make it suitable for future generations, and how we have to act so that our actions are consistent to the presumed actions of yet unborn people. The idea of consistency entails the obligation to act as if it were already fully clear how consistency will be achieved in future times. If we do not assume this obligation, consistency will again be limited arbitrarily.[50]

We can compare the formal notion of the good to a window on the world. In any specific constellation of the world, a window can only show a certain number of things. It includes some of the things that exist in the outside world, others not. But we can always assume that the world continues outside of the range of our view. While the other parts of the world may be less relevant compared to the things we currently see, we have to assume that they are there and will be impacted by what we do to the things that are in front of us. It is impossible to say "I want the whole world to be good," as no individual can have such a goal. But an individual can say "This cannot be good unless these other things are good too," meaning that the good they strive to achieve has to be seen as incomplete if it cannot be extended to respect the possible concerns of others who are involved.

Following Moore's terms, we can distinguish between "the *best state* of things conceivable, the Summum Bonum or Absolute Good," which would be equivalent to Heaven, and "the best *possible* state of things in this world," the "Human Good."[51] The idea of a maximum state of the good, or Heaven, suggests that nothing can be good unless the world changes in radical ways and all limitations that prevent it currently from being fully good have been eliminated. In this case, the realization of the good would be deferred to a point that is completely beyond our practical reach. The idea of Heaven also implies that the good can only be reached once a certain uniformity of individuals has been achieved. It suggests that unless individuals are all alike and unified, no consistency will exist. If this were the case, consistency would be a condition for the dead, not for the living. It would even make the very idea of consistency superfluous, as there can be no deviations, and no inconsistencies, in Heaven. Consistency becomes trivial up there.

For our approach, consistency is relevant precisely because particular things and persons are as different as they can be. With an idea that can be found in Leibniz's *Monadology*, we can say that the totality of things should entail "as much variety as possible, but with the greatest order possible."[52] Consistency allows for the greatest possible harmony combined with the greatest possible freedom, the greatest uncoerced variety, of things. One could even say that the more opposed things are, the more desirable consistency becomes. Full consistency means that every part and element could potentially tear the coherence to others apart, that every part and element could find itself completely isolated and in contradiction to others but eventually does not. This means, again, that there is no reason to limit the assumption of consistency just because at first some parts are difficult to fit into it. If consistency seems impossible to achieve in a given case, we only need to expand the way in which we conceive of it. We may have conceived of it too narrowly. From a moral point of view, we are never allowed to assume that consistency could not be found in challenges that arise in the encounter with others. "Be consistent" means, among others, "be consistent even where you think you cannot be," or "be more consistent than you think you can be."

Part Two

Failures

6

Five Ways of Failing the Good

Disregard, Evil, and Cognitive Failure

Having now achieved an understanding of the two main elements of morality, self-determination and the good, we are in a situation where we can address the inevitable failure of the good in moral decisions, attitudes, and actions, and in the respective moral theories. In the present chapter, we will start from an overview of what "failure" means in our case. Five ways will be distinguished in which it can occur. Terminologically, we will use the "failure," or the "failing of the good," as synonym for the "failing of the moral good" and the "failing of morality" proper. A failure of the good implies a failure of morality as a whole, and insofar as we deal with moral theories here, only the moral good will be relevant for us.

One possible objection has to be addressed right away. In the previous chapters, we have shown that the good is always at least potentially given in human practices insofar as actions are performed according to reasons. If all forms of normativity lead back to moral normativity, then the moral good is always at least implicitly given in them. There is, in other words, always *some* good achieved in human practices. Does not even aggression often stem from a perceived lack of goodness in others and can act as a stimulus for the shared promotion of moral goals? How is it possible then for anyone ever to fail the good? Two answers can be given to address this concern. First, the good is failed not insofar as it does not exist but insofar as it exists. Agents fail the good while trying to realize it, or because they realize it in some way. Failure, in other words, is no mere deficiency or lack but the result of the inner contradictions of the good itself.

Second, it was important to stress the implicit and potential presence of the good against the objections of skeptics. We had to show *that*, and *how*, the good is real in human action. Now, we need more than an implicit good because we cannot understand the actual phenomenon of morality by looking at it merely as a conceptual structure. We have to look instead at moral determinations. The term "determination" has a double meaning which we are happy to exploit: it refers to the particular content that determines what an action is about and to the fact that it is actually determined to occur in such-and-such way. The term "determination" reflects the correlational nature of morality as it refers both to the individual's act and to the content that it bears. What agents fail is not the notion of the good but the good as it is determined to exist.

Agents can first fail to be moral because they *disregard* moral self-determination altogether. There can be many reasons for this: a lack of confidence in one's abilities, overwhelming anxiety, a cynical detachment from moral aims, or a skeptical attitude for which every strong moral determination appears as problematic. Agents can also limit themselves to other forms of normativity, to practical, conventional, and legal normativity. One can fail morality if one thinks that normative questions are merely questions of practical matters, of the conventions that one has to follow in a given social context, or of the existing laws. In all these cases, disregard for morality is not a *moral* failing proper: morality is not explicitly denied, it is rather not considered at all. Obviously, there can be cases in which disregard becomes a moral failure. "They saw that I was offended but pretended not to be aware of it." But in such cases, the indifference toward the moral dimension of an action is in itself morally bad or even evil. This leads to the second point.

Agents act in an *evil* way if they know the good but decide explicitly for a course of action that stands in opposition to it. Evil is the conscious attempt at destroying the good, or at least the voluntary decision not to let the good, although it would be possible, prevail. We have mentioned the notion of evil previously and like before, we cannot engage in a more thorough discussion at this point.[1] In any case, evil has to be distinguished from all cases in which actions carry unintendedly bad consequences. These cases are covered under the following point.

The remaining three points represent morality's own ways of failing what it is supposed to be: they all presuppose an individual wanting to be good. One might remark that the distinction to the previous two cases is often difficult to make insofar as agents may never be entirely free from a certain disregard of moral aims or even from a certain willingness to be considered evil, if only in marginal ways. There are infinite ways in which moral actions can coexist with evil intentions, for example, when the donation to a charity is accompanied by a certain pleasure in the humiliation of those who cannot donate as much. But despite such potential co-intentions, we have to assume that decisions, attitudes, and actions are eventually determined by one specific reason that outweighs or subsumes all other reasons that might be involved. If this were not the case, that is, if there could not be one primary, sufficient reason, we would have to assume that actions are determined by all reasons that are possibly related to them, which would mean that they are not determined at all.

The third way of failing the good includes actions that are meant to achieve the good but ultimately turn out to be bad. It also includes cases in which some good is achieved that turns out to be different from how it was meant. The common factor in these cases is *cognitive failure*: the agent does not properly understand either the consequences of the action they perform, or the way in which their action concretely realizes the good, or the practical situation that requires them to perform a moral action in the first place. We could even imagine the extreme case of someone who fails completely in their understanding of the good, which would happen in a situation in which the agent is unable to see what they should do, even if they have decided to do what is good. However, it is hard to think of such a case as possible. If the only thing that an agent knows is that they want to do some good, without knowing what the good entails in the given situation, they know in fact nothing at all but merely declare to have an interest in the good. The cognitive failures mentioned here imply that the agent has at least some knowledge of the good, even if this knowledge is ineffective, confused, or unrelated to the case at hand. That is, the cognitive failures do not contradict or destroy the individual's intention to be good; they only prevent it from becoming fully clear, specific, and effective. We should also note that the possibility of cognitive failures follows from the very notion of the good. The absolute good is an arrangement of human practice that can be described by assertive statements which are either true or false. It is entirely possible to have incorrect beliefs about the good as quality of actions, like it is possible for agents to have incorrect beliefs about their own ability to reach this quality.

False Absolutes

The fourth and fifth cases are most important for our inquiry. In both of them, moral self-determination takes place and no cognitive failure occurs, so that all conditions for realizing the good are met. Agents fail morality inherently, because of its inner structure. We will see that there is no way for individuals not to fail morality, even if they want, and honestly try to be, good. As said before, they fail morality precisely because they want to achieve it. In the fourth case, the failure happens inadvertently whereas in the fifth case failure is explicit and even embraced. The fourth case will be at the center of the following analyses; it will allow us to take a deeper look at the limitations of morality itself. The fact that the failure of morality is inherent means that it does not occur because of some individual deficiency of agents. Or better: the individual deficiencies of agents do not matter at this point. Morality entails the assumption that an individual's determination is *in principle* sufficient for the good and that the good can be sufficiently completed and achieved through it. If the agent wanted to be only a little bit moral, or moral only in a tentative, doubtful way, they would in fact not be moral at all. It is also important to keep in mind that there is no practically relevant distinction between the absolute good in the sense of the one, encompassing good that has no limitations whatsoever and the good that can be intended and realized in a particular situation. We mentioned this before.[2] Particular realizations of the good are all direct manifestations of the absolute good, and it is neither possible nor necessary to seek for an absolute good beyond the good that can be conceived as absolute in a given case.

A remark made by Foot can help us illustrate this point. Raising the question of what it is that makes something good, she refers to Aquinas according to whom, she claims, "of any individual action" we can say "that *if it is no way bad then it is good*." For Foot, this means that being good is synonymous to the way in which things naturally are: "a plant, after all, is growing well if there is nothing wrong with its development."[3] We can take this to mean that the good is nothing extraordinary, in the sense of an addition to the way in which things usually are. We do not have to assume that the absolute good is foreign to the ordinary practices that humans follow. As consistency of purposes, the good is rather the consistency of all that humans can and do pursue. We could even say that if something extraordinary is pursued it is likely to be inconsistent to the other purposes and therefore bad.

Aquinas' own point is slightly different from the way in which it is presented by Foot. Aquinas raises the question whether there are actions that are indifferent, that is, neither good nor bad.[4] If there were such actions, the good would indeed be extraordinary, something for which agents would have to decide over and beyond the things they usually intend to do. For Aquinas, this is impossible because goodness is inherent to the notion of an action.[5] His argument against indifference is based on the fact that actions are particular, characterized by individual "circumstances." An agent has to choose what is best according to reason in any given situation, which is also what is good; if they do not choose that, they are evil. In order to make this argument, Aquinas has to exclude two kinds of activities from the definition of an action: activities that are not directed by reason, "as when a man strokes his beard," and activities that are considered "in their species," that is, in a general way.[6] Walking is morally indifferent as a general ability of humans and becomes either good or evil depending on where one goes and when. One might ask: "Isn't it morally indifferent if I walk into my bedroom to fetch a piece of clothing?" but even then one can ask, for example, whether one does not disturb anyone by entering the bedroom or whether one should not rather tend to one's sick child, not to mention that speaking of "my bedroom" presupposes the various ways in which private property is regulated and assigned. No particular action can be truly indifferent if all its relevant circumstances are taken into account. In our analysis, we will follow Aquinas and Foot and also assume that the good is embedded in the structure of actions unless they are manifestly bad in one way or another.

Coming back to the problem of individual deficiencies, an important distinction has to be made. We have to distinguish between the qualitative and the quantitative failing of the good. The former is the one that will be considered in the following. The latter stems from the fact that it is unlikely for a single act of self-determination to bring about the good in all its particular elements, even if the agent makes the best effort they can. Their failing is quantitative because the good does not include all persons and things that would have to be considered in a given situation. We have to assume that this failing is a universal and unavoidable condition of any attempt at being moral. But precisely because it is unavoidable it is also irrelevant for an agent's determination. One could avoid the quantitative failing only by not acting at all. More important, the fact that the good is incomplete does not mean that no good can be realized. The good has to be absolute, and therefore complete, *for the individual's determination*, whether it is eventually complete or incomplete from a quantitative point of view.

The qualitative or inherent failure of the good means that the good is prone to an inner dialectic. As an absolute good, it is false because it contradicts its own absoluteness. We have already encountered a set of dialectical structures in the previous chapter where we explained the different forms in which a fragmentarian position can appear.[7] The same structures can be found in the failing of the good.[8] Like before, the structures involve a progression from one position to the next, a progression which potentially goes on forever given that no position is unaffected by the dialectic. In its most basic form, the dialectic means that the good is either not determined enough or too determined. If the good is not determined enough, it can fail to achieve real meaning and appear as empty and ineffective. If the good is too determined, it can first contradict itself by turning into its own opposite. This does not mean that the good turns into evil: it rather means that moral determinations turn into the opposite of what they are intended to be. Second, the good can become antagonistic, excluding more or less aggressively other determinations which would be equally moral to have. For all positions, it is important that the good is intended and realized as absolute, that is, as fully determined. There is nothing in the very idea of a determination that would indicate why it cannot be adequate. The following chapters will show that it is the particular form and content of moral determinations that lead to the inner dialectic. One might ask: if the failure of the good that stems from its dialectical nature happens inadvertently because the good is intended as absolute, is it then not also a cognitive failure? In a certain sense it is, but a cognitive failure can be corrected whereas a false absolute cannot.

The idea of dialectics that will guide us in the following is based on Hegel's understanding of the term. We adopt some of his fundamental intuitions which are valid, we believe, beyond the more specific systematic structures of his thought. Dialectics is often represented in a simplified, schematic way, for example, as a sequence of thesis, antithesis, and synthesis. Such a schematic understanding makes it seem as if it were merely a technical matter and an almost mechanical procedure that forces ideas to unfold in a uniform way. But for Hegel, the essence and primary phenomenon of dialectics lie in the fact that antithetical structures emerge at all. Negativity, he states, "constitutes the *turning point* of the movement of the concept. It is the *simple point of the negative* self-*reference*, the innermost source of all activity, of living and spiritual self-movement; it is the dialectical soul which everything true possesses."[9] No concept or notion can be taken in an isolated, atomic way, as if its meaning were ever only the one particular thing to which it refers, as if it were "fixed."[10] On the contrary, concepts are connected to one another, "held together in organic unity"[11]: any conceptual reflection that starts with only one concept will be moved along to other concepts, merely by means of the implicit conceptual richness that each single notion contains. Negativity, therefore, does not mean that a given concept is simply negated, replaced by its antithesis or turned "into a nullity."[12] Negativity is "positive"[13] because it leads to new contents. It shows that any given concept can "prove[...] to be the other of itself"[14] so that its meaning eventually includes the aspects it was first meant to exclude. Terminologically, Hegel speaks of "determinate negation"[15] as the main logical operation that provides both the dissolution of a given, fixed position and the transition to a diverging, more inclusive concept which then leads to a wholly new position. As already said, we do not adopt his systematic intentions which make all dialectic come together in a totality of conceptual structures, or an "absolute idea." We rather take dialectics as a procedural phenomenon, as the never-ending "self-movement" of conceptual positions, which in our case means that the field of morality is organized as a series of theoretical alternatives which all contain their own negativity and can be transformed into one another by means of "determinate negation."

Some might be tempted to object: why bother? If the dialectic is inevitable, we can adopt whatever position we wish. Being a false absolute does not turn the good into evil. But still, the fact that each determination of the good is dialectical means that each can be replaced by another. An agent cannot want this as long as their desire for the good is genuine. On the level of moral theories, the fact that one theory can be replaced by another creates a lack of unity and may lead to skepticism and relativism. If we realize that all forms of the good are replaceable by others, we may lose confidence and interest in morality altogether.

Recent literature has also paid attention to the failure of morality and identifies it in various forms. One line of thought describes morality as a pragmatic, though fictional construct, as a "myth."[16] Some proponents of this position endorse a form of "abolitionism" with respect to moral obligations; others suggest choosing "amorality."[17] Another line of thought assumes that agents inevitably fail moral demands, which is evident, presumably, in unsolvable moral dilemmas. Moral obligations are then often described as "over-demanding."[18] For all these approaches, the failing of morality implies the abandoning, or at least a far-reaching loss, of the validity of moral demands. Our analysis follows a rather different direction. We think of morality as a real and irreducible phenomenon that cannot be taken as a construct. Neither do we believe that moral obligations represent an external, unachievable standard. We could say that the approaches mentioned here diagnose the failing of morality from without, whereas our approach diagnoses it from within. For us, being moral means to be caught in contradictions, but these contradictions do not imply that morality's claims are fundamentally meaningless or impossible to adopt. Morality, if genuine, is the way in which humans desire the absolute good. Humans cannot not be moral, even if they fail at being so. We have to be aware, therefore, that not all theories of the failure of morality amount to the same.

Rescue Attempts

In the last case, the agent acknowledges the dialectical structures that determine the good. The failure has become explicit for them. At the same time, they hold on to their desire of being good and strive to achieve the good despite its contradictions. There are several ways in which this can happen. Agents can either accept the dialectic and try to interpret it as a potential, as a stimulus for the creation of the good, or reject it, trying to compensate for the failure of morality through a new form of the good. We will analyze and explain at least some of these attempts in *Part Three* of our inquiry. Rescue attempts are foolish, but in a conscious, deliberate way, because they think that the moral good is worth the contradictions which their positions have to incur.

We will see that none of the attempts goes back to the standard model of strong moral theories. Examples of the standard model will be mentioned in the next chapter. Strong moral theories assume that an absolute good can be reached through the appropriate use of human abilities. On the contrary, attitudes such as idealism, responsibility, and forgiveness, which we will describe in *Part Three*, usually play no role in standard theories, not only because they cannot be generalized, but also because dialectical structures are obvious in them. One forgives what can and should not be forgiven, one assumes responsibility for a specific issue but can only do so through a forceful intervention, and one develops an idealist anticipation of the good precisely because the world denies its reality. But before we can understand what this means, we have to see what strong moral theories typically try to achieve.

7

What Moral Theories Try to Achieve

Four Steps toward the Sufficiency of the Good

Preliminary Remarks

The dialectic of moral determinations that we are about to reconstruct in detail presupposes that the good is fully determined in the agent's decisions, attitudes, and actions, or that it is at least intended as fully determined. The dialectic would not occur and the good would not be failed if the latter were not supposed to be absolute. Our approach does not imply any specific understanding of the good. We assume the absolute good to have a guiding role both in the various moral determinations of agents and in the theories that are used to conceptualize the phenomenon of morality. With respect to the latter, we assume that it is the purpose of a moral theory to determine a form of the good as fully sufficient, even if the notion of the good is not employed explicitly in it. We refer here to what can be called classical, or strong moral theories. As already said, in *Part Three* we will discuss theories in which the dialectic of the good is acknowledged and no claim is made that an absolute good can be reached. But such theories are rather the exception, not the rule, we believe. The theories to which we refer in this part, *Part Two*, are the classical ones.

Our approach does not present yet another theory that would add to the series of already-existing theories but describes the target state that all strong moral theories pursue, in one way or another: a specific quality of the world of human practices, taken in its most undiminished and complete form, which agents both have reason to desire and are obliged to achieve. This approach calls for further explanation. We have to show in which sense moral theories, even if they do not use the concept in any explicit way, can be analyzed as bearing a structural equivalent to the absolute good. We have obviously shown this with respect to Plato but it is now time to gather evidence from other major theories in the field. We will mention the theories of Kant, Hume, and Mill to illustrate our claim. In doing so, we have to be briefer than we ideally should be insofar as each theory would deserve a more in-depth analysis than we can give. On the other hand, the theories are well-known and do not need to be explained at great length.

We have to point again at the historical nature of morality which makes it impossible to say what "all" or "most" moral theories do. We can only hope that the examples which we have chosen are paradigmatic of the existing tendencies in moral thought. We will start from a general outline as we believe that there are four steps through which each theory has to go in order to reach the sufficiency of the good.

Generality

Theories first have to establish the good insofar as it provides a reason to act. This requires the articulation of a general principle. Some principles are not only general but universal; however, we do not have to bother at this point with the difference between generality and universality. In the widest possible sense, "general" means that a principle is not limited in a way that would be arbitrary in the given case. A principle that demands, say, that women should not be harassed by men is limited because men can also harass other men, but the principle is not limited *in an arbitrary way* if it refers to every woman in relation to every man. Insofar as general principles are not limited, they are expressive of the absolute good, taken in the form of reason.

It is important to distinguish generality from generalization. Generalization means that a particular action, or a particular feature of actions, is serialized and repeated in all following instances in which it can occur. Generalizations help to see and establish patterns in human behavior, and they also allow for the introduction of standards into otherwise varied and unreliable practices. For example, in medical practices it is required by law that doctors ask patients for their consent before a procedure begins. The interaction between doctor and patient has been regulated to unfold based on a predictable pattern. However, generalizations can also be abused and may then lead to stereotypes and prejudices. It is not always easy to distinguish standards from stereotypes. Stereotypes, we can perhaps say, are the result of a merely descriptive use of generalizations—one assumes, for example, that all members of an ethnic group carry the same trait—whereas standards are the result of their normative use. Following a certain standard, doctors always *ought* to ask for consent, and patients always *ought* to be treated as if they were fully competent to make a medical decision, even if the circumstances of the given situation would occasionally warrant a different behavior.

In contrast to generalizations, generality is not a pattern but a focus. It says in which sense individual cases are to be approached, or what should be of concern in them. No standard is established this way and it is up to the agent using the general view to decide what it entails for the case at hand. Moral principles are often confused with generalizations but it is not difficult to show the difference between them. The principle "Honor your parents" requires children to treat their parents with consideration and respect but it does not say what exactly children should do. Generalized rules say precisely what should be done, for example, "Never disobey your parents" or "Never move away too far from your parents when they are old." Such rules are no moral principles because their concern is not to establish an overall relation of respect (as a focus) but to regulate behavior by establishing a pattern. From a moral point of view, one has to ask how parents are respected best, which may at times require or allow that one disobeys them or moves away from where they live. Moral principles establish what can be called a hierarchy of ends according to which particular actions are not important in and of themselves but only insofar as they reflect an overall concern. Generalizations are therefore also more important in conventional and legal normativity where the goal is to ensure that certain actions are repeatedly performed.

The distinction between generality and generalization aligns with the distinction between formal and classificatory notions, although the two pairs are not fully congruent. While generalizations always correspond to the classificatory use of notions, general notions can be both classificatory and formal. We should also add that there is an inherent connection between generality and generalization. The principle "Do not kill" implies that in all cases in which there is no apparent need we are not allowed to kill other human beings. The general principle entails a generalization of our behavior. But it would be absurd to assume that the generalization extends to cases of self-defense in which we should let ourselves be killed. The hierarchy of ends that underlies the principle not to kill does not apply if it is impossible to respect an attacker's life without losing one's own. While the general principle entails a certain generalization of behavior, this generalization is not strict. We should note, however, that the difference between generality and generalization is *not* that the former would allow for exceptions while the latter would not. Generalizations allow for deviations in special cases, too, and general principles, like the principle not to kill, are as strict as they can be. The difference rather lies in the way in which particular actions are conceived. While generalizations require specific actions to be performed, principles see actions are expressive of an overarching concern. We are not allowed to kill other human beings because we have to respect them in conducting their lives independently from us, not because it is strictly forbidden ever to be causally involved in ending another person's life.

We can call the assumption that moral principles are generalizations the application fallacy. The fallacy consists in assuming that moral principles would dictate a certain automatism of behavior. "Do not lie" would then mean: "Never ever lie." But obviously, if a moral theory could tell us what to do in each particular case, we would not need it. We could then stick to the standards of conventions and the law. Moral principles entail the self-determination of agents who have to decide in which way principles apply to a given situation. In choosing not to lie, the agent does not simply and automatically tell everything they know and think. Again, this does not mean that the following of principles cannot be strict. From a moral point of view, choosing not to lie means choosing to be truthful *in each situation*. The application fallacy may be due in part to a confusion between the normative and empirical interpretation of rules. Moral principles are normative, saying what ought to be done, and do not include statements about their empirical realization. Morality cannot guarantee that agents always act in moral ways. Another confusion may exist between morality and the law. Some may be tempted to take moral principles for another kind of law that tells agents what to do in each given case, but morality does no such thing. It only tells agents what to *consider* when they choose a course of action, which leaves the burden of choice on them.[1]

The misunderstanding of moral principles as generalizations also drives the problem of codification prominently raised by McDowell. According to him, general principles would be modeled following a "deductive paradigm" of practical reason[2] and so imply a machine-like, "mechanical application of the rules" in each case.[3] McDowell emphasized the "uncodifiability" of moral determinations which depend for him not on principles but on the cultivation of virtues, that is, on "being a certain kind of person."[4] This account of general theories has rightly been called a "caricature."[5] No serious approach to morality has ever made the claim that a strict codification of behavior would be possible, let alone desirable. General theories are able to reflect on the problem of application in various ways. One can say, for example, that "the implementation of a universalizable maxim, in specific historical and cultural circumstances, requires extensive reliance on forms of perception and intelligence."[6] On the other hand, McDowell is not completely wrong: if moral theories entail at least some generalization of behaviors, then it is hard to see how the application of principles would *not* be some sort of subsumption of particular cases under a general category. The strength of generalizations is precisely that they prove themselves useful in a variety of cases, which means that they can be applied repeatedly, not perhaps in a purely mechanical manner but with a certain degree of predictability. It may then seem a little disingenuous to claim that of course "extensive reliance on forms of perception and intelligence" would still be needed, as quoted above: identifying cases in everyday life to which a certain pattern of behavior can be applied, like the resolution never ever not to tell the truth, is not really hard and does not require much intelligence. The predictability of certain forms of behavior can even be considered a moral obligation, for example, in cases in which someone depends on our care. One can then always demand that agents are rigorous in their adherence to moral rules. Still, even in such cases morality is far from attempting to cement behavior in the way that McDowell suggests. He did not consider the fact that moral principles, eventually, are based on formal notions.

We have said that general principles are expressive of the good because they are not limited in ways that can be considered arbitrary. Although the principle "Honor your parents" is not strictly universal, given that not every human being is a parent or a child, it is general insofar as it applies to everyone who is a parent or a child. It also does not allow for some actions to be honoring and others not. We can interpret generality to entail consistency in the sense that all particular actions have to reflect an overarching concern. Principles do not say how consistency is achieved, for example, they do not say what it means to honor one's parents, but this is precisely the reason why they allow for consistency in all possible ways that are relevant for a given situation. Generalizations, instead, cannot be absolutely good because one generalized pattern of behavior can contradict another. In and of themselves, generalized accounts of actions do not imply that consistency is achieved or that it is even desired.

Method

In the second step, theories have to establish the good insofar as it is articulated or experienced by the individual. All moral theories need to identify what can be called a method in the etymological sense of the word: a way through which the agent becomes aware of moral principles and incorporates them in their determinations. While the first step stated the "what" of moral determinations, the second step states the "how." The need for this step is most obvious in cognitivist theories which have to indicate the specific rational procedure through which the agent grasps the required principles. But even theories that are based on emotions have to be methodical, in one way or another: experiences of sympathy or compassion do not just occur, and if they occur it is not always clear what they mean. At the very least, non-cognitivist theories have to state which kinds of situations are most conducive for the experience that is targeted and how the agent can become aware of their ability of making this experience. There also has to be a minimal cognitive content without which emotions and the like would hardly be determinate and relevant for moral theories. Emotions may already be transformed if one becomes aware of them, and they can also be cultivated to occur reliably in agents.

Absoluteness

In the third step, theories have to establish the good as absolute. One might think that the absoluteness of the good has already been achieved in the first step. But the articulation of general principles only states the particular content in and through which the good is realized, not whether it is in fact absolute. For this, an additional step is needed, which is twofold and involves both self-determination and the good. From the perspective of the former, moral theories have to ensure that the choice of principles corresponds to certain fundamental attitudes and abilities in the agent. Agents can find many reasons to act, but if their choices do not occur with a certain degree of necessity, then they have to see them as result of a merely individual stance. Such a stance can always be taken in other ways, by either the same individual or others, which eventually destroys their commitment to the good. (We can only assume "degrees of necessity" here, as there is no strict, logical necessity that links fundamental attitudes to actions.) Moral theories have to validate the agents' determinations and can only do so if these determinations can be shown as expression of a more or less general, that is, not individually limited condition of human agency. Cognitivist theories have to show, for example, that certain assumptions and forms of reasoning have to be adopted if agents take seriously what is implied in their practical intentions and thoughts, and non-cognitivist theories have to state certain emotions and experiences as typical and appropriate in practical matters. Otherwise, what would be the significance of these experiences or these forms of reasoning, and how could one be able to say that agents ought to engage in them? We do not have to assume, however, that the account of the conditions of human agency has to be elaborated to become a full anthropological theory. Moral theories only have to state what is necessary for the articulation of practical determinations, without having to consider all aspects of human nature.

From the perspective of the good, theories have to show how it can be achieved as fully sufficient. Many instances of the good can be chosen in any given case, especially if some general principle is involved, but for theories to fulfill their purpose the good has to be either an end in itself so that no other good is desired or needed beyond it, or provide the criterion for all other aspects of goodness that may be concerned.

Perpetuation

In the fourth step, theories have to establish the perpetuation of the good. Moral determinations cannot remain singular events but have to be consistent to an agent's overall orientation in life. We mentioned before that self-determination requires the consistency of one's preferences over time.[7] Theories can explain the perpetuation of determinations in various ways, through efforts at establishing one's moral character, methods of moral education, or the mutual support in the community of others. Not all theories include this step given that it is possible to make moral judgments without bothering about their perpetuation. However, singular judgments and decisions cannot really be sufficient without at least some outlook on their consistency over time. If one decision contradicts other decisions that the agent has made, or if the agent does not know whether they will make the same decision again in the future if the same situation occurs, then they have no reason to make the decision in the first place. It is an empiricist idea to think that moral judgments are made as isolated events and as reaction to particular empirical data, and not rather as a result of a reflective process that stands in a larger context of preferences, values, and ideas about oneself. Still, all we can say here is that moral theories have to consider the problem of perpetuation, not how far they have to go in doing so.

In the brief reconstruction of Kant's, Hume's, and Mill's approach, we will follow the steps from generality through method to absoluteness and finally to perpetuation. Insofar as all three theories claim to be sufficient for both the conceptualization and the realization of the good, we think of them as strong.

Strong Moral Theories

Kant: The Moral Will as Object of Itself

The notion of the good plays a substantial role in Immanuel Kant's approach to morality. His *Groundwork for the Metaphysics of Morals* famously opens with the claim that the "good will" is the only thing in the world that can be unrestrictedly good.[8] To achieve this quality, the will has to adopt principles that can be universalized and conceived as a law for all beings endowed with reason.[9] A universally determined will is not only the necessary but also the sufficient condition for an action to be moral. In adopting the moral law, reason "should need to presuppose only *itself*,"[10] and the will that follows reason can be strictly self-determined, focused only on its own principle and unaffected by external circumstances.[11] Kant points out that although the will is self-sufficient in the use of reason, it is not void but rather has an object in each case.[12] There cannot be a will that is not the will *of something*. Still, the will is not moral because of its object but because having a certain object, and having it in a universally valid way, is the moral thing to do.

Kant's answer to the question how the agent can achieve a universally determined will—the question of method in the widest possible sense—is necessarily simple. The moral law can be grasped through the mere exercise of reason; agents "become immediately conscious" of it.[13] Kant can therefore also say that "the moral law is given, as it were, as a fact of pure reason of which we are a priori conscious and which is apodictically certain."[14] The emphasis on the "fact of pure reason" mainly concerns the validity of the law and does not imply that other aspects of human nature are unimportant for Kant. He states, for example, that if one asks "in a human being ... the judge within him, ... the human being will pronounce a stern judgment upon himself."[15] The moral law entails a measure, or a standard, for the inner relation of a person to themselves. Agents also experience the moral law emotionally, even if the feeling that it causes is first and foremost a feeling of pain.[16] The moral law infringes on all personal "inclinations," "*strikes down* self-conceit altogether,"[17] and is so experienced as "humiliating."[18] But precisely because it has this effect, it also entails a positive "moral feeling": respect for the law.[19] The positive feeling toward the law arises out of the negative one; it is respect for both the dignity of the law and the effect that the law has on the agent in enabling them to be morally determined.

The universally determined will eventually amounts to what can be seen as absolute good. The argument in which this is shown is complex and cannot be reconstructed here. It is based on the second and third formulations of the categorical imperative. According to them, a being endowed with reason is an end in itself and so becomes the primary object and the realization of moral ideas.[20] It becomes its own primary object, to be precise. At the same time, a being endowed with reason finds themselves among others who share the same quality, in what Kant terms "the kingdom of ends." This way, the will, or practical reason, is taken as the good both subjectively and objectively; it is the absolute good both as activity that follows universally valid reasons and as the content and ultimate end of all practical pursuits, which is at the same time attributed to all others. The absolute good, in other words, is me insofar as I am and behave as a reasonable being together with all other reasonable beings.

The last point, the perpetuation of the good, is also based on the will. It entails the notion of character, which consists in the readiness to give oneself definite moral principles.[21] A character proves itself through the ways in which consistency is maintained, which for Kant requires first of all the agent's commitment to "truthfulness."[22]

Hume: The Mutual Enforcement of Moral Feelings

The notion of the good plays no foundational role in David Hume's theory and is rarely ever mentioned. Still, he recurrently states that morality's goal lies in the promotion of "the good of mankind."[23] Although such statements reflect no more than a common and generic use of the term, they show that an idea of the good, seen as the final end of human practice, is not wholly absent from his theory. The theory is naturalistic, based on an analysis of the presumably natural forces that drive moral commitments. At the same time, Hume believes that his approach yields "universal principles"[24] even if strict, logical universality cannot be achieved.[25] Like Kant, Hume establishes a formal criterion on which all particular moral qualities depend. This criterion lies in the fact that the qualities of decisions, attitudes, and actions produce a positive feeling and are approved by agents.[26]

What is approved, however, in each case cannot be stated a priori, which means that although moral validity can be *described* formally, it is not *determined* formally. The agent's positive attitude toward a particular moral quality is always limited to that case, unlike in Kant, where the agent is asked to look at their decision from a universal point of view. One could ask, therefore, whether the variety of personal experiences allows for the generalization that Hume intends. It could seem that his theory is no more than casuistic. But moral qualities, for Hume, are evident in social interaction, unlike for Kant who sees the agent in an isolated way, as decision-maker in a situation that requires the unique choice of the appropriate maxim. Hume assumes that a certain consensus, a common understanding of the value of actions and attitudes, exists among agents, which supports any theoretical generalization. The assumption of such a consensus leads to a certain conventionalism in his approach.[27]

The conventionalism also prevents the theory from falling into relativism. As an empiricist, Hume cannot define moral properties generally. The moral approbation does not rely on a particular quality in the object to which it relates. Rather, the object is revealed as bearing a moral quality through the agent's approbation.[28] This implies that all positive emotional experiences, whatever causes them, can be seen as equivalent to a moral judgment, which would be impossible if one could not expect humans to possess a shared normative framework.[29] For the same reason, Hume can believe to have a sufficient method for achieving moral action, which relies on his emotivism and the famous dichotomy between reason and sentiment as the only moving force.[30]

The structural equivalent to the idea of an absolute good lies in the assumption that sentiments and emotions can commonly and reliably embrace a moral content. Although all approving attitudes are technically moral, it is important that one set of attitudes is directed explicitly toward the good. Moral feelings are experienced as an emotion that humans regularly and willingly embrace; they lie in "the true interest of each individual."[31] Hume believes this to be the case because the emotion is inherently motivating: "the genuine charms of social virtues [can] create a mutual feeling of sympathy in humans."[32] However, from the perspective of the absolute good, it is also necessary that feelings have the requisite force and are *fully* sufficient for the good. For example, self-love could severely limit the ability of moral feelings to engage in mutual sympathy, which would require additional factors and methods to support these feelings.

The main argument that Hume presents relies on the belief that self-love is simply too limited a feeling to matter. He compares the community that sympathy creates "to the building of a vault, where individual stone would, of itself, fall to the ground; nor is the whole fabric supported but by the mutual assistance and combination of its corresponding parts."[33] We have to be aware that the argument made here is descriptive, not normative. The comparison to a vault does not mean that individuals have to submit to some vaguely determined greater good. The comparison rather means that *if* sympathy is cultivated, then a different type of social cooperation emerges, which can overcome the impulses of self-love. Self-love simply drops away if the strength of "mutual assistance" takes on. The absolute good emerges this way as successful cooperation of agents who can be trusted to have positive feelings toward one another. This argument can also be used to explain the perpetuation of moral sentiments, which for Hume help to secure the happiness of agents and lead to an inherently desirable "peace of mind."[34]

Mill: Moral Standard and Social Reform

For John Stuart Mill, the "greatest-happiness principle" is the "first principle" and "ultimate standard" of morality.[35] "Happiness," for him, is co-extensional to "utility" and "pleasure,"[36] and all three qualities can be taken as synonymous to the good.[37] The greatest-happiness principle is universal because happiness has to be "secured to all mankind; and not to them only, but, so far as the nature of things admits, to the whole sentient creation."[38] We can see in this statement the articulation of an absolute good, in the sense of a good that is not arbitrarily limited. Mill emphasizes its objective character: "As between his own happiness and that of others, utilitarianism requires [the agent] to be as strictly impartial as a disinterested and benevolent spectator."[39]

Utilitarianism is often categorized as a teleological theory which is then contrasted to deontological theories, such as Kant's. But the principle of happiness defines both the "end of human action" *and* the moral quality of "rules and precepts for human conduct."[40] It can be understood in both a teleological and a deontological sense. Mill calls the promotion of the greatest happiness of all a "duty."[41] This means that we have to change the order of our overview because method and absoluteness have to be discussed twice, from both a teleological and deontological point of view. We will see that in the teleological approach, the good is taken as a whole, while in the deontological approach, it is a sum.

If the absolute good is seen as a whole, then the subjective and objective dimensions of happiness coincide, so that the happiness of all concerned is also in the individual's own interest. For Mill, this coincidence can be reached through the appropriate organization of society.[42] "Education and opinion" can direct individuals to embrace "the good of the whole."[43] This means, however, that as a teleological theory, utilitarianism has no method in proper sense, that is, in the sense of a particular form of reasoning or feeling that would be at each individual's disposal. Moral self-determination is conditional, depending on whether "human affairs continue to improve."[44] It will be achieved, eventually, through a social transformation, which has to be developed in steps and over the course of time.[45] In its teleological dimension, the approach amounts to a theory of social and political reform, not a moral theory. A moral theory cannot and must not wait for society to improve. Also, the teleological approach only states an overall end without specifying the means through which it can be reached. The approach does not specify, for example, any particular abilities that humans should possess, except for a widely conceived "fellow feeling with the collective interests of mankind."[46]

Given that no ways to act are specified, it follows that the teleological approach is in no way *sufficient* to secure the absolute good. This leaves the question whether it can at least show that it is *necessary* for agents to pursue utility and happiness. Here too the theory is lacking. Mill suggests that any "consciousness of pleasure" related to actions counts as proof that happiness is the universal end of human practice: "There is in reality nothing desired except happiness."[47] It seems that with such a statement he conflates two meanings of happiness: as a formal concept, happiness is related to all actions (insofar as all practical intentions can be described as desire), but this does not mean that agents pursue the utilitarian good in the sense of a general and shared state of satisfaction. The teleological dimension of utilitarianism shows how important it is to consider method and absolute goodness as two separate elements of a moral theory. The conception of the latter does not imply a sufficient definition of the former.

In the deontological approach the good is the sum total of happiness in all sentient beings who are concerned. The agent is required to assess the outcome of their actions in a strictly impartial way, discounting their own interest in happiness. This seems impossible to do: if the standard of actions can only be stated in an objective way, it is subjectively contingent. From the interest in *my* happiness the interest in the happiness of *others* follows only partially. I need to make at least some others happy if I want to be happy myself, but how far does this go? One can of course say that the sum total of happiness is intrinsically more valuable than my isolated happiness but this does not make it a necessary goal for the individual agent.[48]

In fact, Mill conceives the absolute good only as a "standard," not as the "motive" of action.[49] "The great majority of actions are intended, not for the benefit of the world, but for that of individuals."[50] There are extraordinary cases of virtuous behavior in which the good of all is intended; for all others, the method consists in making sure that the good of others is not harmed.[51] Put in a positive manner, agents have to act so that their individual good is compatible, or in "harmony with the interest of the whole."[52] All that Mill can require from agents is that the absolute good is either not excluded through their actions or that it is at least indirectly intended. We see here again that a conception of the good does not need to translate itself into an effective method.

Mill also states that "in the golden rule of Jesus of Nazareth, we read the complete spirit of the ethics of utility."[53] This statement is somewhat surprising, given that the Golden Rule requires mutually benevolent behavior but no maximization of happiness. From this angle, utilitarianism appears not as an ethics but a meta-ethics that is concerned less with the rules for actions than with their justification. The happiness principle could then only be used to explain why deontological rules are valid but would again not serve as a method to determine their content.

Much more would need to be said, of course, for a proper analysis of Mill's approach, as well as of Hume's and Kant's approaches to moral philosophy. We only mentioned them as examples of what we call strong, or classical, moral theories so that we could illustrate the ways in which such theories are guided by the idea of an absolute good, or at least a structural equivalent to it. Our primary intent was not to discuss particular principles and their justification, or the lack thereof, or any specific argument on moral matters, but to indicate what theories do *as theories,* that is, as systematic attempts at a fully sufficient determination of the good as moral quality of decisions, attitudes, and actions. As said at the beginning of this chapter, the fact that the good is fully determined, or at least intended as such, in theories and actions is the starting point for the dialectics of moral determinations which we now have to examine a little closer.

8

The Dialectics of Generality

Generality

Preliminary Remarks

The present chapter, together with the following two, will explore the failing of morality and the good. As said before, agents do not have to be aware of this failing, and it may or may not have practical consequences for them. We aim at a formal structure that allows us to see the nature and scope of moral determinations, taken as such. The three chapters will be aligned according to the three main components that are necessary for a moral theory: generality of principles, method, and absoluteness (perpetuation will be left out). For each component, dialectical contradictions arise. The chapters will be subsumed under the titles of The Dialectics of Generality (Chapter 8), The Dialectics of Reason (Chapter 9), and The Dialectics of Inherent Goodness (Chapter 10).

As also said before, the failures follow a dialectical progression. Moral determinations are either not determined enough or too determined. In the case of the former, they remain empty and ineffective. In the case of the latter, they either turn into their opposite or become antagonistic, discriminating against other determinations which it would also be moral to have. We will find this dialectical progression in each chapter. Strictly speaking, we will find it twice in each chapter: within each component, the contradictions lead to the emergence of the opposite position. Generality turns into particularism, reason into the prevalence of non-cognitive factors, and inherent goodness into consequentialism. In these three opposite positions, the dialectic then repeats itself and is again threefold. That is, although an alternative, opposite position emerges in each case, the contradictions remain. In each component, the need arises for a solution that would overcome all contradictions. The possible solutions that emerge are virtue ethics, pragmatism, and the law, respectively. But as we will see, the solutions cannot overcome the dialectic either but rather lead right back to it. All approaches fail, even when or better: precisely when they try to present an alternative that does not fail. As already said, dialectics is for us no rigid logical scheme but the dynamic of "determinate negation," in Hegel's terms.[1] Through this dynamic, each notion and position comprises, all by itself, a negative moment which makes it possible for it to appear, eventually, as other than itself, or as the opposite it was initially meant to exclude.

Tracing the dialectic of moral theories presents us with a methodological challenge. The dialectic is rarely visible from within each determination. There is no immediate progression that forces anyone to abandon one position and adopt another. The progression becomes necessary only once the conceptual assumptions in each determination are further expressed. This implies in many cases that we have to add an external point of view. The external view may seem abstract and arbitrary, unrelated to what is positive and valuable in a particular determination. But as every determination can be further expressed, we believe that external points of view can never be avoided. Every determination stands in a network of conceptual and practical implications and can be interpreted as answer to the contradictions that emerge in other determinations. The fact that there is almost always controversy in the field of moral philosophy seems a sufficiently strong proof for this assumption.

The framework of dialectical structures that we present may also appear lifeless at first, but dialectical oppositions acquire real force in human life, in dialogues, controversies, and social struggles, and in the self-mortification of agents. The inner contradictions that we describe are not merely logical and epistemic, they rather bring divisiveness and strife to moral action. One can understand the contradictions as exclusions: as exclusion of what cannot be if something other is, or as awareness that something is not what it claims to be. Dialectics entails negativity, which can be painfully experienced in human life.

Why Start from Generality?

We begin with the good insofar as it is expressed in moral principles. Principles instantiate the good insofar as it provides a reason to act and they determine decisions, attitudes, and actions to be taken or performed in such-and-such way. We assume that all moral principles are general, but as said before, not all general principles are universal in proper sense.[2] One can make general claims regarding all human beings, all women, all refugees, all residents of Beijing, and so on. The only requirement is that the claim concerns all agents that are subsumed under the respective point of view. General principles express an absolute good insofar as the good that is articulated is not withheld arbitrarily from others but includes at least potentially all purposes, and all individuals, that are concerned.

One might object that general principles only express the absolute good if we take them to be moral, which would make our definition circular. Non-moral principles can also be general and it may seem that they also contain no arbitrary limitations. For example, I can say that I want to clean all shoes in my house. But in this case there is either no reason to do so and the use of the general idea is meaningless (why all shoes and not just the ones that were worn?) or there is a practical consideration that motivates me to do so, for example, the fact that the soil around the house has been contaminated for some time. This practical consideration does provide an arbitrary limitation because I do not think that all shoes should be clean, simply because they are shoes, but only a sub-group—shoes in our house—and only under a certain condition. The general statement that I make, "All shoes in my house," is not inclusive insofar as shoes are concerned (e.g., I do not want to clean my neighbor's shoes), whereas a general *moral* principle would consider all individuals to which it pertains. If we say, for example, "All homeless people should be given a home," we refer to a limited group of people compared to other groups; however, we refer to all members of this group in the same way, regardless of their reason for not having a home. We think of all of them as equally deserving. Our definition is therefore not circular and only general principles that contain no arbitrary limitation are moral.

General principles are expressive of the absolute good insofar as they are unconditional. There are obviously many factors that can influence a moral judgment on homeless people, which means that one's judgment is always conditioned in some way, by experience, empathy, feelings of justice, and the like. It is also likely that one has particular individuals in view in making such a judgment. But insofar as a moral principle is used in it, it is applied unconditionally to all homeless people because of the nature of their condition. In a moral judgment, particular persons are considered *because of the general principle*, even if the principle may initially be adopted because of an individual encounter with them. General principles also entail bindingness and the validity of moral judgments. Arbitrary limitations depend on contingent factors, which make bindingness impossible. If all homeless individuals deserve a certain treatment, then agents have the obligation to give it to all of them. If a principle were not binding for everyone at all times, it would not really be binding for anyone. One could then always ask: "Is this binding for me here and now?" Finally, general validity and bindingness do not stand in opposition to the idea of self-determination. Quite the opposite is the case: only because principles are unconditionally binding can they be grasped as reason for my self-determination. No one tells me to adopt them: if I do, then only because of my desire to be good. The act of moral self-determination does not depend on practical constraints or the requirements of conventions and the law; content-wise, it has no other reason than the good.

Perennial Ought

The dialectics of generality is set in motion once the claim can be made that moral principles are not determined enough. We have to be aware that there are at least two ways in which this claim can be articulated. The first way is based on a misunderstanding and cannot be relevant here. It states that moral principles can never be determined anyway. If this were true they would have no practical meaning, because a principle that is not in itself determined cannot serve as determination for a course of action. There simply could not be such a thing as a moral determination. The claim often arises in reaction to highly abstract principles. We can take, for example, the statement that is made in the first article of the *Universal Declaration of Human Rights*: "All human beings are born free and equal in dignity and rights." The statement disregards all differences among humans which may result from cultural practices, political conditions, geographical factors, and the like. It also seems to disregard the fact that equality "in dignity and rights" does not and perhaps will never exist to a uniform degree. One could then say that it provides no more than a vague generalization. Generalizations are always somewhat wrong because they cannot cover all individual cases that exist. It would no doubt be wonderful if all human beings were "born free and equal," but no one is obliged to adopt this idea given that the current state of the world seems to make a mockery of it. Likewise, one could say that no one is obliged to provide housing for all homeless people given that some of them might not even want it.

The misunderstanding that causes such statements, although common, should be obvious from our previous analyses. Moral principles do not result from the generalization of empirical properties but represent a formal property, for example, the property according to which each individual life has to be considered the same in dignity and freedom.[3] "Being born free" means that an individual's existence does not depend on the purposes of others. This property is always fully present in them and as determined as it can be. For moral purposes alone, agents are not allowed to take the adverse condition of the world as an argument against the validity of principles. One might object that the principle only implies that one looks at agents *as if they were born equal*, but this still means that the principle is treated as real in all relevant practical matters.

For the determinedness of principles, it is also irrelevant that agents often experience a great deal of uncertainty. Ross made the same point when he suggested the notion of "prima facie duties." *Prima facie* duties can be adopted even before the moral nature of an action is fully examined or clarified.[4] Such "duties at first sight" are "an objective fact involved in the nature of the situation."[5] Ross claims: "That an act, *qua* fulfilling a promise, or *qua* effecting a just distribution of good, or *qua* returning services rendered, … is *prima facie* right, is self-evident."[6] Even if there is an empirical limitation in the use of principles, insofar as one can never exclude that a situation, if examined as a whole, reveals more morally relevant features than initially assumed, the principles present themselves as determined enough to guide one's course of action.

The second way in which it is possible to claim that moral principles are indetermined assumes that indeterminedness results from the very structure of determinations. This assumption is most relevant here. Several arguments can be made in its regard. In the present section, we can start from the fact that moral principles state an obligation and present themselves as imperative to the agent. From a temporal perspective, they require consistency in future actions. For example, "Keep your promises" means "Act according to the promise that you made under all future circumstances, even if those circumstances could make you reconsider what you said that you would do." The meaning of obligations is non-trivial because it is never guaranteed that an agent acts in particular ways and retains consistency over time. Whoever claims that they always hold their promises can therefore be objected that they might not take promises all-too seriously. Holding promises requires effort and attention, which means that the agent has to recognize the obligation as being constantly ahead of them, demanding that they stay consistent even if new situations present themselves. With each new challenge that presents itself, the obligation can be considered as unfulfilled.

The meaning of obligations and imperatives is thus characterized by an inner contradiction. On the one hand, obligations are as determined as they can be: they instantiate the good insofar as it is translated into a principle for action. In being determined, principles entail that specific actions are performed and that the reality of practical matters corresponds to their content. Not acting according to a stated moral obligation can be considered a violation. On the other hand, principles have to be understood as *not* being fully and definitely instantiated in the future world of practice. Their very meaning entails that the agent embraces them in renewed acts of self-determination. If an agent says, for example, "I kept my promise, what else do you want?" the person to whom the promise was made can interpret this statement to mean that the agent does not want to have further obligations toward them. The relationship of trust that was established in making the promise can then appear to be broken. There may of course be cases in which all that mattered was that a particular promise was made. But in general, promises cannot be made as isolated events. They imply at least a certain degree of consistency beyond the point in time to which they refer. The same can be said for other principles. The obligations they entail require to be considered as a constant demand: one should *always* fulfill promises, *never* kill, *always* refrain from lying, etc. A one-time fulfillment of a moral obligation is in most cases no moral action at all. Agents, therefore, have to deny themselves the right to claim that they will ever have met their moral obligations.

Indeterminedness is for this reason an inherent condition of general moral principles. In adopting such a principle, the agent at the same time has to say "no" to themselves and assume that their decisions, attitudes, and actions are precisely not as good as they are intended to be. They are at least not yet as good as they should be and at risk of not being sufficiently good in the future. For moral reasons alone, one can never think to be moral enough. Obviously, it is not only the agent who denies themself the right to be considered fully moral. Such denials often arise from the outside as a criticism of moral claims. Others really like to point out the discrepancy between the principles we claim to follow and our actions, and they may reject our moral claims as unrealizable and empty. But such criticism from the outside is mostly random and malicious. It would not carry much weight if moral determinations could not also be criticized *from within*. The dialectics of generality means that moral principles result in contradictory structures through their own adoption. Others criticize us because they know that everyone can be criticized, including themselves, and we take their criticism to heart because we know that there is always an aspect under which it may be true, even if it feels unmotivated in a given case. For the misunderstanding that we discussed in the beginning of this section, no one acts morally anyway and there can be no contradiction because moral determinations do not really exist. Here, we see that contradictions are inevitable precisely because a well-determined form of the good is supposed to be realized.

The contradictory nature of the good that emerges at this point of view has been emphasized by Hegel. Hegel sees Kant as representative of the modern approach to morality. "The merit and exalted viewpoint of Kant's moral philosophy," he states, is to have captured the good in relation to the subjective will, as obligation.[7] This viewpoint forces morality to remain on the level of a "perennial *ought*," that is, on the level of imperatives whose very meaning is to remain unfulfilled.[8] The moral subject can never know whether their actions are sufficiently moral, and they must not even try to know because their focus should be on following the imperative instead on trying to confirm personal achievements. Moral self-determination has to be "thought of as sheer restless activity, which cannot yet arrive at something *that is*"[9] and so ends up as an "empty rhetoric of *duty for duty's sake*."[10] Hegel also claims that insofar as moral determinations project a practical reality without being able to assert its existence, they result in a hypocritical stance: not in the sense that moral principles are intentionally used in a deceptive way but because the necessary refusal of any practical reality makes moral determinations indistinguishable from the mere pretense at being moral.[11]

Exceptions

Another argument to show that moral determinations are not determined enough starts from the presumed necessity of exceptions. Ross states: "As almost all moralists except Kant are agreed, and as most plain men think, it is sometimes right to tell a lie or to break a promise."[12] This statement is echoed by Gert who writes that "no rational person favors any simple general rule being obeyed without exception."[13] Kant's own view is most prominently expressed in his short essay "On a Supposed Right to Lie from Philanthropy." For Kant, a person who has to ponder whether or not to tell the truth in a given situation is already a liar, "for he shows that he does not recognize truthfulness as a duty in itself but reserves for himself exceptions to a rule that by its essence does not admit of exceptions, since in doing so it would directly contradict itself."[14] If the duty not to lie would allow for exceptions, it would simply be no duty anymore. Kant famously denies the "right to lie" with the example of a murderer who comes after a friend hidden in one's house. Even in such a situation of threat, one cannot assume to have the right to lie about the whereabouts of one's friend. The position seems contra-intuitive, as Ross points out, and brought Kant the accusation of being a cold moral rigorist. His point is, however, subtler than it may seem: "Although indeed I do no wrong to him who unjustly compels me to make the statement if I falsify it, I nevertheless do wrong in the most essential part of my duty in general by such falsification."[15] The person who is asked about their friend is obviously forced to respond and the person forcing them cannot complain if they make a statement that tries to save their friend. Even Kant thinks that it would be natural to say whatever is needed in encountering a violent murderer.[16] The person who is asked cannot believe, however, that they are doing something that is morally good: even if they are forced to react and the lie would be excused by anyone who takes a serious look at the situation, their reaction violates a principle they otherwise would have to follow. At the very least one has to say that duty is violated *conceptually*. If exceptions were morally legitimate, then generality would only be an approximation, a rule of thumb devoid of bindingness, and the very notion of a duty would be undermined. Through the idea of a rightful exception, one ends up with two duties: the duty not to lie and the duty to lie when needed. Individuals can then "reserve for themselves exceptions," as Kant says, because they can decide which one of the two duties applies. This way, Kant's position remains consistent, while positions like Ross's and Gert's cannot explain how exceptions are to be reconciled with duties.

Ross and Gert present another example of what we call the application fallacy. This fallacy consists in assuming that moral principles dictate a certain automatism of behavior, so that "Do not lie" means "Never ever lie." Ross and Gert claim a right to exceptions because they think that moral obligations would otherwise lead to absurd results. But in so doing they fail precisely to distinguish between principles and their application. Lying remains in itself an immoral act, just as the killing of the murderer would be in itself immoral (unless it occurred in self-defense or for the defense of others). The one who lies cannot absolve themself through a presumed right but has to take the violation upon themself. If one thinks that acting immorally is the only way to resolve a really bad situation, then one should of course act this way, but one cannot think that there is a principle of exceptionality that helps one out. To take an example used before: as a doctor, I can have doubts about how I should communicate with a terminally ill patient who might experience great distress if all details of their situation are disclosed. I may eventually resort to lying out of sheer benevolence toward the patient but I cannot think that my lying is ever morally legitimate. If I end up deceiving the patient, and the case has a different outcome than foreseen, I cannot simply claim that I was entitled to lie. At the very least I have to admit that I violated a duty because I felt forced to do so in the face of another person's distress. Mistakes made out of benevolence are still mistakes.

Still, the idea that principles should allow for exceptions is not without any validity. The idea is eventually a symptom of the inherent indeterminedness of principles. If one can never claim one's obligations to be fulfilled, then the application of moral principles is always somewhat insecure. For the agent, it may not be clear which principle needs to be applied to a given situation and whether there is more than one principle that pertains. Perhaps the duty that one follows is indeed too rigorous and needs to be balanced by greater concern for the well-being of others. As before, we believe that the problem of application is produced by moral determinations themselves: insofar as morality entails determined behavior, it creates the possibility of behavior being determined otherwise than it is. And if my behavior *can* be determined otherwise, *should* it then not be determined in other ways? If I assume that the moral principles which I follow will never force me to make an exception, I might not take them seriously enough. On the other hand, if I do in fact assume that an exception will have to be made, I have not taken them seriously either. The idea of exceptions is the somewhat confused expression of an inner contradiction that each determination can face in its practical realization.

Arbitrary Limitations

A contradiction is something that ought not to be. It entails the impulse to be overcome. Following this impulse, one may claim that the indeterminedness described before does not exist and that moral principles are in reality always fully determined in an agent's decisions, attitudes, and actions. Principles are general and at the same time content-bearing and concrete, one can say. Claims like these inadvertently produce yet another contradiction, one that arises from the fact that principles are not only determined but actually too determined. Are moral ideas, if they are fully determined, really still general and not rather particular, limited to particular groups and applications? Generality can appear to have vanished into concreteness, which then means that there is reason to suspect it as a veiled form of particularism. For example, Kant's second formula of the categorical imperative cannot express the absolute good if it sees agents as end in themselves only because they have reason. The imperative seems to disregard other qualities that give them moral worth. Who says that one could not also derive moral principles from the vulnerability of agents, or their gendered nature, instead of the capability of reason? Why prefer one over the other? And if there are several competing general principles, none can be truly general but all appear in one way or another limited, so that choosing one over the other is always an arbitrary decision.

The contradiction mentioned here may need some explanation. There is obviously nothing contradictory in assuming general principles for a particular group. As said before, one can use principles related to all residents of Beijing, all newborns, all males, etc. What makes the principles moral is the fact that they are not arbitrarily limited within that group. Moral principles are indeed both general *and* concrete, and there is no contradiction from this formal point of view. The contradiction only arises once all that is contained in the meaning of the principle is made explicit and expressed. One then begins to see that although generality is embedded in concreteness, it cannot be limited to it: insofar as a principle is general, it can always become more general. One can ask for further clarifications and eventually justifications of the principle that is used. All residents of Beijing deserve to be protected from air pollution, but why only residents from this city and not also from others? And why are residents of Beijing entitled to clean air: because they live in Beijing or because they are citizens of a country that has obligations toward them? Or because they are humans beings? The more we make explicit what is contained in a principle, the more we face the difficulty of stating it either in the outmost general way—"All human beings deserve clean air"—which makes the principle indetermined again, or to restrict it to a particular group: "My main concern is with Beijing's residents here." The concreteness can then only be saved at the price of a limitation that appears as arbitrary compared to the generality of the principle itself. The contradiction that arises is so again an inner one, produced by the very assumptions implied in moral principles: we have to deny ourselves the right to say that we have applied the principles as generally as they would need to be applied if we followed the implications of their meaning. There is nothing wrong with Kant's idea of placing moral worth in reason, and yet we suspect that the reliance on reason misses some important moral aspects that cannot be captured by reason alone.[17]

Another example of general rules that are too determined can be found in Gert's approach to morality. Morality, for him, is "an informal public system that applies to all rational persons."[18] Gert assumes the existence of a "common morality" that is widely, if not universally, followed, even without the support of a moral theory. In fact, moral theories should first of all find justification for common morality.[19] He suggests a list of ten "justified general moral rules," which go from "Do not kill" to "Do not cheat" and "Obey the law."[20] Referring to this list of rules, he says: "These rules have just the content that everyone takes the justified general moral rules to have. The perennial debate between formalists and those who demand content can now be seen to be like most other debates in philosophy: both lacked an adequate account of some more basic concepts."[21] However, the notion of a common morality is an untenable hybrid: it combines a formal account of rationality with an empirical assumption about shared human beliefs. We can show this in relation to another rule that is listed in the approach: "Do not cause pain." Gert states: "All rational persons would take the same attitude toward the rule 'Do not cause pain.' I use the term 'pain' to include not only physical pain but also all kinds of mental suffering, such as anxiety, disgust, displeasure, and sadness."[22] Following this explanation, the rule is on the one hand too determined. Pain is an inevitable element of many activities, such as sports that involve bodily contact. If no rational person could accept suffering pain, no student would ever have to take an exam. If taken seriously, the rule entails an arbitrary limitation of human practices. One could try to work around this limitation by referring to "unjustified pain," but this would only beg the question. On the other hand, the rule can be made plausible if it is stated in a more general way, for example, as rule not to impair the well-being of agents. But in this case it is again indetermined because it is not clear how well-being is defined in relation to each individual agent. The assumption of a content-laden and yet general rule clearly fails in this case.

Negativity

From the claim that moral determinations can be too determined to achieve an absolute good it is only a small step to the next position in the dialectics of generality. If determinations are arbitrarily limited, then they can also be antagonistic toward other determinations which it would be moral to adopt. One can suspect that general principles not only disregard other moral qualities but downright discriminate against them. Moral determinations can be seen to entail non-moral effects, which are again a contradiction that arises from within, as an accusation of moral determinations for equally moral reasons. In its most classical form, the idea that moral determinations are antagonistic can be found in the sophist conception of justice. In the *Republic*, Glaucon describes this conception as follows:

> This, then, is the genesis and being of justice; it is a mean between what is best – doing injustice without paying the penalty – and what is worst – suffering injustice without being able to avenge oneself. The just is in the middle between these two, cared for not because it is good but because it is honored due to a want of vigor in doing injustice.[23]

For the sophists, justice and all related moral ideas are mere means to achieve social control, favored by those who are unable to subdue others and strive for their greatest personal advantage. At the first glance, the sophist conception of justice seems naturalistic, based entirely on psychological or biological assumptions about human nature. But the psychology that it involves is quite rudimentary. The sophist position rather stems from the assumption of rational preferences and the good that humans pursue. It comprises a moral theory about the justified use of self-interest.

In modern times, the most prominent example of such a theory can be found in Nietzsche's distinction between master and slave morality. Master morality, according to him, is based on the "pride in yourself," it rejects the obligation to be selfless and consider others as equal. Masters have "duties only towards their own kind." Slave morality, in turn, is a set of ideas needed by those who cannot protect themselves in other ways, "people who were violated, oppressed, suffering, unfree, exhausted, and unsure of themselves."[24] All moral theories in proper sense, that is, all theories that involve general principles and a more or less egalitarian conception of agents, result from the impulse of slave morality and represent but an ideology of the oppressed.

For the purpose of our analysis, it is not important whether there is really a desire for social control hidden in the use of moral principles. Moral principles can clearly be abused in many ways, but the psychological motives for such an abuse are of no interest to us. We rather assume that the positions mentioned here reveal another aspect in the dialectic of general principles. Nietzsche's claim that general moral ideas are a product of the resentment of the oppressed toward the more powerful concerns the very structure of moral determinations, not only the psyche of agents. Slave morality entails a fundamental distinction between actions as a vehicle of self-realization and actions as reactions to the challenges presented by others. It is essentially negative, created in contrast to master morality, which in turn is positive, based on the spontaneity of agents and a "triumphant affirmation of itself." As the "imaginary revenge" of someone who cannot act otherwise in reality,[25] slave morality articulates the good only insofar as it involves the protection of agents from harm and the restriction imposed on others who are believed to be obligated to follow general rules. The dichotomy of master and slave morality does therefore not lead to a moral pluralism, as it is sometimes assumed, but to a competition between, and mutual exclusion of, the two moralities, because each one is defined in opposition to the other.[26] Or, to be more precise: while each morality can be adopted with unrestricted validity if the respective determinations are taken in an isolated manner, further analysis reveals that their meaning is based on what they exclude. Following Nietzsche's example, general moral principles discriminate against attitudes that pursue self-realization as a legitimate expression of individual life.

From the perspective of our analysis, we can take this to mean that moral determinations fail the good because they are adopted as a reaction against the injustice and aggressiveness that is experienced in human practices. Insofar as they are meant to counter the negative, moral determinations can appear negative themselves, as a mere tool in the fight against the lack of goodness in the world, which is unable to realize an absolute good of its own. There are many ways in which agents can feel that their determinations are determined by what they exclude. Emancipatory discourses constantly face the suspicion of being merely destructive, unable to achieve a positive relationship between all members of society. General moral determinations, as justified as they may be, may seem to destroy the forms of good that are sedimented in traditions, institutions, and social practices. The reflection they entail dissolves the integrity of habits and actions that would otherwise be performed without questioning. Our point is here obviously not that emancipatory discourses are indeed merely destructive and should therefore be avoided. We are also far from accepting Nietzsche's pejorative and classist characterization of general moralities as "slave" morality. The point is rather that the accusation of destructiveness can arise because the structure of moral determinations contains at least implicitly a negative dimension, which then can be further expressed. The suspicion of negativity arises again out of morality itself, not from the outside. Even if moral claims are made in an innocuous way ("I only want to say that in this situation it may be better to do x."), they still deny existing practices the privilege to be fully justified. The agent can find themselves involved in a dialectic that makes the good they strive to achieve appear as antagonistic despite their best intentions. At least it is always possible to ask whether their moral determination may have such non-moral effects.

Another way in which morality can be seen as antagonistic stems from the fact that it is needed. General principles can be used to protect others and establish the respect that we owe them. However, this implies that protection is in fact lacking and that respect is not given as deserved. One can then suspect that moral principles express a position of asymmetry between those who adopt them and the others who are meant to be included in the good. The statement: "I respect your dignity" can then be countered by asking: "Why do you think that you need to tell me *that*?" Moral determinations can be perceived as humiliating: agents may not want others to think that they have a moral obligation toward them, as they may not want to be the recipient of good intentions. Treating others morally can turn into a discriminatory stance because general principles entail a categorization of others which may not correspond to their normative self-image.

Particularism

The Need for a Particularist Position

The inherent contradictions in the use of general principles that we have shown can lead to the adoption of an anti-generalist approach. A particularist or contextualist form of morality can seem to provide an alternative that avoids both the vagueness and over-determination of general principles. For such a form of morality, the good would ever only be individual, realized and expressed in the attitudes and abilities of particular agents, their relation toward others, and in shared practices. (In the following, we will prefer the term "particularism" over "contextualism." While every contextualism is a form of particularism, the latter can also refer to individual agents, independent of any context to which they belong, and is so the wider term.) It is important to distinguish particularism as it appears now in the dialectics of generality from the fragmentarianism that we encountered and refuted in *Part One* of this inquiry.[27] Fragmentarianism claims that there can be no absolute good because all forms of the good are in one way or another limited. Particularism, instead, assumes the existence of the good by claiming that it occurs exclusively in specific abilities, individual actions, and practical contexts. In this sense, particularism emerges as the truth of general principles. If general principles can be applied to particular situations, then their content has to be included in the elements of these situations. We have to assume that general principles express the meaning of particular practices and determine their moral content. That is, although principles are general, we have to believe that they are able to capture at least some of the circumstances of a given situation. Obviously, particular circumstances exist independent of and prior to the use of general principles. They must certainly not be forced into a conceptual scheme. But if general principles apply to them, then we can eventually reverse the point of view and say that it is wrong to assume that principles are "applied" to situations. Principles express the content of particular practices only because these practices invite them, so to speak. Principles would have no meaning if their content would not already be present in the situation at hand, if only in an implicit way. The conceptual content of principles is only the abstract version of a practical constellation in which agents are always already involved. Particularist approaches can so claim to capture a more fundamental, more authentic good than approaches based on general principles.

Compared to the fragmentarian position, the position that emerges in this way is not self-refuting because it does not force us to deny the validity of general principles. It only indicates the inevitable dialectic that comes with their use: principles can always be suspected to have left out a genuine reality of human life because nothing that is relevant for humans occurs in a general way. We can call this the paradox of generality: principles are needed to express the good that can possibly exist in a given situation and that presents itself as an obligation to agents. Principles overcome the pain that stems from all practical and individual limitations and acknowledge the good that agents deserve and can strive to achieve. But the good that principles entail only replaces the pain; it cannot make it not exist. The best thing would be not to need general moral principles at all, which is impossible because the world is not simply good as it is. What makes general morality necessary is therefore the same thing that prevents it from reaching its goal. This also means that particularism results from a *moral* criticism of principles: if general principles have their truth in particular circumstances, then admitting one's particular point of view is in itself a moral obligation.

The fact that a moral argument against the use of general theories can arise from within these theories themselves has been articulated most emphatically by Nietzsche. With respect to the universal commands of Christianity, he states: "After Christian truthfulness has drawn one inference after another, it must end by drawing its most striking inference, its inference *against* itself." Christianity is "*as a dogma* was destroyed by its own morality."[28] Nietzsche is one of the clearest proponents of a particularist theory of human action: "At bottom, all our actions are incomparably and utterly personal, unique, and boundlessly individual, there is no doubt; but as soon as we translate them into consciousness, *they no longer seem to be* …"[29] The moral quality of decisions, attitudes, and actions can consequently also only be conceived in an individual way: "Our visible moral qualities, and especially those that we *believe* to be visible, take their course; and the invisible ones, which have the same names but are neither ornaments nor weapons with regard to others, *also take their course*: probably a totally different one."[30] Truly individual virtues exist only for the respective agent, whereas virtues that correspond to general moral principles are the result of an external perspective that follows social conformity and constraint. Nietzsche rejects all forms of morality that are based on the obligation of selflessness[31] and suggests a positive, self-elevating form of morality that stands in contrast to approaches based on prohibitions.[32] Still, whatever form of morality is adopted by agents, authentic as it may be, it is important not to consider it as yet another, generalizable position, because this would turn one's individual virtue again into a socially oriented one: "Our genuine honesty, we free spirits, – let us make sure that it does not become our vanity, our pomp and finery, our limitation, our stupidity!"[33] A particularist morality requires first of all the distance to oneself, or better: the distance of one's individual to one's social self: "Solitude is a virtue for us … Somewhere, sometime, every community makes people – 'base.'"[34]

A similar distinction between the individual and social self can be found in Lévinas's account of the origin of ethics. For Lévinas, true individuality is encountered in the communicative function of language. Language entails "the transcendence, radical separation, the strangeness of the interlocutors."[35] Only humans can be absolutely foreign to each other, and the separation that appears precisely in their attempt at communicating escapes "every typology, to every genus, to every characterology, to every classification."[36] That is, although language uses general terms, no such term captures the individual nature of the interlocutors, even if their separation made the use of language necessary in the first place. The same experience can be made through the encounter with the face of others. For Lévinas, the face is nothing that is simply seen, it is no object that lies at the disposition of the subject's gaze. The face rather addresses and challenges the perceiving subject: "There is here a relation not with a very great resistance, but with something that is absolutely *other*: the resistance of what has no resistance—the ethical resistance."[37] The resistance of a face is no matter of physical force. The face, like the whole person, is vulnerable and can be injured in many ways. The resistance that it offers is intangible: in the "nudity and destitution" that appears in the other person's face lies the origin of all morality, whose first obligation is not to kill.[38] General principles cannot substitute but in turn rely on the impact that the face provides, which necessarily presents itself in a singular and unique event.

The encounter with others is also the basis for a morality that focuses on responsibility and care. Gilligan states: "While the ethic of rights is a manifestation of equal respect, balancing the claims of other and self, the ethic of responsibility rests on an understanding that gives rise to compassion and care."[39] Gilligan's approach makes it necessary to consider each person individually and respond to their unique and particular needs. General principles, insofar as they require treating every agent as the same, cannot provide "the recognition of the reality of human pain and suffering,"[40] and they certainly cannot lead to an attitude of compassion that would give one person more attention than another. The emphasis on responsibility also implies that agents cannot *not* respond to the other's needs. Human beings are connected, which means "that the self and other are interdependent and that life, however valuable in itself can only be sustained by care in relationships."[41] The ethics of responsibility and care has first been developed from a feminist point of view, but the "interdependence" of self and other is given in other inter-personal contexts as well, between co-workers, roommates, doctors and patients, guests and hosts, etc. Other particularist approaches to morality have therefore taken the form of a social and political philosophy but we cannot discuss them here.[42]

False Certainty

Particularist approaches face the same dialectic that emerges for general principles. Positions can first be seen to be not determined enough. It might be unclear, however, why this is the case: if anything, particularist positions are closer to the lived experience of agents than general ones. But from the fact that one responds to the suffering of others it does not follow what should be done for them in each case. Is it our responsibility to work as much as possible for the benefit and well-being of others, or should we be anxious not to interfere with their autonomy, even if this means that they don't benefit as much as they could? There is undoubtedly such a thing as caring too much for others. Proponents of a particularist approach would probably say that the situations of life in which we find ourselves connected to others determine what we should do. The needs of others are obvious to us in each case. But this argument would only prove our point: the particularist position, in and of itself, does not determine a specific course of action. It only determines the overall attitude toward others but does not provide a criterion for the choice of actions.

The point that is made here is by no means formalistic, we should add. If it is important to develop a certain attitude toward others, then it is also important to prove the reality of this attitude through particular actions that are performed. Without practical consequences there is no value in a caring attitude, and the attitude might not even really exist. The fact that particularist approaches do not provide a criterion for actions is therefore first and foremost a moral concern: it is unclear whether the position is able to determine human practices as an instance of the good.

Particularist positions also rely on the quasi-instinctual ability of agents to sense what is appropriate in each case. They assume that agents simply know how to determine their actions as good whenever there is need. This means that particularist approaches are indetermined also insofar as the actual determination of the good occurs beyond their control. Strictly speaking, the approach makes itself unnecessary: if agents care for the suffering of others, they do so because of particular circumstances, not because they endorse, say, an "ethics of care." The approach also claims a false certainty, as it cannot guarantee that we react to such circumstances at all, or that our reaction is even a moral one. For Lévinas, the basic moral phenomenon lies in the encounter with the face of a particular other, and yet hate is as much a reaction to others than care. For Nietzsche, radical individuality eventually exists in a realm beyond moral constraints.

Hidden Generality

Like before, the indeterminedness of the position needs to be overcome. One way to do so is to claim that particularist positions can be adopted in a fully determined form. I can open myself to the radical individuality of my existence and find out which actions are most appropriate for it, and I can open myself to the suffering of others, recognizing them in their needs and choosing the requisite course of actions. Who can say, after all, that a caring attitude cannot really prove itself through actions? By acknowledging my connectedness to others, I make the relations that I entertain with others stronger and more effective, which means that I find and foster the determinedness of moral contents in the particular circumstances of my life. And if everyone joined me in this effort, would our mutual relationships then not become sufficiently good? Nothing seems to make it impossible for a particularist approach to lead to a good that is as complete as it can be in a given situation.

But despite the plausibility of such claims, particularist positions do not escape the dialectic of moral determinations. While general principles can be accused of being in reality particular, particularist approaches can be described as making general claims. It is impossible to say why one should care about others without using a conceptual scheme that could also be applied to others, and potentially to everyone. Otherwise, care and the experience of others would be random and hardly evidence of a moral attitude. We can say that if particularist principles are determined at all, they are actually too determined and turn into their opposite: the particularist position can be expressed as bearing a generalizable meaning and as articulating yet another general principle in the guise of a concern for particular others. All moral concepts are general, even the ones that are used in a particularist way.

The point made here also follows from the distinction between formal and classificatory notions. If general principles were classificatory, they would subsume every individual under a given criterion and thereby reduce their very individuality. The idea that particularist approaches are opposed to positions based on general principles stems from the erroneous assumption that principles are classificatory. Following this assumption, particularist approaches have the task of saving the authenticity of individual existence from the alienating effect of general moral ideas. (As said before, such assumptions fall into what we have called the application fallacy.)[43] Principles, however, are formal, which means that they can be applied to everyone without reducing their individual nature. Care, for example, means that one cares for everyone as they need to be cared for. The principle that it entails is general *and* particular at the same time. The same is true for all moral principles: whoever says "Do not kill" assumes that *no single individual* should be killed, not that *no one in general* should be killed. There is no contradiction between general principles and their applications to unique others. Whatever moral attitude can be developed in relation to one particular person can also be developed in relation to another. It would not only contradict the conceptual content of one's attitude but also be downright immoral if one were to claim that there is only this one particular person who must not be killed while all others presumably can.

Similar arguments can be used in relation to the moral particularism suggested by Dancy. According to him, "morality has no need for principles at all."[44] Moral judgments and distinctions function perfectly well without them. Judgments are based on what he calls "holism," which means that "a feature that is a reason in one case may be no reason at all, or an opposite reason, in another."[45] Generality, or "generalism," in his terms, presupposes instead a form of "atomism" according to which one particular reason can hold across different cases.[46] The holism of reason makes it possible to decide the moral quality of each particular case, without the need of involving a higher, more general moral concept and a more fundamental method of justification. This approach is clearly also based on a classificatory understanding of moral terms. Dancy seems to understand principles as standards that prescribe the very same reason to act, and therefore the very same action, throughout a variety of situations. Such a conception is obviously wrong because actions that would follow the same exact reason would not even be actions in proper sense but mere repetitions. The form of particularism that he suggests refutes "generalism" only insofar as the latter implies the application fallacy, that is, it only refutes a wrong idea of generality, not generality as such.

A more detailed reading of the approach can show why this is the case. Insofar as Dancy admits what he calls "default reason," he shows that particularism can in fact not exclude *all* generality. A "default reason" is "reason-giving unless something prevents it from being so."[47] As an example he mentions: "If an action is just, that is always a reason in favour of doing it."[48] Dancy is quick to add that this sort of reason does not imply, say, the existence of a "true principle of justice": it only means that justice usually provides a plausible reason to act and can so be invoked in a variety of situations.[49] Evidently, he does not go all the way to argue for casuistry and some sort of radical particularity, which would also be difficult based on his assumption that there is such a thing as acting according to reasons. In other passages, he even admits to "the possibility of some invariant reasons."[50] Invariant reasons are truly atomistic, according to his terminology, and stay the same in all contexts to which they are applied. As an "obvious" example he mentions the "causing of gratuitous pain on unwilling victims."[51] This raises the question: if "default reasons" provide no genuine principles, are at least the "invariant reasons" capable of doing so? The fact that inflicting "gratuitous pain" is universally impermissible for Dancy seems to indicate that he could also accept other, related principles, such as the autonomy and dignity of humans. But he denies that, stating that the assumption of one invariant reason does not lead to "a complete set" of moral principles.[52] For him, it remains an exception in the field of moral judgments, which is otherwise structured in a holistic way. Dancy seems to suggest that the assumption of some genuine moral principles would force one to accept the existence of a whole scholastic system of principles, which would then determine moral thinking one time for all. But no such system needs to exist in order to assume the existence of principles. Dancy again only refutes a wrong idea of generality, a hyper-generality, so to speak, which is a straw-man. The form of particularism that he suggests can therefore offer no real alternative to the assumption of general moral principles and rules.

Exclusion

Against the possibility of converting particularist approaches back into general ones, one might want to hold on to the particularist position and declare it to be fully determined precisely in its particularist nature. If that happens, particularist approaches become antagonistic and discriminate both against the self and others. With respect to the self, discrimination ensues if the fixation on particular others, on care and responsibility, stands against the legitimate interest in the well-being of oneself. The dialectic that emerges at this point can be expressed as dichotomy of egoism and altruism: if altruism is the sole criterion to be morally good, then egoism needs to be overcome and broken. Instead of a comprehensive good one only posits the good of others and suppresses the good that the subject can achieve. It is obvious that such a position is self-refuting: if I am not worthy to be included in the good of others, then why should the others be worthy to be included in mine? The idea of altruism assigns a moral privilege to others that cannot be justified, or that can only be justified if self-interested behavior were in general morally illegitimate, which cannot be justified either. Altruism, as the opposite of egoism, is just a different form of the latter; it is the egoism of the others, one could say. The absolute good, on the contrary, includes the legitimate purposes both of the self and others and does not require the former to be sacrificed.

With respect to others, particularist approaches can easily fall into an exclusionary preference of certain individuals and groups. The care that specific others need and deserve can come at the detriment of more remote others who would need and deserve at least comparable attention. Particularism derives its moral value from a presumed need for protection, but all need for protection implies that there is reason to treat one or more individuals in a preferential way. We should be careful not to trivialize this point. It is of course always necessary to prefer some individuals over others; otherwise, it would be impossible to act. But for particularist approaches, a less trivial condition holds: the good is attainable for them not while but *because* others are excluded. Some of the purposes of others need to be seen as indifferent, because if they were not there could be no particular good. If no differences between the good of various persons or groups could be made, the approach would be general, not particularist. It is necessary then that each particularist approach involves a certain trade-off between different instances of the good. One can even suspect that the particular good is based less on a genuine experience of the suffering of others than on the interest to realize the good that is most attainable and most promising for the agent. "I can only care for one person, and that is all that I will do." Care can so turn into a calculating stance toward the purposes of others. It is important to note that this stance does not need to be reflected in a motivational disposition of the agent. We do not have to assume that all agents whose main focus is care have this focus only because they are secretly calculating their best chances at some practical success. Our point is valid on the level of concepts alone: any particularist approach is conceptually an anti-generalist approach, which means that it implicitly denies the interest of those who would be covered under a broader, general point of view. In other words, insofar as general principles are never logically impossible, particularist approaches *have to* deny them, which is one way of acknowledging their significance for one's decision.

One might ask why a trade-off or a calculating stance is necessarily discriminatory. It could also be the result of a quantitative failing of the good, for example, if the agent has to decide between two possible courses of action. But the trade-off mentioned here concerns different instances of the good, not different practical options. Insofar as one good is chosen over the other, the latter is suppressed as good. For example, in a situation of emergency only one of two patients may receive care in a hospital. It may be practically impossible to care for both. Still, whoever is not chosen can also say that their well-being was valued less. It is at least conceptually possible to see the choice as rejection of an instance of the good. That is, even if the hospital staff will not be blamed for choosing one patient over the other, one can never say that not being able to choose the other is morally good. The motivation of the agents does again not factor into the analysis here. What counts is that the very content of the action entails a discriminatory stance toward other contents. A determination based on a particular good cannot *not* be dialectical.

Summary

In sum, the dialectics of generality shows that there are two equally coherent and plausible but contradictory positions in morality: one position that claims general principles to be the main expression of the good and another position that emphasizes the contradiction between principles and the individually instantiated good. Moral practices and arguments cannot avoid involving general principles and yet any use of general principles drives one to acknowledge the particular conditions of the world of practice. Conversely, one can easily see the need for a particularist approach to morality but is then driven back to general principles if the conceptual content of one's actions is properly expressed. There is no point of view from which one could escape the contradictions. Moral determinations entail a permanent movement between generality and particularity, a tension which forces one to go back and forth between the two. Any reconciliation that moral theories could reach would only be illusionary. This back and forth will repeat itself in the discussion of theories in the following two chapters. It characterizes the field of morality as a whole, we believe.

Some might be tempted to take the perspective of this field in its entirety. They could then say that morality is precisely this, a dialectical web of arguments in which we always have to take one position and its opposite. If that is the case, then all one needs to do is add contradictions until a more coherent picture emerges, like a mosaic that acquires meaning as a whole despite the many disparate pieces of which it is composed. "I determine myself morally by adopting a general principle or a particularist perspective whenever I see fit, and sometimes I combine them for a richer and perhaps even more moral stance." But there can only ever be one moral determination if it is taken seriously. Adding determinations leads to a reduced, not to a richer moral stance. One can also not adopt the perspective of morality as a whole because morality only exists in specific determinations. There is no such thing as being moral in general. The dialectic is experienced from within moral determinations, once the decision for a specific position is made and the conceptual structure of that position begins to unfold.

Attempts at a Reconciliation: Ethical Life and Virtue Ethics

The history of moral thought offers many examples that can be seen as attempts at a reconciliation between particularist theories and approaches based on general principles. Contradictions are supposed not to exist and entail the need to be resolved. One can do so by ignoring them, by escaping to some higher point of view (as discussed at the end of the previous section), or by trying to argue that they can be overcome. The most prominent example for an attempt to do the latter can be found in Hegel who assumed that if moral obligations have meaning at all, they must be expressive of a reality of human practice that at least at some point actually exists: "The abstract good which merely *ought to be*, and an equally abstract subjectivity which merely *ought to be good* – ... have their opposite present *within them*, the good its actuality, and subjectivity ... the good."[53] If this is the case, then the relation between moral determinations and reality can eventually be turned around: one has to give up the idea that reality is unable to incorporate moral ideas and should on the contrary assume that it is morality which has failed to conceive of an adequate realization for itself. Obligations have to be re-interpreted as the imperfect articulations of a "living good,"[54] of a good that already exists. Hegel's term for this form of the good is "ethical life," *Sittlichkeit*. Ethical life is morality insofar as it "*has become the existing world*,"[55] an "objective sphere" that has a "fixed content" in laws and institutions.[56] In state, economy, and family moral obligations are incorporated into existing practices. The normative standards that guide behavior in these institutions realize the good concretely and effectively.

In Hegel's conception of ethical life, all general moral ideas are instantiated individually. I am a moral agent insofar as I am a mother, a citizen, a business person, a member of a political group, and the like. The normative standards, or "duties" in Hegel's words, that institutions require allow for the convergence of general principles and particular acts:

> The individual … finds his *liberation* in duty. On the one hand, he is liberated from his dependence on mere natural drives …; and on the other hand, he is liberated from that indeterminate subjectivity which does not attain existence or the objective determinacy of action, but remains *within itself* and has no actuality. In duty, the individual liberates himself so as to attain substantial freedom.[57]

As an isolated individual, the agent sees the particular conditions of their existence in contradiction to the requirements of moral ideas, and they see their moral ideas as forever deficient of any substantial reality. When they participate in institutional behavior, moral ideas turn into inherent rules and conditions of the practices that are performed. The individual is then certain that they can be a worthy and effective moral agent. The constant battle against their "natural drives," which made it difficult for them to be moral, is now gone, simply because these drives have no power over the requirements of shared practices.

Ethical life is morality's best-case scenario, or in our terms: the realization of a truly absolute good. We can hardly object to Hegel's basic assumption: if morality could not be realized, then all principles and theories would eventually be meaningless, and if there could be no truly absolute good, then there could be no good at all. A similar assumption underlies the dialectics of generality: if this dialectic exists, then a reconciliation of its contradictions also has to exist, or at least one has to act as if such a reconciliation could exist. The dialectic is only possible if each contradiction that emerges also tends to be resolved, for example, insofar as each position is taken to hold the promise of a full realization of moral principles and their fusion with the particular circumstances of the situation at hand. The dialectic, in other words, results from the strife for the true reality of morality, either in general or particularist terms, and if there were nothing to fight for, then there would be no such thing as a sequence of contradictory arguments. The reconciliation outlined here is therefore by no means the effect of some wishful thinking. We can even say that assuming a reconciliation of generality and particularism is in itself an obligation if morality is to be taken seriously.

In more recent times, MacIntyre has defended a similar approach as Hegel. For MacIntyre, modernity went wrong in developing "the project of an independent rational justification of morality," distinct from the rules provided by theology, the law, and aesthetics.[58] Moral ideas have no meaning outside of the historical and social context of practices. The attempt at a rational justification failed, and in its disembodied, ahistorical form, morality inevitably fell into relativism.[59] Nietzsche, with his radical subjectivism, became "*the* moral philosopher of the present age."[60] The counter-model to Nietzsche is Aristotle and his account of virtue. For MacIntyre, only the recourse to the idea of virtue can restore substance and validity to moral ideas. Virtues express "goods which are internal to practices"[61] and so allow for a descriptive foundation of morality. Practices, in turn, have to be understood as part of a living tradition, because "to enter into a practice is to enter into a relationship not only with its contemporary practitioners, but also with those who have preceded us in the practice."[62] The focus on virtue overcomes the isolation of the modern individual: it takes away the burden and conflict that come with the need for self-determination, connects the individual with others, and offers a repertoire of decisions and behaviors which guarantee the realization of normative ideas.

Other philosophers have presented "virtue ethics" as a moral theory independent from deontology and utilitarianism. We are not concerned here with the plausibility of this suggestion.[63] Only one point is of interest for us, the fact that virtue ethics too assumes that general principles can be fully absorbed by individual behavior. In Hurthouse's words: "The concept of a virtue is the concept of something that makes its possessor good; a virtuous person is a morally good, excellent, or admirable person who acts and reacts well, rightly, as she should—she gets things right."[64] Insofar as I possess a specific virtue, I am determined morally: I incorporate a generally recognized, paradigmatic trait and act so that all particular actions fit perfectly to the underlying disposition of my character, as well as to the moral principle that my virtue implies. No dialectic remains because there is no contradiction between my moral ideas, the experience of the given situation, the moral preferences that I want to uphold, and the particular actions that I perform. Strictly speaking, I do not even need to determine myself because I simply *am* determined to continue the actions fitting my disposition.

Hursthouse even assumes that virtues can be used as a criterion for the moral goodness of actions: "An action is right iff it is what a virtuous agent would characteristically (i.e. acting in character) do in the circumstances."[65] She has to admit that it may not always be clear what the appropriate virtue is in a given situation, and she also has to account for variations in the way that particular agents behave. But her point is that deviations in behavior can eventually be disregarded because agents can always default to the standard of virtuous practices: "When I am anxious to do what is right, and do not see my way clear, I go to people I respect and admire."[66]

Virtue ethics too represents morality's best-case scenario. But the theory seems to confuse the scenario with the reality of human practice. It seems to overlook that in a world characterized by contingency, self-determination has to occur. The agent has to be determined to be virtuous, not the other way around, in the sense that virtue would guarantee the determination to act in specific ways. A virtuous character cannot guarantee that every action is determined morally, and the idea that "what is right" in a given situation would be self-evident from the virtuous dispositions of others and their past behavior seems quite preposterous on a closer look.

Three objections can therefore be raised against the attempts at a reconciliation of generality and particularity outlined here. First, the reliance on virtue as compliance to the standards of institutional behavior makes the very idea of virtue superfluous. Hegel states: "The ethical, in so far as it is reflected in the naturally determined character of the individual as such, is *virtue*; and in so far as virtue represents nothing more than the simple adequacy of the individual to the duties of the circumstances to which he belongs, is *rectitude*."[67] From morality's point of view, this statement is paradoxical. It means that if morality is realized it ceases to be morality and becomes a form of socially regulated, conformist behavior. The idea of ethical life, it seems, harbors the wish to have one's cake and eat it: ethical life is supposed to be the ground for a fully sufficient moral theory but without the burden of finding oneself in opposition to conventions and the law. The dialectic is resolved, not because all contradictions are overcome, but because the individual would not even be able to articulate a position that would be moral in proper sense. The inner efficiency of social practices is never disturbed.

Second, both Hegel's approach and virtue ethics seem like a retrospective fantasy, a classicistic idealization of the theories found in ancient philosophy. They leave out that we can find the dynamics of modern life already in Plato and Aristotle: none of their accounts of virtue would have been necessary if people's behavior at the time would have been inherently moral. Nietzsche, who saw in Socrates the dissolution of traditional morality and the emergence of genuine self-determination, rightfully emphasized the rupture that made morality possible. Once morality has set new standards, the unquestioned integrity of human practice is lost, or better: the integrity is visible only after it has been broken. It remains an object of aspiration that can never be reached.

Third, the attempted solutions all require the belief in the existence of moral facts: one has to assume that communities and the various roles of its members truly realize moral ideas. For example, one has to assume that a citizen has an inherent concern for the public good, that a religious believer is devoted to moral values, and that parenthood is inherently guided by a concern for the well-being of one's children. None of these assumptions is necessarily true. It cannot be excluded that each reconciliation that is found reveals itself eventually as merely contingent, so that general principles enter again in contrast to their individual realization. Citizens can oppose the laws of their state, religious followers can become intolerant, and parents can interpret their roles to the detriment of their children. Attempts at a reconciliation of generality and particularity seem but an example of the dialectics of generality rather than a means to overcome it. The elements that are bound together in the conceptions of virtue ethics and ethical life fall apart quite easily, or have never been as tightly bound as the approaches assume. We therefore have good reasons to accept the dialectics of generality as an ultimate condition. As long as the good exists in and through individual determinations (and how else would it be able to exist?), the dialectic that arises in them will be inevitable, we believe.

9

The Dialectics of Reason

Reason

Preliminary Remarks

The second form of dialectics is the dialectics of reason. It shares basic features with the previous form. Reason concerns the method of moral theories, the procedures and specific experiences through which moral determinations can be reached. While the previous component, generality, concerned the content, or the *what*, of moral determinations, the present one concerns their *how*. The two components are closely related insofar as each type of principle entails a specific method of adoption and cannot be fully understood without it. Some of the arguments that we have shown in the previous chapter will therefore be made again, which allows us to be more succinct. However, the dialectics of reason raises questions that warrant an analysis of their own. Like before, we will see that the dialectic is driven ultimately by the idea of an absolute good: the contradictions that emerge are not merely the result of logical inconsistencies but stem from the fact that determinations are not sufficiently good. At the same time, all attempts at overcoming contradictions are attempts at finding a fully sufficient good through other determinations. We never assume that serious approaches at being moral fail because of simple mistakes.

For the sake of our analysis, any articulation of an agent's practical intents will be understood as exercise of reason, whether concepts and inferences remain implicit or are clearly expressed. The arguments made in the present chapter are not limited to any method in particular. In its most rudimentary form, reason is embedded in the linguistic articulation of intents. Even if agents only announce their intention—"I won't do this because it simply isn't right"—others can make a request for clarification or even justification. In one way or another, we always say more than we think, and each normative statement allows for further examination and dialogue. Whoever engages in reasoning can do so again at a later time, and reasoning is often driven by a concern for consistency over the course of one's life. The notions of reason and method that we use here are functional, not normative. We do not expect moral determinations to meet a specific standard of rationality, in the sense that all conceptual contents have to be well-defined and all inferences logically sound. We only expect *some* level of articulation and the potential for further elaboration.

Ineffectiveness

To begin, one can say that an agent's reasoning is not determined enough to make their decisions, attitudes, or actions moral. Arguments based on reason can be deemed meaningless and ineffective with respect to the requirements of practice. Reason inevitably creates a distance to the particular circumstances of a situation and may not allow the agent to capture what is most relevant in a given case. For example, it is reasonable to say that one does not want one's life to be unnecessarily prolonged through the use of medical machinery but such a statement leaves open when exactly the use of medical machines becomes futile and unnecessary and when it would be good to carry it on a little further. Arguments based on fairness often encounter a similar problem: it is reasonable to say that great inequalities of wealth in a society are unfair, but the idea of fairness does not determine by how much inequality should be reduced and which arrangement of social and economic conditions embodies the concept of fairness in the most adequate way. The agent's reasoning, despite being coherent and plausible in itself, may not lead to an effective determination to act.

In the field of moral philosophy, we have to distinguish between positions that deem reason ineffective and others that deem it meaningless. The former has its most prominent representative in Hume who believed that the operations of reason "have no hold of the affections or set in motion the active powers of men."[1] A more recent proponent is Williams who stressed the distinction between "internal" and "external" reasons. For Williams, moral ideas are external, not internal reasons because they lack "some psychological link" which would allow them to connect to the ways in which agents feel motivated to act.[2] For him, reasons that are articulated in an objective manner are also practically inert. Taken in itself, the distinction between internal and external reasons is flawed because it strips practical intentions of their content and reduces actions to an expression of non-cognitive impulses. Internal reasons, in the way that Williams understands them, allow for no better explanation of actions than external reasons do.[3] Morality is never only internal or only external but requires internal *and* external factors, that is, the personal act of self-determination *and* the content of the good, to coincide. Hume and Williams both miss the correlational approach that is needed to grasp morality as whole.[4] Also, there simply is such a thing as acting according to a reason. At one point or another, it becomes impossible to distinguish motives that are articulated based on reason from other, more personal ones that may also play a role in the causality of actions. Still, the very fact that such a distinction can be made shows the dialectic of reason-based determinations. Morality constantly falls apart, so to speak, into an inner and outer dimension. For moral reasons alone, agents have to be wary that their arguments achieve a fully determined, practically relevant meaning, which means that they have to doubt whether any of their motives is sufficient. We can therefore refute Hume's and Williams's arguments but we cannot prevent anyone from suspecting that they may be true nonetheless.[5]

Positions deeming reason as meaningless can be found, for example, in the criticism of Kant's categorical imperative. Locating the morality of the will in the mere form of lawfulness amounts to an "empty formalism," Hegel famously states. If morality is not based on a specific content, like the rules of institutional behavior, then "it is possible to justify any wrong or immoral mode of action."[6] This criticism is untenable. For Kant, the form of lawfulness, which turns individual maxims into universal duties, assumes that every being endowed with reason can accept these duties. An "immoral" maxim that would entail the harming of others cannot be universal, if only for the reason that agents would then have to accept that others can legitimately harm them, which is impossible. The categorical imperative is formal but not empty because it carries as a minimal content the harmony of each and every reasonable agent's will.[7]

We can, however, translate Hegel's criticism also into a moral concern. If agents cannot be certain that their reasoning captures what is morally relevant in a given situation, then they cannot be certain that reason allows them to be moral, which means again that they may fail the good. Perhaps they are able to achieve the good nonetheless in their course of action, but their own determination may not be determined enough. In other words, while Kant's categorical imperative *intends* the absolute good, it may not be able to *realize* it as such in and through its determination, which creates the dialectical tension that Hegel and others point out.

Reason as Fact

As we just mentioned again, if there is such a thing as acting according to reason, then it seems absurd to think that forms of reasoning should never lead to an adequate determination to act. One can say that in many cases an agent's reasoning is indeed well-determined or at least determined enough. But the presumed determinedness of reason does not escape the dialectic either: the closer one looks, the more it becomes evident that reason, insofar as it determines actions, is actually too determined, which means that it turns into its opposite. Determinations then appear as based on non-cognitive factors, that is, on factors that cannot be understood as an articulation of reason in any form. For example, certain assumptions have to be made about the purpose and the condition of actions ("I cannot do this today") and at least some normative ideas have to be accepted as valid without the need for further justification. Humans could never act if they had to conceptualize every step they take. In addition, there are traditions and shared practices that allow agents to act morally without much reflection. Getting married, for example, entails heavy moral commitments toward another person. At the same time, it involves a ritual that unfolds according to a logic of its own. The ritual allows one to express moral commitments without having to explain and justify them in any elaborate way. The burden that lies in the exercise of reason is taken away from agents to make their practices smoother and more efficient. But then, insofar as reasoning is embedded in rituals, habits, tacit assumptions, and the like, it turns into a non-cognitive activity.

We should add that there is nothing wrong in relieving agents of the burden of reason. Human practice would be very difficult without such relief. We also have to note that the opposite of reason as it is presented here is not irrationality, in the sense of erratic behavior, but attitudes and decisions that are not constituted by reason alone. We have to remember that we only ask *how* determinations come about. The idea of irrationality presupposes more, as it would assume that whatever is not constituted by reason is therefore also logically defective. Behavior that is based on shared practices and habits does not have to be deficient in any way. This may raise the question why the fact that reason turns into its opposite should be problematic at all. The answer is that if reason turns into its opposite it has no control over itself, which means that it is unclear whether it is still reason or an unreflected impulse. Such an uncertainty makes it impossible for a determination to be fully good. Again, the determination does not have to be deficient, in the sense that it would negate or exclude the good. But the very fact that its meaning is uncertain is already enough to create a dialectical tension, which forces us to say that the determination fails the absolute good. The absolute good includes the agent's determination to realize it as such.[8]

An example that illustrates this dialectical tension can be found in Kant's understanding of reason. Insofar as the capability of reason is always present in agents, he can say that "to satisfy the categorical command of morality is within everyone's power at all times."[9] At the same time, the moral law manifests itself as a "fact," which we have mentioned before.[10] Kant can say: "Consciousness of this fundamental law may be called a fact of reason, … because it … thrusts itself upon us of itself as a synthetic a priori … [The moral law, M.S.] is not an empirical fact but the sole fact of pure reason which, by it, announces itself as originally lawgiving (*sic volo, sic iubeo*)."[11] At one point or another, a certain form of reasoning has to be adopted in order to provide the arguments that are necessary for a moral determination. All moral reasons, insofar as they are moving, appear intuitively and are therefore indistinguishable from non-cognitive factors. That moral judgments are binding *for me* does not follow from the many reasons that I may have; it rather takes a personal decision to identify with one of them. "I think that one should never steal, and I want to follow this principle here." As said before, there can be no reason that forces one to accept a specific reason. But if this is the case, then it cannot be true that the categorical imperative is "under everyone's control at any time," as Kant says. It is generally "under control" insofar as competent agents can engage in reason-based arguments at any time, but the particular act of its adoption is not. Agents are eventually passive with respect to the "lawgiving" that morality entails for them. This dialectical ambiguity makes it impossible to say with certainty whether the agent determines themself to be good or is not rather driven by other motives.[12]

The two previous sections can also be seen as illustration of a dilemma that is often taken to affect the notion of free will. If the will is truly free, it is undetermined, which makes it ineffective as will. If the will is determined, it is no longer free and therefore no longer the specific impulse causing the action. In a sense, it is then no longer a will, because a will without causal force is a mere wish. The free will, similar to reason, is either transcendent with respect to actions, which creates a disconnect to practice, or immanent, which makes it indistinguishable from the many other factors that are involved in the unfolding of an act. This means that the idea of free will is dialectical, too. We cannot, however, engage in a further discussion of it.[13]

Destructiveness

Finally, in being too determined reason can be suspected to become antagonistic. If actions, attitudes, and decisions have to be based on arguments, then agents may feel they are forced to give up other factors they find valuable, such as tacit assumptions, emotions, and shared behavior. Reason can be seen as an alienating element in human practice: it can appear not only as ambiguous, like it did in the previous section, but as downright harmful. One can say that the use of reason destroys the good that agents would otherwise produce habitually or based on their individual impulses. In reasoning, agents have to distance themselves from a given situation, which means that they eventually may even lose any genuine interest in the good.

In its most pointed form, the opposition between reason and personal impulses has been expressed by Nietzsche. For him, reason and rationality go against the very instincts of humans. The Greeks became "absurdly rational" under the influence of Socrates, he states.[14] "The harshest daylight, rationality at any cost, life bright, cold, circumspect, conscious, without instinct, in opposition to the instincts, has itself been no more than a form of sickness, another form of sickness."[15] Compared to Greek rationalism, a natural and "healthy" form of morality would be one that is "dominated by an instinct of life."[16] Nietzsche's criticism is not limited to ancient ethics. An egalitarian system of laws, as it has been conceived in modern thought, is "hostile to life" too, because it tries to put an end to the struggle for power.[17] The idea of a fully naturalistic morality is evidently paradoxical, because a moral theory that would try to promote the "instinct of life" would already start abandoning it. An instinct-driven morality can only be one that does not know that it merely follows an instinct.[18] (One could add that it is not really clear what the instinct of life requires individuals to do and whether it could not also include a certain desire for the good.)

We can translate Nietzsche's polemic too into a moral concern. The problem that he emphasizes can be attributed to the unlimited nature of reason which, if not otherwise restrained, may demand an ever-greater degree of clarity, coherence, and justification and so end up eroding human practices with their inherent abilities and tacit normative goals. Nietzsche is part of a modern tradition that points at the destructive effect of reason—a tradition that can be traced back at least to Rousseau who famously held that "a state of reflection is a state against Nature, and the man who meditates is a depraved animal."[19] But we can find similar awareness of the dialectics of reason already in classical ancient philosophy. In the *Nicomachean Ethics*, Aristotle points out:

> The mass of mankind, instead of doing virtuous acts, have recourse to discussing virtue, and fancy that they are pursuing philosophy and that this will make them good men. In so doing they act like patients who listen carefully to what the doctor says, but entirely neglect to carry out his prescriptions.[20]

What the presumed philosophers miss is the practice of virtuous actions, which is the only thing that could make their character virtuous. "In order to become just men must do just actions."[21] Reason is of course not wholly destructive for Aristotle. But the exclusive focus on it can be harmful if it makes agents neglect the care they should devote to themselves. Reason can guide but not create moral character, or even maintain its overall "health."[22]

Another way in which determinations by reason can become antagonistic results from them turning into evil. The connection between the morally good and evil has been pointed out by Hegel (we mentioned this briefly before).[23] For him, morality is based on "subjective universality," that is, on the will insofar as it intends the good but does so *as will*, that is, as a mere capability of the subject.[24] Insofar as morality is rooted in the subjective will, it shares the same origin with evil. And not only that, moral and evil determinations can easily morph into one another: "Conscience, as formal subjectivity, consists simply in the possibility of turning at any moment to *evil*; for both morality and evil have their common root in that self-certainty which has being for itself and knows and resolves for itself."[25] Although the moral will is conceptually different from evil, it may in practice be indistinguishable from it insofar as both are characterized by extreme "self-certainty." A determination by and through reason alone can be as self-centered and opposed to the absolute good than evil. It may also have effects that can be considered as evil because the moral determination, in its self-centeredness, cannot be consistent to purposes of others that are involved in a given situation. It may become destructive toward these purposes, or may discount some destruction as a means that is necessary to achieve its goals. In Hegel's terms, both conscience and evil "directly transition into one another"[26]; they oscillate in a sense, which means that it can be difficult to say whether a determination is still moral or has already begun to be evil. In a weaker sense, those who assume certain moral arguments oppose those who do not, or at least disregard those who do not, which is discriminatory toward other determinations it would also be moral to have, even if there is no active intention to discriminate involved.[27]

Moral Arguments in Favor of Emotivism

The inherent dialectic in the use of reason leads to the adoption of non-cognitivist approaches to morality and the good. The approaches on which we will focus are subsumed under the term of emotivism. We use this term in a wider sense than it is typically used. "Emotivism" seems the appropriate label for all moral theories that assume emotions as primary factor in decisions, attitudes, and actions, not just from a meta-ethical but also from a normative point of view. The label of non-cognitivism includes obviously more than emotivist approaches: claims, for example, that normative claims are based on intuitions.[28] But we will leave other versions of non-cognitivism out, because only emotions stand in opposition to reason and allow us to describe a dialectical relation. Reason entails an intentional articulation of arguments which is at least somewhat under the agent's control. While emotions do not exclude intentions and can also be controlled to a certain degree, their very origin is passive. Emotions carry a motivational force which the agent has to acknowledge as given, not as constituted by them.

In the previous chapter, we said that particularism is the truth of generality insofar as principles are applied. We can now say analogously that emotivism is the truth of reason insofar as it motivates actions. The articulations of reason have to be the determining factor in actions, by providing content and the moving impulse. But in order to function as a determining factor, reason has to have a force that is immediate and does not depend on the conclusiveness of articulations. Where the action begins, articulations have to have come to an end. The immediate force that is needed for this is then not given by reason but by an affection that is simply felt. It may appear as reason but stems ultimately from emotion. The truth of our reasoning lies in its emotional basis without which the meaning of the various arguments could not be fulfilled (assuming that meaning does not rely on semantics alone but also on the pragmatic effect of arguments). Emotivism so appears as the most natural and simple explanation of actions and as a much more plausible and reliable factor than reasoning.

We will not enter into a discussion of the meta-ethical theories that are typically labeled as emotivist because these theories do not allow for a full account of morality. We also do not believe that these theories are tenable. Ayer summarizes the main position as follows:

> We can ... see why it is impossible to find a criterion for determining the validity of ethical judgements. ... We have seen that sentences which simply express moral judgements do not say anything. They are pure expressions of feeling and as such do not come under the category of truth and falsehood. They are unverifiable for the same reason as a cry of pain or a word of command is unverifiable.[29]

This argument is wrong on many accounts, mainly because it limits truth to verifiability. If the sole purpose of statements is verification, then only propositions based on "empirical facts"[30] can be objective, which neglects the fact that statements about the good can also be examined in their truth and achieve the degree of validity that is appropriate for them. Ayer is of course consistent when he says that "ethics, as a branch of knowledge, is nothing more than a department of psychology and sociology."[31] Moral theory, for him, is best practiced as one of the sciences if it is supposed to be objective at all. That is, moral theory is objective for him only if stripped of all normative force. Another, equally inconclusive argument for meta-ethical emotivism is provided by Stevenson. It is based on the experience of disagreement about moral questions. Disagreements can stem both from diverging personal attitudes and beliefs. Only the latter are truth-related and can be overcome. Stevenson assumes that the factor most responsible for making moral debates impossible to resolve lies in the non-cognitive attitudes of agents.[32] This argument conflates the use of moral arguments for the promotion of personal goals with the descriptive content of statements about the good.

Still, there are other factors which support emotivism as the basis of moral theory. We mentioned before that all moral reasons, insofar as they are moving, appear intuitively and may therefore be indistinguishable from non-cognitive factors.[33] There are several conditions that make cognitive and non-cognitive factors indistinguishable. First, agents can never be certain that they are able to distinguish which part of their motives comes from reason and which from emotion. Second, making such a distinction may be irrelevant for practical purposes. Third, many considerations that are based on reason are not strictly impartial and include desires, interests, and the like. Fourth, it may even be immoral to separate reasons and emotions. Many reasons relate to deep emotional and personal bonds, such as parental love, which would be treated in a reductive way if one said that they are only based on reason, not on emotion. In the previous section, the indistinguishability meant that there is a dialectical tension which makes arguments based on reason turn into their opposite. We did not go beyond this tension then. Now, we can resolve it and say that if such a tension exists, it speaks in favor of emotivism. If the moving factor of actions cannot be decided definitely, then we have to decide for the most plausible one. Emotions are a more plausible force than reason: they are effective through their inner strength and immediate in their impact on the agent. Compared to them, the motivation from reason has the higher burden of proof because of its need for articulation. For the sake of theoretical economy, we have to decide for the more evident and simpler of two moving forces. We will see later that this argument is not as conclusive as it seems. It shows, however, that the choice for emotivism can be well justified and that it results from inherent problems in the reliance on reason.

Meta-ethical theories typically include no account of specific emotions that drive moral statements. Hume's approach also treats emotions quite generally, as a variety of affective reactions, both positive and negative, within a social context. We conclude our introductory remarks with an approach that is based on one particular emotion, Schopenhauer's theory of compassion. The theory is based on the assumption that "the discovery of a self-interested motive entirely removes the moral worth of an action if it was the only motive, and reduces it if it had an accessory effect."[34] This assumption is of course dialectical because it captures the absolute good, which includes legitimate self-interest, only in part. But be this as may: Schopenhauer concludes that from a moral point of view, actions have "to happen simply and solely *for the sake of the other, ... his well-being and woe* must *be my motive immediately. ...* This requires that I *be identified with him* in some way."[35] The cause of such identification "is the everyday phenomenon of *compassion*, i.e. the wholly immediate *sympathy*, independent of any other consideration, in the first place towards another's *suffering*."[36] Only determinations that are driven by and represent the agent's compassion for another person's suffering are genuinely moral.

From the existence of compassion, Schopenhauer deduces two main attitudes, "all *free* justice and all *genuine* loving kindness."[37] The attitudes arise from the distinction between right and virtue, or "between the negative and the positive, between non-harming and helping."[38] Justice prevents the suffering of others, while loving kindness promotes their well-being. All other duties and virtues can be subordinated to one of the two. Compassion is directly moving because it reacts to a basic experience in human existence, to pain and suffering. While empirical knowledge presents us the other from the outside, separated in time and space, love transcends all separations. In compassion, the "dividing wall" of individuality is broken through, Schopenhauer thinks.[39] The affection of love is therefore unprovable in itself, only its effects in the empirical world are.[40] We will come back later to this point.

In Schopenhauer's theory, we can find additional arguments for emotivism as the truth of reason-based morality. He states that "nothing outrages our moral feeling in its deepest ground so much as cruelty."[41] Any instance of reasoning can be suspected to be only the result of the pressures of social conformity, and the arguments that we adopt may not represent who we are. The almost instinctual reaction to cruelty, instead, shows and realizes what moral principles and arguments can only intend. In addition, compassion can provide the perpetuation of morality in agents. Schopenhauer thinks that "boundless compassion with all living beings is the firmest and safest guarantor of moral conduct and requires no casuistry."[42] Compassion can create a stable disposition toward moral determinations by giving weight and specificity to them. Concern for the others' suffering means that we are present for them and inclined to act for the sake of their well-being. These arguments also show that the main reason for emotivism, as we find it in Schopenhauer, is moral. It stems from the question how we can be truly and positively engaged in moral considerations, whether we can be sure to have such considerations in the first place, and what gives them their particular direction. We see, in other words, that the dialectic of moral determinations which leads to the focus on emotions is driven ultimately by moral concerns, not by epistemological questions about the moving factors of actions.

Insufficiency

Emotivist theories do not escape the dialectics either. One can say, first, that emotions are not determined enough to provide the origin and content of moral actions. Like particularist approaches, emotivist ones are undetermined in two ways: first, they only determine the attitude of agents but cannot give a criterion for the choice of particular actions. The agent has to translate their attitude into specific activities, but no emotion can be linked unambiguously to only one kind of actions. Second, emotivist positions are undetermined insofar as the agent is determined by emotions while the emotions themselves are not determined by them. It cannot be guaranteed that an emotion is the basis of a moral attitude if the emotion first has passively to occur. There can also be no method that guarantees for an emotion to occur at all when a moral response is needed. One may object that these concerns about the limitations of emotivism are mostly academic and that in the reality of human practice emotions do provide a motivational background that allows agents to cultivate moral attitudes. But it is again for moral reasons that agents can suspect the motivational background to be insufficient for moral determinations. Some people, for example, may have abundant and positive moral feelings but repeatedly fail to act on them. Positive emotions can also erode and turn into their opposite if agents feel that their attitudes are not reciprocated. In addition, one's emotional responses may fall short of what the notion of the absolute good would require in each case. Agents know that they can have only so much genuine compassion and love for others. The reliance on emotions may therefore provide a false sense of security with respect to the morality of one's actions.

Formally speaking, emotivism can be suspected to state only a necessary condition for being moral. Agents have to be affected in their emotions if they are supposed fully to identify with, and commit to, moral determinations. But emotivism fails in being sufficient for the realization of the good. We came to the same conclusion in our analysis of Hume, where we pointed at the conventionalism of his approach. Emotions are morally conclusive only if we can believe that they are common among individuals, which depends on the assumption of certain stereotypical conditions of social life. Hume's analogy of a vault in which individual elements mutually support each other shows that sentiments cannot be considered in isolated ways.[43] The realization of morality does not happen through single feelings but depends on patterns of behavior, which then need additional factors in order to be determined appropriately.

Parasitism

It is possible to object against the idea that emotions would be deficient in providing moral determinations. If one does so, then one has to show them as determined enough. But then, the determinations appear as too determined, which makes them turn into their opposite. (To be precise, emotions cannot turn into their opposite, only emotions that are taken as moral determinations can.) We will mention four ways in which this can occur. First, there has to be an implicit conceptual content if it is possible to distinguish morally appropriate emotions from others that are not. One could say that emotions, if they are supposed to carry the weight of a moral theory, have to be reasons in disguise: they have to do everything that reasons do, only without being articulated through principles and arguments. In fact, emotivist theories seem to assume some magical ability by which emotions are able to deliver the required moral determination. It is not difficult to see that what is expected from emotions either cannot be achieved or needs the support of abilities that are not acknowledged as such. Emotivist theories are parasitic with respect to conceptual contents because they have to assume such contents as present in agents' feelings.

The defenders of an emotivist theory could object that even if some conceptual contents have to be involved, emotions simply occur as emotions. One can only have an emotion or not, or so the defense goes, whereas arguments and principles can be captured in degrees. The reality of emotions is both primary and irreducible. In addition, all conceptual contents are eventually subordinated to a final end that is given only in and for emotion. This would mean that even if emotions have to be linked to conceptual contents, there is a hierarchy of sorts and emotions are eventually always primary.

These objections beg the question because they assume that emotions are an ultimate fact that cannot be further analyzed. By saying that emotions are simply emotions, one does not explain why there can be no conceptual contents embedded in them. The problem is avoided but not solved. After all, emotions are intentional, too: one is angry at *someone*, glad that *something* happens, and the like. The strategy of taking emotions as ultimate fact repeats the error of meta-ethical emotivism, which looks at moral statements in an isolated way, as simple and unique events. The difficulties that arise from this approach have often been pointed out.[44] For example, one cannot deny that it is possible to integrate single moral statements into more complex arguments. "If you don't approve of what they are doing, let them know!" This means that if complex moral statements can be made, the meaning of the initial statements cannot be merely emotional: if this were the case, then one could only iterate them and no further arguments and inferences could be made. The initial statement must have contained an argument, if only in an unexpressed way. Agents talk and debate about their claims and do not just signal the feelings they have.

It is even to a certain extent immoral to take the occurrence of particular emotions as an ultimate fact. There is nothing, for example, that should make disagreements final, as even Stevenson assumes. From a moral point of view, one has to search for further consistency between different notions of the good. Disagreements can be only contingent. With respect to the final end of actions, one could say that even if it were only accessible through emotion (which can be debated), it has no direct impact on particular behavior. I may desire happiness in all I do, but what exactly is it that I want to do *here*? And will what I do at this moment really make me happy in the future? Actions happen here and now and need sufficient determination, which final ends cannot provide. There is obviously more to say about the role of final ends, especially happiness, but all we need to say is that the existence of final ends does not force us to assume that emotions are the sole driving factor in actions.

This leads to the second point, which concerns the perpetuation of emotions in practices. Besides Hume's conventionalism, we can see that Schopenhauer too combines emotion with conceptual contents in order to secure the steadiness of moral determinations:

> It is by no means required that compassion is actually aroused in every single case, where anyway it would often come too late: rather, out of the recognition of the suffering that every unjust action necessarily brings upon others, … the maxim 'Harm No One' emerges in noble minds, and rational deliberation elevates it to the firm resolve, formed once and for all, to respect the rights of every one.[45]

Before, in mentioning the arguments that speak in favor of emotivism, we said that emotions can provide a reliable ground for moral attitudes toward, say, cruelty. Now we see that such a ground only provides a rather general effect and is unable to deliver a moral determination "in every single case." The agent needs to rely on principles that guide their behavior throughout various situations. The passage quoted here shows why emotivism cannot provide a complete and sufficient moral theory: it is very much only a theory of the original impulse for actions. As soon as it claims to be more, claims to be determined enough for moral action as a whole, it becomes the opposite of an emotivist theory. Dialectically speaking, reason then appears as the truth of emotion.[46]

The third point shows that in claiming emotion as sufficient origin and content of action, emotivist theories tend to overstate its untouchable nature. The more determined emotion has to be, the more one has to emphasize that it is inaccessible for any non-emotional factor. Schopenhauer, for example, overstates the mysterious quality of compassion: "This occurrence [of compassion, M.S.] is certainly worthy of astonishment, and indeed mysterious. It is in truth the great mystery of ethics, its ur-phenomenon and the boundary stone beyond which only metaphysical speculation can dare to step."[47] The assumption of a "mystery" somewhat contradicts the practical effectiveness of compassion, which shows itself in actions after all and cannot be all that inaccessible. One can think here of a point that Nietzsche made against Schopenhauer's notion of the will: "Willing strikes me as, above all, something *complicated*, something unified only in a word."[48] An emotion like compassion is most probably also "complicated," comprising not just one relation to others but rather a bundle of relations, which then may include, among others, an awareness of the moral quality of situations that could also be expressed through arguments and reason. Following Nietzsche, we can say that if emotions are determined as only *one thing*, it is most likely because of the use of *one name*.

The fourth and last point is closely related to the previous one. Emotions can not only be linked to conceptual contents, in certain cases they may be their direct result. We have seen that for Kant the moral law can cause feelings of respect.[49] Kant made sure to distinguish these feelings from mere sensations of pleasure and pain. Respect is for him no mere enjoyment of oneself, or the lack thereof, but intentionally directed toward another person that is held in high esteem.[50] Other feelings, such as awe, pride, anger, and gratitude, can also not be reduced to pleasure and pain. They all can comprise a normative attitude. Anger, for example, can be rash and uncontrollable, but it can also arise as indignation about a perceived violation of moral expectations. In this case, it is impossible to distinguish the intentional content of the agent's attitude from its emotional underpinnings. This is also evident from the fact that we request agents to have the right emotions. "I want you to show a little gratitude to them." Although an emotion cannot be produced at will, it can at least be awakened and triggered in agents. To be disgusted and appalled by acts of torture, or to be tender toward a child is not "just a feeling," but a sign that one understands the issues that are at stake. The lack of this reaction is a moral failure or at least the cause for moral concerns. "Because I feel this way" is usually not accepted as response to such concerns. We can also learn not to indulge in negative feelings toward others (e.g., during a divorce), or we can learn to adopt positive feelings toward other people (e.g., in overcoming prejudice). Very often, emotions decide about the very possibility of living together with others: "How can I be together with someone who laughs about such jokes?" One may excuse the occasional occurrence of certain emotions, of hate, envy, resentment, and the like, but one is less likely to excuse them as inherent part of another person's character and stance toward the world. Kant points at the indistinguishability of emotions and normative attitudes when he states: "Respect for the law is not the incentive to morality; instead it is morality itself subjectively considered as an incentive."[51] Emotions can represent moral determinations as a whole, if only in an agent-related way.

Latent Aggression

In being too determined, determinations based on emotions can also become antagonistic. The dialectical step that we described with respect to reason occurs for emotions as well. We do not refer here to negative emotions, such as hate, envy, and resentment, because it is obvious that they carry an antagonistic meaning. What we refer to are moral determinations based on positive emotions, on emotions that support and motivate an agent's commitment for the good. There are two ways in which the dialectic can unfold in them.

The first way results from the emphasis on one's emotions. Accepting them without reservations carries the potential to become a discriminatory attitude toward the emotions of others. I believe that I should follow my emotions, express and act on them, and I also believe that they are important enough to be brought to the attention of others, whom I then ask to respect my feelings: in all this there is at least a latent aggression toward the emotional determination of others. Like before, this does not mean that the agent explicitly harbors an aggressive intention. As a matter of fact, the discriminatory effect might even occur against their best intentions. The dialectic is visible only once we adopt the perspective of the absolute good. Concern for the authenticity of my feelings in practical matters is concern for what is only mine. It cannot be distinguished from an act of egoistic self-determination as long as someone else's emotions are also involved. Or, to explain this in a different way: my emotion, which I see as only positive, as simply given, is actually, insofar as it is put in question through the presence of others and yet affirmed, only the negative of its own denial. It can provide my determination only insofar as it is embraced against other motivating factors. Our point is not, of course, that emotional variety should be suppressed, or that individuals have a moral obligation to disregard their feelings. The point is only that the influence of emotions on moral determinations cannot be seen as an innocent, natural event which must be left intact. If emotions translate into determinations, they can entail the failure to make one's feelings consistent to the feelings of others who are involved. After all, emotions are vital for an individual's life and relate to the purposes that they pursue in their actions. Others follow their purposes too, and if the affirmation of my emotions means that others have to start feeling differently, or that their feelings cannot matter as motivation to have their purposes realized, then I cannot believe that relying on my emotions helps to realize the good among us.

For the defenders of an emotivist theory in the sense of, say, Schopenhauer, this may sound absurd. They may ask: can there ever be a problem in having compassion for the suffering of others? Feeling offended by the fact that someone is harmed seems to have an intrinsic moral value. But again, there is nothing that prevents the respective determination from becoming antagonistic either. Who says that my emotional response is not a matter of self-indulgence, and who guarantees that the response is not triggered in an idiosyncratic way which disregards the good of others who are involved? We simply cannot assume that consideration for the good should *not* lead agents to control their feelings in specific situations. A defense of our analysis can be found, surprisingly, in Stevenson. He points out that an emotivist theory, for which moral statements are mere expressions of personal feelings which the speaker wants others to share, can well attribute to moral statements an aggressive meaning. Insofar as meta-ethical emotivism assumes the meaning of normative statements to be prescriptive and imperative—as if all statements implicitly said "I approve of this; do so as well"—they can be seen as a sort of command. Whoever "wishes only to propagate his preconceived aims, without reconsidering them" would follow a desire for "conquest," which amounts to a reductive use of moral language.[52] The use of emotions for moral determinations may then turn from a mere expression of preferences to an exclusionary assertion of one's position.

For the second way in which an antagonistic effect can occur, we can again rely on remarks made by Hegel:

> It is *suspicious* or even worse to cling to feeling and heart in place of the intelligent rationality of law, right and duty; because all that the former holds more than the latter is only the particular subjectivity with its vanity and caprice. ... So long as we study practical feelings and dispositions specially, we have only to deal with the selfish, bad, and evil; it is these alone which belong to the individuality which retains its opposition to the universal.[53]

For Hegel, the assertion of one's emotions entails the denial of claims based on reason, which are universal and include, among others, the "rights and duties" of every agent. It may not be obvious, though, that the reliance on one's emotions implies a discrimination of reason. Following Nietzsche's stance against reason, discrimination is usually thought to occur the other way round. Many suspect reason and claims to "intelligent rationality," in Hegel's words, to discriminate against personal desires and feelings. But a statement of the kind "What I do is good because I feel it is" actually entails the suppression and closing out of requests based on reason. Denying the validity of reason means to deny others the validity of their arguments and to interrupt and prevent the exchange, the dialogue that comes with the use of reason. Saying "Don't try to convince me!" means, among others: do not think that you can have an argument for the good that would force me to change my position. Such a stance is a denial of the very possibility of an absolute good. But to say this one more time, the analysis does not imply that whoever makes such statements has an active desire to discriminate against others. The point is that the affirmation of one's feeling can entail the denial of other determinations, and the potential to realize the good to the greatest possible extent can become suppressed insofar as arguments from reason eventually remain excluded.

And to say this, too, again, the point is also not that the negation of emotions would be in itself a morally worthy goal. We obviously cannot assume that all requests from reason are legitimate, which means that in a given situation the individual may have good reasons to react in an emotionally self-assertive way. In addition, the suppression of emotions would also be a violation of the good because the absolute good includes and respects all legitimate feelings. In some cases, emotional reactions can be a defense against a perceived violation of the good. "I cannot feel otherwise after what you have done to me." It may often be necessary to let emotions run its course. However, if emotions arise out of a defensive stance, they are merely an expression of the absence of the good and so carry a negative meaning. The higher viewpoint of the good requires us to overcome the fixation on particular emotions if their primary meaning is determined by an antagonism in the perceptions of the good. One last point to mention concerns the social dimension of emotions. The exclusion of reason not only occurs on the inter-personal level but can also affect groups of agents. The social and political effects of the assertion of group-specific emotions, in relation to one's nation, race, religion, and the like, sadly do not need much explanation.[54]

Attempts at a Reconciliation: Pragmatism

Like before, the contradictions that emerge from positions that are either based on reason or emotion call for a reconciliation. Attempts at reconciling the positions can be found in pragmatist approaches. We understand pragmatism in as wide as possible a sense. For the sake of our argument, the main criterion for pragmatist approaches lies in the assumption that successful practice, not individual determination, decides about the moral status and content of actions. If you want to determine yourself morally, look around at what works in your community of agents. Pragmatism has the advantage of being indifferent toward both reason and emotion as determining factors: as long as practices occur successfully, whereby success includes their moral acceptability, all capabilities of agents can be involved, or better: all capabilities can contribute equally to them.

An example for such an approach can be found in Descartes' idea of a *morale par provision*, or "provisory code of morals." In his *Discourse on Method*, Descartes famously explains that in the course of his examination of all knowledge he adopted three maxims to define the moral dimension of his conduct. According to the first maxim, which contains a subset of more specific rules, he "was to obey the laws and customs of my country."[55] He would do so by following the opinions "of the most judicious," although strictly speaking he did not want to follow their opinions only: "I ought to pay attention to what they did rather than to what they said, not only because in the corruption of our morals there are few people who are willing to say everything they believe, but also many do not know what they believe." Finally, "among many opinions that are equally accepted, I would choose only the most moderate, … because they are always the most suitable for practical affairs."[56]

The first maxim shows already what a pragmatist approach entails: it starts within a given community of agents by accepting their basic normative standards and seeks out role models who are thought to embody these standards in the best possible way. The maxim also shows the pragmatist concern about the reality of practice, which is assumed to be distinct from any cognitive component and reflective attitude. Descartes' goal is to minimize the role of reason as a guiding and justifying principle of actions: the agent follows determinations that are given and displayed in the actions of others and do not have to be articulated through their own effort of reason. Strictly speaking, the agent does not have to try to determine themself. The same minimization is visible in the attempt at adopting the most moderate option in every case. Moderate positions can be translated into practice more easily than isolated and more extreme ones, which would force the agent to disrupt existing patterns of behavior and require a higher degree of articulation and justification.

Parallel to the minimization of reason, Descartes also strives to minimize the impact of emotions.

> My second maxim was to be as firm and resolute in my actions as I could, and to follow the most doubtful opinions, once I had decided on them, with no less constancy than if they had been very well assured. In this I would be imitating travelers who, finding themselves lost in some forest, should not wander about turning this way and that, nor, worse still, stop in one place, but should always walk in as straight a line as they can in one direction and never change it for feeble reasons, even if at the outset it had perhaps been only chance that made them choose it; for by this means, even if they are not going exactly where they wish, at least they will eventually arrive somewhere where they will probably be better off than in the middle of a forest.[57]

The comparison to a traveler who is lost in a forest shows how limited human abilities are for Descartes. If the world of practice is not fully intelligible and reason cannot ever be sufficient to guide human action, but only "chance" can, then emotions cannot be sufficient either because it can never be assumed that humans find their desires satisfied. Emotions cannot be a criterion for choice. It is therefore necessary to minimize the impact of motivational engagement. Emotional reactions are to be controlled so that they do not disrupt the successful completion of actions. Descartes' pragmatic principles were "able to free me from all the regret and remorse that usually agitate the consciences of ... frail and irresolute minds."[58] Especially negative emotions can induce a reflective detachment from actions, which the agent has to avoid.

For Descartes, reason and emotion are meant to support each other mutually: efforts at a reason-based justification of actions are substituted by the reliance on emotional steadfastness, while emotive forces are regulated according to the general maxim of moderation and the rational insight in the irrationality of the external world. This way, the pragmatist approach escapes the failings of all strong moral theories, whether they are based on reason or emotion. It lets go of theory in order to rely on practice only. Parallel to that, the agent has to renounce any claim at being sufficiently equipped to reach the good by themself. This can of course not mean that pragmatism amounts to a complete negation of the attempt at finding conditions that are sufficient for the good; it only relegates this task to factors that are outside of the agent's direct control. Given the appropriate sensitivity for context, moderation, and steadfastness, the circumstances of each actions will make it at least probable that some form of the good can be reached.

A similar approach can be found in Toulmin's more recent attempt to determine "the place of reason in ethics."[59] According to him, ethical or moral theories provide little less than "partisan slogans."[60] They compare given principles and situations to each other but do not achieve genuine knowledge. In addition, despite the opposition between various approaches that are based on either reason or emotion, moral theories are "less incompatible with one another" than they might seem.[61] Their theoretical differences are eventually irrelevant. Like Descartes, Toulmin assumes that one does not really need theories in order to conduct morally acceptable actions. Feelings and personal attitudes are relevant as "logically independent participants" in decisions about the course of action.[62] Principles and reason-based justifications may be used but enter practices only "as part of the procedure for minimizing the effects of ... conflicts" that can arise between the members of a community.[63] If all goes well, one does not need them.

It is not difficult to show why the attempts presented here are also bound to fail. Pragmatist approaches rely mainly on a negative idea insofar as their basic maxim is, in one way or another, not to disturb what works. They seem to say that if practical success is *not* taken as basic criterion, then all practice would need to be structured according to reason. This argument puts undue burden on the opponent. No one could claim that all human practice can be fully regulated by reason; however, accepting this does not leave one with the pragmatist position as the only viable alternative.[64] Like non-cognitive theories, pragmatist ones are also in essence parasitic. They have to assume that the moral quality of actions is self-evident and that requests for the clarification and justification of contents are a dispensable aspect of human practice.[65] This way, the problem of the appropriateness of moral contents is not solved but simply assumed to be solved by some mysterious ability that can be found in communal interaction. Descartes may be right in saying that extreme positions are not always morally good while moderate ones have a higher chance of being so, but who decides what is extreme? Toulmin states: "There is no more general 'reason' to be given beyond one which relates the action in question to an accepted social practice."[66] Statements like his either say too much or too little. They say too little if they only refer to the "accepted practice" in a small section of the world, say, in parts of Western culture. And even within such a part, it is not clear, for example, that all social classes accept a given practice. The statement says too much if it assumes that there is a clear idea of what "accepted" means. It tacitly assumes that practices are "accepted" not just in a conventional but also in a morally viable sense. But again, who decides that they are? One should not neglect the possibility that at least some participants reject the given practices or would request a more sustained justification if they were asked. Against this possibility, it is hard not to sense that "accepted practice" is just another word for "reasonable practice" insofar as it implies the shared and general validity of normative standards.

Pragmatist positions typically leave the question open why the request for justification and further theoretical reflection arises within practices at all. If practices are as successful and as sufficiently moral as the approaches make it sound, why has anyone then even tried to reflect on them and adjust them to more stringent standards? Pragmatists seem to confuse cause and effect when they believe that it was theories that made practices questionable, while it may well be that practices, because they have become questionable in advanced modern societies, gave cause to engage in theoretical reflection and are less wholesome than it seems.

These remarks do obviously not imply that pragmatist approaches are simply flawed. Toulmin, for example, rightly emphasizes the semantic problem of the meaning of moral ideas. These ideas can only have meaning if they relate to particular types of actions.[67] Pragmatism is an inevitable product of the dialectic of moral determinations and an excellent diagnostic of it. But diagnosis is different from moral guidance, and pragmatist approaches amount to wishful thinking if they declare the problem of the moral determination of actions already to be solved so that all conceptual and practical disputes can be minimized and revoked. The problem is never solved in reality but only in the persuasive writings of the pragmatists themselves.

10

The Dialectics of Inherent Goodness

Inherent Goodness

External Conditions

The third and final form of dialectic will be subsumed under the notion of inherent goodness. Strictly speaking, inherent goodness is always involved in moral theories as the quality that makes someone or something good. It is also part of the principles and methods we discussed in the previous two chapters. But as shown before, strong moral theories do not just aim at *some* good that is reached but at the good insofar as it is absolute, at the fully sufficient good.[1] They have to identify attitudes and actions that can be inherently good, which means that we have to focus on inherent goodness as a separate element of moral theories.

Moral determinations that are deemed inherently good can first seem not determined enough to become sufficient for the good. There are two ways in which this can happen. The first way results from the relation of an individual's determination to the outside world. The agent's abilities can seem futile and ineffective compared to the constraints and the resistance they encounter in the realm of human practice. Kant was well aware of this. He distinguishes between the supreme good and the highest good.[2] The supreme good is realized in and through the morally determined will,[3] whereas the highest good, which represents the entire, or complete good, includes both the moral will and the happiness of the agent. Happiness is a necessary part of the good, an experience that beings endowed with reason cannot not desire, because they cannot desire that despite their best, most worthy efforts things do not end well in the world.[4] Happiness, however, involves the "harmony" of the will and nature, as the totality of external things, which requires an intelligent cause, or God, to arrange nature in the appropriate way.[5] Harmony cannot be achieved through the individual will alone. The agent has to assume the existence of another, higher form of agency which will eventually guarantee the effectiveness of their determinations. The problem articulated by Kant is obviously not an empirical one, as the question is not whether the will is sometimes effective and sometimes not, or to which degree it is effective in each case. At its core, the problem is moral because there is no way in which the world of human practice, with its multitude of other wills, can correspond to one morally determined will. The agent has to be aware that despite the inherent goodness of their resolve, their abilities may eventually not be sufficient for the absolute good. Attitudes, decisions, and actions may be determined in themselves but they are not determined enough, that is, are ineffective and empty from the perspective of the good.

The dialectic pointed out by Kant echoes famous remarks in the *Nicomachean Ethics*. For Aristotle, happiness lies in the activity of the soul according to virtue, an activity that needs to be extended and maintained over time. However, the circumstances of life are contingent and open to misfortune, which means that in principle one would need to consider a person's life as a whole in order to say that they are happy. Strictly speaking, one can only say of someone that they *have been* happy, not that they simply *are*.[6] The only way for a person to be happy presently is therefore when they make themself happy through their soul's virtuous activity. But life's inevitable dependence on fortune has an impact on this activity, too. Humans need "external goods," such as certain material means in order to exert their virtues, and they also depend on other people. Someone "childless and alone in the world is not our idea of a happy man, and still less so perhaps is one who has children or friends that are worthless, or who has had good ones but lost them by death."[7] Like in Kant, the individual's determination, their virtuous attitudes and actions, are deemed sufficient for the good and at the same time insufficient because they cannot secure the completeness of the good through their own activity.

Both Aristotle and Kant assume that the dependency on external conditions can be turned into a stimulus for the true independency of virtue and the moral will. For Aristotle, virtuous activity is the final end of actions. External conditions add to its goodness, but virtue is always good in itself. Even in adverse events, virtue "shines through, when a man endures repeated and severe misfortune with patience, not owning to insensibility but from generosity and greatness of soul."[8] For Kant, the existence of God is a postulate of practical reason that does not need to be translated into an empirical reality. In order to maintain one's moral determination, it suffices to assume that life could *in principle* accord to moral ideas. God is not needed to make moral self-determination possible; on the contrary, it is moral self-determination that entails the postulate of a higher being and through this postulate secures itself. This way, Kant acknowledges the contradiction that emerges for an independent will and yet claims that the will provides its own solution to this contradiction.

Both answers to the problem of external conditions show that the dialectic of moral determinations does not always have to strike positions behind their back. It can well be acknowledged in them. Still, a contradiction remains even if it is recognized. Aristotle's and Kant's attempts at countering the indeterminedness of moral determinations cannot restore full self-sufficiency but only present a way to cope with its absence.[9]

Abstract Rights

The second way in which instances of inherent goodness can be deemed not determined enough can also be explained in relation to Kant, namely in relation to his second formula of the categorical imperative, "*So act that you use humanity, whether in your own person or in the person of any other, always at the same time as an end, and never merely as means.*"[10] As said before, the idea of human beings as universal ends represents the absolute good insofar as it entails the coincidence of the good in both its subjective and objective form. Moral self-determination constitutes the very content of the agent's will and is attributed to both themself and all other beings endowed with reason.[11] The idea has often been criticized. Some of the arguments that have been made can be understood as indicating a lack of determinedness. In the following, we will consider not only the notion of humanity in one's person but also the idea that persons, in contrast to mere things, are "an object of respect"[12] and have dignity, an "inner worth," according to which they are "raised above all price and therefore admit ... of no equivalent."[13] For the sake of our argument, we will treat the notions of humanity, personhood, and dignity as closely related and mutually implicative of each other.

Some critics have raised the concern that Kant's idea of human beings as ends could amount to the self-deification of persons. Following a latent theological influence, Kant would have conceived of the human capacity for autonomy, for giving oneself a law, in analogy to God as the "divine lawgiver."[14] Insofar as human dignity resides in the unlimited capacity of giving laws, he could then not have excluded that some laws may be devoid of moral content or even contrary to the good. There would be a "tension between the potential and the actual in justifying respect for humans."[15] We can disregard this argument here: first, it is not clear that such a problem really exists in Kant, given that for him the only law that humans truly give themselves and do not adopt because of empirical circumstances *is* the moral law. Second, and more importantly, we are interested in the dialectics of moral determinations and therefore assume lawgiving as an actual and not just potential expression of inherent goodness. It is of course right to suspect that autonomy, taken as such, could well result in the unrestricted ability to decide whatever one pleases to do, whether it is good or not. We are, however, not interested in a lack of determinedness of this particular kind.

Another argument that can be found thinks of the idea of humans as ends as impractical. In the typical context of actions, others are hardly ever respected as ends. Interactions of all kinds require humans to take each other as means. Teachers and students, for example, are means for each other, and even moral philosophers need to take taxis and have someone provide them a meal when they are unable to cook for themselves. After all, why would humans interact at all if they were not useful for each other? In a society of divided labor everyone is but a means, in one way or another. However, even if all this is true it still does not provide an argument against the idea of humans as ends. We can rather see in it another case of what we call the application fallacy.[16] According to this fallacy, moral ideas are thought to determine actions directly and in their particular content. One assumes that Kant's second formula of the categorical imperative tells us specifically what to do in particular situations, which would be to consider others for all practical matters and purposes as an end. Obviously, if one were to try this, absurd things would follow because it would be unclear how anyone could be of use to anyone else. But Kant's formula does not tell agents what to do; it only requires them to use others "at same time" as an end and "never merely" as a means. Being an end is a formal, not a classificatory notion, because it refers to all sorts of contents indistinctively and does not touch the many concrete ways in which persons make use of each other. What Kant requires agents to consider can be described as a "limiting condition"[17]: in whatever we do with respect to others, we have to be aware that there are things that we cannot do to them because these things would prevent them from having the status of ends in themselves. We have to be polite to taxi drivers and must not treat them as if it were natural for them to drive us around, and we also have to pay in order to compensate them for their time and effort. In its most basic sense, treating others as ends means to respect them in having their own reason to act. The second formula of the categorical imperative is as determined as it can be by adding an additional, moral perspective to the usefulness that individuals provide for each other. We can therefore disregard this argument too and have to look for yet another kind of indeterminedness.

An example of what we are looking for can be found in the notion of dignity as it is used in the context of human rights. The Kantian inspiration for this notion is obvious if we read one more time the first article of the Universal Declaration: "All human beings are born free and equal in dignity and rights. They are endowed with reason and conscience and should act towards one another in a spirit of brotherhood."[18] Arendt criticized the idea of human rights in her work on *The Origins of Totalitarianism*. For Arendt, human rights articulate freedom and equality in a merely abstract form. They need to be translated into civil rights, because only civil rights ensure that rights are established in a realistic and reliable way. The main right is therefore not freedom and equality, but the "right to have rights (and that means to live in a framework where one is judged by one's actions and opinions) and the right to belong to some kind of organized community."[19] Arendt's idea of a "right to have rights" reacts to the plight of stateless people who, like the Jews in Germany, have been stripped precisely of their civil rights. They find themselves in a state of utter rightlessness because no country other than their native one is legally obliged to grant them any rights. Such rightlessness does precisely not exclude or contradict the fact that they retain their human rights: "There is no question that those outside the pale of the law may have more freedom of movement than a lawfully imprisoned criminal or that they enjoy more freedom of opinion in the internment camps of democratic countries than they would in any ordinary despotism."[20] Ultimately, for Arendt human rights are no genuine rights, only civil and political rights are: "We are not born equal; we become equal as members of a group on the strength of our decision to guarantee ourselves mutually equal rights."[21]

We are interested in this argument from a conceptual point of view. Historically, there is no absolute rightlessness of refugees anymore since documents like the Refugee Convention of 1951 have spelled out the rights of such groups.[22] (Of course, insofar as human rights largely depend on the enforcement by nation states, Arendt's argument is in many cases still valid.) The reason why she can say that dignity, or the idea of humans as ends, is not determined enough, is *not*, however, that there is a variety of ways in which dignity can be translated into civil rights. This problem is not limited to human rights but arises for all laws and general rules. The reason for her criticism lies in the fact that dignity may not be translated into civil rights at all and yet remain the expression of an innate human right. Like Kant's idea of humanity as end, human rights can be understood as limit. Human rights imply that "some abuses … are genuinely intolerable."[23] This limit can be preserved even if few of the instances that support the implementation of human rights are preserved. The limit is independent of the quantity of legal protections enclosed by it, because there is always one element or another that can be deemed dispensable in the realization of human rights. Is it, for example, a violation of human rights if women are not given equal rights in education? Human rights require respect for the religious and cultural preferences of nations, which might include differences in the rights that are attributed to certain groups.[24] And does a situation of emergency, or a situation of civil unrest, temporarily justify the suspension of some human rights? One cannot deduce the answer to these questions from the mere idea of human rights because this idea is not determined enough to exclude cases in which human rights are claimed to be preserved without the corresponding civil rights.

In our terminology, this means that one can claim the inherent goodness of decisions, attitudes, and actions without being able to secure the particular circumstances that have to be in place in order to realize it.[25] Actions, attitudes, and decisions can be deemed good because of an element of inherent goodness that they contain, and one may assume that this element represents all other elements that are involved and makes them good by association to it. But complete goodness does not follow and the inherent goodness that is emphasized may appear painfully deficient. "You say that you respect my dignity but you do not know what I need." As before, the dialectic outlined here does not have to result from an intentional misuse of moral notions but is rooted in the structure of inherent goodness, taken as main focus of one's attitudes and actions.

Self-Elevation

Some might object and say that instances of inherent goodness are in fact determined enough to allow for the realization of an absolute good in practical matters. The ideas of dignity and of humans as ends are entirely realistic, they may say, if only one takes them as a means to transform human practices toward the good. Is it not cynical to say that the world could never accept the implementation of human rights? After all, everyone knows what is needed to respect and protect human beings in their dignity. Giving up the idea of a quality in humans that would be inherently good only helps those who have an interest in harming and oppressing others. Seen from this angle, affirming the determinedness of the inherently good is in itself a moral obligation. We defend morality as a whole by rejecting the claim that the assumed goodness in decisions, attitudes, and actions would not be determined enough, both in itself and in its impact on the world.

This desire to affirm inherent goodness, however, cannot avoid becoming dialectical. It eventually turns determinations into their opposite. There are two ways in which this happens, within moral determinations themselves and in the relation between moral determinations and the practical world. The first dialectical turn parallels another one we mentioned in the dialectics of generality. In echoing a sophist position, Nietzsche famously argues that universal moral obligations are only a means to prevent the spontaneous self-realization of others.[26] We can use this argument one more time. Following Nietzsche's line of thought, what is deemed good in itself is always only good for someone. This argument represents the most common and also most trivial objection against any moral determination: "You claim to be moral but you only benefit yourself." The objection is usually raised by those who do not believe in morality anyway and can only see the deficiency in others. But we can state the argument in a more refined way. If the inherently good is an absolute good, it includes the benefit of the agent, at least insofar as it is consistent to the benefit of others. It can then be too determined because it can include more than it should. For the agent, it would amount to a moral failure if they claimed innocence and said that they honestly only intend the good and nothing else. The good that I realize elevates me, but perhaps it elevates me too much over others? It is important that this suspicion arises for moral reasons and not out of a general rejection of moral ideas. The suspicion arises through the application of moral criteria to one's own moral determinations.

(We should add that in its most common form, the objection "People claim to be moral but in doing so they only benefit themselves" is not only trivial but also self-refuting. It assumes that there should be a moral determination that does not benefit the agent. At the same time, it claims that such a determination is impossible to have. This is clearly a contradiction, at least insofar as the statement is taken in a general sense. One can avoid this contradiction only if one believes that moral ideas have no real meaning anyway. Perhaps one thinks that they are only a means in the struggle for ideological domination. But in that case, one cannot criticize people for abusing moral ideas because one does not possess a moral standard oneself. Either way, the mere possibility of an agent's benefit provides no argument against the validity of their moral claims.)

If attitudes and actions that are deemed inherently good are seen as too determined, it may also seem that they are no moral determinations in proper sense but a particular way of leading one's life. Perhaps one can only imagine living in a specific way and sees certain practices as inherently good, simply because no alternative presents itself. After all, are we not all bound to the experience of specific cultures and their presumed achievements? Due to their cognitive biases, humans tend to find reasons to justify what they are doing anyway. From a political perspective, it may seem that an agent's assumptions of inherent goodness rely on their enjoyment of bourgeois privileges, of a well-secured life. Inherent goodness, one could say, is for those who can afford it. Those living in poverty and under oppression have to give priority to the fulfillment of their needs. They have to bother about the tangible consequences of actions, not about the realization of capabilities for their own sake.

The second dialectical turn, which concerns the relation between moral determinations and the world, results from the way in which inherent goodness is maintained against a background of adverse phenomena. For example, the idea of dignity can be grounded in the fact that all humans "are capable of suffering."[27] Humans have dignity and share this dignity universally, because in one way or another they are all victims of the circumstances under which they live, or so the argument goes. Everyone suffers from someone or something. In this case, attitudes and actions achieve inherent goodness solely by elevating themselves above a state of affairs that is deficient. They are too determined because it is eventually too easy for them to be fully determined.[28] Agents might even harbor a secret temptation to see more suffering in the world because it is one way to make the inherent goodness of their attitudes and actions shine.[29]

Diminishing the Good

The dialectic that emerges from assuming the full determinedness of the inherently good already contains the seed for its antagonistic meaning. The antagonism can happen in three ways: as discrimination against my own good, or at least against my ability of achieving the good; as discrimination against the good of others; and as tendency to use the moral good as a means for discrimination. The first form of discrimination may not be obvious. We find it if we follow the classical argument according to which the fully sufficient good is desired for its own sake. It is the highest good beyond which no other good can be desired or attained. For Aristotle, the highest good provides happiness and self-sufficiency, *autarkia*. Self-sufficiency can only be reached through an activity that is independent from any external object. This activity is contemplation, *theoria*.[30] In it, the object of thought and the process of thinking coincide. We have already seen that Aristotle is well-aware of the dialectic that emerges from the idea of the highest good. All activities need the necessities of life and so depend on external conditions. Contemplation is no different because those contemplating also need to eat and depend on the support of others, he concedes.[31] However, once these conditions are provided, contemplation can become fully self-sufficient whereas practical virtues continue to depend on external circumstances.[32] Also, only contemplation is completely leisurely and does not have to produce any result, compared to practical endeavors whose goal always lies beyond themselves.[33] Although it may sound paradoxical, we can say that the non-practical activity of contemplation is the fulfillment of all other practical interests insofar as it provides the degree of inherent goodness that the other activities only intend to achieve but cannot reach.

Human beings are connected to each other, through their birth, their gender, the necessity for food, shelter, protection, and so on. They also depend on practical activities, if only for the sake of maintaining their physical existence. Contrary to that, inherent goodness, for Aristotle, is established in and through an activity that is both independent of all practical activities and supposed to help the individual overcome the need of connecting to others. This way, the focus on inherent goodness contradicts both the good that is achieved in human practices and the good that stems from their connectedness. It effectively diminishes the quality of this good which can no longer be desired as absolute. Agents may then fall into indifference toward their practical interests and needs, or at least think that these are eventually not worth considering. The inherent goodness of the intellect drains the goodness out of practical activities. We have to be careful not to limit this conclusion to Aristotle's focus on the intellect. Every conception that is focused on the goodness of specific capabilities can have this effect, because inherent goodness is then always maintained against other forms of goodness that are deemed deficient, in whatever way. For example, one could turn Aristotle's argument around and say that inherent goodness is located in human vulnerability as a basis for love and solidarity, and that pursuits of the intellect alienate humans from their deep-seated needs. This would discriminate against the good that is created through the intellect. The dialectic that emerges this way stems from the very idea of inherent goodness, not from the specific capability in which it is supposed to reside.

The second form of discrimination is more directly manifest. One of the most famous arguments in which inherent goodness is maintained despite the possibility of doing harm to others is made in Kant's text "On a supposed right to lie." We have already discussed this text with respect to the problem of exceptions.[34] For Kant, the consequences of an action must not be considered in one's decision because they are external events that cannot be determined with any degree of certainty, compared to the agent's capability which is always at their disposition and is therefore sufficient to be inherently good. The uncertainty of decision-making is especially high in the case of the murderer who comes to one's door: it is impossible to justify lying simply because one does not know whether it will be effective in preventing the friend from being hurt.[35]

To give Kant credit, it would be wrong to believe that he thought of the friend's well-being as morally irrelevant. His argument is not discriminatory against others insofar as it would imply that we should disregard the impact of our decisions on them. After all, even Kant assumed that we have let the friend hide in our house. Still, his argument is unfortunate, to say the least, because it goes counter to the idea of the absolute good. Kant focuses exclusively on the agent who is asked and on the question whether they should lie or not, but the situation as a whole includes many more elements and allows for a variety of reactions. For example, given that the potential murderer threatens the complete loss of the friend's good, that is, the loss of his life, Kant's attempt to preserve the inherent goodness of the agent's decision seems arbitrarily limited. From a broader point of view, the agent should have considered their good as related to the good of their friend so that their reaction to the potential murderer would have included the responsibility for their well-being. In that case, they could have done a number of things, for example, they could have remained silent and refused to give an answer. If Kant is right in saying that the circumstances of the situation are inherently uncontrollable, then refraining from choosing any determinate outcome might have been an adequate reaction. On the other hand, refusing to react to the challenge of a given situation can be a moral failure, too. One could argue that refusing to answer also only preserves the agent's good, very much like the refusal to lie, even if the intention would be to mark the inability of achieving the good in the given situation.

A more complete good may have required, say, following the potential murderer in their way through the house, waiting for the opportunity to intervene and prevent them from going further. After all, the situation can be described as one that requires self-defense or the defense of another person who is in immediate danger. Situations of self-defense are notoriously difficult to decide but morally speaking, the agent should at least have felt obliged to examine whether such a situation has arisen for them.

The inherent good that corresponds to a threatening situation like the one laid out by Kant can perhaps be described as the optimal outcome by which it would be possible to prevent harm from being done to everyone involved. That is, the inherent good would have been the resolution and overcoming of the threatening behavior itself. From the perspective of the absolute good, there should be no murderers, period, and whoever knows of one has the obligation to prevent them from carrying out their plans. Compared to this, Kant's focus on the good of the agent opening the door seems even more limited. We could perhaps say that if the optimal outcome cannot be achieved, it is one's obligation to achieve the good with the smallest amount of limitations.

We should be careful, though, not to imply that Kant's refusal of the need to lie was simply wrong. What we point out here is a dialectical structure according to which the contradictions that emerge are inevitable. The refusal to answer, as well as the attempt to tie down the intruder, may lead to similar difficulties than the refusal to lie. By attacking the intruder, I might endanger myself, which may amount to a case of unnecessary heroism that ultimately hurts others depending on me. If we cannot assume with certainty that the refusal to lie preserves the absolute good, then we cannot assume so for the other reactions either. This means that in such unclear situations we cannot prevent moral determinations from achieving a discriminatory meaning. There may always be one instance of the good that is preserved at the cost of diminishing and violating others. On the other hand, any morally conscious agent will have the intention of preserving at least something that is inherently good. The dialectical tension is inevitable first and foremost for moral reasons, because agents care for the good, not because they do not.

Feelings of Guilt

In the third form of antagonism, the discriminatory meaning of the good is directly manifest insofar as moral determinations are used to show the lack of goodness in others. Morality is used for the purpose of attributing blame. It is of course always possible to attribute blame once a specific moral determination has been made. The possibility of wrongdoing is given with the very notion of the good. What interests us here is the attribution of blame merely for the sake of attributing blame. The blame has no other purpose than to make others feel guilty and bad. In all other cases, blame is supposed to induce a different course of action: others are made aware of their wrongdoing and are asked to change their behavior, or a sanction is carried out to balance the harm that was done. In such cases, once the required changes have been made and the sanction has been imposed, there does not need to remain a feeling of guilt. There may of course be cases in which the harm is too great to be compensated by any subsequent action. But in such cases there is an objective reason to feel guilty, different from the present case in which the agent would not feel any guilt if it were not for the blame attributed by others. Formally speaking, in the present case the main purpose of the moral determination is to preserve inherent goodness by pointing out its absence in the actions of others.

In its most prominent form, the use of moral determinations for the sole purpose of attributing blame to others has been emphasized by Nietzsche. The purpose even defines the morality that originates from Judeo-Christian beliefs: "It is *not* necessary for a man first to be sinful, but for him to *feel* himself sinful."[36] Morality has been created by "priestly people, who in opposing their enemies and conquerors were ultimately satisfied with nothing less than a radical revaluation of their enemies' values, that is to say, an act of the *most spiritual revenge*."[37] Morality became an effective weapon by changing the self-evaluation of one's opponents. It made use of accusations that were unrelated to any objective wrongdoing by others.[38] Among the examples that Nietzsche cites there are, however, at least some cases in which the accusations have not been completely baseless. He tempers his own claims when he admits that the powerless had in fact good reasons to think of certain actions as harmful and bad.[39] Our analysis is therefore limited to those accusations that can indeed be shown as baseless, such as the assumption of sin in sexual activity.

Another example of such accusations can be found in arguments against abortion. Many think that for practical and political reasons it is impossible to withhold the option of abortion from women. Any general prohibition would go against liberal attitudes that are prevalent in today's society. However, the same individuals may still think that abortions are inherently bad. Therefore, even if access to the procedure cannot be prevented, they may want women to be aware that what they choose to do is not good and feel guilty about it. As a matter of fact, many assume that women feel naturally guilty about abortions, or at least should feel so. From our perspective, this means that a form of inherent goodness has been maintained, at least conceptually (or "spiritually," in Nietzsche's words), because one has succeeded in making sure that others feel the lack of goodness in their actions. Any more serious action, like the attempt to establish prohibitions on abortion, is much less likely to succeed because it will most certainly be met with resistance.

On the other hand, there is no resistance possible against the attribution of guilt because one can never conclusively show that one has not done something bad. For moral reasons alone, agents have to assume that they are more often guilty of wrongdoing, or at least of failures of the good, than they are aware of. The attribution of blame can count on a moral disposition in them. Conceptual attributions of blame are also much harder to defeat than factual ones, because factual attributions can be falsified, whereas conceptual ones remain valid unless they are shown as baseless and inconsistent, which is not always easy to do. A feeling of guilt is therefore likely to remain, which makes the accusation of women in the case of abortion a particularly vicious act.

Besides the attribution of blame, morality can become antagonistic if its standards are too high. If this is the case, then everything in the world of practice appears as deficient: the higher the goodness of moral determinations, the lower the reality of human actions. The good turns bitter, so to speak. Gehlen has coined the term "moral hypertrophy" for positions that request a higher moral standard than the existing social practices allow. He postulates the "law of the release of aggression through the radicalization of morality."[40] Radicalized morality leads to a "polarization of ethical impulses" which has an aggressive effect on others and leads to equally aggressive reactions which in turn exacerbate the perception of normative disputes.[41] For Gehlen, the aggressive use of morality is only possible for "privileged classes" who "do not have to be responsible for the consequences of their agitation. Because they are lacking real contact with practical matters, they cannot understand these consequences and are entitled to do whatever they want."[42] Even violence may be justified for them.[43] We do again not assume that those holding strong moral positions are intentionally aggressive or even behave in this way. It is sufficient that their determinations, when further examined and expressed, can have such an effect.[44]

The examples presented here show that the focus on inherent goodness can be seen as dialectical because it lacks any real concern for the consequences of one's actions. It seems that in order to take goodness seriously, one has to devote particular attention to the practical implications of what is done. This means that goodness is eventually not determined inherently but through its impact on oneself and others. The focus on inherent goodness leads so inevitably to the assumption of a consequentialist position.

The Strength of Consequentialism

Consequentialism locates the good in the outcomes of decisions and actions, which means that an agent can never claim to have achieved the good through the inherent goodness of the action they perform. Consequentialist theories derive their plausibility from the fact that the outcomes of actions are empirically real and measurable: whether something useful has been achieved or not can be verified once the appropriate criteria are defined. Obviously, this does not mean that any positive outcome counts, because if this were the case, then consequentialism would not be different from technical disciplines, or from economics, and could not represent a moral theory at all. In its most comprehensive form, consequentialism is a universal moral theory that intends to increase well-being either for some or for the greatest possible amount of people. Subjectively, the approach is supported by a benevolent attitude whose interest is to reduce the suffering of others and create more happiness in the world. We prefer "consequentialism" over "utilitarianism" here because the former highlights the distinctive features that are relevant for our analysis. We also ignore the differences between the various versions of consequentialist and utilitarian theories that can be found.

Before we can show the dialectical structures that emerge, we have to make consequentialism as strong as possible. One could say, for example, that despite its rich and nuanced history, morality has not succeeded yet in making life better than it is. This is proven by the fact that it still seems necessary to be moral. Morality is vain, and if it is supposed to retain any meaning, then we have to become able to effect real change in the world instead of stating, say, mere obligations which are easily disregarded and forgotten. This means that we have to base moral determinations on the consequences they achieve. With consequentialism, morality finally becomes real and touches the ground of human existence. Consequentialism is also able to counteract the elitism and destructive individualism that characterizes so many other approaches to morality, for example, Aristotle's claim that contemplation is the highest good or Kant's refusal to let go of general principles even in light of potentially lethal consequences for others. Following this line of thought, consequentialism is simply the most practical and meaningful moral theory. It does not so much appear as an alternative to other types of theories but rather as the theory that best articulates what other theories try to achieve. For example, Mill believed that utilitarianism captures the meaning that is implicit in previous, traditional forms of morality so that for him there is no difference between "the golden rule of Jesus of Nazareth" and the "ethics of utility."[45]

Variability

Decisions, attitudes, and actions that follow consequentialist principles can first seem not determined enough, despite their attempt at capturing the real, empirical effects of actions on others. There are two ways in which this can happen. The first way results from a well-known criticism according to which consequentialism does not allow for practical decision-making because it does not provide a clear criterion for achieving the good. What exactly increases people's well-being, and which one among the many quantifiable improvements that are possible at any given time constitute a real improvement of their lives? For example, is it good if the overall income of citizens is raised? Certainly, an increase in income would not be perceived as bad by anyone but how does it relate to other improvements that could be made? Would everyone perceive it as a priority? The presumed strength of consequentialism, its emphasis on empirical outcomes, is also its weakness, as no empirical assessment can be indubitable.

The empirical orientation also entails that agents are able to determine the appropriate increase in well-being all by themselves, which adds further complexity to the picture: not only are experiences variable between individuals, they are also dynamic and can change over time, even within one individual. The arguments that are presented in this regard have a long tradition and can be traced back, among others, to Kant who thought "that the concept of happiness is such an indeterminate concept that, although every human being wishes to attain this, he can still never say, determinately and consistently with himself what he really wishes and wills."[46] Against this, consequentialists can say that the indeterminedness of the over-arching goal ("Always produce the best results overall") is precisely the point: as a formal concept, it can relate to all projects of improvement that humans may find adequate in their given situation. This way, consequentialism states a limit condition, very similar to the way in which we explained the idea of humans as ends to be a limit for moral determinations.[47] But as we have seen, the problem with limits is that all kinds of decisions may be acceptable in the way leading up to the ultimate line, in this case even small and ineffective improvements. The risk is then that consequentialism cannot give agents more than the vague and meaningless recommendation "Try your best" or "Even if you can do only little, it is great."[48]

The second way in which the indeterminedness of consequentialism can be evident is also based in its empirical orientation. Williams notes that "many of the qualities that human beings prize in society and in one another are notably non-utilitarian." If these preferences "are not to be legislated out, then utilitarianism has got to coexist with them, and it is not clear how it does that."[49] Consequentialism cannot "legislate out" individual preferences without betraying its empirical orientation and turning into some form of dogmatism. If agents have to be compelled to act in optimific ways, consequentialism loses its normative force. From this perspective, the approach appears as indetermined because it has to allow for actions that contradict its very principle.

Counting on Indeterminedness: Some Remarks on Moral Luck

Indeterminedness also plays a role in the discussion of what has been called moral luck. We can see in this discussion an attempt at using indeterminedness as a positive condition in morality. This attempt fails because even if indeterminedness is acknowledged and embraced, it retains a dialectical structure and cannot *not* be seen as a condition that should not exist.

In his famous essay, Williams criticizes the tradition of moral thought for trying to make the agent "immune to the impact of incident luck."[50] All major theories face the problem that contingency cannot be kept subordinated and controlled.[51] There can be no such thing as responsibility for all conditions and outcomes of one's actions. A conception that would account for this fact would be twofold, depending on whether luck is good or bad.[52] Bad moral luck leads to regret. For Williams, the main point is here that agents may assume responsibility, and therefore feel regret, even for outcomes that they have not directly caused.[53] Good moral luck, or just moral luck in his use of the term, can be felt when actions that are morally bad lead to good results. The well-known example that he uses is Gaugin, who left his wife and children but subsequently produced admirable works of arts. Gaugin can in retrospect feel justified.[54] However, had he failed to produce respectable art, he would have had no reason to assume this retrospective justification.

It is not immediately clear how good moral luck has to be understood. Gaugin's justification can of course not be a matter of the changing tastes of museum goers, or of mere reputation. Williams therefore distinguishes between extrinsic and intrinsic luck: the latter means that Gaugin was lucky to have been the kind of person who had a profound and original vision of the world and was able to translate it into an impressive series of works.[55] We can paraphrase this by saying that in the case of good moral luck the agent knowingly violates moral obligations and harms others but at the same time makes some sort of promise to themself not to do this wantonly but to begin a new course of actions, or a new chapter in their life, whose outcome will be valuable and so restore their integrity as a moral agent, if only retrospectively.

From the idea of intrinsic luck, Williams derives a particularist perspective on morality. Indeterminedness allows agents to develop personal moral projects, either by becoming more regretful and considerate than external norms require or by making decisions that may be harmful to some but amount to a way of achieving a particular form of the good. Williams seems to want his cake and eat it: he wants personal projects to be individually authentic and at the same time moral, leading, among others, to a genuine feeling of justification. The latter is rather questionable. If bad actions could appear justified in retrospective, "it would imply the truth of a hypothetical judgment made in advance, of the form 'If I leave my family and become a great painter, I will be justified by success; if I don't become a great painter, the act will be unforgivable.'"[56] If actions could be seen from such a hypothetical point of view, it would become unclear whether there is even an obligation, say, to care for one's family. Moral considerations would be open to some sort of gambling insofar as the agent would have the chance of becoming justified later for morally problematic acts. Williams seems to be aware of this point when he emphasizes that the "moral cost" of certain decisions is decided by those who are affected by it. It would be "patronizing" to tell them that they have no reason to complain.[57] But if this really were the case for him, then moral luck would be purely incidental and of no particular interest: who cares after all whether Gaugin feels justified or not? The harm to his family would be all we care about.

From a moral point of view, retrospective assessments are irrelevant: what counts is the moral determination at the time the agent acts. What Gaugin's case positively shows is perhaps best described as a conflict of moral obligations, obligations toward one's family *and* obligations toward oneself insofar as Gaugin, like any other individual, has a responsibility to realize his most essential abilities and desires. For example, who says that he would have cared adequately for his family had he stayed and become depressed because he did not feel that he led a life that was truly his? Williams makes a valid point in emphasizing the need to lead one's life in an autonomous and self-respecting way, but contrary to his approach one does not have to think that this need stands in opposition to general obligations. We rather have to see it as another obligation that is relevant for the situation at hand. This means that contrary to Williams we do not believe that contingency should be involved in the idea of justification. Luck is beside the point in moral matters. If Gaugin was justified in doing what he did, he had to be justified at the time of his decision. Both normative points of view, the one related to the family and the one related to himself as individual, have to be seen as sufficient moral determinations. Indetermindness is obviously involved whichever determination one follows, but its impact is behind the agent's back: at the time of the decision, one cannot count on it and think that it may work in one's favor. Gaugin's situation is fundamentally dialectical: he is not allowed to leave his family, morally speaking, and he is allowed to do so. Whatever he does, he cannot claim to have achieved an absolute good.

We can generalize the problem that presents itself here and ask whether agents are ever allowed to take moral risks. Taking moral risks means that they count on indetermindness to work in their favor and make an action good after the fact. For example, we may wish to accuse a co-worker of wrongdoing but do not have enough evidence unless we make the accusation and force them to reveal certain aspects of their behavior. We have enough reason to make the accusation and think that it is relevant enough, but we might also falsely accuse them. Should we take the risk? One might also want to support an authoritarian form of government because there is a perceived crisis in one's country. Is there ever a situation in which such a risk can be taken because there is a realistic chance that the authoritarian government would be more effective than a democratic one? It seems again that counting on indetermindness in one's decision is problematic from a moral point of view. Agents need to base their decision on a moral determination that is sufficient under the given circumstances, in the sense that this determination provides the strongest reason for them to act. Otherwise they decide for the possibility of a bad outcome (a hostile work environment, an oppressive regime), tacitly assuming that they will not be responsible for it because the events could have turned out differently. Counting on indeterminedness would so mean that the agents distance themselves from the moral weight and the possible outcomes of their decision.

For moral reasons alone, one should also not exaggerate the indeterminedness of actions. It may indeed be the case that many, if not all, factors in our actions are "beyond our control."[58] Should we therefore give up the responsibility for what we do?[59] We can describe the problem that arises with the issue of control as a dialectic of parts and wholes. Each single action is a whole and also has parts, and all parts can be isolated and related to elements outside of the action. The action is always one and many at the same time. For example, we buy a new house in a larger city but one day a helicopter falls on it. Nothing in our decision was risky or reckless and yet we put ourselves in harm's way by moving to a large urban area. Are the two events connected? Can we say that we were unlucky *because* we moved? Consequences are parts of an action too, and sometimes it is unclear how far an action reaches into the future through its various parts. If a murder attempt fails, is the agent still a murderer? In some regards they are, in others not. They obviously wanted to commit murder, but a completely different outcome was achieved. This dialectic of parts and wholes may be difficult to resolve in particular cases. Still, dealing with it belongs to the usual assessment of actions and is rooted in our common practical experience. One could perhaps say that practical experience is mostly this, knowing how the different factors of actions, how parts and whole, can be distinguished and managed in relation to each other. Agents only have to be specific enough in their analysis of the circumstances of an action. The combination of parts and whole may be contingent, but it is never random with respect to an individual agent. That is, it is always intelligible to agents what they intend to do and why they intend it. They are not allowed to invoke indeterminedness and say that they did one thing one but also indirectly wanted to achieve another.

Coming to an End

Proponents of a consequentialist approach to morality may claim that the approach is in fact well-determined and can be meaningfully applied in particular situations. After all, do we not all know more or less what would be needed to make our lives better at such-and-such a place and time? And can we not trust all others to know this as well? Objections against utilitarianism are created out of mere sophistry, it seems, pretending that humans are less knowledgeable than they actually are. However, in attempting to maintain the determinedness of consequentialism, the approach appears as too determined and also turns into its opposite.

All assessments of a given situation have to come to an end. At one point or another, a determination has to be found that is likely to yield the greatest possible amount of well-being. Although all empirical assessments are open to revision, there has to be a moment at which further examination would not lead to a different result. This also follows from the limitations of human knowledge. If we have good reasons to assume that our knowledge of the world is finite, we have to reach the point, from time to time, at which our beliefs will not easily change and have to be accepted as they are. Wittgenstein's rhetorical question "Doesn't testing come to an end?" speaks to this limitation.[60] But if this is the case, then there is no guarantee that the consequentialist assessment of a given situation is not arbitrary. Consequentialism may then turn from an open-ended and truth-related empirical inquiry of the greatest possible utility for humans into the dogmatic stipulation of maximal outcomes. "Increase GDP" is such a dogmatic stipulation because it assumes that objectively good consequences are equivalent to monetary ones, which is in itself no empirical idea but a conceptual decision that has been made before the facts are assessed.[61] Consequentialism also favors the majority of those who benefit from the outcome of actions over those who cannot in the case at hand, which too introduces a conceptual distinction before any empirical factors are taken into account. From a moral point of view, there is no reason why one should not always consider everyone as deserving. Instead of being dogmatic, one could also say that consequentialism ends up as a form of casuistry, despite its claim to universality. Here, one could benefit so many people, there, one could benefit so many others, and so on, but which benefits are chosen depends entirely on the capabilities of the particular agent who assesses the situation. Finally, consequentialism is at risk of turning from a moral theory into a non-moral one. If particular outcomes, such as increased GDP, are given normative preference, then consequentialism can end up making itself superfluous: if the increase in well-being can be determined, say, economically or psychologically, no further moral assessment is needed.

Impartiality as Moral Privilege

Finally, consequentialist determinations can acquire an antagonistic meaning. They do so by requiring agents to make sacrifices that are needed to achieve the greatest possible good. In the following, we will distinguish between real and moral sacrifices. The latter will be discussed in the following section. The question of sacrifices is openly addressed in approaches to consequentialism. Mill concedes that utilitarianism could "attain its end" if all agents made "other people happier" without thereby becoming happier themselves.[62] However, he finds such a scenario an "absurdity,"[63] which means that although the utilitarian standard does not depend on, or is supposed to promote, the individual agent's happiness, it does not exclude it either. In other words, it is not the purpose of utilitarianism to make the agents adopting it unhappy. Mill also emphasizes that despite its altruistic character, utilitarianism does not see self-sacrifice as a good in itself.[64] If such a sacrifice occurs, it is only justifiable if it helps to increase the happiness of others. Still, these remarks imply that there can indeed be situations in which a self-sacrifice would be required from a utilitarian point of view:

> Though it is only in a very imperfect state of the world's arrangements that any one can best serve the happiness of others by the absolute sacrifice of his own, yet so long as the world is in that imperfect state, I fully acknowledge that the readiness to make such sacrifice is the highest virtue which can be found in man.[65]

The utilitarian tradition that followed Mill's thought affirmed this position.[66] In all fairness to consequentialism, the question of sacrifices is mostly discussed with respect to situations in which there is urgency to prevent harm, or the need to choose among several harmful options. The mere opportunity of increasing the well-being of some is rarely presented as a valid reason to harm others. Still, sacrifices of oneself or others are at least potentially considered moral and there is no restriction on discussing them as one justifiable option that agents have.[67]

The reason for this readiness to accept sacrifices lies in the standard of impartiality which states "that the good of any one individual is of no more importance, from the point of view ... of the Universe, than the good of any other."[68] Consequentialist positions have to neglect the needs and pains both of the agent and of others if those contradict the overall good. Individual suffering has to make way for the good, so to speak. On a purely conceptual level, it seems evident that self-sacrifice and the sacrifice of others are inherently coercive and cannot be seen as realization of the absolute good. Impartiality is different from universality because it does not aim at a good that is established equally for all. It constitutes a neutral point of view, detached from any individual interest, which then can be used to weigh the benefits it may be possible to achieve against the disadvantages that have to be accepted in a given case. Consequentialist calculations are therefore often presented as a trade-off. Although the very term "impartiality" suggests otherwise, consequentialism is a theory of moral privilege because it accepts and even embraces the fact that not everyone can be included in the overall good which is determined as a worthy goal. The main rule of consequentialism seems to say: "Create as much good as you can for whoever is able to benefit at this point and do not bother about the rest." In addition, impartiality means here that nothing can be considered inherently good but everything can potentially be given up if the calculation of outcomes indicates that it should. "Consequentialist rationality ... has no ... limitations."[69]

The proponents of a consequentialist approach could object that our argument is circular because we assume from the start that there has to be something that is inherently good. But this is in fact the case if there is supposed to be a good at all. Without it, sacrifices would be potentially endless, given that there can always be a greater good. Not even the proponents of a consequentialist position can require an open-ended increase of utility.

We can also notice a certain ambivalence between the subjective disposition toward consequentialism, which is typically driven by benevolence and a concern for effective changes in well-being, and the objective criteria that are used to reach decisions. It is unclear whether consequentialism is eventually a cold form of social engineering, hidden behind a benevolent façade, or a mere tool of thought that will always be subservient to morally acceptable ideas and goals, despite some vagueness in its application. However, if consequentialism is driven by benevolence, it may not have any considerable impact because benevolence exerts a limiting effect. No drastic strides toward the overall good can be made. This would mean that consequentialism is not determined enough. If it is determined, and the objective calculations are not limited by subjective reservations, then it cannot avoid being discriminatory, for the reasons mentioned above. There is no way, it seems, to avoid this dialectic.

The dialectical nature of consequentialism is particularly manifest in the question how numbers should be factored in. Consequentialists assume that the number of people who are affected by a decision is of moral relevance. Impartiality entails the use of quantitative measures and requires the agent to care for the well-being of the greater number if they have the choice. In a hypothetical situation in which a life-saving drug can be administered either to one person or to five, but not to all, consequentialism requires it to be distributed to the greater number. Taurek uses this example to explain why he refuses to take numbers into account for the moral determination of decisions. Counting "the relative numbers of people involved as something in itself of significance, would have me attach importance to human beings … in merely the way I would to objects which I valued."[70] The presumed objectivity of the quantitative evaluation disregards the uniqueness of each person who is concerned. The one person in this case has no duty to give up their interest in life, and the five others do not have any right over the single one to be saved.[71] That is, the greater number does not give each member of that group a comparatively greater right to live than the person who is considered alone. If we consider each life in its own right, the decision to prefer the greater number does not appear tenable: "five individuals each losing his life does not add up to anyone's experiencing a loss five times greater than the loss suffered by any one of the five. … Suffering is not additive."[72] In other words, it is a category mistake to assume that the number of individuals would matter because we can add up what is valued by each individual. Parfit has objected to that solution, claiming that different instances of pain can in fact be compared and that the "urgency of moral claims" may well depend on one harm being "much greater" than another.[73] We have to take numbers into account, not because they matter as such, but because "we *do* give equal weight to saving each. Each counts for one. That is why more count for more."[74] Precisely because each agent's suffering can be looked at in a unique way it matters if more of this unique suffering can be prevented.

Parfit is certainly right in pointing out that a greater number matters insofar as it multiplies the normative concerns that one can have with respect to persons. If a person is guilty of neglecting their children, it matters whether they have three children or only one child. Taurek's claim that there is no reason to prefer the five over the single person would be untenable from this angle. And yet, it seems equally problematic to justify one's decision in favor of the five simply because they form a group. This shows again that impartiality is in reality an expression of moral privilege: an isolated agent would not be given moral preference simply because they are isolated, whereas the same person, if they switched sides and became part of a group, would all of the sudden deserve such a preference. In the case of the neglect of children, it might matter for jurisprudence how many children one has, but morally speaking even the neglect of one child is morally wrong. In fact, in the neglect of three children, each one of them counts only for one, not as one resulting from a division of three. Parfit's argument can be turned against his own conclusion insofar as we can say that in greater numbers there are simply more ones, so that there is in a sense more concern to be had, but that this concern is qualitatively always only the concern for one. It does not become greater because it is repeated several times. It may be the case that one has to save the five because of circumstances that belong to the particular case at hand, but in this case it should at least be clear that one discriminates against the isolated individual. The consequentialist position seems to suggest instead that, taken objectively, the isolated individual could not even complain because there can be no moral reason to consider saving the smaller number. Impartiality is an expression of privilege also insofar as it pretends that there would be no regret or remorse in a situation in which one has to decide against particular individuals or groups.

Moral Sacrifices

Moral sacrifices are made when consequentialist determinations discriminate against the preferences of agents, either by requiring them to give up preferences or by attributing blame and guilt. The consequences that agents suffer from moral sacrifices might eventually be only conceptual. However, the sacrifices alter an agent's belief about the good that they are able to achieve, and such beliefs may well end up being practically relevant. The first form of discrimination, which requires the renunciation of preferences, has been diagnosed in Williams' famous criticism of consequentialism. For him, impartiality "abstracts from the identity of the agent."[75] An agent is not allowed, morally speaking, to treat situations as uniquely relevant for them, for example, because they concern others for whom they care or because they feel individually involved. All situations and agents have to be given equal weight, which has an alienating effect.[76] Having to give up one's preferences means to give up the ability to pursue moral goals on one's own account, which is also the ability for self-determination. Individuals then stop being moral agents and become, so to speak, servants of a higher authority. Obviously, not all moral preferences that individuals maintain are worthy of being preserved. Quite the contrary is often the case. But the point is that bad preferences should be replaced by better ones, not by an impartial standard that is presumably objective and makes it unnecessary to develop preferences in the first place.

The second type of moral sacrifices follows from the rigor that lies in the application of an impartial standard. Consequentialism has often been felt to be over-demanding: if we look at our achievements impartially, we realize that we all should make more sacrifices than we do to achieve an even greater good. Everyone is guilty for the potential positive outcomes they have failed to produce. Williams, again, points out that impartiality entails the idea of negative responsibility. If all outcomes are given equal weight, morally speaking, then it does not matter exactly how the agent is practically involved in them. They can be held morally responsible even for things they have not brought about themself because at the very least they have let them happen.[77] An argument that exemplifies this approach is presented by Singer:

> If it is in our power to prevent something bad from happening, without thereby sacrificing anything of comparable moral importance, we ought, morally, to do it. ... The principle takes, firstly, no account of proximity or distance. It makes no moral difference whether the person I can help is a neighbor's child ten yards from me or a Bengali whose name I shall never know, ten thousand miles away.[78]

According to Singer, it is downright immoral if agents prefer particular others in their efforts toward the good. There is no morally significant difference between anyone on earth. Sacrifices are only allowed to stop once the agent would find themself in a situation that is as bad as the one they want to remedy.[79]

If agents accept Singer's use of the standard of impartiality, they have to accept that their relation toward others is always and inevitably discriminatory. This entails that they have to stop discriminating, which is only possible if they discriminate against themselves and commit to significant sacrifices. The agents cannot simply stop discriminating without sacrifices because their very existence, say, as members of an affluent society is unjustifiable as long as poverty exists in some parts of the world. As a concrete application of this argument, Singer explained that each member of the Western world should donate at least 5 percent of their yearly income to charities addressing problems in the Global South.[80]

The question is what such a demand is able to achieve. Singer is of course right in pointing out that the affluence of Western societies is made possible by the poverty of other nations which are exploited and prevented from rising to the status of equals. But the exploitation means that Western societies have to acknowledge the asymmetry in their relation to the Global South as well as their privileged position. If they do, drastic remedies have to be found. For example, developed nations have to cut their fossil fuel emissions because these emissions contribute to the rise in temperature that affects the living conditions of poorer nations. The privileged position of Western societies is a violation of global justice, not a failure to produce more well-being from an impartial point of view. Also, Singer's focus on charitable donations instead of, say, increased taxation frames the question along the lines of a supererogatory act. Charity, by definition, cannot be required. Agents would then only face an obligation because they have applied a neutral standard of impartiality, not because they have acknowledged both their current and historical responsibility as members of a privileged group. While the latter is definite and based on undeniable facts, the former is hypothetical because it leaves open how the overall amount of good can be increased and distributed in the world. In this sense, Singer's rigorous demand, paradoxically, is too vague. At the same time, it is too strict: if a hypothetical assessment is used, one could also be blamed for not having prevented a murder in a country very far from one's own, simply because there is the logical probability that one could have been at the place where the murder occurred.

The main purpose that Singer's demand seems to achieve is, again, the instilling of guilt in agents. It is unrealistic to expect that the call for charitable donations will be answered universally. Singer's argument seems similar to the Christian condemnation of sexuality and the call to abstinence that it entails, which can also never succeed on a universal scale. The only thing that is achieved by such calls is that they produce the awareness in agents of having failed in significant moral matters, which makes them feel regretful and dependent on the forgiveness of those who have diagnosed their guilt. The calls, eventually, only help those making them because it lets them appear as experts and authority in moral excellence. Whoever shares Singer's argument becomes morally unassailable: no one can meet their standard and they are the first ones to admit guilt, which makes them superior over all others.

This way, we come back to the point from which we started. We have seen that determinations based on inherent goodness can be used to induce feelings of guilt, which was one of the reasons for which consequentialism seemed a better option. It may be surprising to see that consequentialist positions can have the same effect. But this should not be surprising at all. Consequentialism is the dialectical counter-point to inherent goodness. Both are based on a distinction between existing practices and a particular moral content against which they are measured. What differs between them is only the place of the good. For both, the good is realized only in one part of an action, which makes the other parts, and the agent's involvement in them, appear as deficient. It is possible, therefore, to swing back from the focus on future outcomes that we find in a position like Singer's to the assumption that something in one's immediate action has to be inherently good. The dialectic of moral determinations, eventually, convinces us that among two opposing theories the better option is always the other one that is not chosen.

Attempts at a Reconciliation: The Law

Like in the previous chapters, the dialectic between inherent goodness and consequentialism calls for a reconciliation. In order to restore the integrity and effectiveness of morality, the contradictions that have emerged need to be resolved. This brings us one more time to Hegel's practical philosophy. His attempt at overcoming the dialectic of generality and particularism through the idea of "ethical life" has been described before.[81] Ethical life culminates in the reality of state. This point is most relevant for the present analysis. For Hegel,

> it is only through being a member of the state that the individual himself has objectivity, truth, and ethical life. ... The destiny of individuals is to lead a universal life; their further particular satisfaction, activity, and mode of conduct have this substantial and universally valid basis as their point of departure and result.[82]

We can read this passage in light of the dialectical contradictions presented here. In the state and the lawful behavior that it establishes—the state is not just a political institution but first and foremost a legal entity insofar as it resides on a constitution[83]— the goodness of practices is guaranteed as inherent. Agents unconditionally adopt rules-based practices and the corresponding personal roles that they play as citizens and members of representative groups. At the same time, individuals can pursue their interest in well-being and "satisfaction." They are even encouraged to do so as it is the nature of the modern state to be based on "concrete freedom."[84] Agents can adopt consequentialist positions precisely because their content is limited to what the laws allow. The dialectic of inherent goodness and consequentialism has become indifferent as both ways of realizing the good coexist in the lawful sphere of the state. In addition, neither consequentialist positions nor positions based on inherent goodness have to face indeterminedness anymore because the law takes the burden away from agents to determine individually the content of their action. Finally, insofar as institutional roles and the purposes that they fulfill are well-defined, at least in in principle, no determination can become too determined or antagonistic.

The law thus realizes what morality strives to achieve but cannot achieve by itself. Morality, insofar as it is based on individual self-determination and cultural practices, needs to be subordinated to the sphere of law. For Habermas, this is especially the case in the modern conception of the law.[85] Following the law is required by moral reasons, as the individual cannot claim to be a moral person if they violate rules that all others have legitimately established among themselves. If moral self-determination would try to affirm itself outside of or against the state it would appear not only as irrelevant but even as evil. Lawful and institutional behavior *is* the fulfillment of the demands that morality makes. Morality, if it takes itself seriously in establishing general adherence to principles, has to acknowledge its feebleness and turn the task of realizing normative ideas over to the state.[86]

Similar arguments can be found in the field of legal positivism. Not all approaches are relevant for us here. What interests us is the fact that legal positivism can also be based on a moral argument. For example, Kelsen states: "The realization of natural law becomes dependent upon the knowledge and will of men by whose doing alone abstract natural law is transmuted into a concrete legal relationship."[87] We can take "natural law" and morality as synonymous in this quote. Like Hegel, Kelsen assumes that moral principles remain empty and ineffective without their translation into specific laws. As an example, he cites the notion of equality.

> The question ... whether, in a given case, A and B are 'equal' or not, and that means, which differences, actually existing between A and B, are irrelevant, cannot be answered by natural-law doctrine. The answer is given exclusively by positive law. The principle of equality as a principle of justice implies only that if A is to be treated in a certain way and B equals A, it follows that B must be treated in the same way.[88]

The notion of equality contains a hypothetical element because it is *a priori* unclear in which way it can be established between individuals. Some of the activities and qualities of agents have to be disregarded because relying on them would make it impossible to achieve equality, but it does not follow from the very notion of equality which ones these are. As a mere notion, unrelated to concrete behavior, equality is devoid of meaning. This means again that legal procedures do the job that morality only proclaims to do. The law provides a "normative system" and a "positive regulation of human relationships" which do not need assistance or justification by moral ideas.[89] Morality and the law are eventually no "simultaneously valid orders."[90]

For the purpose of our analysis, we can leave out questions that often arise with respect to legal positivism, for example, the questions whether the law is to be followed simply because it is the law and what happens in the case of unjust laws. "Laws may be law but too evil to be obeyed."[91] Legal positivism is compatible with the idea that laws can be revised or even broken if there is need. The point is only that if laws were an expression of moral ideas *at all times*, they would not be laws at all. There simply would be no rules, properly speaking, if the existing rules depended on moral self-determination and the randomness of consensus between various individuals and groups.[92]

Evidently, the question how the law relates to morality is much more complex than we can treat it here. We can see this, for example, when Kelsen states: "From the point of view of a consistent positivism, which regards the positive legal order as supreme, non-derivative, and therefore non-justifiable by reference to a superior system of norms, the validity of a natural law cannot be admitted."[93] While it is possible to see statements like this as a mere clarification of the conceptual status of a legal system, it seems unclear whether such a system is wholly "non-derivative," as he states. Could moral ideas not have been important for the creation of a legal system?[94] If so, when do they cease to have an impact? And if the existing laws can sometimes be disobeyed, how can the necessity of such an act be decided if there is not "a superior system of norms"? Again, we cannot unpack the complexities of legal positivism here. These questions show, however, that while legal positivism provides *one* solution to the dialectics of inherent goodness and consequentialism, it cannot provide the *final* one. The legal system is the expression of morality's self-limitation but it cannot, and must not, amount to its self-effacement. In the law, the dialectics of morality is not so much resolved as paused. The law is never simply given and complete, unless one would claim that the factual completeness of a legal system is equivalent to the completeness of the good, which would lead to the crude form of legal positivism that even its proponents try to avoid. At the very least one can say that for moral reasons alone one should never accept a given legal system as beyond the need for questioning and reform. Morality has to let rules be rules, but those representing or benefiting from the legal system cannot hide from questions of legitimacy behind the pretense of mere functionality. The question can always arise whether the law yields acceptable consequences or whether certain established laws are still inherently good. The dynamic nature of the law is essentially a moral one and becomes inevitably affected by morality's own dialectic.[95] It seems impossible for morality *not* have an impact on the legal system at some point, and if that is the case then no definitive reconciliation of morality's inherent dialectic is found in the law.

Part Three

Foolishness

11

Moral Nonetheless

Introductory Remarks

The last chapters seem to have driven us into a desperate position. All attempts at providing a moral determination that would be sufficient for the good fail insofar as none can avoid inner contradictions. Moral determinations, and the theories by which they are articulated, lead to an endless progression of dialectical structures, as each one of them turns into the opposite of what it claims to be or can be given up for another one which then suffers the same fate. Moral determinations fail the good precisely because they are meant to achieve it, as we have said repeatedly before. The question is then whether this is the end of story for the desire to be good. Where could we go from here? In distinguishing the different ways of failing morality, we have already indicated the answer to this question. There are what can be called rescue attempts which seek to remedy the contradictory nature of moral determinations. Agents undertake these attempts either by trying to restore the good under a form that compensates for its failure or by holding on to moral determinations despite the obvious contradictions that they incur.[1] The present chapter will show in detail what this entails. But before we can do so, we have to explain a little more how it is even possible to move on despite the awareness of the dialectical nature of moral determinations. How can one be moral nonetheless?

There is a first and simple answer to this question: all determinations that we analyzed were moral, that is, all were possible determinations of the good. The inner contradictions that emerged did not turn them into immoral or evil ones. Neither were the determinations made by mistake or logically inconsistent. As we have mentioned, dialectical structures only emerge once a moral determination is fully expressed in its conceptual assumptions and implications.[2] The dialectic leaves the initial determinations with their moral contents and intentions intact. A second answer can point at the fact that the contradictions too were not logical but moral. Agents have to deny themselves *for moral reasons* the claim of realizing the absolute good. They produce dialectical structures as a result of the self-application of moral criteria. This means that agents eventually do not have to give up their desire to be good. They can legitimately retain it as long as they are aware that they retain it *nonetheless*. At the first glance, this may seem like a way to avoid the problem: is the desire for the good supposed to make the contradictions go away? In fact, there is only a fine line between an agent who is aware of the tensions in their determination and another one who goes on as if there were no problem at all. From a practical point of view, both attitudes can be indistinguishable. But as also said before, we are not bothered by wrongfully used moral positions. We assume that there is such a thing as attempting, honestly and genuinely, to achieve the good while reacting to its failure. At least we hope that the examples presented in the following sections will prove that such attempts can exist.

We will describe three types of rescue attempts, each of which can be exemplified by a number of positions and moral theories. The types will be aligned according to the dialectal progression that was at the basis of the previous analyses. As we have seen, moral determinations are either not determined enough or too determined. In the case of the latter they either turn into their opposite or become antagonistic.

Rescue attempts that start from the awareness that moral determinations may not be determined enough will be called *idealist*. The positions resulting from these attempts acknowledge the contrast between the world of practice and the emptiness and ineffectiveness of moral determinations. The positions state, however, that the good can be realized if agents only anticipate it and act as if it were present. Rescue attempts which are based on determinations that are too determined will be subsumed under the idea of *responsibility*. These positions are aware that general principles might turn into particularist ones, thereby contradicting their own meaning, but they conclude that if all moral determinations are particular, then the agent has to act in a particular, individual way, too. The responsibility that agents assume lets go of principles and engages in actions that address specific circumstances in the world, often guided by feelings of urgency. The last type of rescue attempts tries to overcome the dialectic altogether. It rejects the antagonistic nature of moral determinations. The positions that emerge from this will be described as attempts to reach *forgiveness*. Forgiveness is redemptive insofar as it counter-acts the divisiveness that comes with moral determinations. It tries to establish a fresh, untainted ground on which agents can achieve the good in a more consistent way.

These rescue attempts evidently cannot escape the dialectic either, whether they embrace it openly or try to act against it. Positions that are meant to compensate the failure of the good cannot all of the sudden become fully sufficient. They are marked by the conditions that they strive to overcome. The different theories that will be mentioned in the following are mostly unaware that they can be qualified as "rescue attempts." We believe, however, that our analysis allows us to diagnose such motives and tendencies working tacitly in them.

One may think that at this point we would finally reveal our own, positive morality, the forms of moral self-determination that would incorporate the necessary failure of good in such a way that they can be suggested as the new normative standard. But we cannot present such a thing. There is no solution, practical or conceptual, to the failing of the good. Whatever we would suggest would only be a variation of the determinations that we have analyzed in the previous parts. If an agent were to ask in light of the inquiry conducted up to this point, "Is there anything specific I should do?" the only answer we can give is *no*. We can only tell them: "Do whatever you want, you will fail the good whether you are aware of it or not." By all means do we want to avoid promoting a certain pragmatic indulgence that would allow the agent not to be bothered with their own contradictions. Just as no one is allowed to let go of the idea of an absolute good, morally speaking, no one is redeemed of its failing either. We could even say that it would be evil to assume that one's own way of being moral does not entail the contradictions that the ways of others do. As a rule of thumb, it is always *my* moral self-determination that fails, even if I have good reason to prefer it over the determination of others.

Others might think that being aware of positions as rescue attempts undermines the agent's honesty in moral affairs. After all, the agent has to take a certain personal risk in trying to promote the good against its apparent contradictions. They have to convince others that it is still worthwhile doing so and they also have to go against the pressures of social groups that habitually tend to appease and pretend that "everything is okay" so that no one has to be blamed for any failure. Their attitude may then easily become a mere posturing that turns failing into a fancy and exquisite attitude of sorts. Admitting failure could even become a sign for the agent's special moral quality. There is of course nothing that could prevent this from happening. All we can say is that agents should not spend too much time focusing on their failures, given that there is no reason not to be good. The awareness of failure should not become a separate, intellectually attractive attitude but has to work as a sort of conscience that goes along implicitly and silently with moral attitudes.

Finally, whoever is determined to let the good prevail has to become the victim of their own determination. "I wanted to follow this principle at all costs, now I have to see it through." Agents have to be willing to make a fool of themselves by embracing contradictions that would convince others to go for a less controversial option. The idealist might look foolish to those who have decided that there is nothing to expect from morality anymore, and so might the agent who assumes responsibility in a difficult case. Forgiveness, in turn, is often admired but can secretly be seen as foolish because the agent gives up the right to pursue their own advantage. All positions can easily be criticized and even ridiculed in the eyes of those who find it more interesting and comfortable to dwell on the obvious failures and limitations of moral determinations. Foolishness, however, is no negative term for us here. It rather designates both the quality and intensity of a non-trivial commitment to morality's cause. Our use of the term echoes Paul who called the apostles fools.[3] We believe that agents who embrace the positions we are about to describe are fools too—not for Christ's sake, but for the sake of the good.[4]

Each of the following three parts of this chapter proceeds along a certain schematic order—not, of course, because we think that moral theories and positions properly fit into any scheme, or any typology for that matter, but because the scheme allows us to show the variety of options that exist for all approaches based on idealism, responsibility, and forgiveness. The main theories and positions in each part are the foolish ones which let their inner contradictions come to the fore. We will contrast them, first, to theories and positions whose overall tendency is to reconcile the contradictions, sometimes up to the point at which they seem to disappear or at least become invisible. These approaches are less foolish but also less cognizant of, and responsive to, the dialectical nature of the good. The theories and positions will in turn be contrasted to approaches we consider vulgar. Instead of reconciling the contradictions, these approaches simplify things too much and completely ignore or overlook dialectical tensions. Finally, there are approaches which are simple and pragmatic without at the same time being vulgar. The problems in the world of practice to which idealism, responsibility, and forgiveness react can also be countered by activism, community, and humor, respectively. In the latter, the scope and the ambition of moral determinations are much reduced.

First Attempt: Idealist Anticipations

Factual Contra-factuals

The positions and theories described in this section acknowledge that moral determinations may appear either empty or ineffective, or both. Moral determinations might not have real meaning and cannot by themselves guarantee their realization. The positions and theories turn this lack of reality into a promise. Given that no one is forced to give up moral determinations as delusional or inconsistent, one can think that morality retains an inexhaustible potential. This potential only needs to be explored in order to anticipate the realization of morality in the future, or better: *as a future* in which human practices will be transformed. We can show what this means by using the example of Habermas' moral theory.

The theory, called "discourse ethics," is a reformulation and adaptation of some of the basic features of Kant's moral philosophy. All "variants of cognitivist ethics," Habermas believes, assume "the impersonal … character of valid moral commands"[5] and incorporate, in one way or another, the idea of the categorical imperative insofar as it entails the "generalizability" of principles.[6] He is well aware of the dialectical tensions that arise in Kant's conception of morality. Relying on autonomy as individual exercise of reason can be problematic in two ways. First, autonomy can only be expected from agents if it occurs in a social context which allows for practices that are guided, at least partially, by reason. Otherwise, the agent can only ever be moral at their own detriment.[7] Habermas follows Hegel's criticism of Kant insofar as he too believes that morality has to be embedded in, and realized through appropriate institutions and social behavior.[8] Second, reason alone cannot guarantee the neutrality of the agent's point of view.[9] Kant's theory, like many others, postulates an "ideal observer," but this observer is in reality only an "isolated subject, collecting and assessing his information in the light of his own individual understanding of the world and of himself."[10] For Habermas, there is a "residuum of Platonism"[11] in Kant's approach: each subject endowed with reason, insofar as it is a member of an ideal community, a "kingdom of ends," can all by themselves articulate a universally valid determination of the will. The subject so "arrogates to himself the authority to examine norms on behalf of all others."[12] This means that norms are only assessed "in monological fashion"[13] and in an "egocentric" manner,[14] whereas a "radical generalization" would require the assessment to be conducted in an intersubjective way.[15] In their traditional form, moral determinations are for Habermas either not determined enough and ineffective or become too determined. In case of the latter, moral theories fall prey to the dialectic of generality and particularism.

The fact that it is required, for Habermas, to justify norms in an intersubjective way means that he is first and foremost concerned with the method through which moral determinations are found. His discourse ethics does not allow for any claims regarding the content of determinations and cannot *a priori* answer the question whether there are specific principles and moral ideas that should be preferred over others.[16] The method that he suggests relies on two principles: first, the principle of universalization, "U," according to which a norm can only be accepted "unless all affected can *freely* accept the consequences and the side effects that the *general* observance of a controversial norm can be expected to have for the satisfaction of the interests of *each individual*"; second, the core principle of discourse ethics, "D," according to which "only those norms can claim to be valid that meet (or could meet) with the approval of all affected in their capacity as participants in a practical discourse."[17] "D" is crucial because it states the only way in which valid moral determinations can be achieved. However, it may not be clear why an agent should feel compelled to engage in a "practical discourse" with others and work effectively toward the "approval of all." For Habermas, the obligation to adopt principle "D" can be justified because the principle is rooted in the ordinary interaction of agents. Anyone who "seriously" enters into a discussion with others about the validity of given norms has to accept, at least intuitively, "procedural conditions" that determine how they interact.[18] There are tacit rules that participants in any open and honest conversation have to respect. One only needs to spell these rules out to show agents that they have actually already accepted the conditions under which they ought to approach and endorse moral ideas.

In our terminology, the two principles of discourse ethics are formal, not classificatory. "D" does not entail a "standard interpretation" of cases,[19] but rather allows for the "extension and reversibility of interpretive perspectives."[20] It is indeed merely "procedural" and assumes that all arguments that are introduced will be transformed in the mutual evaluation of positions.[21] We cannot enter at this point into a detailed discussion of Habermas' approach. What interests us is that the approach can be described as an attempt at rescuing the good against its manifest contradictions. Following the intersubjective meaning of the principles "U" and "D," it has to be "recognizable" in any discourse that is held that all those who are concerned do indeed accept the norm in question.[22] The "actual participation" of all relevant agents is required, a "real discourse" in which norms are publicly discussed.[23] Otherwise, the assessment of norms would not be truly intersubjective.[24] Habermas would not even accept a procedure by which the agents would communicate their positions to others, because then they would not know, or at least could not be sure, that they have really found an agreement.[25] Discourse ethics requires a transformation of human practice, or a new practice altogether, the establishing of a mutual understanding of agents and a new form of cooperative behavior. We can see again the heritage of Hegel at this point, insofar as a truly intersubjective and inclusive discourse among agents would mean the full presence of universal moral ideas in the attitudes and intentions of agents (not of course in their actions, or at least not necessarily).

There is, however, no way in which such a fulfillment can be guaranteed. "Rational discourses have an improbable character, existing like islands in the sea of everyday practice."[26] Agents are no "intelligible characters,"[27] Habermas states, they are driven by personal interests and have been socialized in particular cultures and forms of life.

"These barriers must first be breached in rational discourse."[28] In this sense, the ethics of discourse is built on a pessimistic attitude toward the abilities of human beings, at least insofar as they act and think as individuals. For moral reasons alone, individuals have to deny themselves the capacity to be morally determined. This raises the question how the "real discourse" that the ethic requires can happen at all.

As already said, no one can engage, for Habermas, in a serious process of argumentation without presupposing, at least tacitly, equal respect for all participants in the conversation.[29] Any discourse that happens, however rudimentary, already contains the seeds of a truly intersubjective clarification of norms. In every concrete process of argumentation, "*idealizing* assumptions" are made: the participants must believe, "*as a matter of fact*," that everyone who takes part in the exchange does so as an equal and without coercion.[30] "The standpoint of morality" entails the "anticipation of, and approximation to, a regulative idea."[31] This idea, the truly intersubjective discourse, can obviously be no mere projection; if it were, it would be indistinguishable from an illusion. The conversation has to follow certain course; it has to "present itself as a form of communication that adequately approximates to ideal conditions."[32] On the other hand, no one other than the participants in the conversation can actually know that such an approximation is taking place. From an external point of view, it has to remain unclear "whether and to what extent [their] assumptions are contrafactual in a given case or not."[33] Habermas lays much emphasis on the fact that the implicit rules of communication are not constitutive for it, like the rules of chess. The communication does not have to adopt a certain pattern and the participants do not engage in it as if they were following a rulebook or a script.[34] The rules of communication are only "intuitively known."[35] With respect to the actual statements that are made, the rules are contra-factual and anticipatory of a complete agreement that is never actually reached. The rules are, in other words, no objective quality of the discussion that occurs, but subjective, a projection which allows participants to give their statements an additional meaning. Agents have to talk to others as if it were already clear that an agreement can be reached and that everyone's stance will eventually be acceptable to all others, but no one is allowed to declare individually whether an issue is resolved or not, or whether there is now sufficient agreement.

The heart of discourse ethics lies in the idealizations that are made by agents in their conversation with each other. A real and truly intersubjective discourse is of course the final end of the approach, but this discourse cannot be directly achieved by individual agents or groups or even directly intended by them. Discourse ethics confronts the individual with a moral obligation which is precisely the obligation to engage in idealizations. Agents can only be moral, for Habermas, if they anticipate, purely contra-factually, how their own point of view will be absorbed in the mutual agreement with others. "The moral principle articulates a notion of transcendence or self-overcoming already contained in assertoric validity claims," he states.[36] For his theory, which starts from the failure of the good in ordinary practice, morality is a perpetually transcending movement toward an intersubjective understanding that is not yet real and not at any individual's disposal.

But again, morality's idealization is for Habermas no mere projections but a real factor in the discourses that occur. "The transcending force of validity claims that are dealt with in a straightforward manner has an empirical impact as well."[37] The ideal, in other words, does not stand in opposition to the real but represents the ideal dimension of the real itself. Idealizations are factually contra-factual,[38] and the anticipation of a moral reality contains the reality of a moral anticipation. At the very least, agents have a moral obligation to adopt effectively an anticipatory stance in the conversation with others. They must not claim, for example, that it would be impossible anyway to work toward greater mutual understanding. Conversely, it is important that the realization of the principles of discourse ethics remains contra-factual. The principles are valid only *because* they are contra-factual in each individual determination and in any concrete conversation. Universality would be lost if one could think of it as achieved, because then it could only be assumed in a particular, personally and culturally limited situation. The "communicative practice … operates in a self-reflexive and self-correcting manner and results in a progressive derelativizing of the conditions under which validity claims … can be redeemed."[39] The universality of moral principles has to present itself in a dialectical way, as a perpetual negation of any position that the agents may have achieved.

Habermas rescues the good precisely because no individual determination is determined enough. He embraces, from our point of view, the deficiency that the dialectic of moral determinations reveals. Insofar as my determination is an idealization, I leave room for others. A new moral practice is always just about to begin and will never be complete. If a truly intersubjective discourse would instead be achieved, morality would have become superfluous, it would have become the ladder that gets thrown away. As an idealization, morality guides the agents' engagement in the reality of practice, but at the same time, it is safe from the limitations of the real. Morality immunizes itself, so to speak, from any contradiction that occurs by assuming that it is in fact ever only that, a contradiction. In the form of discourse ethics, morality is possible because it is impossible to achieve, because it represents a commitment that is always made *nonetheless*. But the commitment does not only relate negatively to the real. Like a promise, the anticipation of a moral reality lets that reality at least *begin*. A new practice emerges which is ever more secure as it is only the practice of the agent's moral determination. The impulse to be moral, which would otherwise be frustrated, finds a release insofar as it recognizes that one only needs to anticipate a moral practice in order to be in it. The idealist is never disappointed, even if they may not be aware that they are not disappointed only because they can never be satisfied. On the other hand, they can rightfully feel empowered because they do not fall into resignation, or sheer indeterminedness, and also do not let contingent facts decide about their desire for the good.

As-Ifs

The inner contradictions that we have identified in Habermas' position are of course not limited to his approach. We assume that in one way or another all idealist positions in morality end up with similar structures, even there is no way to prove this here. We also do not want to single out Habermas' approach as particularly problematic. On the contrary, his merit lies precisely in making the contradictions manifest by showing them in their most extreme form. Not all idealist positions articulate their moral determinations as contra-factual idealizations, which means that not all idealist positions present themselves as a sort of sacred foolishness for which morality emerges as response to its own impossibility within the world of practice. Other approaches want to maintain an idealist commitment while trying to avoid the dialectic it entails. An example for this can be found in Vaihinger's *Philosophy of As If*.[40] Vaihinger presents his philosophy as an "idealist positivism": positivism because nothing exists for it besides the "empirical contents of sensation", and idealism because it recognizes the "intellectual and ethical needs" of humans, which have led to the creation of the many ideas in epistemology, science, morality, and religion.[41] Ideas have proven to be "useful" and "valuable" for humanity even if they are, eventually, all fictions.[42] Some ideas, like the logical functions of thought, are used to give structure to sensations and make them predictable,[43] others, like our practical and ethical ideas, go even further: not only do they contradict reality as it is perceived, they are contradictory in themselves.[44] For Vaihinger, these are the true fictions.[45] He declares to follow Kant who, for him, had already recognized the fictitious character of human ideas. It takes "courage," Vaihinger believes, to align with the "radical orientation" in Kant and not with his "traditional" image as it is presented in the textbooks of the discipline.[46]

The most prominent example for a self-contradictory moral idea is free will. Free will either contradicts the laws of nature or is random, causing events "from nothing," which makes it "ethically … valueless."[47] The idea was first seen as a dogma, then became a hypothesis, and now reveals itself as fiction.[48] As a hypothesis, the idea of freedom would still have referred to something real, whereas a fiction has meaning only in relation to practical needs.[49] Being a fiction, however, is no deficiency because ideas that would be refuted as a hypothesis remain valid if one sees them as a human figment and creation.[50] As already said, *all* general moral ideas, such as the ideas of duty, virtue, and equality, stand in contradiction to reality and are also contradictory in themselves: general principles are adopted as binding although one knows that agents do not obey them, and moral ideals are proclaimed although one knows that they are not attainable.[51]

Vaihinger's analysis of the dialectical nature of moral obligations is similar to the role of idealizations in Habermas' approach. But contrary to Habermas, he does not assume that the dialectic is manifest in the use of moral ideas. It only reveals itself from an analytic point of view. The self-contradictory nature of moral ideas is even irrelevant in actions and cultural practices. There are several reasons for this. First, the evolutionary role of ideas: human thought is an "organic function"[52] which helps to cope with a contradictory and hostile reality[53] and so preserves organic life.[54] This implies that, second, morality loses nothing of its imperative meaning. "We include as fictions … ideational constructs emanating from the noblest minds, to which the noblest part of mankind cling and of which they will not allow themselves to be deprived." Moral norms "perish only as *theoretical truths*."[55] Third, fictions are examples of inherent goodness precisely because they do not correspond to an external reality. The moral character of principles would be destroyed were they understood as hypothetical, not as fiction, because then principles would only be adopted to avoid sanctions and punishment: "As soon as [the] *as if* is transformed into a *because*, … it becomes simply a matter of our lower interests, mere egoism."[56] Vaihinger concedes that "only a few, only an élite" can accept that human dignity lies in the use of fictions, all others have to adopt a less sophisticated view.[57] This means that, fourth, from a pragmatic point of view, the distinction between fictions and hypotheses is merely semantic. Whether a principle is endorsed as fiction or in the traditional way of an obligation does not really matter and leaves the principles untouched. Compared to Kant, nothing changes in Vaihinger's approach besides his descriptive language. If Kant had used another language, he would have been able to present the very same ideas in the manner of fictions.[58]

Whereas idealizations in Habermas' sense go directly counter to reality and are determined as a contra-factual, anticipatory stance, fictions establish a reality of their own and are therefore indistinguishable from traditional morality. Everything changes in Vaihinger's interpretation and yet everything remains the same. He does not lay bare the inherent contradictions in morality. Vaihinger is no sacred fool, in the way we understand it here, but almost too clever for his own good. His analysis develops a higher perspective on moral ideals but does not lay any demand on agents which would force them to question and transcend their own moral position.

Progress

We should not be too critical of Vaihinger's approach given that it is based at least on a certain awareness of the dialectical nature of moral determinations. This sets him far apart from any vulgar interpretation of moral idealism. We define an idealist stance as vulgar if it sees a tendency toward the realization of moral ideas as actually existing in society. According to such a stance, the world of practice is indeed becoming better and slowly incorporates more universal standards of justice and equality. One term that can summarize these ideas is progress. For us, the belief in progress is the vulgar form of moral idealizations.

Historically, the belief in progress was spurred by enlightenment ideas. Condorcet thought, for example, that "the perfectibility of man is absolutely indefinite."[59] The future of humanity that he envisioned could "be reduced to three points: the destruction of inequality between different nations; the progress of equality in one and the same nation; and lastly, the real improvement of man."[60] He believed that this future could be predicted based on the observation of the history of humans up to the present point. While progress may be faster in the European nations, the global connection of the world will make sure that once Europe leads the way all other nations follow.[61] In recent times, Pinker has claimed that enlightenment ideals can be maintained and even revitalized based on data.[62] Data show that adverse events and suffering are decreasing around the globe and that progress is indeed real.[63]

The problem with such assumptions is not only that they are debatable. Condorcet's grotesque miscalculation of the colonial cruelty that European nations have inflicted on the world, and the lasting damage that they have produced, shows that one should never underestimate the bias that results from the presumed achievements of one's culture. Even if there are "data" that show improvements, the underlying parameters that are chosen for their collection may be random and culturally limited. There may also be no guarantee that the progress that is made will not be reversed. What is worse, however, is the fact that once real progress has been identified, the individual has no longer the obligation to work toward it. Why should I try to be moral if the society in which I live is already moral as a whole? No other than Kant distinguished between the improvement of human behavior and the possession of an inner, moral disposition. Humans can learn to behave in more socially adequate ways but they cannot become more moral.[64] Even if there is a certain moral progress in human society, virtue, insofar as it is based on self-determination, "always starts *from the beginning*."[65] For a genuine, that is, a non-vulgar idealist, all moral determination require a never-ending projection into the future. Non-vulgar idealizations can be compared to a headlight which has an illuminated area ahead of it only insofar as it is moving forward and only up to certain point beyond which nothing can be foreseen for sure.[66]

Of course, not everyone can be an idealist. If another outlet for one's moral impetus is sought, then a different attitude is needed. There is a pragmatic and compensatory version of idealism which puts all emphasis on the desire to act. This version is represented by the activist. The activist wants to effectuate some good, no matter how random it may be. They think that if the world is made better in one tiny part, it may become better in all others. The activist manifests the restlessness of the commitment to morality, which cannot remain satisfied with the fact that it runs into contradictions. The underlying logic of the activist is: if not everything, then anything, that is, if not the fully inclusive and universal good, then at least some.

What unites the pragmatic activist with the more ambitious idealist is the belief that even if a world governed by moral principles will never be achieved, nothing makes it impossible to hold an attitude governed by principles. As said before, idealism is immune to refutation because it can prove itself as real all by itself and emerge against all objections as an exception to prevailing practices. Both the activist and the idealist follow the idea that moral contents do not have to be given up just because they contradict reality. Contingent facts cannot decide about the reality of the good. Neither does the moral good allow for cynicism. Even if the existing reality might well make us cynical, one can retain an idealist outlook on life, as the idealist is eventually only a cynic turned positive (and vice versa).

Second Attempt: Force and Responsibility

Responsibility as Devotion

In the previous analyses, we have seen various ways in which positions and theories can become too determined: general principles can be used in ways that lead to arbitrary limitations, and determinations based on reason can appear to be driven by non-cognitive factors. The positions and theories that we analyze here, which are centered around the notion of responsibility, accept this dialectical turn: they emphasize the agent's individual commitment and call for an engagement in particular cases either without the support of general principles or against the obligations that general principles would entail. Moral determinations can then appear as too determined because they are indistinguishable from non-moral ones. Agents who act out of responsibility continue where the activist stops. As said before, the activist wants to realize at least some good, even if it is only a limited one. There is a certain randomness in this stance as each realization of the good can be replaced by another. Those acting out of responsibility see one cause as most relevant compared to others: either because they have a special ability, or an opportunity, to achieve a particular instance of the good, or because that instance of the good outweighs all others for them. An extraordinary commitment is required, they assume, in *this* particular place with respect to *this* particular condition and in *this* particular way.

We find such a position articulated in Weber's analysis of political action, presented in his famous speech on *Politics as Vocation*.[67] In it, he lays out the attitudes and abilities that are necessary to engage in politics as a distinct and typically modern activity. He believes there is a certain type of morality that is most appropriate for this activity, which he calls an "ethics of responsibility." Throughout the text, the term "responsibility" is used in a variety of ways. At least four aspects can be distinguished. The term refers first to the "exclusive *personal* responsibility" that a leader has to assume.[68] They are responsible insofar as they are the one who decides in matters of political scope. Second, responsibility means that the leader has the power to carry out their decisions.[69] Their decision-making has to have causal force. Third, the term implies that a leader is accountable for their decisions, that they can be held responsible by others.[70] Finally, responsibility involves an attitude of respect and care toward particular issues, a personal "sense" that counteracts all narcissistic tendencies a leader might have.[71] As the following will show, Weber uses the different meanings of the term to highlight the dialectical tensions in political action. For us, the focus on political leadership captures responsibility in a heightened form. As a moral commitment, it is not limited to this domain. All sorts of actions can have the structure that Weber lays out, we believe, and the use of institutional power can be replaced by any kind of forcefulness in an individual's engagement. There is at times a certain fascination with male dominance and strength in his approach, but as a formal notion responsibility does not have to be limited to particular gender roles.

On a side note, the notion of responsibility did not play a role in classical moral theories and is not "well-established within the philosophical tradition."[72] Responsibility became more commonly used in the late eighteenth century, as a topic relevant precisely in the realm of politics.[73] Compared to other notions, such as duty, right, and virtue, responsibility seems to have retained its place at the margins of moral philosophy until now.

Ethics, for Weber, concerns the character that a political leader needs to have.[74] He mentions three "pre-eminent qualities":[75] "passion," which designates the individual impulse driving political action; "a feeling of responsibility" which makes sure that passion is no mere emotion or excitement but the "devotion to a 'cause,' to the god or demon who is its overlord"[76]; and a "sense of proportion" which provides the "ability to let realities work upon [oneself] with inner concentration and calmness."[77] Not all attempts at gaining political power are justifiable in Weber's theory: "The sin against the lofty spirit of his vocation ... begins where this striving for power ceases to be *objective* and becomes purely personal self-intoxication."[78] The normative quality of responsible action is not determined by the mere act of self-determination but by its content, the particular instance of the good to which it is devoted.

The dialectical tensions that arise in actions based on responsibility are not difficult to show. If the actions are supposed to have any effect at all, that is, if they are to succeed in addressing given problems in the world of practice, there are certain means they need to employ. In the realm of politics, power is the "unavoidable means"[79] which in turn is based on force.[80] The very effectiveness of responsible action can then make it seem as if the agent desired power for its own sake. In a sense, they *have to* desire power for its own sake, at least insofar as the immediate steps of their intervention are concerned. But the dialectic does not stop there and more contradictions can emerge as responsible actions can have antagonistic effects. Even if the agent does not take the consequences of their actions "lightly,"[81] they cannot avoid inserting themselves forcefully into an existing context of practices. (To say this again, we assume that similar effects can occur in all realms of practice and outside of politics in proper sense.) At the same time, political projects are difficult to realize, which means that the agent's determination may well seem not determined enough. Weber mentions, slightly vaguely, the "knowledge of tragedy with which all action, but especially political action, is truly interwoven."[82] At the very least, the outcomes of one's actions are likely to turn out other than intended: "The final result of political action often, no, even regularly, stands in completely inadequate and often even paradoxical relation to its original meaning."[83] Agents have to be ready to face "the ethical irrationality of the world,"[84] a "world of undeserved suffering, unpunished injustice, and hopeless stupidity."[85] From a moral point of view, this means that the agent's devotion to their cause is all the more important. The action, if it is likely to fail or to be antagonistic, or both, at least needs to have the right focus and "inner strength."[86] Precisely because actions based on responsibility are inherently dialectical, the agent has to act as if they were not, otherwise they would not take them (and themself) seriously enough.

Like Habermas, Weber not only registers the dialectical tensions but makes them manifest in his approach, intensifies them even. He does so through the distinction between two types of ethics: his own ethics of responsibility and the "ethics of ultimate ends." The latter can also be called an "ethics of convictions," an ethics of strong value-oriented, inner attitudes (the German word *Gesinnung* is impossible to capture in one term). The two types are based on "two fundamentally differing and irreconcilably opposed maxims," Weber contends.[87] The distinction implies that morality as a whole is dialectical because there are two mutually exclusive ways based on which agents can desire to be good.[88] Formally speaking, the difference between the two types of morality is established by the role that consequences play in the agent's determination. Whereas responsibility is focused on achieving certain outcomes and effects, the ethics of convictions holds it most important that the agent is determined according to what is inherently good. For Weber, those who mainly follow their convictions even disregard the consequences their actions might have:

> You may demonstrate to a convinced syndicalist, believing in an ethic of ultimate ends, that his action will result in increasing the opportunities of reaction, in increasing the oppression of his class, and obstructing its ascent—and you will not

make the slightest impression upon him. If an action of good intent leads to bad results, then, in the actor's eyes, not he but the world, or the stupidity of other men, or God's will who made them thus, is responsible for the evil.[89]

Weber's description of the ethics of conviction seems polemical or, even worse, a caricature. Can there be agents who really do not care about the outcome of their actions? Also, if the outcome of an action is indeed never fully under one's control, as he assumes himself (see the previous paragraph), then the ethics of convictions has at least the one advantage that it allows the agent to hold on to as much good as they can. If I do not realize the good at least in my own actions, who else realizes it? In a world of "ethical irrationality" the irrationality of personal convictions could be the only way in which the good prevails. We therefore have to be careful not to follow Weber's polemic and see one type of morality as less consistent or legitimate than the other.

His main example for an ethics of convictions is the Sermon of the Mount, which he calls "the absolute ethics of the Gospel."[90] Jesus' ethical stance is unconditional, whereas the ethics of responsibility is based on hypothetical considerations, allowing the agent to adjust to changing situations. Weber does not believe that responsibility can be bound by universal principles. For a politician, it may be not responsible, say, to tell the truth about a certain matter. They may even have the responsibility to lie to the public at times.[91]

Given the rejection of inherent goodness, the ethics of responsibility seems to amount to a form of consequentialism. But this is not the case because the focus on responsibility does not lead to a universal moral theory, as consequentialism does. It does not pursue, say, an overall increase of well-being. The situations that are addressed are always particular ones. In addition, the focus on responsibility does not mean that all actions can be justified as means to an end. "Whosoever contracts with violent means for whatever ends ... is exposed to its specific consequences."[92] The effect of one's use of force is never justified in proper sense. Unlike consequentialism, the ethics of responsibility has no conceptual tools to justify sacrifices in the name of a general conception of the good. Responsibility means that the agent has to define the good that needs to be achieved all by themselves and cannot shift the blame for any harm that has occurred.

On the other hand, the ethics of responsibility is not alone in producing, at least potentially, harmful effects. An ethics of convictions can produce them too if it seeks to prevail in the reality of practice. If the ethics of convictions entails more than the self-sacrifice of its proponents, then these proponents have to use the same means that would be used if they acted from responsibility, Weber believes:

> No ethics in the world can dodge the fact that in numerous instances the attainment of 'good' ends is bound to the fact that one must be willing to pay the price of using morally dubious means or at least dangerous ones—and facing the possibility or even the probability of evil ramifications. From no ethics in the world can it be concluded when and to what extent the ethically good purpose 'justifies' the ethically dangerous means and ramifications.[93]

This statement has to be taken again with a grain of salt. It is hard to assume that all proponents of an ethics of convictions end up using "dubious" means, as he suggests, or use it as excuse for discriminatory and oppressive practices. The means which are employed may be "dangerous" only because changes to existing practices, if they are meant to be substantive, can always lead to unintended consequences. The proponents of an ethics of convictions may succumb to harmful consequences simply because they cannot anticipate them, because the consequences are not part of their determination. The "diabolic forces which enter the play remain unknown to the actor. These are inexorable and produce consequences for his action and even for his inner self, to which he must helplessly submit, unless he perceives them."[94]

Weber's remarks have to be seen in their historical context and against the background of his own political convictions. He repeatedly references the violent consequences of the Soviet revolution[95] and also suggests that an ethics of convictions may lead to some sort of ethical nihilism for which all kinds of destructive forces would become acceptable.[96] We cannot discuss these beliefs. As said before, the main point, for us, is that the ethics of responsibility makes its own dialectical tensions manifest. The action of a political leader, or of anyone acting from responsibility, always happens *nonetheless*; they act under, and anticipate, the bad and irrational conditions of the human world as well as the moral ambiguity of their decisions, attitudes, and actions. At the same time, they are convinced that they are the one who has to act because otherwise the intolerable conditions of the world would not be properly addressed.

Responsibility is also not justified along the lines of any given moral theory, whether such a theory would be consequentialist or based on the inherent goodness of certain duties and obligations (e.g., the duties of a leader). In fact, it is not justified at all, at least not by way of a general principle. Responsibility is chosen *because* one believes that a universal ethics of convictions and of moral principles is not helpful in the given case. It is chosen, in other words, against the apparent superiority of a position that would allow one to maintain the absolute good as the focus of one's commitment. Responsibility lets go of a purer morality for morality's sake. It is adopted as the foolish compensation of the failure of universal theories, or as a tribute to morality in the face of its failure. "Whoever wants to engage in politics at all, and especially in politics as a vocation, has to realize these ethical paradoxes. He must know that he is responsible for what may become of himself under the impact of these paradoxes."[97] Again, the "ethical paradoxes" mentioned here must not be taken as an excuse to indulge in the abuse of force. As said before, precisely because all actions are bound to fail the agent has to act as if theirs were the only ones who will not, otherwise their actions would lack moral content. Harmful consequences, for both others and oneself, can ever only be unintended ones, morally speaking, even if one can foresee them. The individual acting from responsibility has to adopt two attitudes, as it were: one in which there is no paradox and they are fully devoted to their cause and one in which they are aware of the paradoxes they cannot avoid.

In a sense, actions done from responsibility want to capture an absolute good too, but they can only capture it as this good or that. The truly absolute, general good is postponed. Those acting from responsibility have to assume that future actions will continue to achieve the truly absolute good. "Perhaps if I do this now, other will do x later." The dialectical tension that characterizes responsibility is justified only if the absolute good is at least intended as real, but the intention is of course what keeps the tension alive because responsibility is motivated only insofar as the absolute good remains, at least for the moment, denied.

At times, there is a certain heroism in Weber's descriptions, for example, when he suggests that "only he has the calling for politics who is sure that he shall not crumble when the world from his point of view is too stupid or too base for what he wants to offer."[98] In such formulations, it almost seems as if the inner strength of the political leader would be sufficient to justify the dialectical tensions because they overcome all moral contradictions by directing them back at themself. It is "something genuinely human and moving," Weber says, if a responsible agent truly feels the impact of their actions and then "reaches the point where he says: 'Here I stand; I can do no other.'"[99] These formulations show that there is a certain risk in positions which make their own dialectical tensions manifest. If some actions are to be performed, then one cannot forever contemplate the contradictions in one's stance but simply has to act, come from it what may. It is also not easy to focus on contradictions without wanting to resolve them in one way or another. At some point, the dialectical structures may seem indifferent in light of practical pressures and needs. Ironically, it may then be that not the proponent of an ethics of convictions but the one acting from responsibility appears as a moral nihilist. Still, the contradictions *are* laid open in Weber's approach, if only because he thinks that responsibility requires one to go against one's own moral convictions.

Responsibility as Choice

We can show to what degree Weber is aware of the tensions that arise in his approach by contrasting it to another use of the notion of responsibility, one that falls short of acknowledging the dialectic. We find this use in Sartre's work, especially in his programmatic essay, *Existentialism Is a Humanism*. Compared to the focus on the realm of politics, responsibility, for Sartre, is a universal quality of actions. Our analysis refers to his approach only insofar as it involves responsibility. We cannot engage in a discussion of the underlying existentialist philosophy.

The guiding idea of existentialism is well-known: "There is at least one being … whose existence comes before its essence, a being who exists before he can be defined by any conception of it. That being is man."[100] Humans beings are radically free to give themselves an essence; they are, according to the famous formulation, "condemned to be free."[101] A human being is "responsible for everything he does":[102] no action can be motivated or excused through the recourse to external circumstances. If the agent is influenced by others, it is because they have adopted a disposition that allowed them to be influenced.[103] The same holds for weaknesses and flaws in one's constitution.[104] This way, responsibility not only applies to actions but to one's being as a whole. Cognitive acts are included in it, too, because how one interprets the world is for Sartre also the result of one's decisions.[105] The only thing for which the agent is not responsible is responsibility itself.[106] We should also note that responsibility not only concerns the agent and their decisions, attitudes, and actions, it also involves the world of practice in which they find themself: "There are no accidents in life" and "everything take place as if I were compelled to be responsible."[107] Responsibility cannot simply end at a certain point because then it could be limited from the start. If the agent is fully responsible for one thing, they have to consider everything else as if they were responsible for it as well.

It seems, however, that this conception of absolute freedom does not go well together with the idea of responsibility. The individual chooses who they are, which in turn determines what they do, but there is no one there who can be thought to be responsible for that choice. "What we mean to say is that a man is nothing but a series of enterprises, and that he is the sum, organization, and aggregate of the relations that constitute such enterprises."[108] The person simply was not there before the choice. Also, based on the idea of freedom, there is for Sartre no reason to prefer one action over the other. Any single choice that is made could have been made otherwise, but this very fact does not imply that responsibility was involved in the act of choice. One can of course say that humans become responsible after the fact, so that someone can be blamed for having cultivated, say, a cowardly character, but in this case the responsibility would be extrinsic and not inherent to the act of choice itself. Sartre wants responsibility to be rooted in freedom, or to be co-extensional with it, which makes the perspectives of others as well as retrospective considerations irrelevant.

In the text, Sartre pursues different strategies to give the idea of responsibility plausible meaning. One strategy lies in assuming that an individual's determination is no isolated act but the choice of one of many possible ways to be.[109] The choice answers, albeit implicitly, to the question of how one should live:

> When we say that man chooses himself, not only do we mean that each of us must choose himself, but also that in choosing for himself, he is choosing for all men. ... Choosing to be this or that is to affirm at the same time the value of what we choose, because we can never choose evil. We always choose the good, and nothing can be good for any of us unless it is good for all. ... If I decide to marry and to have children ..., I am ... committing not only myself, but all of humanity, to the practice of monogamy. I am therefore responsible for myself and for everyone else, and I am fashioning a certain image of man as I would have him to be. In choosing myself, I choose man.[110]

With these remarks, Sartre evidently, but perhaps inadvertently, takes recourse to a theory of the good. There is no reason prior to an act of choice, but the choice itself, as a practical pursuit, involves a reason and a purpose for which it occurs. It is nothing other than the adoption of a reason. This means that it has to be the choice of what is best (in the Platonic terms that Sartre uses here) because one cannot have a reason to do what is worse if a better option is available (if there is not, then what is worse overall is relatively best). One may of course wonder why the good should play a role in an account of existential freedom. The only answer seems to be: what else could play a role if some normative content is required? There is nothing in the individual's nature that could provide guidance, let alone a moral determination. Their act can only follow the most formal determination possible, which is the good. As a formal account of freedom, Sartre's theory can only involve formal contents.

Following his remarks, the good that individuals choose entails that the choice can be generalized. The idea that one "commits humanity as a whole" to the practice one has chosen can obviously not mean that every other human should follow suit. It rather means that every other human being who would find themselves in the same situation would choose the same thing, or that the chosen course of action is not only a valid choice, one that is possible to make, but the most adequate one all things considered. Whoever marries says implicitly, according to Sartre: "Yes, it is good that human beings marry." This way, the text also echoes Kant. The act of choice does not follow a general imperative, or any imperative for that matter, but it is made as if it were an imperative itself, that is, as if it were a paradigm whose adoption is binding for all.[111] The formal notion of freedom goes again well together with formal accounts of morality, such as the categorical imperative. Seen from this angle, existential freedom is first and foremost the freedom to choose the moral content of one's action: "Man makes himself; ... he makes himself by choosing his own morality, and his circumstances are such that he has no option other than to choose a morality."[112] We cannot go into further detail here and show the different aspects of the good that Sartre uses to explain the normative dimension of freedom, for example, the need for consistency both in one's own determinations and in relation to the determinations of others,[113] or the fact that freedom itself can become an obligation as the truth of human agency which can be invoked against agents who declare themselves unfree, either as an excuse or out of fear.[114] Coming back to responsibility instead, we now see that it arises merely from the awareness of the meaning of one's choice. An individual's act is always more than an individual act; it attracts normative implications like a magnet and has a content that can be further analyzed and expressed as an instance of the good. The individual, all by themselves, has to respond to the tacit question of whether it is good what they want to do.

Still, even if it is possible to think of one's awareness of the good as a feeling of responsibility, the question remains why such a feeling needs to be involved in action at all. Why is Sartre's account not simply another, slightly dramatized theory of the good, or a heightened and intensified version of Kant's conception of autonomy as moral self-determination? The answer lies in his conception of action. The good, for him, is always chosen in a particular act. It is always only *me*, or *you* who chooses. The adoption of a reason breaks apart, so to speak, into its two elements, into the very act of self-determination, or its origination from a strictly individual source, and the content which it assumes and which connects it to the world of practice as a whole. Sartre emphasizes the hiatus that often remains implicit in the realization of moral contents, the hiatus between the contents, which are general and common, and their realization, which is necessarily a unique event that cannot be transferred to others or deduced from any previous condition. The agent feels this hiatus subjectively as it causes for them an "anguish pure and simple, of the kind experienced by all who have borne responsibilities."[115]

We can undoubtedly believe that there is a gap between the act of determination and its content, but to what extent do we have to do so? How fundamental or how relevant is this gap? Compared to the reality of human action, Sartre's analysis seems exaggerated.[116] We can see this, among others, in the well-known case of the young man who consulted him about a decision he had to take. The young man was uncertain whether he, as the only remaining child, should stay with his mother and support her, or whether he should go to England to join the resistance against the occupation of French. For Sartre, the young man "was vacillating between two kinds of morality: a morality motivated by sympathy and individual devotion, and another morality with a broader scope, but less likely to be fruitful."[117] In this choice, no consideration could provide any help: "Values are too broad in scope to apply to the specific and concrete case under consideration" and "the strength of a feeling" that could pull him in one direction or the other would ultimately depend on his choice as well.[118] In morality, but actually in all practical matters, the individual finds themselves permanently at a crossroads, and all actions require a more or less explicit effort to decide. All determinations are a choice. The example of the young man shows this only in a more dramatic way.

As we said, this account of action seems exaggerated. If agents always found themselves in a situation of choice in which they have to decide between two equally plausible actions, all action would come to a halt. Agents would be immobilized like Buridan's ass. Sartre places the agent outside of practice, on a vantage point removed from action, and then cannot explain how they would be able to get back into it. The agent is conceived as an isolated Cartesian *ego* which contemplates actions without being involved in them.[119] In the reality of practice, decisions are most likely always already made: if the young man is not much of an adventurer and cares deeply about his mother, he will stay, and if he feels instead that he has a moral duty to help in the defense of his country, he will leave. The good, for him, will take shape based on his past dispositions. Or he will change course and leave, overcoming his fear and his desire to stay: in that case, he may have realized that the good of an entire nation must have a greater weight. It is artificial to think, like Sartre does, that all types of morality are equally viable and valid in each situation.[120]

This means, again, that it is hard to see whether the idea of responsibility has any real meaning in Sartre's approach. If agents are supposed to be responsible only because there is absolutely nothing that would indicate what they should do, then they are not really responsible for what they decide. Their choice does not have the weight that comes with responsibility, so to speak. From another point of view, Sartre's account does not go far enough. If there is indeed a certain responsibility in choosing between different versions of the good, he fails to explore its dialectical structure. Compared to Weber, for whom the agent's responsibility is inevitably either not determined enough or too determined and antagonistic, there are no contradictions in his approach. Responsibility, for him, is mainly the awareness of the normative dimension of one's choice. Agents can feel the questionability of their decision, they can sense how much strength is needed to see it through, and they might experience the loneliness that sometimes lies in making a commitment to the good. All these feelings are possible aspects of self-determination but despite the vividness of their impression they leave no impact on its structure. The agent's responsibility does not appear as inherently contradictory, as it does in Weber, just because there is a certain focus on the individual impulse from which it stems. The only dialectical structure that could arise would result from the fact that the agent's choice is too determined.

The agent chooses the good but the choice is only theirs, which means that the good turns into its opposite and becomes the expression of a mere idiosyncrasy. But Sartre does not explore this dialectic. He also cannot do so because if he did, the existential freedom of the agent would no longer be absolute. The content would then have to be considered independently. For Sartre, freedom *is* absolute and cannot be measured against given principles and ideas. Freedom sanctifies itself so that all contradictions that may occur are absorbed and revoked in its ultimate positivity. I may feel anxious and lonely in my choosing but it is my choosing after all. There is no moral quality outside of it against which it could appear as deficient or unduly violent. Whereas for Weber responsibility entails the burden of committing to a cause, and to the potentially harmful consequences through which this cause has to be reached, for Sartre it amounts to the self-empowerment of the agent. The responsibility, if there is any, is always only mine and therefore always rightfully mine.

The inherently positive nature of responsibility is evident in many of Sartre's remarks. For example, he compares moral self-determination to an act of artistic creation when he says that the student seeking advice "was obliged to invent his own laws."[121] Like a work of art, the act of self-determination has the criteria for its rightness all in itself. There can of course be failure but it is irrelevant if this failure is diagnosed from the outside. The outcomes of actions are indifferent to the individual's determination, as they "cannot count on anything."[122] Compared to Weber's pessimism, Sartre emphasizes the "sternness of our optimism."[123] Existentialism sets humans free because they are able to have all good in themselves.

Like Vaihinger, Sartre is no sacred fool but too clever for his own good. With his focus on freedom, he wants to conceive of morality in a different, more radical and more individualistic way than classical theories. However, what gives normative weight to responsibility is what makes it at the same time indistinguishable from Plato's and Kant's conceptions of morality. On the other hand, insofar as there is truly individual responsibility it is impossible for Sartre to see any inner contradictions in it. Responsibility, for him, is not in itself tragic or questionable, as it is for Weber. The only thing that Sartre adds to classical theories is the awareness of the precariousness that lies in an agent's commitment to the good. The agent has to accept their responsibility because they cannot obtain justification from higher principles or external sources and because each practical situation presents a unique challenge to them.[124] But this aspect was at least implicitly present in Socrates' idea of self-determination, so that it is only a nuance that has changed.[125]

Responsibility as Virtue

Despite its limitations, Sartre's approach, again like Vaihinger's, is far from the vulgar understanding of responsibility. We can only discuss one form in which such an understanding can be found. It lies in the belief that responsibility amounts to a lasting moral quality of agents, a virtue, which they possess in such a way that a certain type of behavior can be expected from them. Responsibility, in this view, "can be learned and developed. ... A good politician is one who is recognized as knowing better than others how best to deal with the typical threats to politics."[126] The problem with such an understanding is not only that it confuses responsibility with other moral qualities which can indeed be lasting, for example, with prudence and a moral conscience.[127] More problematic is the fact that this understanding empties responsibility of its proper moral content altogether: by assuming that agents simply possess responsibility, one does not assume any longer that they have to commit explicitly to particular issues or cultivate their sense of devotion to a specific cause. One simply expects that when a certain issue presents itself, they will act appropriately. This way, responsibility becomes indistinguishable from the fulfilling of institutional roles which may require some personal commitment but also provide a standard that agents can follow: "Clearly, the virtue is closely related to conscientiousness in fulfilling one's responsibilities. With some circularity, one might say that responsibility suggests an agent who lives up to their, or its, position within a division of responsibilities."[128] Eventually, responsibility amounts to the agent's readiness to respond to the expectation of others, not to their own impulse to act. The account is vulgar because it wants to benefit from the merit that follows moral effort without burdening the agent with this effort in any serious way.[129]

There is here also a pragmatic attitude that compensates for the tensions in responsibility without flattening it into a vulgar account. This attitude belongs to those who assume responsibility for a particular group of people: people in one's neighborhood, fellow parishioners, one's family and friends, etc. We can call agents who possess this attitude communitarians. Compared to the responsibility that lies in a *radically* individual decision, in the sense of Weber's and Sartre's conceptions, the communitarian acts as member of a group and does not devote their energy to issues of more general relevance. The logic that they follow is again: I could devote my responsibility to this and to this and to this as well; therefore, I can devote it simply to this, the issue that is right in front of me. There is at least *this* instance of the good for which I can care. The communitarian also does not think of their commitment as one that only depends on their individual effort and choice. They rather derive the impulse to take care of things from the practical context to which they belong. Still, compared to the vulgar conception of responsibility, their commitment is unique and cannot be reduced to a certain professional excellence. Being a good neighbor or a supportive family member requires one to play an irreplaceable role.

Third Attempt: Forgiving Morality

Burdens

Eventually, moral determinations that are too determined can become antagonistic. The positions that we will describe in this final part, positions that are centered around the act and attitude of forgiveness, can be understood as attempts to compensate this effect. Moral determinations are antagonistic if they discriminate against other determinations which it would also be moral to have. "The good can only be achieved in my way, not in yours." In such cases, moral determinations have immoral effects. As said before, the suspicion that morality may have effects that contradict its own intentions and contents is relevant for us only insofar as it stems from moral reasons, too. Although much could be said about morality's effects, say, from a psychological, sociological, and historical perspective, we are not interested in an empirical analysis here. The point is that morality, in suspecting determinations to be antagonistic, turns on itself, or better: applies its own criteria to determinations and sees the contradiction to the good precisely in the attempt at realizing it.

Antagonistic effects can be felt in different ways and to varying degrees. We have mentioned many examples in the previous analyses. Moral determinations, although they are positive as a way to realize the good, can be understood to carry a negative meaning. They can seem to be conditioned by what they exclude. Moral positions can then appear, among others, as a subtle form of revenge. Strong moral determinations, especially the ones based on reason, can be suspected to undermine emotions and habitual practices. They can also appear as destructive because of the heightened self-centeredness of moral agents or the feelings of guilt and deficiency instilled in others. Agents can therefore for various reasons believe that they have to remedy the antagonistic effects of morality. They can use forgiveness as an attempt to overcome and renounce the negativity of moral principles insofar as they are applied to a given situation and to individual persons. Like before, in the cases of idealism and responsibility, we can obviously not assume that all instances of forgiveness follow this purpose. But we have no ambition to present a general theory of the phenomenon. All we want to show is that some approaches to forgiveness involve a more or less explicit renunciation of the dialectical effects of moral determinations.

We start from Arendt's conception of forgiveness which she presents in her work on *The Human Condition*.[130] Arendt's understanding of the world of practice is not as pessimistic as Habermas' and Weber's but she also emphasizes the limits of individual determinations, both moral and non-moral ones. Human beings know

> that he who acts never quite knows what he is doing, that he always becomes 'guilty' of consequences he never intended or even foresaw, that no matter how disastrous and unexpected the consequences of his deed he can never undo it, that the process he starts is never consummated unequivocally in one single deed or event, and that its very meaning never discloses itself to the actor but only to the backward glance of the historian who himself does not act. All this is reason enough to turn away with despair from the realm of human affairs and to hold in contempt the human capacity for freedom, which, by producing the web of human relationships, seems to entangle its producer to such an extent that he appears much more the victim and the sufferer than the author and doer of what he does.[131]

Arendt refers to the 'web of human relationships' as a technical term. On the one hand, all action is a beginning, a new and unforeseeable way of shaping the world of practice. Each agent, insofar as they are born into the world, is a "beginner."[132] On the other hand, all individual action is shaped by the plurality of the human world. Humans can ever only "insert" themselves into a world inhabited by others.[133] The world of practice is a web in the double sense of a structure that supports individual action and initiative and a net in which they are hopelessly caught and in which no action can be realized simply as planned.[134] Agents control neither the consequences nor the meaning of their actions because all action depends on, and is impacted by, the presence of others. Actions are no longer ours once they have started to unfold in the common web. Even the fact that no action can be undone means something more for Arendt than the otherwise trivial insight that the past can never be changed: actions cannot be undone because they have impacted others who now remember them or have already reacted to them in their own way. Only with respect to mere objects humans have the privilege to replace what is faulty and go on as if nothing had happened. For the question of morality, this means that moral determinations are either not determined enough or have to become antagonistic if they want to have a real effect in the web of relationships. In what follows, we will focus on the latter.

Forgiveness has a particular place in Arendt's conception because it alleviates the "enormous capacity for endurance" that actions possess, the "burden of irreversibility."[135] "Without being forgiven, released from the consequences of what we have done, our capacity to act would, as it were, be confined to one single deed from which we could never recover; we would remain the victims of its consequences forever."[136] Forgiving, for Arendt, enables action as a new beginning and is therefore a fundamental necessity for humans in their dependence on others. Because humans inevitably obstruct and limit each other's freedom, they need a mechanism that allows them to re-adjust the web of relationships. Forgiveness is granted through the constant re-interpretation of actions. Although Arendt does not draw this conclusion herself, one could perhaps say that all action, insofar as it is inter-action, contains an element of forgiving: it anticipates the reactions of others, gives them room, and tries to achieve what is possible based on their respective interests. Forgiving also indicates the plurality of the world of practice, the inevitable co-existence with others, because one needs others to be forgiven. No one can forgive themself.[137]

Contrary to what one might expect, forgiving, for Arendt, is not defined as moral act. It rather constitutes an attempt at keeping moral demands away from the realm of action. She makes this clear by contrasting this realm, which for her is also the realm of the political, from the institutional arrangement that is laid out in Plato's *Republic*. There is for her a tyrannical and violent element in Plato's vision of politics insofar as the plurality of human interaction is reduced and a structure is imposed that conceives of the community as one. "Plato can see the whole public realm of the many in the image of the inner soul of the one, projected to a greater scale."[138] The analogy between the individual soul and the *polis*, which the *Republic* uses to explain how a political body can become virtuous as a whole, shows that morality, for Arendt, remains a solitary perspective, external to the plurality of humans who cannot be expected to act according to one, common principle. Morality, thus, cannot *not* become antagonistic if it suggests standards that all interactions should adopt. The act of forgiving, therefore, does not follow from a specific principle or because a moral theory would have been established which defines wrongdoing, blame, and the appropriate retribution. Forgiving, for Arendt, is rather the renunciation of moral categorizations altogether. It leaves moral demands behind for the sake of a new beginning.[139]

Forgiveness can be opposed to revenge "which is the natural, automatic reaction to transgression and which because of the irreversibility of the action process can be expected and even calculated."[140] We could add that revenge can also be expected because it implies the blameworthiness of the initial act and so follows the logic of moral categorizations and retribution. The fact that forgiveness escapes this logic means that "it can never be predicted" and always occurs "in an unexpected way."[141] Forgiving is "provoked" but not conditioned by the initial act.[142] Forgiving, in other words, is an act of freedom which has the double purpose of liberating the forgiver from vengeance and the forgivee of the burden of their past.[143] But this does not mean that forgiving is for Arendt without any moral categorization. "Men are unable to forgive what they cannot punish."[144] After all, if there were no moral torts, forgiveness would not need to exist. For Arendt, there is even a parallel between punishment and forgiving. Both acts want to put an end to the impact of past actions, that is, want to put an end to the reactions that these actions have provoked. They are also both unable to deal with radical evil, which for her can be neither punished nor forgiven.[145] Her conception of forgiveness, therefore, is by no means relativistic: it respects a limit beyond which it would not be meaningful, let alone morally appropriate to forgive. This limit, however, is not all-too relevant for the realm of practice. "Crime and willed evil are rare," Arendt states,[146] they belong more as an exception than a rule to the web of human relationships. The cases that can trigger moral blame and may so call for forgiveness are much more frequent because they are rooted in the interactive nature of practices itself.

The fact that forgiveness has to be unpredictable and unexpected in order to escape the logic of retribution and revenge raises the question whether there are specific reasons for which it occurs. As an individual act, forgiving may be incalculable, but this does not mean that it is devoid of proper motive. For Arendt, the motive lies in the relation to the other agent: "Forgiving and the relationship it establishes is always an eminently personal ... affair in which *what* was done is forgiven in sake of *who* did it."[147] This statement is no doubt plausible from a linguistic point of view: one always forgives someone and cannot forgive animals or things. But the question is whether there needs to be a special relation to the forgivee. Arendt mentions love as a feeling that may lead to forgiveness but does not believe that it is the only motive that exists. Love is intimate and transcends "the larger domain of human affairs," which means that it does not really touch the realm of action.[148] Within this realm, Arendt contends that the feeling for which others are forgiven is respect.[149] It seems, however, that the dependence on respect would contradict the very meaning of forgiveness. Not only is it possible to respect a person without forgiving their actions, respect is also a lasting relation, based on a person's character as a whole, while forgiveness can ever only be a singular act. Respect also introduces a moral perspective insofar as it bears an evaluative attitude toward others, which could imply that forgiveness fits into a general moral theory after all, something that Arendt certainly would have wanted to avoid. It also seems that forgiveness often is a way to restore the respect toward someone, not the other way around.

Transactions

The questions that arise in regard to Arendt's conception allow us to discuss in a more general way the tensions that affect forgiving. As a determination that tries to overcome the dialectics of morality, forgiveness cannot be other than dialectical itself. We can describe the dialectic in the following way: if forgiveness is granted for a specific reason, then the determination is too small, that is, deficient from a moral point of view. If forgiveness is instead granted for no reason, in the sense that the events preceding the act of forgiving provide no reason that would allow one to infer that the act had to be granted, then the determination is too great and either escapes or transcends a moral point of view. In the present section, we start with the first of these possibilities.

In an extensive analysis, Griswold has listed "the conditions that offender and injured would ideally meet" in an interaction that leads to forgiveness.[150] "The offender must acknowledge responsibility and show regret," among others, and the injured has to give up their resentment.[151] The injured, according to this analysis, "requires reasons" and must not forgive past actions on a whim.[152] Or better: if the injured forgave the offender on a whim they would fail to grasp the normative dimension in the act of forgiving. "Forgiveness comes with certain conditions or norms, else it would collapse into forgetting, or excusing, or condonation, or rationalization, as the case may be."[153] Forgiveness is a moral act only if it follows the repentance of the person who committed the initial tort.[154] The scenario that follows from these ideal conditions is no doubt a beautiful one. It seems to encapsulate what Arendt had in mind when she described forgiving as a new start in the web of human relationships: both the offender and the injured have been changed and leave their fixation on the past behind. However, the conditions listed here involve the use of moral notions: offenses need to be considered with regret, resentment ought to be overcome, and the adequate and fair reaction to a genuine form of repentance is the forgiveness that one grants. This understanding of forgiving is problematic precisely from a moral point of view. At least two reasons can be mentioned for this.

For the first reason, we can refer to some remarks made by Derrida. Derrida rejects the "conditional logic of the exchange" as it is outlined in Griswold's analysis because this logic turns forgiving into "an economic transaction," a sort of trading of gestures and attitudes:[155]

> Each time that it [forgiveness, M.S.] aims to re-establish a normality (social, national, political, psychological) by a work of mourning, by some therapy or ecology of memory, then the 'forgiveness' is not pure—nor is its concept. Forgiveness is not, it should not be, normal, normative, normalising. It should remain exceptional and extraordinary.[156]

Derrida's focus lies on the political use of forgiveness but his criticism is valid beyond this realm. If forgiveness is granted because of an ulterior moral purpose, for example, to remove the disturbing effects of the past and restore the presumed normalcy of interaction, then the act itself becomes instrumental, "economic." One could then suspect that forgiveness loses its morality altogether: "The simulacra, the automatic ritual, hypocrisy, calculation, or mimicry are often a part, and invite parasites to this ceremony of culpability."[157] Like for Arendt, forgiveness has to remain "exceptional" and unpredictable if it is to retain its genuine moral quality.[158]

The problem is not only that forgiveness may be abused. It can also acquire an antagonistic effect. For the side of the injured, there may arise a certain expectation or even an obligation to forgive. If the offender repents, does one then not have to forgive them? Clearly there can be no such requirement, if only for the reason that the very meaning of repentance makes it impossible to expect such a reward, at least as long as the repentance is genuine, too: "To be sincerely repentant implies the view that forgiveness is inadequate. And if the wrongdoer himself thinks that feelings of resentment towards him are apt, why should the victim, in this respect, think otherwise?"[159] In other words, one has to repent without being forgiven, and if that is the case, then one also has to forgive without relying on someone else's repentance. The injured person must not be forced to grant their forgiveness. On the side of the offender, making oneself worthy of forgiveness may also be felt as an undue constraint. "The offer of forgiveness, though seemingly so attractive and gracious, all-too often displays ... a list-keeping, inquisitorial mentality that a generous and loving person should eschew."[160] The injured person may use forgiveness to humiliate the offender ("I can forgive you because I am a better person than you") or draw benefits from their seemingly gracious act ("I forgive you so that you do what I say").

One might be tempted to ask from where Arendt and Derrida retrieve the normative force of their claims that define forgiveness exclusively as an unpredictable act. As a term used in everyday practices and in natural language, one could well think of practices in which forgiveness is part of some sort of exchange. In politics, which is Derrida's own example, can it ever be otherwise? We should undoubtedly refrain from imposing normative restrictions on semantics and be careful not to reduce the variety in the meaning of forgiving. But it seems that there are indeed cases that transcend any logic of exchange, and it also seems that there is a distinction between forgiveness and, say, excuses which are given according to a much more predictable pattern. If this is the case, then we can say that what Arendt and Derrida are interested in is the emphatic understanding of forgiveness as a unique and personal act, and that the emphatic understanding marks the specific difference that distinguishes forgiveness from acts and attitudes that are similar or related but ultimately distinct.

This methodological reflection leads to the second reason for which the conditional understanding of forgiveness is problematic. Griswold, as we have seen, was concerned that forgiveness would lose its moral meaning if it were not linked to repentance. It might then even "collapse into forgetting," he believed. But the link to repentance, eventually, amounts to an undue generalization.[161] While it may be possible to find cases in which repentance and forgiveness are bound together, these are not the only instances that can be imagined and must not be taken as paradigmatic. Insofar as forgiveness has to happen as a singular, unpredictable act there cannot be a way in which one can say that it generally has to occur. It is possible, for example, to continue to have resentment and not expect any remorse in the offender.[162] Repentance may also follow, and not precede, the act of forgiving. In addition, forgiveness does not entail any specific act toward the offender; it can simply be a mental stance. Renouncing any "transactional" meaning may even be the only way to grasp what can be called "pure forgiveness."[163] Actions toward others may already invite a certain instrumental use of forgiveness, whereas forgiveness first and foremost has to exist as a mental stance in the agent, before and beyond any practical application.

In moral philosophy, we can find references to what is called the paradox of forgiveness. This paradox can be summarized in the following way:

> If forgiveness relates to an act of wrongdoing that is regarded as neither justified nor excused, why shouldn't we continue to resent that act? When we forgive, we forgive a person for a culpable wrongdoing, but if the wrongdoing is culpable, there is no reason to forgive him or her for it. Forgiveness, it seems, is either impossible from the start (namely if the act is excused), or it is possible (namely if the act is culpable), but then there can never be reasons for forgiveness and the claim that one ought to forgive is necessarily unjustified.[164]

We find this paradox a construct, and a rather simplistic one for that matter. It fails to capture the meaning of forgiveness both logically and morally. First, it implies a rather superficial logic of wrongdoing and retribution if one thinks that wrongdoing can ever only be followed by blame and that agents who have been wronged never have any reason to react without resentment. No logical restriction is violated if one continues to blame the offender and still decides to forgive.[165] Second, the very meaning of forgiveness implies that there is an action which could at the same time also be blamed. Arendt pointed this out by saying that we can only forgive what we could also punish. Derrida famously rephrased the point by saying: "Forgiveness forgives only the unforgivable. One cannot, or should not, forgive; there is only forgiveness, if there is any, where there is the unforgivable."[166] Taken as a general condition, Derrida's formula is too strong. There are forgivable offenses that are still not forgiven and some unforgivable acts may forever be off limits, as Arendt believed. But Derrida states correctly, we believe, that in order to grasp the meaning of forgiveness one has to reach beyond the desire to blame. There may be no good reason to forgive an offender, but this is precisely the point. Forgiveness is then not simply "unjustified," as if this were all that can be said about it, but constitutes an act of its own which finds whatever justification it can have all in itself.

Ambivalence

We now come to the second way in which the dialectic of forgiveness can play out. In this way, forgiveness is granted for no prior reason. We have said that when this happens forgiveness is too great and either escapes or transcends a moral point of view. In this section, we will first talk about how it escapes morality. To do so, we have to come back one last time to Griswold's concern that forgiveness might slip into a non-moral attitude like forgetting. We dismissed this concern before because it stems from a false generalization and an overstatement of the moral nature of forgiving. But the concern can in principle not be dismissed because it is part of the dialectical nature of forgiveness itself. As an unpredictable new beginning, there is no way to say why forgiving begins and what it entails. For moral reasons alone one can always suspect that it is a careless, empty gesture of generosity. Arendt assumed, as quoted above, that "he who acts never quite knows what he is doing." This ignorance can also affect forgiving as an action that is meant to remedy the flaws of other actions.[167] We therefore have to admit that forgiving carries with it an ineradicable ambivalence and that its moral status can always to some extent be called into question.

Forgiveness even doubles the ambivalence of actions insofar as it shows that the past is ambivalent, open to re-interpretation through another action which is ambivalent in itself insofar as it constitutes a rupture with the logic of blame and retribution. Seen from this angle, one may rightfully suspect that forgiveness risks the seriousness of morality and disregards existing wrongs for the sake of some vague goodness or some purely pragmatic solution. Even worse, there can be cases in which it may be morally objectionable to forgive. "But how could you forgive them *that*?" Finally, one may suspect that forgiveness stems from weakness, from a lack of force and decisiveness in reacting to the harm inflicted by others. Weakness is indeed not easy to rule out: cases in which forgiveness is just a pretense to mask one's inability to confront the other agent may be rare, but all forgiveness means that one relinquishes a potential position of power. The agent lets go of the potential to condemn, blame, and punish that they hold over the offender. There is obviously also power in the ability to forgive, but it may not be enough to rule out the suspicion that one could have pursued one's interests more decidedly.

It is important to note that we talk about a dialectical tension, a mere suspicion here. The idea that forgiveness may be no more than an empty, inconsiderate gesture is a reflection of the moral content that lies in the act. That is, if forgiveness were always a careless act, one would not have to suspect that it is at certain times. We should therefore not over-emphasize its potential emptiness. Forgiving may not follow, or may not be necessitated by any prior reason but it can obviously go along with reasons. It may even attract reasons, much like a center of gravity. The relation between the act of forgiving and moral reasons is eventually quite the opposite of how we described it before: forgiveness does not follow from reasons but gives certain reasons their force. If I do not want to forgive you, you can repent as long as you want. That is, without me forgiving, purely and simply, your repentance would in turn become an empty act. Only because I forgive, in a wholly unpredictable manner, can we see how your repentance fits in as a prior event and provides a retroactive motivation of sorts.[168] The same holds for all other moral reasons that may give content to the act of forgiving: if the act does not happen, the reasons are merely potential, but if it happens then they acquire the weight of a real determination. There is nothing magical in this retroactive force: forgiving, as a new beginning, is a meaning-giving act. It creates a new center in the web of actions from which new relations can be woven, even backwards. Few other acts, like declarations of love, have a similar effect. This shows once more how simplistic the so-called paradox of forgiveness is. It looks at forgiveness in a static way, as an isolated act that is related to some prior, equally isolated act. But forgiveness is dynamic and changes the constellations of past and future. The paradox vanishes up in the air once we recognize that blame is only one of the many ways to react to the past. Forgiveness lets the dead bury their dead and continues life in a new direction.

Transcendence

What remains to be shown is how forgiving may transcend a moral point of view. We will mention two approaches to the phenomenon, the first of which was also used by Arendt. According to her, "the discoverer of the role of forgiveness in the realm of human affairs was Jesus of Nazareth."[169] The religious context of the *New Testament* should not distract us from seeing in his actions an "authentic political experience."[170] Jesus asks humans to forgive each other and only as a consequence of that God may also forgive them.[171] He shows humans a way to achieve "freedom from vengeance" in their interactions.[172] We can follow Arendt's lead and think of Jesus' teachings outside of their religious premises as an attempt at reorienting the moral attitudes of humans. (Like Arendt, we are also happy to eschew all exegetical difficulties and only want to indicate what certain passages in the *New Testament* can mean for our understanding of morality.)

The main justification for Jesus' repeated exhortation to forgive seems to stem from his idea that all humans fail moral standards and that no one is entitled to be the judge of any other: "Judge not, that you be not judged. For with the judgement you pronounce you will be judged ... You hypocrite, first take the log out of your own eye, and then you will see clearly to take the speck out of your brother's eye."[173] With respect to a woman who was supposedly caught in committing adultery, we find: "'Let him who is without sin among you be the first to throw a stone at her.' ... But when they heard it, they went away one by one. ... And Jesus said, 'Neither do I condemn you; go, and from now on sin no more.'"[174] As arguments against hypocrisy, these passages would be rather trivial. But we can also understand them as a demonstration of the meaning of moral principles: principles apply to everyone, including those who use them to judge others, *and* they apply to the way in which they are used. Judging others is as much in need of a moral justification as any other action. Humans, therefore, cannot hide from the self-application of moral principles and they cannot deny that even the simple act of judging requires the overall consistency of their actions and beliefs. They have to realize that if they endorse just any principle they have to endorse them all, which eventually means that they have to realize that they too fail morality in one way or another. Humans then simply have to stop measuring each other's actions against a moral standard that is chosen only because it seems applicable in a given situation. For Jesus, the "works" of the world are all "evil,"[175] which implies that none can be attributed a substantially higher degree of morality compared to any other. If Jesus passes moral judgment, it is from a trans-worldly point of view: "You judge according to the flesh; I judge no one. Yet even if I do judge, my judgment is true, for it is not I alone who judge, but I and the Father who sent me."[176] For this reason, even criminals can be forgiven, as well as those who performed the torturous and deadly act of crucifying: "Father, forgive them, for they know not what they do."[177] If humans are shrouded in ignorance in their moral judgments, then they are also ignorant in their violations.

For us, the question is here: in the name of which morality should forgiveness be granted to everyone? Refraining from judgment because of one's ignorance and guilt is only the negative side of Jesus' moral stance. What does it mean positively for humans to adopt an attitude of forgiveness? Humans should obviously continue to act righteously ("sin no more") but what else follows for their interactions? The "Parable of the Unforgiving Servant" can help us see what it is:

> Then Peter came up and said to him, 'Lord, how often will my brother sin against me, and I forgive him? As many as seven times?' Jesus said to him, 'I do not say to you seven times, but seventy-seven times. Therefore, the kingdom of heaven may be compared to a king who wished to settle accounts with his servants. When he began to settle, one was brought to him who owed him ten thousand talents. And since he could not pay, his master ordered him to be sold, with his wife and children and all that he had, and payment to be made. So the servant fell on his knees, imploring him, 'Have patience with me, and I will pay you everything.' And out of pity for him, the master of that servant released him and forgave him the debt. But when that same servant went out, he found one of his fellow servants who owed him a hundred denarii, and seizing him, he began to choke him, saying, 'Pay what you owe.' So his fellow servant fell down and pleaded with him, 'Have patience with me, and I will pay you.' He refused and went and put him in prison until he should pay the debt. When his fellow servants saw what had taken place, they were greatly distressed, and they went and reported to their master all that had taken place. Then his master summoned him and said to him, 'You wicked servant! I forgave you all that debt because you pleaded with me. And should not you have had mercy on your fellow servant, as I had mercy on you?' And in anger his master delivered him to the jailers, until he should pay all his debt. So also my heavenly Father will do to every one of you, if you do not forgive your brother from your heart.'[178]

One could read this passage in light of what Derrida called an economic exchange: forgiving obliges the forgivee to reciprocate the act and continue it toward others. If one does not reciprocate, then the initial forgiveness is revoked and one has to suffer punishment for one's deeds. Jesus does of course not refer to punishment that is inflicted by humans but to the punishment that his heavenly father will eventually mete out. Even then, the parable seems to be driven by a logic of equivalence. However, the fact that it is God who will punish, not another human, indicates that the parable transcends the ordinary view of actions. The servant in the story does not do much to gain our sympathy, for sure, choking his own servant and throwing him in jail. He seems a standard hypocrite, and a violent one for that. But he also may have acted according to what the customary practices of lending money and collecting debt allowed agents to do. After all, each epoch has their share in cruel punishments. Perhaps the individual who owed him money borrowed it under false pretenses, or at least could not have expected to be treated any different. We do not really know, but we also should not rule out that the servant's reaction might be a somewhat normal, foreseeable one. What Jesus requires from humans is instead a transformation of their whole attitude toward others, a transformation of their "heart." Humans are asked to disregard all debt, all obligations that result from regular interactions, and forgive unconditionally. Moral principles, as they may relate to promise-making, responsibility, honesty, and the like, should be cast away and all focus has to be laid on removing negative categorizations from the view of others. Humans have to forgive, not because the other agent may be worthy of it but despite or even because they are not, because they have to understand that they too "do not know what they do."

The transformation of practice that Jesus wants to initiate does not amount to a new standard for the way in which actions are conducted. Humans are called to elevate themselves above their own practical purposes, distance themselves from their involvement with others and from the focus on moral principles as they may be violated by the things that others do. Their attitude has to transcend morality as a set of specific and practically relevant principles for the sake of an exclusive focus on forgiveness which embraces everyone and so constitutes a true community of sinners, that is, a community of humans who are all deficient in their moral determinations and all fail according to their own standards. The servant in the story is therefore not punished because he did not reciprocate forgiveness; he is punished because he was pleading for forgiveness without understanding what it means. Forgiveness has to be sought for its own sake, and once one has captured that, then all trading for economic benefits has to stop.

(This also means that forgiveness would still be inadequate if it were given out of indifference. It is not merely an act, something that simply needs to be done to get over with it. Cold forgiveness is worthless and more like disdain. "I don't think you are worthy to be taken seriously and punished." Forgiveness, again, has to come from the heart, as a gesture that accepts the other person without reserve.)

One should for these reasons be careful to term Jesus' call for a transformation of human hearts a new morality in proper sense, as if it were a new principle which could be followed by adopting a new pattern of behavior in the relation to others. "Do always forgive" may be possible to say but it would fail to indicate that each act of forgiveness is exceptional insofar as it goes counter to moral ideas which it would be more ordinary to have. "Do always forgive despite all evidence and even if you don't want to" would be more adequate but it would mean precisely that what one is called to do goes against reason, as "a madness of the impossible."[179] Jesus indicates the extraordinary character of forgiveness when he asks to forgive not "seven times, but seventy-seven times," as quoted above.[180] The number indicates the sheer multiplication of the acts of forgiving, which are all unique and extraordinary but have to be repeated over and over again because there is always reason in human practice to engage in the logic of retribution and blame. The number indicates, in other words, the sheer foolishness that forgiving represents from a worldly perspective. It may be acceptable to grant it once, but granting it again, and then again, is that no wholly unreasonable?

At times, Jesus talks as if he was indeed using a new moral standard, for example, in forgiving another woman who was deemed a "sinner":[181]

> Do you see this woman? I entered your house; you gave me no water for my feet, but she has wet my feet with her tears and wiped them with her hair. ... Therefore, I tell you, her sins, which are many, are forgiven—for she loved much.' ... And he said to the woman, 'Your faith has saved you; go in peace.[182]

Humans can save themselves through their faith and love for God. One could then ask whether there is not a contradiction between the demand to forgive unconditionally and the forgiving of those who seem worthiest of it. But the passage again only shows that forgiveness is no impersonal standard (apart from the fact that a person's faith has to be genuine, which can only be known by God): we should rather forgive than not, but forgiveness cannot simply be expected to be given. The woman could not have counted on it. One has to ask for it in each case anew, seventy-seven times and more. Forgiveness only makes sense as a singular act; otherwise, it would turn into a hollow gesture. And as a singular act, forgiveness comes from the heart, which means that those worthy of it might also speak to our heart more. Forgiveness is partial and biased, in other words, and its foolishness consists precisely in extending this bias so that it includes everyone.[183]

Even if forgiveness, as it is understood in this section, cannot and must not be granted in the name of any specific form of morality, we can say that humans are asked to forgive in the name of the truly absolute good insofar as it overcomes the use of morality for the purposes of categorization, blame, and punishment. The good that humans believe to achieve by focusing on particular moral principles and the various ways in which agents meet and violate them is replaced by another, higher one. This higher good not only entails that all blameworthiness is revoked, it also entails that all moral purposes, insofar as they are particular, related to truth-telling, personal property, bodily integrity, and the like, are revoked. To be clear: it is not that these purposes have become indifferent. There is no license to engage in immoral behavior just because one can count on another person's forgiveness. Certain crimes may have to be punished, if only for practical reasons because it may not be safe not to do so. But at least the person who forgives has to be indifferent to the violations of others. Whatever the violation, even after the seventy-seventh time it will be forgiven. At the bottom of one's heart, that is, at the bottom of one's interest for the good the truly absolute good makes all deficiencies and violations of moral principles consistent. The truly absolute good, in other words, comprises the consistency of what is consistent and what is inconsistent. It makes inconsistency consistent, too.

Practically speaking, the consistency of the consistent and the inconsistent can only be achieved if one transcends the realm in which morality is ordinarily applied. The focus on forgiving is an idealizing, pre-emptive attitude: the agent recognizes the personal motives and interests in others as well as the purposes that make up the good for them even it cannot be consistent to their own. Forgiveness gives room to these purposes, waiting for the truly absolute good to emerge once the negative effects that the differences in purpose may have caused have all faded away. Forgiving cannot simply create the absolute good, or pretend that it is already real, because this would mean to disregard all moral distinctions, but it acts as if the absolute good were at least achievable, initiating a transformation that starts from within one's heart and that will eventually radiate into the practical world, even if there can be no expectation that the good will not be failed. Forgiving is therefore always wrong, because it disregards inconsistency and even multiplies it through its own act, but in it lies the belief that inconsistency, if only it is countered by other genuine acts of the heart, will eventually dissolve in the overall consistency of the good. Forgiveness fails the good, both in regard to moral categorizations and principles *and* the absolute good which remains elusive and a never-ending task in each repeated instance of forgiving, but it fails it willingly and happily, because this failing of the good is the only way in which an absolute good can be envisioned beyond its typical, inevitable antagonisms. The dialectical tension in forgiveness can therefore never be overcome. One has to take morality seriously and needs to blame what is to blame in human interactions but for moral reasons one also has to renounce morality's own antagonism, taking morality seriously in this other way, too. No point of view outside of this constellation can be taken. In forgiveness, agents take these contradictions upon themselves. Their foolishness can also be described as a sort of risk-taking because it is not clear in advance how the absolute good will emerge, or even just a higher form of the good than the one available, and whether such a good will emerge at all.

To conclude, we want to mention a more recent approach to the phenomenon of forgiveness which also aims at transcending the limits of morality. We find it in Nietzsche who also embraces the example of Jesus. Like Arendt, Nietzsche stresses the practical, human meaning of Jesus' message. Contrary to her, he sees in Christ not a political but a radically a-political stance:

> The 'glad tidings' are precisely that there are no more opposites: the kingdom of Heaven belongs to children; the faith which here finds utterance is not a faith which has been won by struggle—it is there, from the beginning, it is as it were a return to childishness in the spiritual domain.[184]

Jesus' teachings, for Nietzsche, have to be interpreted in a psychological way. What is divine is precisely the new way of life that Jesus has found,[185] which is based on an "*instinctive exclusion of all aversion, all enmity, all feeling for limitation and distancing.*"[186] The moral concepts of "guilt and punishment" all vanish in Jesus' perspective and human morality as a whole is overcome.[187] Nietzsche is less interested in the phenomenon of forgiving than in this overcoming of morality. In a sense, forgiving is overcome, too, given that it only has meaning in relation to particular wrongdoings that can be identified. We can perhaps say that Nietzsche's interpretation captures the end of all forgiving, a state in which moral differences would cease to exist or at least become irrelevant. From our perspective, there is something problematic in this: fulfilling the transcending meaning of forgiveness risks taking the dialectical tension out of forgiving itself, not to mention the dialectical tension out of morality as a whole.

Besides Jesus, Nietzsche also uses the figure of Zarathustra to proclaim a radical forgiving. Zarathustra preaches, in a manner much like Christ, the overcoming of the need to punish and a higher sort of justice which would allow humans to give up the desire to judge: "I do not like your cold justice; and from the eye of your judges there gazes always the executioner and his cold steel./ … Devise for me the justice that acquits everyone except the one who judges."[188] Avoiding the logic of blame and retribution is simply a matter of 'cleanliness'[189] and moral determinations can be abandoned simply because it is not worth defending a limited position: "How tired I am of my good and my evil!"[190] In telling Zarathustra's story, Nietzsche traces the desire to overcome all moral retribution back to the human desire to overcome time. Similar to Arendt, the relation to the past and the burden of past events are described as the main source of human suffering: "'It was': that is the will's gnashing of teeth and loneliest sorrow. Powerless with respect to what has been done—it is an angry spectator of all that is past."[191] Zarathustra too wishes *"that humanity might be redeemed from revenge,"*[192] which eventually leads him to the idea of the eternal recurrence of everything. This idea, which we cannot further discuss, shows that the overcoming of revenge, as well as the overcoming of the need to forgive, ultimately implies the overcoming of action altogether. As infinitely repeated events, actions lose their character of practical endeavors driven by intent and purpose. A whole new perspective on the world emerges this way: redemption is achieved because there is nothing that one needs to be redeemed from. As said before, this is also the idea of a world without dialectics. We can see it as a limiting idea of human practice, an idea that makes morality unnecessary without the recourse to a higher power. But then again, forgiveness is not at the center of Nietzsche's analyses and his goal is not to render justice to the phenomenon.[193]

Anesthesia

In highlighting the problem of revenge in his *Zarathustra*, Nietzsche shows how difficult it is for humans to engage in genuine forgiveness. Time and the resentment that it brings through the inevitable attachment to the past hold too much power over them. Other philosophers have been much more optimistic and assumed that it would indeed be possible to establish a general and widespread attitude of forgiveness in humans. We think of their approaches as vulgar. The approaches can also be termed relativistic because they claim, in one way or another, that moral categorizations are in principle invalid and therefore useless and irrelevant for human practice anyway. An example of this kind of relativism can be found in Rorty. Rorty describes himself as a pragmatist,[194] which means for him precisely that no moral idea and principle can be given a definite truth value. Moral ideas are "social constructions" which amount to no more than "practical recommendations."[195] Like Jesus, only without any religious commitment, Rorty believes that it is meaningless to strive for the right action or for moral goodness because humans simply cannot know what that is. There is in fact moral progress for him, but it is exclusively "a matter of wider and wider sympathy."[196] In renouncing any claim at holding a valid position, agents can become ever more inclusive with respect to the position of others. They can "minimize one difference at a time" and so slowly achieve greater consistency among them.[197] This way, a welcoming and forgiving attitude toward others can evolve out of pragmatic arrangements, a "process of adjustment,"[198] and a vague and general benevolence whose main driver is the "sensitivity to pain."[199] Rorty clearly wants to overcome any antagonism that could result from strong moral determinations. He achieves this through a sort of moral anesthesia which makes it impossible to feel the sting of contradictions. Contradictions disappear because no agent has a ground to stand on in making moral claims and everyone eventually accommodates to the positions of others which may not be so terrible and serious after all.

The reason why we think of such an approach as vulgar is not that it wants to overcome dialectical tensions or that it aims at promoting mutual sympathy. The reason is rather that it thinks of everyone as morally justified. Agents can never be wrong and are therefore in one way or another always right. Their consistency is guaranteed, at least in the long run. No one needs to be forgiven because something grave or unforgivable would have happened. The question is only how long it makes sense to consider perceived moral flaws, given that they are baseless anyway. Moral contradictions are mere differences between individuals, which exist in degrees and can be diminished if needed. Like in the other vulgar positions that we have shown in this chapter, there is simply no need to be moral in any emphatic, self-determined sense. Rorty states, for example: "To say that respect for human rights demanded our intervention to save the Jews from the Nazis, or the Bosnian Muslims from the Serbs, is to say that a failure to intervene would make us uncomfortable with ourselves."[200] The language that he uses in this quote is telling: moral antagonisms are like disturbances in one's comfortable life. We adopt them temporarily and fight against, say, the Serbs in the name of human rights because we want to go back to a world of minimized pain and differences. Human practice will eventually be sanitized from moral accusations. Dealing with moral controversy is only annoying, like having to wake up from one's sleep to kill a mosquito.

What happens if an agent wants to avoid the antagonism of morality but is not inclined to follow a vulgar, relativistic approach? What is left if they also want to avoid the demanding and contradictory attitude of forgiveness? There is a pragmatic solution for them, which is the way of humor. Humor means to accept the limited goodness of all activities and to relieve oneself and others from the painful feeling that the awareness of these limitations can cause. Instead of focusing on the past and the wrongdoings that have occurred, one looks for the cathartic outlet of a laugh. The past cannot be changed anyway, and one resigns to letting it be. There is an implicit resignation in humor for this reason. Sarcasm can go together with it as one of its darker forms. Where there is reason to laugh, there is often just as much reason to condemn and be bitter. But one may eventually need forgiveness for becoming all-too sarcastic, which means that it is no good solution after all. Humor counter-acts bitterness: a laughing attitude lets everyone have their own foolish point of view and takes none all-too seriously. Contrary to Rorty's relativism, in humor one does not minimize the differences but deals with the potential antagonisms by trying to show what is laughable in them.[201] Like the person who forgives again and again, seventy-seven times and more, the humorous person turns it all into a joke, again and again. The logic that they follow is the one of conjunction: I can laugh about this, and about this, and so on. While in forgiving one may feel the weight of moral seriousness and perhaps a tone of tragedy, because too much is at stake both if one forgives and if one does not, the humorous person prefers comedy and agrees with the final choir of Verdi's *Falstaff* in that "everything in this world is a joke" (*tutto nel mondo è burla*).

Epilogue

It would be tempting to end this chapter, and the whole book, with these remarks on humor. Morality has often been suspected to be too solemn, whether its solemnity is considered genuine or a hypocritical façade. Having an easy, pragmatic escape from the tensions that moral determinations create has for many been a dream. But in the conceptual realm of morality, it never works simply to stop: the dialectic continues to unfold if one only looks closely enough at the assumptions that are contained in any position. Are we allowed to laugh, eventually, or better: are we allowed *only* to laugh? Perhaps we should not laugh about things that are unforgivable? On the other hand, are we not forever locked into a diminished, broken form of the good if we focus on the harm and strife that we experience in the practical world? But then, the good of humor is diminished too, as it can well seem too small. Humor restores the good merely because it lets go of a fuller version. This way, one can find oneself brought back inadvertently to the dialectics of forgiveness in which the agent recognizes and at the same time endures the inevitable tensions: tensions between the inconsistency of purposes that should not be and the consistency of purposes that cannot and should not be considered achieved.

Notes

Introduction

1. See Michael Steinmann, *Die Ethik Friedrich Nietzsches* (Berlin/New York: Walter de Gruyter, 2000) and "Duties towards our Bodies," in *Altruism Reconsidered. Exploring New Approaches to Property in Human Tissue*, ed. Michael Steinmann, Peter Sykora and Urban Wiesing (Aldershot: Ashgate, 2009), 67–86.
2. It is wrong, of course, to think of the variety of moral theories as some sort of competition, but the following words ring true nonetheless: "None of the competing styles of moral theory has what it takes to win. After all, one might think that if one of utilitarianism, deontological moral theory, or virtue theory were a satisfactory rendition of our moral world, there would by now be no remaining dissenters. If none of these theories have gained anything close to consensus, their very able advocates and the amount of time they have had to exhibit their merits notwithstanding, a likely explanation of the persistent dissatisfaction is that there is something seriously and fairly obviously wrong with each" (Elijah Millgram, *Ethics Done Right: Practical Reasoning as a Foundation for Moral Theory* (New York: Cambridge University Press, 2005), 315).
3. For an early attempt at articulating my discomfort, see Michael Steinmann, "What Technology Is Not. On Ethics as Ecology of Human Life," in *Science, Technology, and the Humanities: A New Synthesis*, ed. Lisa Dolling (Hoboken, NJ: Stevens Institute of Technology, 2011), 366–85.
4. See Chapter 6 for a more detailed account of my understanding and use of the idea of dialectics.
5. First Corinthians 4, 10.
6. This commitment can also follow Murdoch's dictum: "'All is vanity' is the beginning and the end of ethics" (Iris Murdoch, *The Sovereignty of Good* (London/New York: Routledge, 1971), 69).

Chapter 1

1. Other forms of normativity are less pertinent to our analysis of morality, such as epistemic, religious, or aesthetic normativity. We do not aim at a systematic analysis of normativity here.
2. For an illustration of the empiricist approach to morality, see Hume's remarks: "The very nature of language guides us almost infallibly … ; and as every tongue possesses one set of words which are taken in a good sense, and another in the opposite, the least acquaintance with the idiom suffices, without any reasoning, to direct us in collecting and arranging the estimable or blamable qualities of man" (David Hume, *An Enquiry*

Concerning the Principles of Morals, in *Moral Philosophy*, ed. Geoffrey Sayre-McCord (Indianapolis: Hackett, 2006), 190).

3   To illustrate the importance of distinguishing between the linguistic and conceptual form of normativity, see Dancy's somewhat undecided remarks: "It is often said that normativity is the characteristic common to everything that appears on the 'ought' side of the distinction between what is and what ought to be. ... Perhaps ... it would be better not to have any single term like 'ought' as the mark of the normative ... I confess, however, that I find it helpful to have an 'ought' in mind when thinking about normativity" (Jonathan Dancy, "Editor's Introduction," in *Normativity*, ed. Jonathan Dancy (Oxford: Blackwell, 2000), VII). What makes matters worse is that "the term 'normativity' itself bears the stamp of but one aspect of such phenomena, leading etymologically back to the Latin term for the builder's square, *norma*" (Peter Railton, "Normative Force and Normative Freedom: Hume and Kant, but not Hume versus Kant," in *Normativity*, ed. Dancy, 1). Apparently, not even "normativity" is always the most appropriate term for what is experienced as normative.

4   John Locke calls it "that most unshaken Rule of Morality and Foundation of all social Virtue," and so implicitly states its twofold meaning as a moral and conventional rule (*An Essay Concerning Human Understanding*, ed. Peter H. Nidditch (Oxford: Oxford University Press, 1973), 68 (Book I, Chapter III, 4).

5   For the definition of, and distinction between, "nonmaleficence" and "beneficence," see Tom L. Beauchamp and James F. Childress, *Principles of Biomedical Ethics*, 6th edn (New York: Oxford University Press, 2009), 149–51 and 199.

6   For the definition of prima facie duties, see W. D. Ross, *The Right and the Good* (Oxford: Clarendon, 1930), 19–20.

7   For a formalistic approach to normativity, see for example Joseph Raz, "Explaining Normativity: On Rationality and the Justification of Reason," in *Normativity*, ed. Dancy, 34: "Aspects of the world are normative in as much as they or their existence constitute reasons for persons, i.e. grounds which make certain beliefs, moods, emotions, intentions or actions appropriate or inappropriate." The complexity of the phenomenon can at best be indicated but not captured this way. In addition, the statement quoted here is circular, because in order to use reasons for the "explanation" of normativity, these reasons have to be seen as "appropriate or inappropriate," which means that they are already taken in a normative sense. Formalist approaches to morality are likely to run into the problem of circularity, although we cannot show here in more detail why this is so.

8   From a slightly different angle, Thomson mentions "that the truth of what people are saying when they say sentences of the form 'A ought to V_{act}' turns on more than just what those of A's immediate circumstances are that provoked their saying the sentence. ... The reason why we are provoked to say these things ... lies also in assumptions we are making about the rest of the world" (Judith Jarvis Thomson, *Normativity* (Chicago and La Salle, IL: Open Court, 2008), 184). Gaita nicely shows that evoking principles in an isolated manner can lead to quite absurd results: "If one puts in the mouth of the remorseful person many of the philosophical accounts of what makes an obligation a moral obligation or a principle a moral principle, ... we get parody. 'My God what have I done? I have violated the social contract, agreed behind a veil of ignorance.' 'My God what have I done? I have ruined my best chances of flourishing.' 'My God what have I done? I have violated rational nature in another.' 'My God what have I done? I have diminished the stock of happiness'" (Raimond Gaita, *Good and Evil: An Absolute Conception*, 2nd edn (New York: Routledge, 2004), xxi; see also 33–5).

Chapter 2

1. See Friedrich Nietzsche, *Daybreak. Thoughts on the Prejudices of Morality*, transl. R. J. Hollingdale (Cambridge: Cambridge University Press, 1997), 10–12 (section 9). For a comparable analysis in Nietzsche's work, see *Human, All Too Human I*, transl. Gary Handwerk (Stanford: Stanford University Press, 1997), 73–4 (sections 96 and 97).
2. See for example the use of the terms in *Daybreak*, section 10 (*Sittlichkeit*) and section 11 (*Moral*).
3. See Avishai Margalit, *The Ethics of Memory* (Cambridge, MA: Harvard University Press, 2004), 8.
4. *Daybreak*, 11 (section 9).
5. Ibid.
6. Nietzsche refers to coercion in *Human, All Too Human I*, 75–6 (section 99). *Daybreak*, 16 (section 18) mentions the element of cruelty in customary practices.
7. See *Daybreak*, 11 (section 9).
8. Ibid. (translation modified M.S.)
9. *Daybreak*, 10 (section 9). There is a remarkable parallel to this analysis in Hegel's *Philosophy of Right*: compared to the sphere of right, which consists of a set of legal rules, morality appears as the standpoint of subjectivity. In order to reach this standpoint, the sphere of right has to be overcome, that is, negated, which happens through crime. Crime provides the logical transition from a given set of rules to moral self-determination. See G. W. F. Hegel, *Elements of the Philosophy of Right*, transl. H. B. Nisbet (Cambridge: Cambridge University Press, 1991), 131–2. (paragraph 104).
10. For the evilness of morality, see also *Daybreak*, 202 (section 496) and Friedrich Nietzsche, *The Gay Science*, transl. Josefine Nauckhoff (Cambridge: Cambridge University Press, 2001), 32 (section 4). For its craziness, see *Daybreak*, 14 (section 14) and 119 (section 199), as well as *The Gay Science*, 115 (section 117). Sometimes an element of cruelty also belongs to it, see *Daybreak*, 22–3 (section 30).
11. For a similar account of the transition from traditional to individual morality, see Jürgen Habermas, *Moral Consciousness and Communicative Action*, transl. Christian Lenhardt and Shierry Weber Nicholson (Cambridge, MA: MIT Press, 1990), 107–8. For a sociological explanation, see Niklas Luhmann, *Die Moral der Gesellschaft*, ed. Detlef Horster (Frankfurt a.M.: Suhrkamp, 2008), 255 and 319–20.
12. For a psychological theory of self-determination as "*intrinsically* motivated activity," see Alexios Arvanitis, "Autonomy and Morality: A Self-determination Theory Discussion of Ethics," *New Ideas in Psychology* 47 (2017), 58.
13. In his *Theory of Justice*, Rawls shows how the rational interest in the good can be present in life-conduct over time: "A rational plan of life establishes the basic point of view from which all judgments of value relating to a particular person are to be made and finally rendered consistent. … We can think of a person as being happy when he is in the way of a successful execution (more or less) of a rational plan of life drawn up under (more or less) favorable conditions, and he is reasonably confident that his plan can be carried through" (John Rawls, *A Theory of Justice*, rev. edn (Cambridge, MA: Harvard University Press, 1999), 359). Williams criticized the idea of a rational plan as too static: "There is no set of preferences both fixed and relevant, relative to which the various fillings of my life-space can be compared" (Bernard Williams, "Moral Luck," in *Moral Luck. Philosophical Papers 1973–1980*

(Cambridge: Cambridge University Press, 1981), 34). It seems indeed unfortunate to think of preferences as fixed ideas which are only "executed" instead as the living and mutual adaptation of actions and beliefs.
14 Christine M. Korsgaard, *Self-Constitution. Agency, Identity, and Integrity* (New York: Oxford University Press 2009), 158.
15 Ibid., 21.
16 Ibid., 25.
17 Ibid., 169.
18 See ibid., 162.
19 See ibid., 73 and 77.
20 Ibid., 160.
21 Ibid., 25.
22 Compare to a recent attempt at defining morality: "The term 'morality' can be used … normatively to refer to a code of conduct that, given specified conditions, would be put forward by all rational persons" (Bernard Gert and Joshua Gert, "The Definition of Morality," *The Stanford Encyclopedia of Philosophy*, Fall 2017 Edition). This definition is either incomplete (because rationality, like normativity, does not only come in moral form) or circular (because one has to assume that "rational persons" are precisely those who choose a certain "code of conduct"). More important, the definition leaves out the subjective impulse of persons who first have to commit to acting rationally and to making morality their primary goal.
23 For a similar view, see Kant's famous remarks: "If we look back upon all previous efforts that have ever been made to discover the principle of morality, we need not wonder now why all of them had to fail. It was seen that the human being is bound to laws by his duty, but it never occurred to them that he is subject *only to laws given by himself but still universal* and that he is bound only to act in conformity with his own will" (Immanuel Kant, *Groundwork of the Metaphysics of Morals*, transl. Mary Gregor (Cambridge: Cambridge University Press, 1998), 40 (Akademieausgabe IV, 432; in the following AA)).
24 Although Nietzsche indicates in several passages that the individual exception from the morality of custom may lead to the creation of new moral norms, he does not say clearly what these are. For the—rather vague—idea of an individual impetus to represent what would be good for all human beings, see *Human, All Too Human I*, 71–2 (section 94); *Daybreak*, 223 (section 552), and *The Gay Science*, 30–2 (section 3). For Nietzsche, only actions that are strictly individual can be authentic, which means that the general morality created by Christianity and Socrates was a misunderstanding from the start. See *Human, All Too Human I*, 72 (section 95) and 82–4 (section 107); *Daybreak*, 209–10 (section 529). General reasons are self-refuting for him; see *Human, All Too Human I*, 78 (section 102), and *The Gay Science* 43–5 (section 21).
25 For a similar conception of moral behavior, see again Rawls: "We cannot have things both ways. We cannot preserve a sense of justice and all that this implies while at the same time holding ourselves ready to act unjustly should doing so promise some personal advantage. A just person is not prepared to do certain things, and if he is tempted too easily, he was prepared after all" (*Theory of Justice*, 498). And: "This sentiment [of justice, M.S.] cannot be fulfilled if it is compromised and balanced against other ends as but one desire among the rest. It is a desire to conduct oneself in a certain way above all else, a striving that contains within itself its own priority" (503). The point here is not, we believe, to decide whether individuals really follow

the idea of justice in their lives (it is impossible to decide this anyway), but to show that justice, if taken seriously, entails the commitment to a consistent conduct of life and to determine oneself in such a way that its principles are maintained as primary compared to other interests and influences.
26 See Søren Kierkegaard, *Either/Or, Part II*, transl. Howard V. Hong and Edna H. Hong (Princeton: Princeton University Press, 1987), 174–5.
27 Ibid., 166–7.
28 Ibid., 214.
29 Ibid., 169.
30 Ibid., 167.
31 Ibid., 176. See also Søren Kierkegaard, *Concluding Unscientific Postscript to the Philosophical Crumbs*, transl. Alistair Hannay (Cambridge: Cambridge University Press, 2009), 287: the transition to the ethical happens "as a break, yes, as a suffering." In a similar vein, Gaita emphasizes "the kind of seriousness that is peculiar to morality" (*Good and Evil*, 33). Morality, for him, requires "a deepened understanding of the *meaning* of our actions" (264), not just of the principles that are involved. Without this focus on the individual agent and their way of acting, moral theory slides into "banality" (213).
32 *Either/Or*, 224.
33 See ibid., 270.
34 Ibid., 219.
35 Ibid., 254 (translation modified, M.S.). See also *Concluding Unscientific Postscript*, 163 and 268.
36 *Either/Or*, 255 (translation modified, M.S.).
37 Ibid., 270.
38 See ibid., 329. "As soon as the single individual wants to assert himself in his particularity over against the universal, he sins" (Søren Kierkegaard, *Fear and Trembling*, transl. Sylvia Walsh (Cambridge: Cambridge University Press, 2006), 46).
39 See ibid., 60. Strictly speaking, "there are at least three senses of the ethical" in Kierkegaard's work (Merold Westphal, "The Many Faces of Levinas as a Reader of Kierkegaard," in *Kierkegaard and Levinas. Ethics, Politics, and Religion*, ed. J. Aaron Simmons and David Wood (Bloomington/Indianapolis: Indiana University Press, 2008), 22). Insofar as ethics can be grounded in faith, the exteriority of the general can vanish. But we are only interested here in Kierkegaard's treatment of the ethical as a sphere *sui generis*.
40 Ibid., 69.
41 As *Fear and Trembling* famously shows, Abraham "suspends" the ethical because his willingness to sacrifice his son cannot be justified in the perspective of moral ideas (52). In faith, an "incommensurable" attitude is reached (47), an interiority that cannot be expressed in the outer sphere of generalizable duties and ideas (60).

Chapter 3

1 The term "the good" is of course inherited from the ancient Greek tradition, which used the nominal version of "good," *to agathon*, in a natural and pre-philosophical way. We also believe that it is the most natural candidate for a fundamental notion in morality. Whoever would prefer a different term would have to shoulder a quite heavy burden of proof to show that it is better suited, it seems.

2   Christine Korsgaard, *The Sources of Normativity* (Cambridge: Cambridge University Press, 1996), 35 and 37.
3   To give an example, one can find moral realists say: "Making the decision is up to you. But which decision is the one it makes most sense for you to make is not. This is something you are trying to discover, not create. Or so, at least, it feels like when deliberating" (David Enoch, *Taking Morality Seriously. A Defense of Robust Realism* (Oxford: Oxford University Press, 2011), 73). While such arguments are plausible, they do not force us to commit to realism. Truth in morality can be explained without reference to a particular sphere of reality, or to such things as "moral facts" (Russ Shafer-Landau, *Moral Realism. A Defense* (Oxford: Clarendon, 2003), 15). The arguments that are presented by moral realists are often unjustifiably dichotomic insofar as they suggest that there are no other options besides either realism or the arbitrariness of moral positions. To us, realism appears as an exaggeration and over-determination of certain conditions that are inherent to all moral reasoning. Realism is not so much wrong as it is superfluous, adding a layer of explanation to the phenomenon of moral reasoning that is not needed to make it work. It seems that we can trust the reality of moral ideas in our practices without needing the theoretical crutches of realism to think of these ideas as effective. From another perspective, moral realism well appears to be under-determined. We see this when we ask for particular moral truths. The examples that are provided are often quite trivial. One can find, among others: "Aren't we ... justified in believing that, absent special circumstances, one's enjoyment doesn't make it right to hurt others?" (ibid., 249). Or: "I believe that there are irreducibly normative truths and facts, facts such that we should ... not humiliate other people" (Enoch, *Taking Morality Seriously*, 1). No one would deny these examples, but that is precisely what is problematic about them. In which sense are the examples "irreducible truths" and not just expressions of common sense? First, one can easily think of instances that would prove the examples wrong, for example, the case of a corrupt politician who would be publically humiliated by being brought to court. Second, the examples are, in the Kantian sense of the term, analytic. Speakers of the English language have to think of humiliation as a hurtful act and have to associate it with being rather wrong than right. They simply cannot talk differently.
4   See the second step of Chapter 5.
5   See the tenth, eleventh, and twelfth steps of Chapter 4.
6   Ross, *The Right and the Good*, 66–7.
7   G. E. Moore, *Principia Ethica* (London: Cambridge University Press, 1903), 142.
8   Moore seems to have adopted Ross' view in later works. See his "Is Goodness a Quality?" in *Philosophical Papers* (New York: Collier, 1962), 89–90.
9   Richard Kraut, *Against Absolute Goodness* (New York: Oxford University Press, 2011), 7.
10 Ibid., 33. See also Richard Kraut, *What Is Good and Why. The Ethics of Well-Being* (Cambridge, MA: Harvard University Press 2007), 71.
11 Kraut, *Against Absolute Goodness*, 76.
12 Ibid., 167, see also 93.
13 See ibid., 9. For the co-extension of good and beauty in our conception, see Chapter 4.
14 Moore, *Principia Ethica*, 183.
15 Ibid., 215.
16 Ibid., 45 and 77.

17. See ibid., 99 and 101.
18. See ibid., 26 and 187.
19. Ibid., 188, see also 187.
20. Ibid., 197.
21. Ibid., 188.
22. Ibid.
23. The fact that absolute goodness and being-good-for-someone are not mutually exclusive is also emphasized by Katja Maria Vogt, *Desiring the Good. Ancient Proposals and Contemporary Theory* (New York: Oxford University Press, 2017), 51.
24. See for example *Republic* 506 d–e.
25. The following is based on Aristotle, *Nicomachean Ethics* 1096 a 11–1097 a 14. For a similar argument, see *Protagoras* 334 b.
26. For a modern defense of Aristotle's argument, see Charles Taylor, *Sources of the Self. The Making of the Modern Identity* (Cambridge: Harvard University Press, 1989), 76–7. It needs, so Taylor, a "historical enterprise" (103) to explore "the goods to which we cannot but hold allegiance in their full range" (107). The theory of the good has to be spelled out as an account of the plurality of goods that are identifiable in human life. Following Aristotle, ethics can describe the "regularities" in human practice but they are just that, "general patterns," which allow for variations (see Vogt, *Desiring the Good*, 189; see also 194).
27. Such an argument is presented forcefully by Thomson, *Normativity*, 37 et passim, who denies that there is a single and general property of goodness.
28. Numbers can be counted, too, for example the amount of numbers written on a page. In this case, numbers are taken in a twofold sense, as objects and as units of measure.
29. See the third step of Chapter 4.
30. *Republic* 509 b.
31. See Jan A. Aertsen, *Medieval Philosophy and the Transcendentals. The Case of Thomas Aquinas* (Leiden et al.: Brill 1996), 25–40.
32. The difference between formal and classificatory, or generalizing, notions was emphasized by Edmund Husserl, *Ideas. General Introduction to Pure Phenomenology*, transl. W. R. Boyce Gibson (London/New York: Routledge, 2013), 72–4. The relevance of the distinction for the analysis of human practice and experience is shown in Martin Heidegger, *Towards the Definition of Philosophy. Freiburg Lecture-Courses 1919*, transl. Ted Sadler (London/New York: Continuum, 2008), 86–9.
33. Korsgaard, *Self-Constitution*, 47.
34. Ibid., 49.
35. Ibid., 48.
36. See ibid., 49.
37. See ibid., 57.
38. Kraut, *What Is Good and Why*, 131, see also 38.
39. Ibid., 132.
40. Ibid., 202.
41. Ibid., 131.
42. Ibid., 203.
43. See ibid., 66.
44. See ibid., 210.
45. Ibid., 272.
46. See for this argument Vogt, *Desiring the Good*, 43.
47. Kevin Kinghorn, *A Framework for the Good* (Notre Dame: University of Notre Dame Press, 2016), 15.

48 Ibid., 59.
49 See ibid., 74.
50 Ibid., 58. Kinghorn also distinguishes between formal and substantive aspects of his approach. The formal aspects deal with conceptual structures, whereas the substantive aspects show concrete ways in which the good is realized (ibid., 57–8 and 167). However, insofar as pleasure is identified as good, the overall character of his theory is substantive. The formal analysis is conducted *within* the given substantive assumptions and does not concern the status of the basic concepts themselves.
51 Ibid., 32.
52 Ibid.
53 See ibid., 36.
54 Ibid., 34.
55 As a matter of fact, Kinghorn states that "for any competent user of the term *good*, her concept of goodness will be derivative of her understanding of flourishing" (ibid., 42). If "good" has meaning only insofar as it interprets, or expresses, the content of "flourishing," then it cannot provide the foundation of the theory that is presented. This is even more so as "flourishing" has more aspects of meaning than can be expressed through "good," as he concedes (see ibid., 43). The good of flourishing, it seems, could be explored on its own account, without much concern for the slim value that can be derived from the (merely hedonistic) notion of the good.
56 Peter T. Geach, "Good and Evil," *Analysis* 17 (1956), 33.
57 Ibid.
58 Ibid.
59 Ibid., 34.
60 This is also emphasized by Kraut, *Against Absolute Goodness*, 179.
61 Charles R. Pidgen, "Geach on 'Good,'" *The Philosophical Quarterly* 40 (1990), 141.
62 C. ibid., 139.
63 Philippa Foot, *Moral Dilemmas: And Other Topics in Moral Philosophy* (Oxford: Clarendon, 2002), 167.
64 Friedrich Nietzsche, *On the Genealogy of Morals*, in *On the Genealogy of Morals and Ecce Homo*, transl. Walter Kaufmann and R. J. Hollingdale (New York: Vintage, 1967), 25–6 (First Essay, section 2).

Chapter 4

1 For the origin of this formula, see Robert B. Brandom, *Articulating Reasons. An Introduction to Inferentialism* (Cambridge, MA: Harvard University Press, 2000), 189–96.
2 For an overview of the recent discussion, see Francesco Orsi, "The Guise of the Good," *Philosophy Compass* 10 (2015), 714–24.
3 Thomas Aquinas, *Summa Theologica* I-II, 1.6 ("quidquid homo appetit, appetit sub ratione boni. Quod quidem si non appetitur ut bonum perfectum, quod est ultimus finis, necesse est ut appetatur ut tendens in bonum perfectum, quia semper inchoatio alicuius ordinatur ad consummationem ipsius").
4 For a general defense of this claim, see Joseph Raz, "On the Guise of the Good," in *Desire, Practical Reason, and the Good*, ed. Sergio Tenenbaum (New York: Oxford University Press, 2010), 112–36.

5   Vogt, *Desiring the Good*, 118.
6   See ibid., 133; see also 117 for her criticism of the analytic philosophy of action which often follows an exclusive preference for single, "small-scale" actions.
7   See David Velleman, "The Guise of the Good," *Noûs* 26/1 (1992), 9–10 and 20.
8   See Kieran Setiya, "Sympathy for the Devil," in *Desire, Practical Reason, and the Good*, ed. Tenenbaum, 91.
9   See Velleman, "Guise of the Good," 18–19; Setiya, "Sympathy for the Devil," 99–100.
10 Velleman, "Guise of the Good," 17. It also seems that such a conception of desire would risk reducing it to a natural impulse. For the idea that the guise of the good warrants a non-naturalistic approach, see Francesco Orsi, "Ethical Non-naturalism and the Guise of the Good," *Topoi* 37 (2018), 581–90.
11 Setiya, "Sympathy for the Devil," 90.
12 See Sergio Tenenbaum, *Appearances of the Good. An Essay on the Nature of Practical Reason* (Cambridge: Cambridge University Press, 2007), 2 and 24.
13 Ibid., 28.
14 See ibid., 38.
15 *Protagoras* 358 c–d. See also *Meno* 77 b–c.
16 *Protagoras* 358 c.
17 This argument paraphrases *Protagoras* 352 b.
18 See *Nicomachean Ethics* 1147 b 15f., with 1145 b 25–30. For a similar interpretation, see Pierre Destrée, "Aristotle on the Causes of *akrasia*," in Akrasia *in Greek Philosophy. From Socrates to Plotinus*, ed. Christopher Bobonich and Pierre Destrée (Leiden/Boston: Brill, 2007), 139–65.
19 *Nicomachean Ethics* 1147 a 1–10.
20 *Nicomachean Ethics* 1147 a 28–1147 b 3.
21 Donald Davidson, "How Is Weakness of the Will Possible?" in *Essays on Actions and Events* (Oxford: Clarendon, 1980), 23, 28, 32.
22 The existence of incontinence has also been denied by Gary Watson, "Skepticism about Weakness of Will," *The Philosophical Review* 86/3 (1977), 316–39.
23 Davidson pays attention to this although we do not agree with his conclusion. He argues that "incontinence is not essentially a problem in moral philosophy, but a problem in the philosophy of action." It is necessary, for him, to "divorce [it] entirely from the moralist's concern" ("Weakness of the Will," 30). For a more recent example of this argument, see Joseph Heath, "Practical Irrationality and the Structure of Decision Theory," in *Weakness of Will and Practical Irrationality*, ed. Sarah Stroud and Christine Tappolet (New York: Oxford University Press, 2003), 251–73. One of the few illuminating, and also deeply understanding, approaches to the problem can be found in Amélie Oksenberg Rorty, "The Social and Political Sources of *akrasia*," *Ethics* 107/4 (1997), 644–57.
24 Davidson, "Weakness of the Will," 11 and 48.
25 Ibid., 13f.
26 For an overview of the various criticisms of Davidson's position, see Daniel Hutto, "A Cause for Concern. Reasons, Causes and Explanations," *Philosophy and Phenomenological Research* 59/2 (1999), 381–401. At times, the objection is raised that reasons are "normative" and can therefore have no causal force. This, however, confuses the content of reasons with the fact of having them. A reason, even if normative, is a cause insofar as *I take it* as reason to act. A similar confusion lies in the suggestion that the explanation from reasons would be teleological not causal (see Scott Sehon, "An Argument against the Causal Theory of Action Explanation,"

Philosophy and Phenomenological Research 60/1 (2000), 67–85). There is nothing wrong in assuming that a goal or purpose causes an action insofar as agents commit to pursuing it. Teleology was traditionally taken as a form of causality and so confirms the claim that reasons are causes.

27 *Timaeus* 28 a.
28 *Phaedo* 98 c–99 a. According to Vlastos, Plato interprets the causality of forms, which are the content of reasons, as logical, not physical necessity. See Gregory Vlastos, "Reasons and Causes in the *Phaedo*," *The Philosophical Review* 78/3 (1969), 320.
29 This is also emphasized by Immanuel Kant, *Religion within the Boundaries of Mere Reason*, in *Religion within the Boundaries of Mere Reason and Other Writings*, transl. Alan Wood and George di Giovanni (Cambridge: Cambridge University Press, 1998), 47, footnote (AA VI, 22).
30 T. M. Scanlon, *Being Realistic about Reasons* (Oxford: Oxford University Press, 2014), 44. "Reasons fundamentalism" also means for him that questions regarding reasons are normative and cannot be settled by way of a psychological explanation (see 10 and 89). For Scanlon too, one does not have to look for "some further element that does the motivating" (56) because it would be a regress to ask for the motivation to have a reason.
31 Davidson, *Essays on Actions and Events*, 4, 39, 49, 59, 98f.
32 Ibid., 41f.
33 See Rosalind Hursthouse, "Arational Actions," *Journal of Philosophy* 88 (1991), 57–68, for an attempt at delineating actions that cannot be analyzed as being caused by reasons: "Anyone who confidently holds the view that ... ascriptions of reasons or 'intention with which' must apply in such cases [of actions following a specific desire and belief—M.S.] is committed to seeing a great disanalogy between them and cases such as feeling frightened of burglars, ghosts, or thunder and burrowing under the bed clothes (to safety?), feeling angry and kicking furniture (to hurt it?), and muttering imprecations under one's breath (for whose ears?), or to making them analogous by ascribing quite lunatic beliefs to the agent" (64). Actions that follow from unconscious or subconscious desires can also be counted among these cases. See Kieran Setiya, "Explaining Action," *The Philosophical Review* 112/3 (2003), 351.
34 *Phaedo* 99 a.
35 We do not claim here that all uses of the notion of the good are comparative, in a sense that "good" would always mean, or at least imply, "better than x." Such an idea is clearly false (for a criticism of the comparative meaning of the good, see Michael David Rohr, "Is Goodness Comparative?" *Journal of Philosophy* 75 (1978), 494–503). We only assume that the good *achieves* a comparative meaning if it is used in the practice of giving and asking for reasons, in which there always has to be a variety of options for an agent. In order to be comparable to other options, a thing first has to be good in itself, otherwise one could only say that it is less bad than other things, which is not how the notion of the good is used.
36 *Republic* 505 a (translation Bloom, 185).
37 *Republic* 519 c. See also *Crito* 44 d.
38 *Symposium* 205 e–206 a.
39 *Symposium* 205 a. See also the idea of the *proton philon* in the *Lysis* according to which there has to be a point of origin (*arche*) which is loved for itself and because of which all other things are loved (219 c).
40 *First Alcibiades* 115 d.
41 *Crito* 46 b.

42 Leibniz makes the same argument with respect to God's choice of the best possible world: if there were not one world that is best, God would not have created any world (Gottfried Wilhelm Leibniz, *Essays of Theodicy on the Goodness of God, the Freedom of Man, and the Origin of Evil*, Part I, 8). A recent version of the argument can be found in Habermas's ethics of discourse: "We can never be certain that the statements we take to be true or correct at this stage of discussion belong among the statements that will withstand all future criticism. But this fallibilism built into the theory of discourse is merely the converse side of the postulate that every sufficiently precise question admits of just one valid answer" (Jürgen Habermas, *Justification and Application. Remarks on Discourse Ethics*, transl. Ciaran Cronin (Cambridge, MA/London: MIT Press, 1993), 165). Moral questions, for Habermas, are such that they can be decided.

43 See Chapter 3.

44 Rawls's theory of the good, which will be further discussed in the following fifth step, is based on a similar combination of agent-centric and action-centric points of view. We have already mentioned his idea of a rational plan (see Chapter 2, footnote 13). The plan has to be rationally chosen (agent-centric) and has to have all properties that make it eligible for rational choice (action-centric): "A person's interests and aims are rational if, and only if, they are to be encouraged and provided for by the plan that is rational for him. ... These principles [of rational choice, M.S.] do not single out one plan as the best. We have instead a maximal class of plans: each member of this class is superior to all plans not included in it, but given any two plans in the class, neither is superior or inferior to the other. Thus to identify a person's rational plan, I suppose that it is that plan belonging to the maximal class which he would choose with full deliberative rationality" (*Theory of Justice*, 359). The quote nicely lays out the mutual dependence of agent-centric and action-centric points of view: for the agent, it is important that there is a "maximal class," whereas from the perspective of the action, the best plan is ever only the one that is chosen in an act of self-determination. For the need to give a reason beyond one's personal desire, see also Taylor, "What Is Human Agency?" 23. Moral concepts make a "qualitative characterization of desires as higher and lower, noble and base, and so on" possible. It introduces a "vocabulary of worth" into the agent's assessment of actions (24).

45 See Chapter 3.

46 Scott MacDonald, "Goodness as Transcendental: The Early Thirteenth-Century Recovery of an Aristotelian Idea," *Topoi* 11 (1992), 173–86.

47 See Kraut on this point: "One needs more than a general conception of what is good; one must also know something about who the potential beneficiaries of one's actions are, and about how one is situated in relation to them. ... In addition to one's general knowledge about the sorts of things that are good, one also needs to know which particular actions will bring it about that something good is done" (Kraut, *What Is Good*, 213).

48 See Chapter 3.

49 See Robert B. Brandom, *Making It Explicit. Reasoning, Representing, and Discursive Commitment* (Cambridge, MA: Harvard University Press, 1994).

50 Ibid., 76.

51 Ibid., 98. For the historical background of the idea of expression, see 94–111, and Brandom, *Articulating Reasons*, 8, 31–4. But the idea can also be traced back to the medieval discussion of transcendentals, namely to the question what further determinations, or *rationes*, transcendental notions entail. For the *rationes* of the good, see Jan A. Aertsen, *Medieval Philosophy as Transcendental Thought. From Philip the Chancellor (ca. 1225) to Francisco Suárez* (Leiden/Boston: Brill, 2012), 697–701.

52 *Republic* 353 a.
53 *Republic* 601 d.
54 See *First Alcibiades* 125 a. For the link between capabilities and the good, see also *Hippias Major* 367 c.
55 Foot, *Moral Dilemmas*, 173. For the attributive understanding of "good," see 162. See also our discussion in Chapter 3.
56 Ibid.
57 Ibid., 166.
58 Philippa Foot, *Natural Goodness* (Oxford: Clarendon, 2001), 27.
59 Ibid., 33.
60 Ibid., 44.
61 Ibid., 48.
62 Ibid., 59.
63 Ibid., 49.
64 Ibid., 63.
65 See ibid., 67. For the descriptive foundation of our uses of "good," see also Thomson, *Normativity*, 36.
66 Foot, *Natural Goodness*, 76.
67 Ibid., 80.
68 See ibid., 79.
69 Foot, *Moral Dilemmas*, 172.
70 This point has been made by David Enoch, "Agency, Shmagency: Why Normativity Won't Come from What Is Constitutive of Action," *Philosophical Review* 115 (2006), 169–98.
71 Foot, *Natural Goodness*, 63.
72 See *Protagoras* 354 b.
73 *Phaedo* 99 a–b.
74 See also Chapter 5 for the question of the reality of the conceptual.
75 *Republic* 353 a.
76 *Republic* 353 b.
77 *Republic* 444 d–e.
78 See also *Gorgias* 506 d.
79 *Nicomachean Ethics* 1103 a 24–6.
80 *Nicomachean Ethics* 1105 b 5–9.
81 *Nicomachean Ethics* 1119 b 27–8; 1122 a 21–3. As a general condition, we should "keep in mind that intrinsic goodness may not be an intrinsic property, and that what is intrinsically good may turn out not to be so in virtue of its intrinsic properties." (Mark Schroeder, "Value Theory," *The Stanford Encyclopedia of Philosophy* (Fall 2021 Edition), ed. Edward N. Zalta.)
82 See *Crito* 48 b and *Philebus* 55 b.
83 *Gorgias* 506 d. See also *Meno* 87 d.
84 *Republic* 427 e. See also *Meno* 79 b–c on the parts of virtue.
85 This, by the way, also solves a Sophistic *aporia* that is left unresolved in the *Hippias Major* (see 373 d–376 c): if one has the capability of being good does this mean that one has the capability for both the good and bad? Whoever knows the good also has to know the opposite of it, it seems. Does this not mean that we have to qualify someone as good precisely because they are also capable of the bad? So that someone who is good would be good and bad at the same time? The answer to this question is that "good" implies the consistent presence of virtue, not the realization of some abstract capability.

86   *Republic* 423 c–d, 442 c.
87   *Republic* 428d, 442 b–c.
88   *Republic* 429 c, 440 b.
89   *Republic* 431 e–432 a.
90   *Republic* 433 b (translation Bloom, 111).
91   *Republic* 443 d (translation Bloom, 123).
92   *Republic* 442 c.
93   See the image of the soul's "inner human" in *Republic* 589 a–d. See also 577 c on tyranny.
94   See *Republic* 444 d.
95   *Republic* 443 d.
96   Plato's ideal of a whole in which all parts are working actively together to support one goal sets too high a bar for ordinary human practice. We rather assume that in many cases one has to be content if purposes that could potentially infringe on others are reduced in their influence and become cooperative by not interfering. Particular activities should be able to explore their freedom just up to the point at which consistency would be impossible to maintain. For a beautiful way to illustrate this point, see Eagleton's remarks: "Take, as an image of the good life, a jazz group. A jazz group which is improvising obviously differs from a symphony orchestra, since to a large extent each member is free to express herself as she likes. But she does so with a receptive sensitivity to the self-expressive performances of the other musicians. The complex harmony they fashion comes not from playing from a collective score, but from the free musical expression of each member acting as the basis for the free expression of the others" (Terry Eagleton, *The Meaning of Life. A Very Short Introduction* (Oxford: Oxford University Press, 2007), 99–100).
97   O'Neill points this out in reference to the consistency that is required by Kant's categorical imperative. See Onora O'Neill, "Consistency in Action," in *Constructions of Reason* (Cambridge: Cambridge University Press, 1989), 96.
98   Habermas, *Justification and Application*, 51–2.
99   Bernard Williams, *Ethics and the Limits of Philosophy* (Cambridge: Harvard University Press, 1985), 177.
100   See Chapter 2.
101   Rawls, *Theory of Justice*, 21.
102   Ibid., 80.
103   Ibid., 78.
104   Ibid., 393.
105   Ibid., 27.
106   Ibid., 350.
107   See ibid., 450.
108   Ibid., 418.
109   Ibid., 453.
110   See ibid., 105–6.
111   Henry Sigdwick, *The Methods of Ethics* (1907), 7th edn (Indianapolis: Hackett, 1981), 105–6.
112   Ibid., 106; see also 34–6.
113   Ibid., 105.
114   Ibid., 106.
115   Ibid., 105–6.
116   See Kant, *Groundwork*, 31 (AA IV, 421).

117 Sidgwick, *Methods of Ethics*, 390.
118 Ibid., 106.
119 Ibid., 390.
120 *Republic* 505 d.
121 *Republic* 536 e.
122 *Republic* 423 e (translation Bloom, 101).
123 *Republic* 413 a. See also 490 c.
124 For the co-extensionality of the beautiful and the good, see *Protagoras* 359 e, *Lysis* 216 d, *First Alcibiades* 116 a. For their co-intensionality, see *Hippias Minor* 294 b.
125 See Chapter 3.
126 *Symposium* 210 b–d, 211 a.
127 *Symposium* 211 e–212 a.
128 *Republic* 402 d.
129 *Symposium* 206 e.
130 *Philebus* 64 e.
131 For a comparable analysis of these passages, see Hans-Georg Gadamer, *Plato's Dialectical Ethics. Phenomenological Interpretations Relating to the* Philebus, transl. Robert. M. Wallace (New Haven/London: Yale University Press, 1991), 208–9.
132 See *Republic* 443 d–e. In Aristotle's words: "We are busy so that we can have leisure, and we go to war so that we can have peace. … No one desires to be at war just for being at war" (*Nicomachean Ethics* 1177 b 5–10).
133 For a similar understanding of beauty, see Hans-Georg Gadamer, *Truth and Method*, 2nd, rev. edn (London/New York: Continuum, 2004), 475–7.
134 *Philebus* 20 d and 22 b.
135 As a summary of the analysis, see *Philebus* 54 e–55 a.
136 *Philebus* 66 c.
137 *Republic* 431 c.
138 *Gorgias* 499 d–e.
139 *Republic* 505 a.
140 *Republic* 379 b.
141 See *Republic* 457 b ("the beneficial is beautiful"); *Protagoras* 358 b ("each beautiful deed is good and beneficial"); *First Alcibiades* 116 c ("good things are advantageous").
142 *Republic* 357 c–358 a. For justice, see also 612 b.
143 Ross, *The Right and the Good*, 74.
144 Ibid., 134.
145 Moore, *Principia Ethica*, 168, see also 187.
146 *Philebus* 51 c.
147 Our claim is not that the moral good would trump all other value judgments. For a discussion of the "overridingness of the morally required," see Owen Flanagan, "Admirable Immorality and Admirable Imperfection," *Journal of Philosophy* 83 (1986), 54. The moral good does not replace or push out practical, conventional, and legal normativity but can be introduced in each case as their ultimate expression and justification. We also do not aim at promoting an ideal of perfection according to which "every action is as morally good as possible" so that one could not engage in practical, conventional, or legal matters without at the same time doing something moral (see the discussion in Susan Wolf, "Moral Saints," *Journal of Philosophy* 79 (1982), 419).

148   It seems wrong, therefore, to distinguish between a class of "pragmatic tasks" which can be addressed solely through instrumental reason and a class of "complex decisions" which involve moral questioning (see Habermas, *Justification and Application*, 3–4). We rather have to assume that all practical matters lend themselves to an increasingly expressive interpretation and that instrumental and moral reasons are always at least potentially intertwined. Their distinction in each case depends precisely on the degree of expressiveness.
149   *Phaedrus* 229 c–e.
150   See, for example, *Apology* 21 c–22 e; *Euthyphro* 15 b; *Laches* 190 e, 191 e.
151   *Republic* 330 d–331 d.
152   As the Supreme Court's judgment states, again with respect to the problem of marriage: "If rights were defined by who exercised them in the past, then received practices could serve as their own continued justification … The right to marry is fundamental as a matter of history and tradition, but rights come not from ancient sources alone" (Supreme Court of the United States, *Obergefell v. Hodges*, No. 14-556, June 26, 2015).
153   Legal rights can be assumed to "represent moral rights" (Ronald Dworkin, *Taking Rights Seriously* (Cambridge, MA: Harvard University Press, 1977), 191).
154   See ibid., 208.
155   For a further discussion of this point, see Chapter 10.
156   *Crito* 49 b.
157   *Crito* 50 b.
158   *Crito* 51 a–b.
159   *Republic* 484 b.
160   *Republic* 501 b.
161   See the seventh step in this chapter.
162   See the ninth step in this chapter.
163   *Gorgias* 507 e.
164   *Republic* 579 b.
165   *Republic* 462 b–d.
166   *Republic* 586 e–587 a.
167   See again O'Neill with respect to consistency in Kant: "To will some end without willing whatever means are indispensable for that end, insofar as they are available, is, even when the end involves no conceptual inconsistency, to involve oneself in a volitional inconsistency. … The business of intending coherently and avoiding volitional inconsistency becomes a demanding and complex affair" ("Consistency in Action," 91–2). Agents cannot rely on the sole intention to be inherently consistent. All conditions of their action have to be consistent too, and not only hypothetically so but in reality. For O'Neill, this means that agents need to focus not only on the necessary but also on the sufficient means in striving for a goal; they need to make the means available through their own effort, not only in general but in all components and details that are involved; they need to make sure that all sub-intentions in a given case are consistent; and they need to consider the foreseeable results or the consequences of their action (ibid.). This list of conditions is not meant to be complete; it only shows how consistency pervades actions *and* their context once it is taken seriously.
168   *Timaeus* 30 c–d.
169   See the last section of Chapter 5.

Chapter 5

1. Moore, *Principia Ethica*, 7–8.
2. See the critical remark by Geach, "Good and Evil," 35: "Nobody has ever given a coherent and understandable account of what it is for an attribute to be non-natural." It is not enough simply to say that the good is *not* like other, natural properties.
3. See Moore, *Principia Ethica*, 7–8. For a similar criticism, see Habermas, *Moral Consciousness*, 53. Moore's emphasis on the naturalistic fallacy (see *Principia Ethica*, 12f.) is also driven by the naturalism of his approach. See, for example, his remark: "Not a single question in Ethics can be answered except by causal generalization" (*Principia Ethica*, 146). If the good is taken instead as a formal concept, the problem of natural fallacy vanishes entirely because then no property of things instantiates the good. Moral concepts *interpret* physical things but are *not derived* from them.
4. See the thirteenth step of Chapter 4. With respect to Kant, O'Neill points out that self-consistency entails the consistency to others: "Whatever cannot be consistently intended even for oneself also cannot be consistently intended for all others" ("Consistency in Action," 94).
5. We can note the closeness to Scanlon's version of contractualism here, despite his emphasis on "right" instead of "good": "According to contractualism, when we address our minds to a question of right or wrong, what we are trying to decide is, first and foremost, whether certain principles are ones that no one, if suitably motivated, could reasonably reject" (T. M. Scanlon, *What We Owe to Each Other* (Cambridge, MA: Belknap, 1998), 189). Contractualism entails the "justifiability" of one's position in the eyes of others (see ibid., 393, note 5). However, the focus on procedural terms such as "rejection" and "justification" brings a certain vagueness into the conception (e.g., it may not always be clear whether an act of rejection is morally relevant). This vagueness can be avoided if one focuses on the target state that all deliberation is supposed to reach, on the consistency of purposes.
6. See also the sixth step of Chapter 4.
7. For Kant, the categorical imperative can also appear in a twofold way: for a being endowed with reason, it is an expression of their will (*Wollen*), whereas for a being affected by sensuousness, it has to appear as an ought (*Sollen*). Humans are both, rational and sensuous, so that the law of morality can appear to them both in a declarative and prescriptive form (*Groundwork*, 54–5; AA IV, 449).
8. Kant, for example, did not think that sacrificing one's life for the sake of a moral action would be a good thing to do (see *Critique of Practical Reason*, transl. Mary Gregor (Cambridge: Cambridge University Press, 1997), 130; AA V, 158).
9. *Republic* 443 d (translation Bloom, 123).
10. We have used this example before in the Introduction.
11. The task that presents itself here is also acknowledged by Murdoch: "How is one to connect the realism which must involve a clear-eyed contemplation of the misery and evil of the world with a sense of an uncorrupted good without the latter idea becoming the merest consolatory dream?" (*Sovereignty of the Good*, 59).
12. See *First Alcibiades* 115 c: *ta megista (agatha) malista*.
13. See *Republic* 402 d: *to kalliston erasmiotaton*.
14. *Crito* 48 b, *Apology* 28 b, *Gorgias* 512 d.
15. We do not touch here on the plurality of worldviews that has been so acutely felt by many thinkers. One could mention Weber who believed that "the ultimately

possible attitudes toward life are irreconcilable" (Max Weber, *Science as Vocation*, in *From Max Weber: Essays in Sociology*, transl. and ed. H. H. Gerth and C. Wright Mills (New York: Oxford University Press, 1949), 77–156, here 152). Berlin famously distinguished "hedgehogs" and "foxes," or monists and pluralists, in a distinction which is in itself testimony to the existence of plurality (see Isaiah Berlin, *The Hedgehog and the Fox. An Essay on Tolstoy's View of History* (Princeton: Princeton University Press, 2013), 3). It seems, however, that the pluralism of overarching worldviews does not need to contradict the unity of the moral good, which can be taken as a basic, limiting condition for the variety of orientations toward the world.

16 *Republic* 409 d–e.
17 *Republic* 582 a–e.
18 *Republic* 445 c.
19 This reading of the passages in the *Republic* presupposes that vice is only a deficiency of the good and not its contradiction. In the case of the latter, the passages could not be used to confirm our argument.
20 See for the following *Philebos* 55 a–c.
21 See the eighth step of Chapter 4.
22 A famous argument presented by Hare suggests otherwise. According to him, it is not permissible "to discriminate morally between actual and possible people" (R. M. Hare, "Possible People," in *Essays on Bioethics* (Oxford: Clarendon Press, 1993), 72). Hare argues in favor of "total utilitarianism," which considers the overall value of utility that is created and not its average (69). Now, if one assumes "that most of us have reason to be thankful for our own existence," and if one looks at a possible person "as if I were going to be that person," then it follows that possible people would also be thankful for being born (73). By promoting the birth of more people the total amount of utility would be increased. This argument is circular, at least in parts (we cannot discuss Hare's version of utilitarianism here). If we say about possible people, for example, that they would need oxygen to breath if they existed, we say nothing that forces us to assume their existence. The argument is purely hypothetical. If, for some reason, there would be no more oxygen in the atmosphere, then no human life could exist. If we say instead that humans would be thankful for their existence, we assume a quality that implies their actual existence. Being thankful means that it is better to exist than not exist. The argument then presupposes what it needed to prove, namely, that possible people should be considered like actual ones. If possible people were just that, *possible*, there could be no discrimination against them. The idea of possible people is also indeterminate and does not allow for specific statements. One could perhaps say that my partner and I discriminate against our third, possible child, assuming that we have two and could consider another one, but do we also discriminate against our fourteenth possible child? Hare mentions this problem himself but says that he would only have "to consider what the consequences of my actions actually would be" (72), which again tacitly counts the possible people that are considered as if they were actual ones.
23 Foot, *Moral Dilemmas*, 42.
24 Rosalind Hursthouse, *On Virtue Ethics* (Oxford: Oxford University Press, 1999), 44.
25 See Foot, *Moral Dilemmas*, 43.
26 John Stuart Mill, *Utilitarianism*, in John Stuart Mill and Jeremy Bentham, *Utilitarianism and Other Essays*, ed. Alan Ryan (London: Penguin, 2004), 297.
27 Notably, Mill's own (see ibid., 298).

28 Hursthouse, *Virtue Ethics*, 45.
29 Foot, *Moral Dilemmas*, 41.
30 Kraut, *What Is Good*, 37.
31 Hursthouse defines an irresolvable dilemma as "a situation in which the agent's choice lies between x and y and nothing would count as the reasonable practical answer to 'Should I do x or y?'" (*Virtue Ethics*, 63). However, if there is no reasonable answer, then the case is undecidable, which means that it is no dilemma. And obviously, a solvable dilemma is no dilemma either.
32 See our discussion in Chapter 11.
33 Hursthouse, *Virtue Ethics*, 70.
34 Some moral philosophers take regret as a sign that moral conflicts and dilemmas exist (see Bernard Williams, *Problems of the Self* (Cambridge: Cambridge University Press, 1973), 175; Jonathan Dancy, *Ethics Without Principles* (Oxford: Clarendon, 2004), 4). Foot, who seems to have sensed the moralizing tendency in this belief (one assumes that some people should really feel guilty about their decisions), has rightfully denied that feelings of regret indicate an objective conflict of obligations (*Moral Dilemmas*, 47).
35 Scanlon, *Being Realistic about Reasons*, 2. See the first step in Chapter 4.
36 Ibid.
37 Ibid., 23.
38 Ibid., 24.
39 Ibid., 70. For the comparison to mathematics, see 85 and 122.
40 It is necessary to distinguish between the psychological and normative properties of the content of mental acts. See Gilbert Harman et al., "Moral Reasoning," in *The Moral Psychology Handbook*, ed. John M. Doris and the Moral Psychology Research Group (New York: Oxford University Press, 2010), 236.
41 Kant, *Groundwork*, 19–20 (AA IV, 407). See the parallel remarks in Immanuel Kant, *Critique of Pure Reason*, transl. Paul Guyer (Cambridge: Cambridge University Press, 1998), 542; A 551/B 579, footnote.
42 Moore, *Principia Ethica*, 185.
43 Ibid., 187.
44 Ibid., 184–5.
45 Murdoch, *Sovereignty of the Good*, 95.
46 Moore, *Principia Ethica*, 187.
47 *Republic* 472 c.
48 *Republic* 473 b.
49 See the thirteenth step of Chapter 4.
50 "There is no reason to pick out only oneself as the person whose good one should aim at. There is no reason to suppose that nothing less than the good of all must be the object of our concern" (Kraut, *What Is Good*, 66). In a more dramatic way, some have argued that we should deeply care about the question whether there will be future generations at all. See Samuel Scheffler, *Death and the Afterlife. The Berkeley Tanner Lectures*, ed. Niko Kolodny (New York: Oxford University Press, 2016), 16–17.
51 Moore, *Principia Ethica*, 183.
52 Gottfried Wilhelm Leibniz, *The Principles of Philosophy, or, the Monadology*, in *Philosophical Essays*, ed. and transl. Roger Ariew and Daniel Garber (Indianapolis/Cambridge: Hackett, 1989), 220 (paragraph 58).

Chapter 6

1. See the first step of Chapter 4.
2. See Chapter 3.
3. Foot, *Natural Goodness*, 76.
4. Thomas Aquinas, *Summa Theologica*. First Part of the Second Part. Question 18, article 9.
5. Ibid., article 1. Kant also denies the possibility of a third, indifferent state between good and evil. See *Religion*, 47–8 (AA VI, 22).
6. Thomas Aquinas, *Summa Theologica*. First Part of the Second Part. Question 18, article 9.
7. Chapter 5.
8. The similarity in structure may appear surprising. But grammatically speaking, in the dialectic of the good the genitive can have both an objective and a subjective meaning, as a dialectic that affects the good as object (and thereby destroys it) and as a dialectic that is produced from within. The former leads to a fragmentarian position, whereas the latter shows the contradictions in the good itself.
9. Georg Wilhelm Friedrich Hegel, *The Science of Logic*, translated and edited by G. de Giovanni (Cambridge: Cambridge University Press, 2010), 745.
10. Ibid., 743.
11. Ibid., 27.
12. Ibid., 33.
13. Ibid.
14. Ibid., 744.
15. Ibid., 33.
16. See Richard Joyce, *The Myth of Morality* (Cambridge: Cambridge University Press, 2001).
17. See the discussion in Richard Joyce and Richard Garner, eds., *The End of Morality. Taking Moral Abolitionism Seriously* (New York: Routledge, 2019), and Joel Marks, *Ethics without Morals. In Defense of Amorality* (New York: Routledge, 2013).
18. See Lisa Tessman, *Moral Failure: On the Impossible Demands of Morality* (New York: Oxford University Press, 2015), and the discussion in Marcel van Ackeren and Michael Kühler, eds., *The Limits of Moral Obligation. Moral Demandingness and Ought Implies Can* (New York: Routledge, 2015).

Chapter 7

1. Mills makes a similar point in his defense of utilitarianism: "There is no ethical creed which does not temper the rigidity of its laws, by giving a certain latitude, under the moral responsibility of the agent … Though the application of the standard may be difficult, it is better than none at all: while in other systems, the moral laws all claiming independent authority, … their claims to precedence one over another rest on little better than sophistry, and … afford a free scope for the action of personal desires and partialities" (*Utilitarianism*, 297–8). Concrete moral problems cannot be sorted out *a priori* without holding arbitrary and dogmatic positions. See also O'Neill's defense of Kant: "What reason can provide is a way of discovering whether we are choosing to act in ways (however culturally specific) that

we do not in principle preclude for others. The 'formal' character of the Categorical Imperative does not entail either that it has no substantive ethical implications or that it can select a unique code of conduct as morally worthy for all times and places" ("Consistency in Action," 104).
2 John McDowell, "Virtue and Reason," *The Monist* 62/3 (1979), 339.
3 Ibid., 336.
4 Ibid., 347.
5 R. Jay Wallace, "Virtue, Reason, and Principle," *Canadian Journal of Philosophy* 21/4 (1991), 480.
6 Ibid., 481.
7 See Chapter 2.
8 *Groundwork*, 7 (AA IV, 393).
9 See ibid., 14–15 (AA IV, 402).
10 *Critique of Practical Reason*, 18 (AA V, 21).
11 See also *Groundwork*, 23 (AA IV, 412).
12 See *Critique of Practical Reason*, 50 (AA V, 34).
13 Ibid., 27 (AA V, 29).
14 Ibid., 41 (AA V, 47); see also 28 (AA V, 31).
15 *Religion*, 93 (AA VI, 77).
16 See *Critique of Practical Reason*, 63 (AA V, 73).
17 Ibid.
18 See ibid.
19 Ibid., 64 (AA V, 75).
20 See *Groundwork*, 37 (AA IV, 428–9).
21 *Anthropology from a Pragmatic Point of View*, transl. Robert B. Louden (Cambridge: Cambridge University Press, 2006), 234 (B 326/A 329).
22 Ibid., 195 (B 270/A 272).
23 Hume, *Enquiry*, 155.
24 Ibid.
25 See ibid., 264.
26 The use of a formal criterion allows Hume to work with an open and unsystematic list of moral qualities. He can say, for example: "No qualities are more entitled to the … approbation of mankind than beneficence and humanity, friendship, and gratitude, natural affection, and public spirit" (ibid., 193).
27 For examples of this conventionalism, see the gender bias in the treatment of chastity and attitudes toward the poor (ibid., 214 and 242).
28 *A Treatise of Human Nature*, in *Moral Philosophy*, ed. Geoffrey Sayre-McCord (Indianapolis: Hackett, 2006), 78.
29 See *Enquiry*, 289.
30 Ibid., 274.
31 Ibid., 265.
32 Ibid., 193.
33 Ibid., 282. In the comparison to a vault we can see a striking similarity to our idea of the good as uncoerced consistency. The stones in the wall support each other in their respective position, different from a wall in which most stones have to carry others and only a few sit freely on top. For Hume's own contrast to a wall, see ibid., 266.
34 Ibid., 267, see also *Treatise*, 183.
35 Mill, *Utilitarianism*, 274f.
36 See ibid., 283.

37 The notion of the good is used throughout the text; see also ibid., 283 and 288–9.
38 Ibid., 283.
39 Ibid., 288.
40 Ibid., 283.
41 Ibid., 300.
42 See ibid., 288f.
43 Ibid., 289.
44 Ibid.
45 See ibid., 286.
46 Ibid., 285.
47 Ibid.
48 From his correspondence, it seems that Mill was aware of this problem, too. See Alan Ryan, "Introduction," in J. S. Mill and Jeremy Bentham, *Utilitarianism and Other Essays*, ed. Alan Ryan (London: Penguin, 1987), 50.
49 Mill, *Utilitarianism*, 289.
50 Ibid., 290.
51 Ibid., 291.
52 Ibid., 289.
53 Ibid., 288.

Chapter 8

1 See Chapter 6.
2 See the remarks on generality in Chapter 7.
3 See also the remarks on generality in Chapter 7.
4 See Ross, *The Right and the Good*, 19–20, see also 28.
5 Ibid., 20.
6 Ibid., 29.
7 Hegel, *Philosophy of Right*, 161 (section 133).
8 Ibid., 163 (section 135, translation modified).
9 Ibid., 139 (section 108).
10 Ibid., 162 (section 135).
11 See Georg Wilhelm Friedrich Hegel, *Phenomenology of Spirit*, transl. A. V. Miller (Oxford: Oxford University Press, 1977), 383.
12 Ross, *The Right and the Good*, 28.
13 Bernard Gert, *Morality: Its Nature and Justification*, rev. edn (Oxford: Oxford University Press, 2005), 121; see also 116.
14 Immanuel Kant, "On a Supposed Right to Lie from Philanthropy," in *Practical Philosophy*, transl. Mary Gregor (Cambridge: Cambridge University Press, 1996), 615.
15 Ibid., 612.
16 It is important to note that Kant does not assume we have a duty not to lie to the murderer at the door, say, because we would do some moral harm toward them. The lie only violates the general duty not to lie. On this point, see Helga Varden, "Kant and Lying to the Murderer at the Door … One More Time: Kant's Legal Philosophy and Lies to Murderers and Nazis," *Journal of Social Philosophy* 41 (2010), 409.

17 From another angle, it is possible to say that the very adoption of a universal principle can ever only occur as particular act, which then raises the question whether the principle is appropriate at all in the given case (see Luhmann, *Moral der Gesellschaft*, 330).
18 Gert, *Morality*, 13.
19 Ibid., 19; see also 115.
20 Ibid., 218.
21 Ibid., 219.
22 Ibid., 164.
23 *Republic* 359 a–b. See also 344 c, for similar ideas expressed by Thrasymachus.
24 Friedrich Nietzsche, *Beyond Good and Evil*, transl. Judith Norman (Cambridge: Cambridge University Press, 2002), 155 (section 260).
25 Nietzsche, *Genealogy*, 35 (Essay I, section 10).
26 For a pluralistic interpretation, see Alexander Nehamas, *Nietzsche. Life as Literature* (Cambridge, MA: Harvard University Press, 1985), 112–13 and 214.
27 See Chapter 5.
28 Nietzsche, *Genealogy*, 161 (Essay III, section 27).
29 Friedrich Nietzsche, *The Gay Science*, transl. Josefine Nauckhoff (Cambridge: Cambridge University Press, 2001), 213 (section 354).
30 Ibid., 35 (section 8).
31 "'Selflessness' has no value in heaven or on earth" (ibid., 202; section 345).
32 See ibid., 173; section 304.
33 Nietzsche, *Beyond Good and Evil*, 118 (section 227).
34 Ibid., 171 (section 284).
35 Emmanuel Lévinas, *Totality and Infinity. An Essay on Exteriority*, transl. Alphonso Lingis (Pittsburgh: Duquesne University Press, 1969), 73.
36 Ibid.
37 Ibid., 199.
38 Ibid., 200.
39 Carol Gilligan, *In a Different Voice. Psychological Theory and Women's Development* (Cambridge, MA: Harvard University Press, 1982), 164–5.
40 Ibid., 103.
41 Ibid., 127.
42 See, for example, Michael Walzer, *Spheres of Justice. A Defense of Pluralism and Equality* (New York: Basic Books, 1983), 4. We also cannot explore here Murdoch's approach which takes up Simone Weil's notion of attention and emphasizes the "just and loving gaze directed upon an individual reality" (*Sovereignty of the Good*, 33). Murdoch's position is also only in part a particularist one.
43 See again the remarks on generality in Chapter 7.
44 Dancy, *Ethics without Principles*, 5.
45 Ibid., 7.
46 See ibid.
47 Ibid., 112.
48 Ibid., 113.
49 See ibid.
50 Ibid., 77.
51 Ibid.
52 Ibid., 82.

53 Hegel, *Philosophy of Right*, 185 (section 141).
54 Ibid., 189 (section 142).
55 Ibid.
56 Ibid. (section 144).
57 Ibid., 192 (section 149).
58 Alisdair MacIntyre, *After Virtue. A Study in Moral Theory* (Notre Dame: University of Notre Dame Press, 1981), 39.
59 See ibid., 117.
60 Ibid., 114.
61 Ibid., 191.
62 Ibid., 194.
63 For example, an approach based on virtues does not necessarily present an alternative to a deontological approach. For this argument, see Roger Crisp, "Does Modern Moral Philosophy Rest on a Mistake?" in *Modern Moral Philosophy*, ed. Anthony O'Hear (Cambridge: Cambridge University Press, 2004), 87.
64 Hursthouse, *Virtue Ethics*, 13.
65 Ibid., 6.
66 Ibid., 35–6.
67 Hegel, *Philosophy of Right*, 193 (section 150).

Chapter 9

1 Hume, *Enquiry*, 189. See also Chapter 7. On Hume as a skeptic regarding practical reasoning, see Millgram, *Ethics Done Right*, 203.
2 Bernard Williams, "Internal and External Reasons," in *Moral Luck* (Cambridge: Cambridge University Press, 1981), 107.
3 See Parfit's argument against Williams and other internalists: "Normativity ... is very different from motivating force. Neither includes, or implies, the other. Other animals can be motivated by their desires and beliefs. Only we can understand and react to reason. ... The fact that we have some desire never, by itself, provides reasons" (Derek Parfit and John Broome, "Reason and Motivation," *Proceedings of the Aristotelian Society. Supplementary Volume* 71 (1997), 127–8).
4 Parfit falls into the opposite extreme when he claims, erroneously, that "reasons for acting ... are all external" (ibid., 130).
5 That is, we cannot prevent statements like the following from being made, dialectical as they may be: "I cannot see any necessary link between the rationality of some action and the psychological phenomenon of feeling impelled to perform some action" (Kinghorn, *Framework for the Good*, 123). If such statements were generally true, there could never be any rational motive to act, which obviously cannot be the case.
6 Hegel, *Philosophy of Right*, 162 (section 135).
7 Other critics have assumed, quite superficially, that Kant's categorical imperative merely requires logical consistency (see MacIntyre, *After Virtue*, 46). These critics also overlook that the logic of the imperative has a material component in the relevance for, and acceptance by all agents endowed with reason. It is not the case that anything goes in the universalization of maxims.
8 See the sixth step of Chapter 4.

9   Kant, *Critique of Practical Reason*, 33 (AA V, 36-7).
10 See Chapter 7.
11 Kant, *Critique of Practical Reason*, 28-9 (AA V, 31).
12 See Crisp on this point: "There is no reason to do what is morally right ... except in so far as there is some ultimate reason that can be stated in non-moral terms. ... The property some action has of furthering the agent's own well-being is a reason for that agent to perform that action" (Roger Crisp, *Reasons and the Good* (Oxford: Clarendon, 2006), 36). Contrary to this quote, the question seems to be how one can decide, both in general terms and in particular cases, that morality does *not* provide the ultimate reason to act. It seems dogmatic to avoid the ambiguity that comes with the dialectical tension outlined above.
13 For the dilemma of free will, see also Hans Vaihinger, *The Philosophy of "As If." A System of the Theoretical, Practical, and Religious Fictions of Mankind*, transl. C. K. Ogden, 2nd edn (London: Routledge and Kegan Paul, 1935), 43.
14 Friedrich Nietzsche, *Twilight of the Idols*, in *Twilight of the Idols* and *The Anti-Christ*, transl. R. J. Hollingdale (London: Penguin, 2003), 43 (The Problem of Socrates, 10).
15 Ibid., 44 (The Problem of Socrates, 11).
16 Ibid., 55 (Morality as Anti-Nature, 4).
17 Nietzsche, *Genealogy*, 76 (Essay II, section 11).
18 Nietzsche makes this point himself; see *Beyond Good and Evil*, 10 (section 9).
19 Jean-Jacques Rousseau, *Discourse on the Origin and Foundations of Inequality among Men*, in *The Discourse and Other Early Political Writings*, transl. Victor Gourevitch (Cambridge: Cambridge University Press, 1997), 138 (Part 1).
20 *Nichomachean Ethics* 1105 b 13-18.
21 *Nichomachean Ethics* 1105 a 17-18.
22 From another angle, Crary uses the term "moralism" to describe the negative impact of "moral judgment-centered theories" on the "rich and variegated sensibilities" of individuals (Alice Crary, *Beyond Moral Judgment* (Cambridge, MA: Harvard University Press, 2007), 233).
23 See Chapter 2, note 9.
24 Hegel, *Philosophy of Right*, 141 (section 114).
25 Ibid., 167 (section 139).
26 See Georg Wilhelm Friedrich Hegel, *Enzyklopädie der philosophischen Wissenschaften im Grundrisse. Gesammelte Werke, vol.* 20 (Hamburg: Meiner, 1992), section 511.
27 In more recent times, the potentially aggressive use of moral ideas has been emphasized by Luhmann: "Whoever moralizes, wants to hurt others" (Luhmann, *Moral der Gesellschaft*, 371; translations M.S.). Moral criteria are by definition exclusionary: "How could one overlook that each strengthening of the good will always induce a strengthening of the bad, a heightening of the difference between the two?" (281). No one asked, according to Luhmann, whether "the distinction between good and bad is in itself good and not rather bad" (360). In the same vein, see also Hans-Georg Moeller, *The Moral Fool. A Case for Amorality* (New York: Columbia University Press, 2009), 186. It seems wrong, however, to see the desire to hurt as essential for the notion of morality. The desire rather constitutes a dialectical development which can but does not have to unfold in the use of moral ideas and which can be limited and revoked by morality's own criteria (because every criticism of morality can eventually be expressed in a self-referential way).
28 See Allan Gibbard, *Reconciling Our Aims: In Search of Bases of Ethics*. Berkeley Tanner Lectures (New York: Oxford University Press, 2008), 23.

29 A.J. Ayer, *Language, Truth, and Logic* (New York: Dover Publications, 1952), 68.
30 Ibid., 64.
31 Ibid., 71.
32 C. L. Stevenson, *Ethics and Language* (New Haven: Yale University Press, 1944), 13.
33 See the first step in Chapter 4.
34 Arthur Schopenhauer, "Prize Essay on the Basis of Morals," in *The Two Fundamental Problems of Ethics*, transl. Christopher Janaway (Cambridge: Cambridge University Press, 2009), 197 (section 15).
35 Ibid., 200 (section 16).
36 Ibid.
37 Ibid.
38 Ibid., 204 (section 17).
39 Ibid., 201 (section 16).
40 See ibid., 218 (section 18).
41 Ibid., 221 (section 19).
42 Ibid., 223 (section 19).
43 See Chapter 7.
44 The difficulties have been described under the title of the Frege-Geach problem which is "at bottom the problem of how it could be that moral and descriptive terms have exactly the same sort of semantic properties in complex sentences, even though they have different kinds of meaning" (Mark Schroeder, "What Is the Frege-Geach Problem?" *Philosophy Compass* 3/4 (2008), 704–5).
45 Schopenhauer, "Basis of Morals," 205 (section 17).
46 See Hegel's remarks on this point: "It is … *silly* to suppose that in the passage from feeling to law and duty there is any loss of import and excellence; it is this passage which lets feeling first reach its truth. It is equally silly to consider intellect as superfluous or even harmful to feeling, heart, and will; the truth and, what is the same thing, the actual rationality of the heart and will can only be at home in the universality of intellect, and not in the singleness of feeling as feeling. If feelings are of the right sort, it is because of their quality or content,—which is right only so far as it is intrinsically universal or has its source in the thinking mind" (Hegel, *Enzyklopädie*, section 471; translation Wallace, open source).
47 Schopenhauer, "Basis of Morals", 201 (section 16, translation modified).
48 Nietzsche, *Beyond Good and Evil*, 18 (section 19).
49 See Chapter 7.
50 See Kant, *Critique of Practical Reason*, 66 (AA V, 77).
51 Ibid., 65 (AA V, 76).
52 Stevenson, *Ethics and Language*, 32.
53 Hegel, *Enzyklopädie*, section 471; translation Wallace, open source.
54 Empathy, for example, can be used both to support a liberal agenda and to justify torture. See Paul Bloom, *Against Empathy. The Case for Rational Compassion* (New York: HarperCollins Eco, 2016), 123.
55 René Descartes, *Discourse on the Method for Conducting One's Reason Well and Seeking the Truth in the Sciences*, in *Philosophical Essays and Correspondence*, ed. Roger Ariew (Indianapolis/Cambridge: Hackett, 2000), 56.
56 Ibid., 56–7.
57 Ibid., 57.
58 Ibid.

59 Stephen Toulmin, *The Place of Reason in Ethics* (Cambridge: Cambridge University Press, 1964).
60 Ibid., 194.
61 Ibid., 189.
62 Ibid., 158.
63 Ibid., 157.
64 It would be tempting at this point to show that many moral theories operate under such dichotomic assumptions. We have already mentioned the distinction between internal and external reasons, which assumes that if reasons are external they cannot be internal in any way. In a similar way, moral realists sometimes claim that if moral ideas do not exist as undeniable facts they are mere social constructs. Such arguments suggest that only two, mutually exclusive alternatives exist, which then forces one to drop one position and accept the other. The fact that many debates in morality almost stupidly revolve around dichotomies is again but a sign of the inevitable dialectics of moral determinations.
65 Eventually, even pragmatism is still too much of a theory for some: "Our commonsense experience of the world doesn't need to be underwritten by philosophy, even by pragmatist philosophy, which can no more shore up the world of common sense than analytic philosophy can break it down" (Stanley Fish, *The Trouble with Principle* (Cambridge, MA: Harvard University Press, 1999), 295).
66 Toulmin, *Place of Reason*, 146.
67 See ibid., 161 and 178.

Chapter 10

1   See the remarks on absoluteness in Chapter 7.
2   Kant, *Critique of Practical Reason*, 100 (AA V, 119).
3   See also Kant, *Groundwork*, 14 (AA IV, 401).
4   *Critique of Practical Reason*, 104 (AA V, 124).
5   Ibid., 105 (AA V, 125).
6   Cf. *Nicomachean Ethics* I, 1100 a 10–11.
7   *Nicomachean Ethics* I, 1099 b 5–7.
8   *Nicomachean Ethics* I, 1100 b 31–3.
9   With respect to Aristotle, this is also the nuanced conclusion in Nussbaum's seminal analysis: "Stable goodness of character ... makes the good life tolerably stable in the face of the world. But this stability is not limitless" (Martha C. Nussbaum, *The Fragility of Goodness. Luck and Ethics in Greek Tragedy and Philosophy* (Cambridge: Cambridge University Press, 1986), 334).
10 Kant, *Groundwork*, 38 (AA IV, 429).
11 See Chapter 7.
12 Ibid., 37 (AA IV, 428).
13 Ibid., 42 (AA IV, 434–5).
14 Avishai Margalit, "Human Dignity between Kitsch and Deification," in *Philosophy, Ethics, and a Common Humanity. Essays in Honor of Raimond Gaita*, ed. Christoph Cordner (London/New York: Routledge, 2011), 115.
15 Ibid., 116.

16 See the remarks on generality in Chapter 7.
17 Kant, *Groundwork*, 39 (AA IV, 430).
18 United Nations, *Universal Declaration of Human Rights*, 1948, online: https://www.un.org/en/universal-declaration-human-rights/. See our remarks on perennial ought in Chapter 8.
19 Hannah Arendt, *The Origins of Totalitarianism*, 2nd enlarged edn (Cleveland: Meridian, 1958), 296–7.
20 Ibid., 296.
21 Ibid., 301.
22 Office of the High Commissioner for Human Rights (UN Human Rights), *Convention relating to the Status of Refugees*, 1951, online: https://www.ohchr.org/en/professionalinterest/pages/statusofrefugees.aspx
23 Michael Ignatieff, *Human Rights as Politics and Idolatry*, ed. Amy Gutman (Princeton: Princeton University Press, 2001), 22.
24 See ibid., 19.
25 In a similar vein, the focus on inherent goodness has been criticized as "unilluminating" because it does not include the particular ways in which things are good (Kraut, *What Is Good*, 202).
26 See our remarks on negativity in Chapter 8.
27 Margalit, "Human dignity," 111.
28 See ibid., 113.
29 One can think here of Hitchens's remarks on the mistreatment of the sick and poor by Mother Teresa. He suspects that the point for her "is not the honest relief of suffering but the promulgation of a cult based on death and suffering and subjection" (Christopher Hitchens, *The Missionary Position. Mother Teresa in Theory and Practice* (Toronto: McClellan and Stewart, 2012), 43–4). For a quite different idea of the purity of Mother Teresa's love, see Gaita, *Good and Evil*, 202. The same point is made by Hegel who assumes that morality needs the world to be bad in order to justify its existence: morality "has to be projected into a future infinitely remote; for if it actually came about, this would do away with the moral consciousness" (*Phenomenology*, 368).
30 *Nicomachean Ethics* X, 1177 a 28.
31 *Nicomachean Ethics* X, 1177 b 25–6.
32 *Nicomachean Ethics* X, 1177 a 28–35.
33 *Nicomachean Ethics* X, 1177 b 4–18.
34 See our remarks on exceptions in Chapter 8.
35 Kant, "Supposed Right to Lie," 613.
36 Friedrich Nietzsche, *The Anti-Christ*, 145 (section 23), in *Twilight of the Idols* and *The Anti-Christ*, trans. R. J. Hollingdale (London: Penguin, 2003).
37 Nietzsche, *Genealogy*, 33–4 (Essay I, section 7).
38 See ibid., 45 (Essay I, section 13); and *Anti-Christ*, 137 (section 15).
39 See *Genealogy*, 40 (Essay I, section 11).
40 Arnold Gehlen, *Moral und Hypermoral. Eine pluralistische Ethik* (Frankfurt a.M./Bonn: Bouvier, 1970), 41 (translations M.S.).
41 Ibid., see also 66, 68, 70, 150.
42 Ibid., 150.
43 Ibid., 172.
44 Following Nietzsche's criticism of pity, Taylor lays out the dialectic that can affect the "ethic of benevolence": "If morality can only be powered negatively, where there can be no such thing as beneficence powered by an affirmation of the recipient as a being

of value, then pity is destructive to the giver and degrading to the receiver" (Taylor, *Sources of the Self*, 516).
45 *Utilitarianism*, 288. Passage quoted before, see Chapter 7, note 53.
46 Kant, *Groundwork*, 28-9 (AA IV, 418). A similar argument is made by Rawls, *Theory of Justice*, 489. See also Nietzsche's polemical argument in *Twilight of the Idols*, 33 (Maxims and Arrows 12). One can also ask whether it is even possible to make anyone happier: if changes in happiness are only measurable in contrast and tend to level out over time, then no one can be made substantially happier than they are. See for this argument Millgram, *Ethics Done Right*, 39. It is unclear, however, whether this conclusion holds: it is likely that in any given case, there is someone who can be made somewhat happier or whose suffering can be reduced. The real problem seems to be that it remains arbitrary, or at least undetermined, to decide who that is and what should be done for them.
47 See the section on abstract rights in this chapter.
48 For this criticism, see Judith Jarvis Thomson, *Goodness and Advice*, ed. Amy Gutman (Princeton: Princeton University Press, 2008), 17 and Thomson, *Normativity*, 63-4.
49 Bernard Williams, "A Critique of Utilitarianism," in J. J. C. Smart and Bernard Williams, *Utilitarianism: For and against* (Cambridge: Cambridge University Press, 1973), 131.
50 Williams, "Moral Luck," 20.
51 See ibid., 29.
52 Thomas Nagel makes this distinction more explicit in his essay on moral luck, but it is present in Williams' text as well. See Thomas Nagel, "Moral Luck," in *Mortal Questions* (Cambridge: Cambridge University Press, 1979), 26.
53 See Williams, "Moral Luck," 29.
54 Ibid., 24.
55 Ibid., 26.
56 Nagel, "Moral Luck," 28 (footnote). See also Gaita's critical comment on Williams' analysis: "It does not follow that if we are glad of an outcome than we are glad about what was necessary to achieve it" (Gaita, *Good and Evil*, 241).
57 Williams, "Moral Luck," 37.
58 Nagel, "Moral Luck," 25.
59 See ibid., 26.
60 Ludwig Wittgenstein, *On Certainty*, ed. G. E. M. Anscombe and G. H. von Wright (New York et al.: Harper Torchbook, 1972), 24e (section 164).
61 This argument has been made prominently by Amartya Sen. See his *Development as Freedom* (New York: Anchor Books, 1999), 291.
62 *Utilitarianism*, 282f.
63 Ibid., 283.
64 See ibid., 287.
65 Ibid., 287-8.
66 See for example Smart, "Outline," 63.
67 See Williams, "Critique of Utilitarianism," 92.
68 Sidgwick, *Methods of Ethics*, 382.
69 Williams, "Critique of Utilitarianism," 93.
70 John M. Taurek, "Should the Numbers Count?" *Philosophy & Public Affairs* 6 (1977), 306.
71 See ibid., 301.
72 Ibid., 307. The same point is made by C. S. Lewis, *The Problem of Pain*. New York: MacMillan, 1973, 103-4.

73 Derek Parfit, "Innumerate Ethics," *Philosophy & Public Affairs* 7 (1978), 299.
74 Ibid., 301.
75 Williams, "Critique of Utilitarianism," 96.
76 See also ibid., 103–4 and 116.
77 See ibid.
78 Peter Singer, "Famine, Affluence, and Morality," *Philosophy and Public Affairs* 1 (1972), 231–2.
79 See ibid., 234.
80 See Peter Singer, *The Life You Can Save. Acting Now to End World Poverty* (New York: Random House, 2009), 152. A similar argument has been presented by Kagan. Although it sounds "extremist," agents are habitually failing the "demands of morality" and avoid promoting the good as it would be "morally required," for example, by going to the movies instead of donating their money to charity (Shelly Kagan, *The Limits of Morality* (Oxford: Oxford University Press, 1989), 2). What he calls "ordinary morality" is used to defend one's limited efforts toward a greater good, but the arguments that this type of morality employs all prove to be untenable (386). Kagan's approach is less practical than Singer's; the main point is for him to say: "What we must not do—is to deny our failure" (403).
81 See the section "Attempt at a Reconciliation" in Chapter 8.
82 Hegel, *Philosophy of Right*, 276 (section 258).
83 See ibid., section 272.
84 Ibid., 282 (section 260).
85 See Jürgen Habermas, *Contributions to a Discourse Theory of Law and Democracy*, transl. William Rehg (Cambridge, MA: MIT Press, 1996), 106.
86 Ibid., 567.
87 Hans Kelsen, *General Theory of Law and the State*, transl. Anders Wedberg (Cambridge, MA: Harvard University Press, 1949), 398.
88 Ibid., 440. See also the parallel remarks on justice and peace, ibid., 441.
89 Ibid., 413.
90 Ibid., 415.
91 H. L. A. Hart, "Positivism and the Separation of Law and Morals," *Harvard Law Review* 71 (1958), 620.
92 Ibid., 615.
93 Kelsen, *General Theory*, 411.
94 See our parallel remarks in the twelfth step of Chapter 4.
95 This can be said against Kelsen who assumes that whereas the law remains dynamic, natural law would be static (see ibid., 400). However, morality, as it is based on self-determination, is dynamic too, both in itself and in its relation to societal and legal rules. For an approach that assumes a shared dynamic of law and morality by integrating the former into the latter, see Ronald Dworkin, *Justice for Hedgehogs* (Cambridge, MA: Belknap Press, 2011), 402.

Chapter 11

1 See Chapter 6.
2 See the opening section of Chapter 8.
3 First Corinthians 4, 10.

4   Our use of the word differs from Moeller's for whom "the moral fool simply does not understand why ethics are necessarily good" (Moeller, *Moral Fool*, 5). Foolishness, in his sense, amounts to moral skepticism.
5   Habermas, *Moral Consciousness*, 63.
6   See ibid., 67.
7   See Habermas, *Justification and Application*, 34; see also *Moral Consciousness*, 61 and 207.
8   See the section "Attempt at a Reconciliation" in Chapter 8. As a reformulation of Kant's approach, discourse ethics can avoid some but not all of Hegel's objections, Habermas admits (see ibid., 210).
9   See *Justification and Application*, 48.
10 Ibid.
11 Ibid., 34.
12 Ibid., 51.
13 Ibid., 49.
14 Ibid., 51.
15 Ibid., 52.
16 See *Moral Consciousness*, 61.
17 Ibid., 93.
18 Ibid., 92–3; see also *Justification and Application*, 32.
19 Ibid., 58.
20 Ibid.
21 Ibid., 58–9. For the difference to Kant, see ibid., 64.
22 *Moral Consciousness*, 65.
23 Ibid., 67–8; see also *Justification and Application*, 49.
24 See ibid., 51.
25 See *Moral Consciousness*, 67.
26 *Justification and Application*, 56.
27 *Moral Consciousness*, 92.
28 *Justification and Application*, 50.
29 See ibid., 31; see also *Moral Consciousness*, 88.
30 *Justification and Application*, 50.
31 Ibid., 51.
32 *Moral Consciousness*, 88; see also *Justification and Application*, 55–6.
33 *Moral Consciousness*, 92.
34 See ibid., 91.
35 Ibid.
36 *Justification and Application*, 58.
37 *Moral Consciousness*, 105.
38 See *Justification and Application*, 53.
39 Ibid., 54.
40 Rather marginal for some time, Vaihinger's philosophy has recently received attention. See Kwame Anthony Appiah, *As If. Idealization and Ideals* (Cambridge, MA: Harvard University Press, 2017).
41 "Preliminary remarks to the introduction," German edition: Hans Vaihinger, *Die Philosophie des Als Ob. System der theoretischen, praktischen und religiösen Fiktionen der Menschheit auf Grund eines idealistischen Positivismus*. 7th and 8th edn (Leipzig: Felix Meiner, 1922), XX (translations M.S).
42 Ibid.

43 Vaihinger, *Philosophy of "As If,"* 5.
44 Ibid., 42–3.
45 Ibid., 16.
46 "Preliminary remarks to the introduction," XVIII.
47 Vaihinger, Philosophy of "As If," 43. See our previous mention of free will in the section on reason as fact in Chapter 9.
48 Ibid.
49 Ibid., 47. Kant would have been able to treat free will completely as a fiction but did not present this idea consistently (ibid., see also 289–90).
50 Ibid., 47.
51 Ibid., 49. This is also the case for the presumed universality of Kant's categorical imperative, see 292.
52 Ibid., 8.
53 Ibid., 12.
54 Ibid., 16.
55 Ibid., 48–9.
56 Ibid., 49.
57 Ibid., 293.
58 A similar conclusion can be drawn with respect to the use of fictions in science. Gravity, as conceived by Newton, is merely a hypothesis and therefore a fiction too—not a made-up one, but a fiction nonetheless (ibid., 41).
59 Marie-Jean-Antoine-Nicolas Caritat, Marquis de Condorcet, *Outlines of an Historical View of the Progress of the Human Mind*, Introduction.
60 Ibid., Tenth Epoch: "Future Progress of Mankind."
61 See ibid.
62 Steven Pinker, *Enlightenment Now. The Case for Reason, Science, Humanism, and Progress* (New York: Viking, 2018), 6.
63 Ibid., 43.
64 See Immanuel Kant, *The Conflict of the Faculties*, transl. Mary Gregor (New York: Abaris Books, 1979), 165 (A 156).
65 See Immanuel Kant, *The Metaphysics of Morals*, transl. Mary Gregor (Cambridge: Cambridge University Press, 1996), 209 (AA VI, 409). See also Sartre's remarks: "We do not believe in the idea of progress. Progress implies improvement, but man is always the same, confronting a situation that is forever changing, while choice remains always a choice in any situation" (Jean-Paul Sartre, *Existentialism Is a Humanism*, transl. Carol Macomber (New Haven/London: Yale University Press, 2007), 47).
66 An exception to the vulgar conception of progress can be found in approaches that see agents themselves as responsible for unlocking the potential of a future development of humanity. Bloch, for example, saw in the phenomenon of hope a utopian dimension of human consciousness: "The point is reached where hope itself, this authentic expectant emotion in the forward dream, no longer just appears as a merely self-based mental feeling, … but in a conscious-known way as utopian function" (Ernst Bloch, *The Principle of Hope. Volume I*, transl. Neville Plaice, Steven Plaice, and Paul Knight (Cambridge, MA: MIT Press, 1986), 144). From Bloch's Marxist point of view, humanity has still not realized all of its emancipatory powers. Real progress is possible, although it has to be brought about through their own actions: "Man is the real possibility of everything which has become of him in his history and, above all, which can still become of him if his progress is not

67 Max Weber, *Politics as Vocation*, in *From Max Weber: Essays in Sociology*, transl. and ed. H. H. Gerth and C. Wright Mills (New York: Oxford University Press, 1949), 77–128.
68 Ibid., 95.
69 See ibid., 112.
70 See ibid., 121.
71 Ibid., 115.
72 Paul Ricoeur, "The Concept of Responsibility: An Essay in Semantic Analysis," in *The Just*, transl. D. Pellauer (Chicago: University of Chicago Press, 2000), 11. For the transformation of responsibility from a legalistic notion to a philosophical one, see Robert Bernasconi, "Before Whom and for What? Accountability and the Invention of Ministerial, Hyperbolic, and Infinite Responsibility," in *Difficulties of Ethical Life*, ed. Shannon Sullivan and Dennis Schmidt (New York: Fordham University Press, 2008), 131–6.
73 See Garrath Williams, "Responsibility as a Virtue," *Ethical Theory and Moral Practice* 11/4 (2008), 457–8.
74 Weber, *Politics as Vocation*, 115.
75 Ibid.
76 Ibid. Although Weber emphasizes the devotion to a cause, which ideally prevents the political leader to be engaged merely for egocentric purposes, his approach is based primarily on the responsibility that the agent, the moral subject, assumes. This sets his theory apart from approaches that understand responsibility as responsiveness to others, as an attitude that puts the concerns of others over one's own (see Robert Gibbs, *Why Ethics? Signs of Responsibilities* (Princeton: Princeton University Press, 2000), 23). We do not explore this aspect of responsibility here. See also the section "The Need for a Particularist Position" in Chapter 8, where we discussed Gilligan's ethics of responsibility and care.
77 Weber, *Politics as Vocation*, 115.
78 Ibid., 116. "Objective" stands here for the focus on a cause.
79 Ibid.
80 Ibid., 119; see also 121. The translation has "violence" for the German *Gewalt*, but "force" seems more adequate. All political action has to be forceful but not all actions resort to actual violence.
81 Ibid., 116.
82 Ibid., 117.
83 Ibid.
84 Ibid., 122.
85 Ibid.
86 Ibid., 117.
87 Ibid., 120.
88 The distinction between the two types of ethics is not merely a cognitive one. There are for Weber various "ultimate *Weltanschauungen*" (ibid., 117) and agents find themselves "placed into various life-spheres, each of which is governed by different laws" (123).
89 Ibid., 120–1.
90 Ibid., 119.

Before the list (top of page):
blocked" (235). For a more recent call to "recognize our shared idealism" and "return to utopian thinking," see Rutger Bregman, *Utopia for Realists. How We Can Build the Ideal World* (New York: Back Bay Books, 2018), 20.

91   See ibid., 120. For a similar argument in favor of lying in politics, see Hannah Arendt, *Between Past and Future. Eight Exercises in Political Thought* (New York: Penguin, 1977), 246. Arendt distinguishes individual lies from the mass deception in totalitarian regimes and dictatorships (252).
92   Weber, *Politics as Vocation*, 124.
93   Ibid., 121.
94   Ibid., 126.
95   See ibid., 119, 121–2, and 125.
96   See ibid., 122.
97   Ibid., 125.
98   Ibid., 128.
99   Ibid., 127.
100   Sartre, *Existentialism Is a Humanism*, 22.
101   Ibid., 29.
102   Ibid.
103   See ibid., 24.
104   See ibid., 38.
105   See ibid., 34.
106   Jean-Paul Sartre, *Being and Nothingness. A Phenomenological Essay on Ontology*, transl. Hazel Barnes (New York et al.: Washington Square Press, 1992), 710.
107   Ibid., 708 and 710.
108   Sartre, *Existentialism Is a Humanism*, 38.
109   Another strategy highlights the comparability of all human existence, "a universal human *condition*" (ibid., 42).
110   Ibid., 24–5.
111   This also means that an individual's decision has an intersubjective dimension, even if it cannot be determined by others: "Everything happens to every man as if the entire human race were staring at him and measuring itself by what he does" (ibid., 26).
112   Ibid., 46.
113   For the former, see ibid., 48; for the latter: "I cannot set my own freedom as a goal without also setting the freedom of others as a goal" (49).
114   See ibid.
115   Ibid., 27.
116   Sartre's conception of responsibility has been called "hyperbolic," which from the perspective of our analysis has a more negative connotation than it has for Bernasconi (see "Before Whom and for What?", 140–1).
117   Ibid., 31.
118   Ibid., 32.
119   See ibid., 40.
120   Sartre actually runs into a paradox similar to the one stated in Plato's *Euthyphro* (10 a): it is not clear whether an action is chosen because it is good or whether it is good because it is chosen. Sartre seems to opt for the latter, when he says about the anguish of leaders: "It is the very condition of their action, for they first contemplate several options, and, in choosing one of them, realize that its only value lies in the fact that it was chosen" (Sartre, *Existentialism Is a Humanism*, 27). The mistake in this formulation, if we read it correctly, is to take moral principles, or values, as an object of choice while in reality they are the reason for which objects are chosen. If principles were objects, then the individual's choice

would determine everything about an action, even its morality. Contrary to that, principles determine and constrain the act of choice.

121 Ibid., 46.
122 Ibid., 36.
123 Ibid., 38; see also 54.
124 Another approach for which the notion of responsibility helps to express the precarious nature of moral commitments has been articulated by Jonas. He believes that "the enormity of powers" that humans now possess through their technologies and the progress of industrialization, powers both over nature and themselves, "forces upon ethics a new dimension of responsibility never dreamt of before" (Hans Jonas, "Technology and Responsibility: Reflections on the New Tasks of Ethics," in *Philosophical Essays. From Ancient Creed to Technological Man* (Englewood Cliffs, NJ: Prentice-Hall, 1974), 9). For Jonas, "the anthropocentric confinement of former ethics no longer holds" because nature now requires "a role of stewardship" for which "no previous ethics has prepared us" (10). The notion of responsibility serves a threefold purpose in this account: first, it reflects the causal force that humans have acquired over nature; second, it expresses their asymmetrical position vis-à-vis nature, the fact that nature itself cannot request to be respected but needs to be attended to in an attitude of self-restraint, devotion, and care; and third, it indicates the situation of emergency that has been created by human powers, which makes an extraordinary commitment necessary. (For the need to develop attitudes of devotion and love toward nature, see also Hans Jonas, *The Imperative of Responsibility. In Search for an Ethics of the Technological Age* (Chicago/London: University of Chicago Press, 1984), 93). It seems, however, that responsibility is eventually a placeholder in his approach. If it were the primary notion, then he would have to examine the dialectical tension that lies in making the very same power that has such destructive effects on nature committed to providing the remedy and protection. Jonas' approach is meant to prepare the way for the articulation of new duties and principles, such as the principle of stewardship, and is therefore like Sartre's theory more classical than he presents it to be.
125 In the *Gorgias*, Socrates refers to a myth according to which the souls who pass on to the underworld have to be stripped off their body and their external belongings so that they can be examined in all nakedness (*Gorgias* 523 c–e and 524 d–525 e; see also *Apology* 41 a). Agents are solely responsible for the moral quality of their soul and cannot justify their wrongdoings by citing physical limitations or outside circumstances.
126 Berry Tholen, "Political Responsibility as a Virtue: Nussbaum, MacIntyre, and Ricoeur on the Fragility of Politics," *Alternatives: Global, Local, Political* 43/1 (2018), 31.
127 See Garrath Williams, "Responsibility as a Virtue," *Ethical Theory and Moral Practice* 11/4 (2008), 459.
128 Ibid.
129 See for a similar point our remarks on Hegel's idea of the ethical as rectitude in the last section of Chapter 8.
130 Hannah Arendt, *The Human Condition*, 2nd edn (1958; repr., Chicago: University of Chicago Press, 1998). German version: *Vita activa oder Vom tätigen Leben* (München/Zürich: Piper, 1981). Passages quoted from the German version are not included in the English version (translations M.S.).

131 Arendt, *Human Condition*, 233–4.
132 Ibid., 177.
133 Ibid., 176.
134 See ibid., 184.
135 Ibid., 233.
136 Ibid., 237.
137 See ibid.
138 Arendt, *Vita activa*, 233 (translation M.S.).
139 The criticism of general moral theories also seems to include consequentialist theories, at least implicitly. See ibid., 238.
140 Ibid., 241.
141 Ibid.
142 Ibid.
143 See Arendt, *Vita activa*, 235.
144 Arendt, *The Human Condition*, 241.
145 Ibid. It is of course possible to say that even acts of evil can eventually be forgiven, but in such cases forgiving is a merely subjective, inner practice. It cannot lead to a new beginning in the world of action because genuine evil needs to be punished in any case, whether the agent is personally forgiven or not. The web of relationships needs to be protected from truly destructive acts.
146 Ibid., 240.
147 Ibid., 241.
148 Ibid., 243.
149 Ibid.
150 Charles L. Griswold, *Forgiveness: A Philosophical Exploration* (New York: Cambridge University Press, 2007), 38.
151 Ibid., 49–50.
152 Ibid., 49.
153 Ibid., 47.
154 For this condition, see also Aurel Kolnai, "Forgiveness," *Proceedings of the Aristotelian Society* 74 (1973), 97.
155 Jacques Derrida, *On Cosmopolitanism and Forgiveness*, transl. M. Dooley and M. Hughes (New York: Routledge, 2001), 34.
156 Ibid., 32.
157 Ibid., 29.
158 In following Derrida, we refrain from conceptualizing forgiving as a supererogatory act, although it often has been understood as such. See David Heyd, *Supererogation. Its Status in Ethical Theory* (Cambridge: Cambridge University Press, 1982), 154. There is of course a certain similarity: "A supererogatory act is an act which is good (right, praiseworthy, virtuous) to do, but not bad (wrong, blameful, evil) not to do" (8). Forgiving at first glance, could be seen as an act that is always right, or inherently good, but this cannot generally be the case. One can also demand forgiveness and think that it is bad not to forgive, for example, in a personal relationship.
159 Oliver Hallich, "Can the Paradox of Forgiveness Be Resolved?", *Ethical Theory and Moral Practice* 16 (2013), 1006. For more arguments against the duty to forgive because of repentance, see 1002–7.
160 Martha C. Nussbaum, *Anger and Forgiveness. Resentment, Generosity, Justice* (New York: Oxford University Press, 2016), 12.

161 For a similar criticism of "definitional stops" in the understanding of forgiveness, see Leo Zaibert, "The Paradox of Forgiveness," *Journal of Moral Philosophy* 6 (2009), 377 and 392.
162 See ibid., 392.
163 Ibid., 384.
164 Hallich, "Can the Paradox Be Resolved?", 1001.
165 See on this point Zaibert, "Paradox of Forgiveness," 388 and 392.
166 Derrida, *Cosmopolitanism and Forgiveness*, 32-3.
167 See Hallich, "Can the Paradox Be Resolved?", 1015: it is sometimes a sign of good character to forgive, sometimes not. Forgiving is a particular act which has a contextual meaning so that no general theory is adequate for it.
168 See also Robert Gibbs, *Why Ethics? Signs of Responsibility* (Princeton: Princeton University Press, 2000), for the idea that forgiveness changes the past (338-9). There lies for him an asymmetry in such an act of forgiving: "Only the other person can repair my past, can forgive me and transform my sins into merits" (353).
169 Arendt, *Human Condition*, 238.
170 Ibid., 238-9.
171 Ibid., 239. For the origin of this claim, see Matthew 6, 12-15; Markus, 11, 25-6, and Lukas 11, 4.
172 Arendt, *Human Condition*, 241.
173 Matthew 7, 1-5.
174 John 8, 7-11.
175 John 7, 7.
176 John 8, 15.
177 Luke 23, 34.
178 Matthew 18, 21-35.
179 Derrida, *Cosmopolitanism and Forgiveness*, 39.
180 See also Luke 7, 4: "And if he sins against you seven times in the day, and turns to you seven times, saying, 'I repent,' you must forgive him."
181 Luke 7, 37.
182 Luke 7, 44-50.
183 As said before, we mostly leave out the religious context here, for example, the fact that actions against the Holy Spirit will not be forgiven (see Matthew 12, 32; Mark 3, 29; Luke 12, 10). Jesus and God can judge and condemn humans if there is need (John 8, 15). We also leave out the problematic claim that forgiveness has to be extended to all peoples, which justifies the missionary domination of other nations (see Luke 24, 47).
184 Nietzsche, *The Anti-Christ*, 156 (section 32).
185 See ibid., 158 (section 33).
186 Ibid., 154 (section 30).
187 Ibid., 157 (section 33).
188 Friedrich Nietzsche, *Thus Spoke Zarathustra*, transl. Graham Parkes (Oxford: Oxford University Press, 2005), 59-60 (Zarathustra I, On the Bite of the Adder).
189 Ibid., 81 (Zarathustra II, On the Virtuous).
190 Ibid., 13 (Prologue, section 3).
191 Ibid., 121 (Zarathustra II, On Redemption).
192 Ibid., 86 (Zarathustra II, On the Tarantulas).
193 Exceptions can be found in passages that envision a "self-overcoming of justice" (Nietzsche, *Genealogy*, 73; Essay II, section 10). From this perspective, the main

purpose of established rules for justice is not to punish but to end "the senseless rage of *ressentiment*" (*Genealogy*, 75; Essay II, section 11).
194 Richard Rorty, *Philosophy and Social Hope* (London: Penguin, 1999), 81.
195 Ibid., 83.
196 Ibid., 82.
197 Ibid., 87.
198 Ibid., 81.
199 Ibid., 82.
200 Ibid., 85.
201 The role of humor mentioned here is limited compared to the one it plays in some of Kierkegaard's works. We can, however, note a structural analogy insofar as humor and also the related attitude of irony for him testify to the contradiction between one's desire for the good and its realization (see *Concluding Unscientific Postscript*, 422–4).

Bibliography

Aertsen, Jan A. *Medieval Philosophy as Transcendental Thought. From Philip the Chancellor (ca. 1225) to Francisco Suárez*. Leiden/Boston: Brill, 2012.
Aertsen, Jan A. *Medieval Philosophy and the Transcendentals. The Case of Thomas Aquinas*. Leiden/Boston: Brill 1996.
Appiah, Kwame Anthony. *As If. Idealization and Ideals*. Cambridge, MA: Harvard University Press, 2017.
Arendt, Hannah. *The Human Condition*. 2nd edn, 1958. Reprint, Chicago: University of Chicago Press, 1998. German version: *Vita activa oder Vom tätigen Leben*. München/Zürich: Piper, 1981.
Arendt, Hannah. *Between Past and Future. Eight Exercises in Political Thought*. New York: Penguin, 1977.
Arendt, Hannah. *The Origins of Totalitarianism*. 2nd enlarged edn. Cleveland: Meridian, 1958.
Aristotle. *Nicomachean Ethics*. Translated by H. Rackham. Cambridge, MA/London: Harvard University Press, 1934.
Arvanitis, Alexios. "Autonomy and Morality: A Self-Determination Theory Discussion of Ethics." *New Ideas in Psychology* 47 (2017): 57–61.
Ayer, A. J. *Language, Truth, and Logic*. New York: Dover Publications, 1952.
Beauchamp, Tom L. and Childress, James F. *Principles of Biomedical Ethics*. 6th edn. New York: Oxford University Press, 2009.
Berlin, Isaiah. *The Hedgehog and the Fox. An Essay on Tolstoy's View of History*. First published 1953. Princeton: Princeton University Press, 2013.
Bernasconi, Robert. "Before Whom and for What? Accountability and the Invention of Ministerial, Hyperbolic, and Infinite Responsibility." In *Difficulties of Ethical Life*, edited by Shannon Sullivan and Dennis Schmidt, 131–46. New York: Fordham University Press, 2008.
Bloch, Ernst. *The Principle of Hope. Volume I*. Translated by Neville Plaice, Steven Plaice, and Paul Knight. German orig. 1959. Cambridge, MA: MIT Press, 1986.
Bloom, Paul. *Against Empathy. The Case for Rational Compassion*. New York: Harper Collins Eco, 2016.
Brandom, Robert B. *Articulating Reasons. An Introduction to Inferentialism*. Cambridge, MA: Harvard University Press, 2000.
Brandom, Robert B. *Making It Explicit. Reasoning, Representing, and Discursive Commitment*. Cambridge, MA: Harvard University Press, 1994.
Bregman, Rutger. *Utopia for Realists. How We Can Build the Ideal World*. New York: Back Bay Books, 2018.
Caritat, Marie-Jean-Antoine-Nicolas, Marquis de Condorcet. *Outlines of an Historical View of the Progress of the Human Mind*. Translator unknown. Philadelphia: M. Carey, 1796. Public domain at https://oll.libertyfund.org/title/condorcet-outlines-of-an-historical-view-of-the-progress-of-the-human-mind (last accessed November 1, 2021).
Crary, Alice. *Beyond Moral Judgment*. Cambridge, MA: Harvard University Press, 2009.

Crisp, Roger. *Reasons and the Good*. Oxford: Clarendon, 2006.
Crisp, Roger. "Does Modern Moral Philosophy Rest on a Mistake?" In *Modern Moral Philosophy*, edited by Anthony O'Hear, 75–93. Cambridge: Cambridge University Press, 2004.
Dancy, Jonathan. *Ethics without Principles*. Oxford: Clarendon, 2004.
Dancy, Jonathan, ed. *Normativity*. Oxford: Blackwell, 2000.
Davidson, Donald. *Essays on Actions and Events*. Oxford: Clarendon, 1980.
Derrida, Jacques. *On Cosmopolitanism and Forgiveness*. Translated by M. Dooley and M. Hughes. New York: Routledge, 2001.
Descartes, René. *Discourse on the Method for Conducting One's Reason Well and Seeking the Truth in the Sciences*. In *Philosophical Essays and Correspondence*, edited by Roger Ariew. Indianapolis/Cambridge: Hackett, 2000.
Destrée, Pierre. "Aristotle on the Causes of *akrasia*." In Akrasia *in Greek Philosophy. From Socrates to Plotinus*, edited by Christopher Bobonich and Pierre Destrée, 139–65. Leiden/Boston: Brill, 2007.
Dworkin, Ronald. *Justice for Hedgehogs*. Cambridge, MA: Belknap Press, 2011.
Dworkin, Ronald. *Taking Rights Seriously*. Cambridge, MA: Harvard University Press, 1977.
Eagleton, Terry. *The Meaning of Life. A Very Short Introduction*. Oxford: Oxford University Press, 2007.
Enoch, David. *Taking Morality Seriously. A Defense of Robust Realism*. Oxford: Oxford University Press, 2011.
Enoch, David. "Agency, Shmagency: Why Normativity Won't Come from What Is Constitutive of Action." *Philosophical Review* 115 (2006): 169–98.
Fish, Stanley. *The Trouble with Principle*. Cambridge, MA: Harvard University Press, 1999.
Flanagan, Owen. "Admirable Immorality and Admirable Imperfection." *Journal of Philosophy* 83 (1986): 41–60.
Foot, Philippa. *Moral Dilemmas: And Other Topics in Moral Philosophy*. Oxford: Clarendon, 2002.
Foot, Philippa. *Natural Goodness*. Oxford: Clarendon, 2001.
Gadamer, Hans-Georg. *Truth and Method*. 2nd, rev. edn. Transl. rev. by Joel Weinsheimer and Donald G. Marshall. First published 1975. London/New York: Continuum, 2004.
Gadamer, Hans-Georg. *Plato's Dialectical Ethics. Phenomenological Interpretations Relating to the* Philebus. Translated by Robert. M. Wallace. German orig. 1931. New Haven/London: Yale University Press, 1991.
Gaita, Raimond. *Good and Evil: An Absolute Conception*. 2nd edn. New York: Routledge, 2004.
Geach, Peter T. "Good and Evil." *Analysis* 17 (1956): 33–42.
Gehlen, Arnold. *Moral und Hypermoral. Eine pluralistische Ethik*. Frankfurt a.M./Bonn: Bouvier, 1970.
Gert, Bernard. *Morality: Its Nature and Justification*. Revised Edition. Oxford: Oxford University Press, 2005.
Gert, Bernard and Gert, Joshua. "The Definition of Morality." *The Stanford Encyclopedia of Philosophy* (Fall 2017 Edition), edited by Edward N. Zalta. URL = https://plato.stanford.edu/archives/fall2017/entries/morality-definition/
Gibbard, Allan. *Reconciling Our Aims: In Search of Bases of Ethics. Berkeley Tanner Lectures*. New York: Oxford University Press, 2008.
Gibbs, Robert. *Why Ethics? Signs of Responsibility*. Princeton: Princeton University Press, 2000.

Gilligan, Carol. *In a Different Voice. Psychological Theory and Women's Development*. Cambridge, MA: Harvard University Press, 1982.
Griswold, Charles L. *Forgiveness: A Philosophical Exploration*. New York: Cambridge University Press, 2007.
Habermas, Jürgen. *Contributions to a Discourse Theory of Law and Democracy*. Translated by William Rehg. German orig. 1992. Cambridge, MA: MIT Press, 1996.
Habermas, Jürgen. *Justification and Application. Remarks on Discourse Ethics*. Translated by Ciaran Cronin. German orig. 1991. Cambridge, MA/London: MIT Press, 1993.
Habermas, Jürgen. *Moral Consciousness and Communicative Action*. Translated by Christian Lenhardt and Shierry Weber Nicholson. German orig. 1983. Cambridge, MA: MIT Press, 1990.
Hallich, Oliver. "Can the Paradox of Forgiveness Be Resolved?" *Ethical Theory and Moral Practice* 16 (2013): 999–1017.
Hare, R. M. "Possible People." In *Essays on Bioethics*, 67–83. Oxford: Clarendon Press, 1993.
Harman, Gilbert et al. "Moral Reasoning." In *The Moral Psychology Handbook*, edited by John M. Doris and the Moral Psychology Research Group, 206–45. New York: Oxford University Press, 2010.
Hart, H. L. A. "Positivism and the Separation of Law and Morals." *Harvard Law Review* 71 (1958): 593–629.
Heath, Joseph. "Practical Irrationality and the Structure of Decision Theory." In *Weakness of Will and Practical Irrationality*, edited by Sarah Stroud and Christine Tappolet, 251–73. New York: Oxford University Press, 2003.
Hegel, Georg Wilhelm Friedrich. *The Science of Logic*. Translated and edited by G. de Giovanni. Cambridge: Cambridge University Press, 2010.
Hegel, Georg Wilhelm Friedrich. *Enzyklopädie der philosophischen Wissenschaften im Grundrisse. Gesammelte Werke, vol. 20*. Hamburg: Meiner, 1992.
Hegel, Georg Wilhelm Friedrich. *Elements of the Philosophy of Right*. Translated by H. B. Nisbet. Cambridge: Cambridge University Press, 1991.
Hegel, Georg Wilhelm Friedrich. *Phenomenology of Spirit*. Translated by A. V. Miller. Oxford: Oxford University Press, 1977.
Heidegger, Martin. *Towards the Definition of Philosophy. Freiburg Lecture-Courses 1919*. Translated by Ted Sadler. London/New York: Continuum, 2008.
Heyd, David. *Supererogation. Its Status in Ethical Theory*. Cambridge: Cambridge University Press, 1982.
Hitchens, Christopher. *The Missionary Position. Mother Teresa in Theory and Practice*. Toronto: McClellan and Stewart, 2012.
Hume, David. *Moral Philosophy*. Edited by Geoffrey Sayre-McCord. Indianapolis: Hackett, 2006.
Hursthouse, Rosalind. *On Virtue Ethics*. Oxford: Oxford University Press, 1999.
Hursthouse, Rosalind. "Arational Actions." *Journal of Philosophy* 88 (1991): 57–68.
Husserl, Edmund. *Ideas. General Introduction to Pure Phenomenology*. Translated by W. R. Boyce Gibson. First published 1931. London/New York: Routledge, 2013.
Hutto, Daniel. "A Cause for Concern. Reasons, Causes and Explanations." *Philosophy and Phenomenological Research* 59/2 (1999): 381–401.
Ignatieff, Michael. *Human Rights as Politics and Idolatry*. Edited by Amy Gutman. Princeton: Princeton University Press, 2001.
Jonas, Hans. *The Imperative of Responsibility. In Search for an Ethics of the Technological Age*. German orig. 1979. Chicago/London: University of Chicago Press, 1984.

Jonas, Hans. "Technology and Responsibility: Reflections on the New Tasks of Ethics." In *Philosophical Essays. From Ancient Creed to Technological Man*, 3–20. Englewood Cliffs, NJ: Prentice-Hall, 1974.
Joyce, Richard. *The Myth of Morality*. Cambridge: Cambridge University Press, 2001.
Joyce, Richard and Garner, Richard, eds. *The End of Morality. Taking Moral Abolitionism Seriously*. New York: Routledge 2019.
Kagan, Shelly. *The Limits of Morality*. Oxford: Oxford University Press, 1989.
Kant, Immanuel. *Anthropology from a Pragmatic Point of View*. Translated by Robert B. Louden. Cambridge: Cambridge University Press, 2006.
Kant, Immanuel. *Critique of Pure Reason*. Translated by Paul Guyer. Cambridge: Cambridge University Press, 1998.
Kant, Immanuel. *Groundwork of the Metaphysics of Morals*. Translated by Mary Gregor. Cambridge: Cambridge University Press, 1998.
Kant, Immanuel. *Religion within the Boundaries of Mere Reason*. In: *Religion within the Boundaries of Mere Reason and Other Writings*. Translated by Alan Wood and George di Giovanni. Cambridge: Cambridge University Press, 1998.
Kant, Immanuel. *Critique of Practical Reason*. Translated by Mary Gregor. Cambridge: Cambridge University Press, 1997.
Kant, Immanuel. *The Metaphysics of Morals*. Translated by Mary Gregor. Cambridge: Cambridge University Press, 1996.
Kant, Immanuel. *Practical Philosophy*. Translated by Mary Gregor. Cambridge: Cambridge University Press, 1996.
Kant, Immanuel. *The Conflict of the Faculties*. Translated by Mary Gregor. New York: Abaris Books, 1979.
Kelsen, Hans. *General Theory of Law and the State*. Translated by Anders Wedberg. Cambridge, MA: Harvard University Press, 1949.
Kierkegaard, Søren. *Concluding Unscientific Postscript to the Philosophical Crumbs*. Translated by Alistair Hannay. Cambridge: Cambridge University Press, 2009.
Kierkegaard, Søren. *Fear and Trembling*. Translated by Sylvia Walsh. Cambridge: Cambridge University Press, 2006.
Kierkegaard, Søren. *Either/Or, Part II*. Translated by Howard V. Hong and Edna H. Hong. Princeton: Princeton University Press, 1987.
Kinghorn, Kevin. *A Framework for the Good*. Notre Dame: University of Notre Dame Press, 2016.
Kolnai, Aurel. "Forgiveness." *Proceedings of the Aristotelian Society* 74 (1973): 91–106.
Korsgaard, Christine M. *Self-Constitution. Agency, Identity, and Integrity*. New York: Oxford University Press, 2009.
Korsgaard, Christine M. *The Sources of Normativity*. Cambridge: Cambridge University Press, 1996.
Kraut, Richard. *Against Absolute Goodness*. New York: Oxford University Press, 2011.
Kraut, Richard. *What Is Good and Why. The Ethics of Well-Being*. Cambridge, MA: Harvard University Press, 2007.
Leibniz, Gottfried Wilhelm. *The Principles of Philosophy, or, the Monadology*. In *Philosophical Essays*. Edited and translated by Roger Ariew and Daniel Garber, 213–25. Indianapolis/Cambridge: Hackett, 1989.
Lévinas, Emmanuel. *Totality and Infinity. An Essay on Exteriority*. Translated by Alphonso Lingis. French orig. 1961. Pittsburgh: Duquesne University Press, 1969.
Lewis, C. S. *The Problem of Pain*. New York: MacMillan, 1973.

Locke, John. *An Essay Concerning Human Understanding*. Edited by Peter H. Nidditch. Oxford: Oxford University Press, 1973.

Luhmann, Niklas. *Die Moral der Gesellschaft*. Edited by Detlef Horster. Frankfurt a.M.: Suhrkamp, 2008.

MacDonald, Scott. "Goodness as Transcendental: The Early Thirteenth-Century Recovery of an Aristotelian Idea." *Topoi* 11 (1992): 173–86.

MacIntyre, Alisdair. *After Virtue. A Study in Moral Theory*. Notre Dame: University of Notre Dame Press, 1981.

Margalit, Avishai. "Human Dignity between Kitsch and Deification." In *Philosophy, Ethics, and a Common Humanity. Essays in Honor of Raimond Gaita*, edited by Christoph Cordner, 106–20. London/New York: Routledge, 2011.

Margalit, Avishai. *The Ethics of Memory*. Cambridge, MA: Harvard University Press, 2004.

Marks, Joel. *Ethics without Morals: In Defense of Amorality*. New York: Routledge, 2013.

McDowell, John. "Virtue and Reason." *The Monist* 62/3 (1979): 331–50.

Mill, John Stuart and Bentham, Jeremy. *Utilitarianism and Other Essays*. Edited by Alan Ryan. London: Penguin, 2004.

Millgram, Elijah. *Ethics Done Right: Practical Reasoning as a Foundation for Moral Theory*. New York: Cambridge University Press, 2005.

Moeller, Hans-Georg. *The Moral Fool. A Case for Amorality*. New York: Columbia University Press, 2009.

Moore, G. E. "Is Goodness a Quality?" In *Philosophical Papers*, 89–100. New York: Collier, 1962.

Moore, G. E. *Principia Ethica*. London: Cambridge University Press, 1903.

Murdoch, Iris. *The Sovereignty of Good*. London/New York: Routledge, 1971.

Nehamas, Alexander. *Nietzsche. Life as Literature*. Cambridge, MA: Harvard University Press, 1985.

Nietzsche, Friedrich. *Thus Spoke Zarathustra*. Translated by Graham Parkes. Oxford: Oxford University Press, 2005.

Nietzsche, Friedrich. *Twilight of the Idols* and *The Anti-Christ*. Translated by R. J. Hollingdale. London: Penguin, 2003.

Nietzsche, Friedrich. *Beyond Good and Evil*. Translated by Judith Norman. Cambridge: Cambridge University Press, 2002.

Nietzsche, Friedrich. *The Gay Science*. Translated by Josefine Nauckhoff. Cambridge: Cambridge University Press, 2001.

Nietzsche, Friedrich. *Daybreak. Thoughts on the Prejudices of Morality*. Translated by R. J. Hollingdale. Cambridge: Cambridge University Press, 1997.

Nietzsche, Friedrich. *Human, All Too Human I*. Translated by Gary Handwerk. The Complete Works of Friedrich Nietzsche, vol. III. Stanford: Stanford University Press, 1995.

Nietzsche, Friedrich. *On the Genealogy of Morals* and *Ecce Homo*. Translated by Walter Kaufmann and R. J. Hollingdale. New York: Vintage, 1967.

Nussbaum, Martha C. *Anger and Forgiveness. Resentment, Generosity, Justice*. New York: Oxford University Press, 2016.

Nussbaum, Martha C. *The Fragility of Goodness. Luck and Ethics in Greek Tragedy and Philosophy*. Cambridge: Cambridge University Press, 1986.

Office of the High Commissioner for Human Rights (UN Human Rights), *Convention Relating to the Status of Refugees*, 1951, online: https://www.ohchr.org/en/professionalinterest/pages/statusofrefugees.aspx

O'Neill, Onora. "Consistency in Action." In *Constructions of Reason*, 81–104. Cambridge: Cambridge University Press, 1989.
Orsi, Francesco. "Ethical Non-Naturalism and the Guise of the Good." *Topoi* 37 (2018): 581–90.
Orsi, Francesco. "The Guise of the Good." *Philosophy Compass* 10 (2015): 714–24.
Parfit, Derek. "Innumerate Ethics." *Philosophy & Public Affairs* 7 (1978): 285–301.
Parfit, Derek and Broome, John. "Reason and Motivation." *Proceedings of the Aristotelian Society. Supplementary Volume* 71 (1997): 99–130.
Pidgen, Charles R. "Geach on 'Good'." *The Philosophical Quarterly* 40 (1990): 129–54.
Pinker, Steven. *Enlightenment Now. The Case for Reason, Science, Humanism, and Progress.* New York: Viking, 2018.
Plato. *The Republic*. Translated by Allan Bloom. 2nd edn. New York: Basic Books, 1968.
Railton, Peter. "Normative Force and Normative Freedom: Hume and Kant, but not Hume versus Kant." In *Normativity*, edited by Jonathan Dancy, 1–33. Oxford: Blackwell, 2000.
Rawls, John. *A Theory of Justice*. Rev. edn. Cambridge, MA: Harvard University Press, 1999.
Raz, Joseph. "On the Guise of the Good." In *Desire, Practical Reason, and the Good*, edited by Sergio Tenenbaum, 112–36. New York: Oxford University Press, 2010.
Raz, Joseph. "Explaining Normativity: On Rationality and the Justification of Reason." In *Normativity*, edited by Jonathan Dancy, 34–60. Oxford: Blackwell, 2000.
Ricoeur, Paul. "The Concept of Responsibility: An Essay in Semantic Analysis." In *The Just*. Translated by D. Pellauer, 11–35. Chicago: University of Chicago Press, 2000.
Rohr, Michael David. "Is Goodness Comparative?" *Journal of Philosophy* 75 (1978): 494–503.
Rorty, Amélie Oksenberg. "The Social and Political Sources of *akrasia*." *Ethics* 107 (1997): 644–57.
Rorty, Richard. *Philosophy and Social Hope*. London: Penguin, 1999.
Ross, W. D. *The Right and the Good*. Oxford: Clarendon, 1930.
Rousseau, Jean-Jacques. *The Discourse and Other Early Political Writings*. Translated by Victor Gourevitch. Cambridge: Cambridge University Press, 1997.
Sartre, Jean-Paul. *Existentialism Is a Humanism*. Translated by Carol Macomber. New Haven/London: Yale University Press, 2007.
Sartre, Jean-Paul. *Being and Nothingness. A Phenomenological Essay on Ontology*. Translated by Hazel Barnes. New York et al.: Washington Square Press, 1992.
Scanlon, T. M. *Being Realistic about Reasons*. Oxford: Oxford University Press, 2014.
Scanlon, T. M. *What We Owe to Each Other*. Cambridge, MA: Belknap, 1998.
Scheffler, Samuel. *Death and the Afterlife. The Berkeley Tanner Lectures*. Edited by Niko Kolodny. New York: Oxford University Press, 2016.
Schopenhauer, Arthur. "Prize Essay on the Basis of Morals." In *The Two Fundamental Problems of Ethics*. Translated by Christopher Janaway. Cambridge: Cambridge University Press, 2009.
Schroeder, Mark. "Value Theory." *The Stanford Encyclopedia of Philosophy* (Fall 2021 Edition), edited by Edward N. Zalta. URL = https://plato.stanford.edu/archives/fall2021/entries/value-theory/
Schroeder, Mark. "What Is the Frege-Geach Problem?" *Philosophy Compass* 3/4 (2008): 703–20.
Sehon, Scott. "An Argument against the Causal Theory of Action Explanation." *Philosophy and Phenomenological Research* 60/1 (2000): 67–85.
Sen, Amartya. *Development as Freedom*. New York: Anchor Books, 1999.

Setiya, Kieran. "Sympathy for the Devil." In *Desire, Practical Reason, and the Good*, edited by Sergio Tenenbaum, 82–110. New York: Oxford University Press, 2010.
Setiya, Kieran. "Explaining Action." *The Philosophical Review* 112/3 (2003): 339–93.
Shafer-Landau, Russ. *Moral Realism. A Defense*. Oxford: Clarendon, 2003.
Sigdwick, Henry. *The Methods of Ethics*. 7th edn. First published 1907. Indianapolis: Hackett, 1981.
Singer, Peter. *The Life You Can Save. Acting Now to End World Poverty*. New York: Random House, 2009.
Singer, Peter. "Famine, Affluence, and Morality." *Philosophy and Public Affairs* 1 (1972): 229–43.
Smart, J. J. C. "An Outline of a System of Utilitarian Ethics." In J. J. C. Smart and Bernard Williams, *Utilitarianism. For and against*, 1–74. New York: Cambridge University Press, 1973.
Steinmann, Michael. "The Axial Age and the Quest for a Secular Religion in Modernity." *Existenz* 14/1 (2019): 98–106.
Steinmann, Michael. "Wertung und Wertwiderstand. Selbsterfahrung und die antinomische Struktur des Daseins bei Jaspers und Heidegger." *Discipline Filosofiche* 27/1 (2017): 75–94.
Steinmann, Michael. "But What Do We Matter!' Nietzsche's Secret Hopes and the Prospects of Transhumanism." In *Nietzsche and Transhumanism: Precursor or Enemy?* Nietzsche Now, vol. 1, edited by Stefan Lorenz Sorgner and Yunus Tuncel, 172–90. Cambridge: Cambridge Scholars Publishing, 2016.
Steinmann, Michael. "Nietzsche, Darwin, and the Greeks: On the Aesthetic Interpretation of Life." *The Agonist. A Nietzsche Circle Journal* 9 (2015/16): 1–42.
Steinmann, Michael. "What Technology Is Not. On Ethics as Ecology of Human Life." In *Science, Technology, and the Humanities: A New Synthesis*, edited by Lisa Dolling, 366–85. Hoboken, NJ: Stevens Institute of Technology, 2011.
Steinmann, Michael. "Determinatio est Negatio. Über Möglichkeit und Unverzichtbareit negativer Freiheit". In *Gegenständlichkeit und Objektivtität*, edited by David Espinet, Friederike Rese and Michael Steinmann, 116–37. Tübingen: Mohr Siebeck, 2011.
Steinmann, Michael. "Under the Pretence of Autonomy. Contradictions in the Guidelines for Human Tissue Donation." *Medicine, Health Care and Philosophy* 12/3 (2009): 281–9.
Steinmann, Michael. "Duties towards our Bodies." In *Altruism Reconsidered. Exploring New Approaches to Property in Human Tissue*, edited by Michael Steinmann, Peter Sykora and Urban Wiesing, 67–86. Aldershot: Ashgate, 2009.
Steinmann, Michael. "Begründung als soziale Praxis". In *Wie funktioniert Bioethik? Interdisziplinäre Entscheidungsfindung im Spannungsfeld von theoretischem Begründungsanspruch und praktischem Regelungsbedarf*, edited by Eve-Marie Engels et al., 53–60. Paderborn: Mentis, 2008.
Steinmann, Michael. "Ein Prinzip für die Prinzipien. Kantische Einwände gegen den Ansatz von Beauchamp und Childress". In *Prinzipienthik in der Biomedizin. Moralphilosophie und medizinische Praxis*, edited by Oliver Rauprich and Florian Steger, 120–44. Campus: Frankfurt/New York, 2005.
Steinmann, Michael. *Die Ethik Friedrich Nietzsches*. Berlin/New York: Walter de Gruyter, 2000.
Steinmann, Michael and Matei, Sorin and Collmann, Jeff. "A Theoretical Framework for Ethical Reflection in Big Data Research." In *Ethical Reasoning in Big Data. An Exploratory Analysis*, edited by Jeff Collmann and Sorin Matei, 11–27. New York et al.: Springer, 2016.

Stevenson, C. L. *Ethics and Language*. New Haven: Yale University Press, 1944.
Supreme Court of the United States, *Obergefell v. Hodges*, No. 14–556, June 26, 2015.
Taurek, John M. "Should the Numbers Count?" *Philosophy & Public Affairs* 6 (1977): 293–316.
Taylor, Charles. *Sources of the Self. The Making of the Modern Identity*. Cambridge: Harvard University Press, 1989.
Taylor, Charles. "What Is Human Agency?" In *Human Agency and Language. Philosophical Papers I*, 15–45. Cambridge: Cambridge University Press, 1985.
Tenenbaum, Sergio. *Appearances of the Good. An Essay on the Nature of Practical Reason*. Cambridge: Cambridge University Press, 2007.
Tessman, Lisa. *Moral Failure: On the Impossible Demands of Morality*. New York: Oxford University Press, 2015.
Tholen, Berry. "Political Responsibility as a Virtue: Nussbaum, MacIntyre, and Ricoeur on the Fragility of Politics." *Alternatives: Global, Local, Political* 43/1 (2018): 22–34.
Thomson, Judith Jarvis. *Normativity*. Chicago/LaSalle, IL: Open Court, 2008.
Thomson, Judith Jarvis. *Goodness and Advice*. Edited by Amy Gutman. Princeton: Princeton University Press, 2008.
Toulmin, Stephen. *The Place of Reason in Ethics*. Cambridge: Cambridge University Press, 1964.
United Nations, *Universal Declaration of Human Rights*, 1948, online: https://www.un.org/en/universal-declaration-human-rights/
Vaihinger, Hans. *The Philosophy of "As If." A System of the Theoretical, Practical, and Religious Fictions of Mankind*. Translated by C. K. Ogden. 2nd edn. London: Routledge and Kegan Paul, 1935.
van Ackeren, Marcel and Kühler, Michael, eds. *The Limits of Moral Obligation. Moral Demandingness and Ought Implies Can*. New York: Routledge, 2015.
Varden, Helga. "Kant and Lying to the Murderer at the Door ... One More Time: Kant's Legal Philosophy and Lies to Murderers and Nazis." *Journal of Social Philosophy* 41 (2010): 403–21.
Velleman, David. "The Guise of the Good." *Noûs* 26/1 (1992): 3–26.
Vlastos, Gregory. "Reasons and Causes in the *Phaedo*." *The Philosophical Review* 78/3 (1969): 291–325.
Vogt, Katja Maria. *Desiring the Good. Ancient Proposals and Contemporary Theory*. New York: Oxford University Press, 2017.
Wallace, R. Jay. "Virtue, Reason, and Principle." *Canadian Journal of Philosophy* 21/4 (1991): 469–95.
Walzer, Michael. *Spheres of Justice. A Defense of Pluralism and Equality*. New York: Basic Books, 1983.
Watson, Gary. "Skepticism about Weakness of Will." *The Philosophical Review* 86/3 (1977): 316–39.
Weber, Max. *From Max Weber: Essays in Sociology*. Translated and edited by H. H. Gerth and C. Wright Mills. New York: Oxford University Press, 1949.
Westphal, Merold. "The Many Faces of Levinas as a Reader of Kierkegaard." In *Kierkegaard and Levinas. Ethics, Politics, and Religion*, edited by J. Aaron Simmons and David Wood, 21–40. Bloomington/Indianapolis: Indiana University Press, 2008.
Williams, Bernard. *Ethics and the Limits of Philosophy*. Cambridge: Harvard University Press, 1985.
Williams, Bernard. *Moral Luck. Philosophical Papers 1973–1980*. Cambridge: Cambridge University Press, 1981.

Williams, Bernard. *Problems of the Self*. Cambridge: Cambridge University Press, 1973.
Williams, Bernard. "A Critique of Utilitarianism." In J. J. C. Smart and Bernard Williams, *Utilitarianism: For and against*, 75–150. Cambridge: Cambridge University Press, 1973.
Williams, Garrath. "Responsibility as a Virtue." *Ethical Theory and Moral Practice* 11/4 (2008): 455–70.
Wittgenstein, Ludwig. *On Certainty*. Edited by G. E. M. Anscombe and G. H. von Wright. New York et al.: Harper Torchbook, 1972.
Wolf, Susan. "Moral Saints." *Journal of Philosophy* 79 (1982): 419–39.
Zaibert, Leo. "The Paradox of Forgiveness." *Journal of Moral Philosophy* 6 (2009): 365–93.

Index

abolitionism 110
abortion 170
absolute (good) 5–8, 60, 77, 85–9, 92,
    99–101, 107–12, 117–20, 112–13,
    136, 139, 146, 161, 177, 187, 200–1,
    217–18
    definition of absolute good 31–5
    absoluteness 35, 115, 117
action-centric 45, 57–8, 66, 69, 71–2, 75,
    85, 88, 232
activism 190, 196–7
aesthetics 77
    modern aesthetics 74
agent-centric 45, 57, 66, 69, 71–2, 75, 85,
    88, 232
altruism 77, 136, 176
ancient philosophy 69, 73, 141, 147
anger 72, 154
antagonistic, antagonism (as result of
    dialectics) 3, 8, 89, 92–3, 109, 121,
    129, 131, 136, 146–7, 154–5, 167,
    169–70, 176, 188, 198, 204, 206–8,
    211, 218–20
application (of moral principles) 26,
    113–14, 126–7, 177, 187
    application fallacy 113, 126, 135, 163
Arendt, H. 164, 207–14, 218
    The Human Condition 207
    The Origins of Totalitarianism 164
Aristotle 36, 50–1, 65, 140–1, 147, 162,
    167, 171
    Aristotelian 25, 40
    Neo-Aristotelian 6
    Nicomachean Ethics 36, 147, 162
assertive statement 15, 107
attributive 41–3, 61. *See also* predicative
autonomy 26, 136, 163, 190, 203
Ayer, A. J. 149

bad 41–3, 48–9, 51, 56, 59, 68, 75, 78–9,
    90, 94, 106–8, 170, 173

beauty 13, 35, 56, 65, 71, 73–5
Beckett, S. 8
beneficence 16–17
benefit 75–7, 82, 165–6, 176–7
benevolence 93, 119–20, 127, 177
bindingness 27, 39, 123, 126
blame 8, 169–70, 179, 208–9, 212–13,
    216–18
Bloch, E. 252
Brandom, R. 59

care 17, 134–7
    care ethics 6, 17, 133–4
categorical imperative 17, 39, 87, 117, 127,
    144–6, 162–4, 190, 203, 237, 244
charity 180
choice 28, 48–9, 57, 66, 72, 113, 115,
    202–5
Christ. *See* Jesus of Nazareth
Christian, Christianity 23–4, 132, 169, 180
classificatory (notion) 37–9, 41, 57–8, 113,
    135, 163, 191. *See also* formal
codification 113–14
cognitivism, cognitivist 114–15, 190
    non-cognitivism 6, 115, 121, 144–6,
    148–9, 158, 196
community 190, 206
compassion 115, 133, 150–1, 153, 155
concept, conceptual 6–7, 15, 31, 34–5, 38,
    41–3, 58–60, 64, 71, 85, 96, 99, 109,
    122, 143, 152
Condorcet, Marquis de 195
conscience 29, 148, 189, 206
consequentialism 17, 77, 121, 171–3,
    175–9, 181, 183, 199–200
consistency 68–70, 72–3, 78, 86–8, 92–3,
    100–2, 114, 217, 221, 236
    uncoerced consistency of purposes 6,
    77, 82, 85–7, 241
contemplation 167, 171
contextualism 131

contradiction (in the dialectic of the good) 1–3, 8, 94–5, 105, 108, 110, 121–2, 124–9, 131, 137–41, 143, 156, 162, 169, 181, 187–91, 193–6, 198, 201, 204–7, 218–20
conventions 4–5, 14–17, 21–4, 34, 79–80, 90, 106, 141
  conventionalism in moral theory 118, 151
correlation (of self-determination and the good) 4–5, 27–9, 33, 45, 70, 85, 105, 144
cruelty 150, 153

Dancy, J. 135–6
Davidson, D. 51–2, 54
deontology 17–18, 70, 89, 119–20, 140
Derrida, J. 210–12, 215
Descartes, R. 157–9
  Discourse on Method 157
descriptive (vs normative) 65, 69, 86, 98, 112, 118
  descriptive meaning of the good 6, 32, 42, 61, 65, 140
desire 50–1, 56, 70, 75, 218
  desire for the good 46, 56, 90, 119–20, 123, 147, 167, 187, 193, 198
  desire for happiness 153, 161
  desire as practical term 6, 45–9, 63, 119
determination (in moral action) 5, 8, 109, 111, 114–15, 120–2, 146, 156, 189. *See also* indeterminedness
  definition of determination 3, 105
  moral determination 125–7, 129–31, 138, 143, 146, 151, 162, 165, 187–91, 196, 206–7
dialectics 2–3, 7–8, 89, 108–11, 121–3, 125, 131–2, 134, 137–41, 143, 148, 151, 161, 165, 181, 187–90, 195, 198, 201, 204, 218, 221
  definition of dialectics 109
dignity 123–4, 163–6, 195
dilemma 94–6, 146
Diotima 56, 74
disagreement 86, 93, 149, 152
discourse ethics 190–3

duty 17, 28, 32, 70–1, 119, 125–7, 145, 150, 194, 197, 200. *See also* obligation
  prima facie duties 17, 124

egoism 136, 155
emotion 76, 118, 149–58. *See also* feeling
  emotivism as metaethical theory 6, 118, 152, 155
  emotivism as moral theory based on emotion 148–51, 153
empiricism 15, 17, 116
equality 6, 123, 164, 182
ergon 60–3, 65–7
ethics 28, 35, 61, 70, 77, 133, 149, 197
  ancient ethics 6, 17, 147
  definition of ethics 22 (*see also* morality)
  the ethical (Kierkegaard) 28–9
  ethical life (*Sittlichkeit* in Hegel) 138–9, 141, 181
  ethics of convictions (also: ethics of ultimate ends) 198–201
  ethics of responsibility 133, 197–200
  meta-ethics 120, 148–50, 152, 155
evil 23, 28, 49, 106, 108, 147–8, 187, 209, 224, 256
exception (to general rules) 126–7
  morality as an exception 23–5, 32
existentialism 201, 205
expression, expressive (in meaning of concepts) 59–60, 65, 74, 76–7, 85, 100, 112–14, 137, 232
expressivism (as meta-ethical theory) 42

failure, failing (of the good) 1–3, 8, 97, 105–10, 121, 143, 187–9, 200, 214, 218
  cognitive failure (in morality) 106–7, 109
  definition of failure 105
  failure of practical rationality (Foot) 62
  qualitative failing of the good 108
  quantitative failing of the good 108, 137
feeling 4, 76, 117–19, 154–6, 209. *See also* emotion
  sentiment 118
  sympathy 118

fiction 194–5
flourishing 39–41, 229
fool, foolishness 8–9, 110, 189, 194–5, 200, 205, 216–18, 241
Foot, Ph. 42, 61–2, 95, 107–8
forgiveness 8–9, 110, 188–90, 206–21
    paradox of forgiveness 212–13
formal (notion) 6, 37–9, 41, 45–6, 57–60, 63–6, 68, 85, 99, 101, 113–14, 124, 135, 163, 172, 191, 197, 202–3. *See also* classificatory
formalism 17, 144
foundation 6, 13, 33, 36
    foundationalism 6, 13
fragmentarianism 33, 88–90, 97, 108, 131–2
free, freedom 6, 67–9, 82, 86, 101, 123–4, 164, 201–3, 205, 209. *See also* free will
Freud, S. 2
future generations 100–1

Gaugin, P. 173–4
Gehlen, A. 170
general, generality 8, 29, 37–8, 87, 94, 108, 112–15, 121–3, 125–43, 148, 164–5, 174, 181, 188, 194, 196, 200, 209
    general vs universal 112, 114, 122
    generalization 37, 118, 123, 190, 203, 211–12
    generalization vs generality 112–14
Gert, B. 126, 128
Gilligan, C. 133
Glaucon 129
God 31, 39, 88, 161–3, 214–15, 217
good 5–8, 39–43, 48–9, 57, 61, 65, 74, 76–7, 82–3, 86, 89–93, 97–9, 105–11, 116–19, 138, 187–9, 202–3. *See also* absolute good
    definition of the good 6, 45–6, 76–7, 85, 98–9, 226
    good as formal notion 6, 37–8, 41, 58–60 (*see also* formal)
    good as fundamental notion of morality 5–6, 32, 35, 69
    good as one 36–7, 60, 73, 75
    good vs right 5–6, 70–1 (*see also* right)
    guise of the good 46–8
    final good 26, 55–7

highest good 161, 167
individual realization of the good 72, 131, 137, 139–41
inherent goodness (definition) 121, 161, 181
the moral good as good proper 34–5, 78–80, 100
Platonic notion of the good 7, 27, 36, 38, 45
self-determination and the good 26–9
summum bonum 101
supreme good 161
Griswold, Ch. L. 210–12
guilt 169–70, 179–81, 207, 214

Habermas, J. 182, 190–5, 198, 207
habit 22, 24, 29, 65, 79, 130, 145–7, 207
happiness 23–4, 39, 100, 118–20, 153, 161–2, 167, 172, 176, 249
Hare, R. M. 238
harm 13, 15–16, 26, 145, 177, 199–200
    do no harm 17
    non-maleficence 16
health 58, 65, 67, 92
Heaven 101, 215
Hegel, G. W. F. 3, 7, 109, 121, 125, 138–41, 144–5, 147–8, 155–6, 181–2, 190–1
historical (as condition of moral theory) 6, 18, 21, 27, 45, 111, 139
humans as ends 39, 163–5, 172
Hume, D. 4, 6, 8, 40, 111, 116–18, 120, 144, 150–1, 153
    Humean 6, 61
humor 190, 220–1, 258
Hursthouse, R. 96, 140
hypocrisy 2, 126, 214

idealism 8, 110, 189–90, 194–6, 207
    the good as ideal 33, 98–100
    ideal vs empirical 7, 193
    idealization 192–6
impartiality 177–80
incontinence 49, 51. *See also* weakness of the will
indeterminedness 124–5, 127, 134, 162–5, 172–5, 181
individuality 131–5, 139, 150, 205
intuition 53, 146, 148–9

Jesus of Nazareth 120, 172, 214
Jonas, H. 255
justice 25, 32, 36, 66–7, 70–1, 76, 80–1, 87, 99–100, 129, 136, 150, 180, 218, 225
justification 4, 16, 18, 23, 26, 47, 62, 64, 80–1, 90, 96, 120, 128, 135, 139, 143, 145, 157–9, 173–4, 182, 200, 205, 212, 214

Kagan, Sh. 250
Kant, I. 8, 17, 21, 28, 39, 71, 87, 98, 111, 116–20, 125–28, 144–6, 154, 161–2, 164, 168–9, 171–2, 190, 194–6, 203, 205
Groundwork for the Metaphysics of Morals 116
Kelsen, H. 182–3
Kephalos 80
Kierkegaard, S. 28–9, 258
Either-Or 28
killing 87, 93, 96, 113, 128, 133, 135
kingdom of ends 117, 190
Kinghorn, K. 40–1
Korsgaard, Ch. 25–6, 32, 39
Kraut, R. 35, 39–40

law, legal 4, 14–15, 21, 24, 66, 70, 80–1, 113, 121, 138–9, 141, 147, 164, 181–3
legal positivism 182–3
legality vs morality 28
modern conception of law 81, 182
moral law 28, 98, 116–17, 144–6, 154, 163
Leibniz, G. W. F. 101, 232
Monadology 101
Lévinas, E. 133–4
logic, logical 3, 7, 19, 41–2, 59–60, 94, 109, 115, 117, 121–2, 143, 187, 194, 212
lying 18, 69, 126–7, 168

MacIntyre, A. 139–40
marriage 79, 87, 145, 202–3
Marx, K. 2
material inference 7, 59–60
McDowell, J. 113–14
metaphysics 5–7, 31, 36, 39, 57, 64, 74
method (in moral theory) 3, 8, 35, 39, 114, 116, 118–21, 143, 151, 191

Mill, J. St. 8, 17, 94, 111, 116, 119–20, 171, 176–7
Moore, G. E. 35, 77, 85, 98–101
Principia Ethica 35
modern (society and life) 23, 88, 93, 140–1, 159, 197
modern philosophy 7, 31, 147
modernity 2, 6, 76, 139
moral philosophy 1–5, 7–8, 14, 18, 22, 39, 54, 69, 98, 122, 197
ancient moral philosophy 71
modern moral philosophy 26, 71, 81, 125
morality 2–8, 13, 17–19, 26–8, 32–4, 70–1, 80–1, 105–17, 109–11, 113, 121, 125, 132, 138–41, 144, 147–8, 169–71, 182–3, 190, 193–4, 198, 200, 204–8, 216–18
amorality 110
common morality (Gert) 128
definition of morality 21–2 (*see also* ethics)
distinctiveness of morality 4, 15, 19, 23–6
immoral 8, 126–7, 145, 187, 206, 217
master morality (Nietzsche) 129–30
moral luck 173–4
moral risk 174, 201, 218
morality of custom (Nietzsche) 21–4
slave morality (Nietzsche) 129–30
Murdoch, R. 99

naturalism, naturalistic 6, 85, 98, 117, 129, 147. *See also* physicalism
negativity 109, 122, 130, 155–6
determinate negation 109, 121
New Testament 214
Nietzsche, F. 2, 4, 21–5, 27, 43, 129–30, 132, 134, 139–41, 147, 153, 156, 165, 169–70, 218–19
Thus Spoke Zarathustra 219
nihilism 8, 200
normativity 4, 14–19, 21, 24–6, 31, 34–5, 37–8, 47, 61–2, 77–81, 90, 105–6, 113, 155
conventional normativity 4–5, 14–17, 19, 24, 26–7, 34, 37–8, 79–80, 90, 106, 113, 123

legal normativity 4–5, 14–16, 19, 26–7, 34, 37–8, 77, 80–1, 90, 106, 113, 123
normative vs descriptive 65, 69, 85–6, 98–100, 112
practical normativity 4–5, 14–17, 19, 24, 26–7, 34, 37–8, 77–8, 90, 106, 123

obedience 22–3
obligations 6, 27, 69–71, 94–6, 110, 124–5, 138–9, 165, 174. *See also* duty
ontology, ontological 36, 96–7

pain 128–9
Parfit, D. 178
Paul 8, 189
perfection 31, 69, 235
perpetuation 115–18, 150, 153
physicalism 64. *See also* naturalism
Pinker, St. 195
Plato 7, 21, 25, 27, 31, 36, 38, 45, 49, 52, 55–6, 60–1, 65–8, 73–7, 81, 87, 90–2, 111, 141, 190, 205, 208
  Crito 57
  Gorgias 82
  Phaedo 54, 63
  Phaedrus 79–80
  Philebus 74–5, 92
  Platonic 202
  Republic 71, 80, 82, 99, 129
  Symposium 57
  Timaeus 82
pleasure 75–6, 92
  hedonism 92
pluralism 6–8, 37, 41, 60, 237–8
pragmatism 121, 156–9
predicative 41–3. *See also* attributive
preference 25, 116, 172, 179
prescriptive statement 15–17
principle 5, 16–17, 26, 28–9, 33, 70–1, 112–15, 120, 122–41, 182, 193–6, 214. *See also* rule
progress 195–6, 252
promise 124–5
punishment 8, 209, 215. *See also* retribution
purpose 38, 59–70, 72–3, 75–8, 85–9, 99, 107, 122, 137, 148, 155, 182, 217, 221

rational, rationality 4–5, 53–4, 56, 61–2, 70, 114, 128–9, 139, 143, 147, 191–2
arational 54, 231
instrumental rationality 78
irrational 54, 145, 158, 198–200
rationalist 34
Rawls, J. 70–1, 224–5, 232
realism 32–3, 227
anti-realism 32–3
reason (as capacity of reasoning) 39, 112, 115–17, 121, 128, 143–50, 153, 156–8, 190
fact of reason (Kant) 116, 146
reason (as motive for action) 6, 45–50, 52–8, 62, 85, 108, 122–3, 135–6, 152, 202, 213, 231
internal vs external reasons 144
practice of giving and asking for reasons 6, 45, 55
reason as cause 51–2
reasons as domain (Scanlon) 97
sufficient reason 24–5, 54–6, 58, 66, 85, 105
regret 47, 173, 239
relativism 89, 91–2, 219–20
repentance 210–11, 213
respect 117, 154, 209
responsibility 8, 110, 133, 136, 173, 188–90, 196–206, 255. *See also* ethics of responsibility
negative responsibility 179
retribution 8, 209, 212–13. *See also* punishment
revenge 207–9, 219
right 126–7, 133, 150, 164–5, 178, 197
human rights 123, 164–5, 220
right vs good 5, 32, 70–1, 140, 219
right to have rights (Arendt) 164
Rorty, R. 219–20
Ross, W. D. 34–5, 76–7, 124, 126
Rousseau, J.-J. 147
rule 5, 16–17, 22, 26, 112–13, 128–9, 192. *See also* principle
Golden Rule 16–17, 120

sacrifice 176–7, 179–80, 199
self-sacrifice 87
Sartre, J.-P. 95, 201–6
Existentialism Is a Humanism 201

Scanlon, T. M. 6, 53, 97, 231, 237
Schopenhauer, A. 150-1, 153, 155
self-determination 4-5, 23-9, 31-3, 69, 106-7, 113, 115, 123, 125, 140-1, 144, 162, 182, 189, 196, 203-5
self-restraint 49-51. *See also* weakness of the will
Sermon of the Mount 199
Sidgwick, H. 70-1
Singer, P. 179-81
Socrates 2, 27, 48-50, 52, 54-7, 63, 65-6, 74-6, 79-82, 87, 90, 92, 99, 141, 147, 205
sophist 2, 129, 165
Stevenson, Ch. L. 149, 152, 155
subjective, subjectivity 4, 26-8, 92
suffering 150-1, 166, 178
sufficient, sufficiency (of the good or the reason to be good) 7, 24-5, 54-8, 63, 75, 80-3, 85, 90-2, 106-7, 111-12, 115-16, 118-20, 125, 143, 153, 158-9, 161-2, 168, 174, 188
self-sufficiency 116, 162, 167
supererogatory 16, 180, 256

Taurek, J. M. 178
teleological 24-5, 68, 70, 119-20
theory (of morality) 1-3, 7-8, 17-18, 26, 33, 39-40, 89, 93-4, 109-16, 118-21, 128-9, 140, 143, 147, 149, 152-3, 158-9, 171, 181, 187-90, 200
strong and classical theories 8, 110-11, 116, 120, 158, 197, 205
Thomas Aquinas 46, 107-8
Toulmin, St. 158-9
transcendentals 38-9, 58, 232
truth 71, 73, 94, 149

universal, universality 3, 5, 22, 25, 39, 50, 85-6, 116-19, 128, 136, 145, 156, 165-6, 171, 176-7, 180, 190-1, 193, 195, 199
universal vs general 112, 114, 122
universalization 114, 116, 191
Universal Declaration of Human Rights 123, 164
utilitarianism 2, 17-18, 39, 61, 89, 119-20, 140, 171, 176, 238
utility 39, 75-77, 119-20, 238
utopia 33, 252-3

Vaihinger, H. 194-5, 205
Philosophy of As If 194
Verdi, G. 230
Falstaff 230
virtue 2, 17, 26, 32, 65-6, 85, 91, 132, 141, 150, 162, 194, 197, 205-6
courage 66, 92
prudence 66, 92
virtue ethics 2, 17, 121, 140-1
wisdom 66-7

Weber, M. 195, 197-201, 204-7
Politics as Vocation 197
well-being 6, 16, 39-40, 76, 150, 172
will 116-17, 144, 153, 161-2
free will 146, 194
good will (Kant) 116
weakness of the will 49, 51, 54 (*see also* incontinence)
Williams, B. 69, 144, 172-4, 179
Wittgenstein, L. 176

Zarathustra 218-19

www.ingramcontent.com/pod-product-compliance
Lightning Source LLC
Chambersburg PA
CBHW062122300426
44115CB00012BA/1769